The Divine Decision

The Divine Decision

A Process Doctrine of Election

Donna Bowman

Foreword by John B. Cobb Jr.

Westminster John Knox Press
LOUISVILLE • LONDON

Book design by Sharon Adams
Cover design by Mark Abrams

First edition
Published by Westminster John Knox Press
Louisville, Kentucky

This book is printed on acid-free paper that meets the American National Standards Institute Z39.48 standard. ⊗

PRINTED IN THE UNITED STATES OF AMERICA

02 03 04 05 06 07 08 09 10 11 — 10 9 8 7 6 5 4 3 2 1

Library of Congress Cataloging-in-Publication Data
Bowman, Donna.
    The divine decision : a process doctrine of election / Donna Bowman ; foreword by John B. Cobb Jr. — 1st ed.
        p. cm.
    Includes bibliographical references and index.
    ISBN 0-664-22494-6
    1. Election (Theology)—History of doctrines—20th century. 2. Barth, Karl, 1886–1968. 3. Process theology—History of doctrines—20th century. 4. Whitehead, Alfred North, 1861–1947. I. Title.

BT809 .B69 2002
234—dc21

                                                                    2001055773

Dedicated to Noel, who chose me

CONTENTS

FOREWORD

Karl Barth was the greatest theologian of the twentieth century. Alfred North Whitehead was the greatest philosophical cosmologist. One might suppose that their work could be viewed as complementary and that together they could provide a larger vision for contemporary Christians.

Unfortunately, matters are not that simple. From a Barthian point of view, philosophical cosmology is virtually irrelevant to theology. From a Whiteheadian point of view, anything approaching fideism is unacceptable. Needless to say, the relations between Barthians and Whiteheadians have not been very cordial! On the whole, at best, they have largely ignored each other's work.

Of course, theologians influenced by Whitehead have not altogether ignored Barth. To be a theologian on the cusp between the twentieth and twenty-first centuries entails some response to Barth. But this response has tended to be a global rejection of his approach in general rather than an engagement of his treatment of particular issues with care. Understandably, this has made it easy for those whose understanding of the theological task has been deeply shaped by Barth to ignore, and sometimes condemn, process theology.

Process theology has often presented itself as an alternative to traditional theology rather than as a development of it or in it. Since those who pursue theology in a more traditional way are committed to its development, process theology has appeared largely irrelevant. Nevertheless, developments in the mainstream of traditional theology have in fact reduced the gap.

Some process themes, such as the capacity of God for suffering with finite creatures, have found their way into mainstream discussion, although process sources are rarely those cited. The emphasis on relationality, so important for process thought, has, for whatever reasons, gained ground. The dialogue between science and religion, central to process theology, is growing. The attitude toward other religions has largely moved away from Barth's position toward that of process theology. There is more emphasis on God's sharing power with creatures than earlier, so the process polemic against divine omnipotence has less evident relevance. That God's power is more often exercised persuasively than coercively is emphasized today more so than in an earlier generation.

On the process side, the polemical attitude that characterized some earlier representatives is less common. Process theologians number some evan-
gelicals among them. The heritage of Daniel Day Williams, the first process
thinker fully to engage the Christian tradition, is alive and well. Process
theologians such as Paul Sponheim work in responsibly traditional ways.

All of this is to say that, although differences of style and attitude often
remain substantial, mainstream theologians and process theologians are not
now as far apart as was once the case. Perhaps the major continuing difference today is that process theologians often work with those in mind who are
most alienated from the tradition. These theologians want to show that there
is a way of being Christian that does not entail the ideas and attitudes that
have driven so many away. More traditional theologians, on the other hand,
want to show that some of the developments they support are fully continuous with the tradition. It is time to recognize that both roles are important.

This book makes a major contribution toward bringing process theology
back into discussion with mainstream traditional theology. It does so by taking as its topic one that few process theologians have considered. For many
process theologians, "election" rings of the unilateral power and action of
God and implies a predetermined outcome. These are just the ideas that
process thought most systematically opposes. Hence, rather than developing
a doctrine of election, process theologians have tended to ignore, or explicitly reject, this doctrine. Meanwhile, recent mainstream theologians, beginning already with Barth, have developed the doctrine in ways that are no
longer vulnerable to the simple, sweeping criticism of process theologians.

The proper response to such a situation is, of course, to engage the work
of these theologians appreciatively. This does not mean that the process theologian will find what traditional theologians have already done completely
satisfactory. But where there are remaining dissatisfactions, the process theologian can enter the conversation and propose further developments.

Carrying out this proper response has awaited the work of Donna
Bowman. She develops a doctrine of election that is entirely appropriate
from a Whiteheadian perspective but can also be understood as a part of
the ongoing mainstream discussion of the topic. Process theology is not an
alternative to mainstream theology but a participant. We can hope that
Bowman's formulation of the doctrine of election will commend itself to
those interested in this doctrine independently of the philosophical cosmology that also supports it.

John B. Cobb Jr.

ACKNOWLEDGMENTS

The members of my dissertation committee at the University of Virginia—Langdon Gilkey, Jamie Ferreira, and Will Power—believed in the worth of this project despite bringing to it very different philosophical and theological suppositions. Their incisive questions and encouragement fostered an atmosphere of scholarly respect that helped me believe I had something to contribute to the discussion on these topics. A separate word of thanks is due to Will Power, my mentor, who introduced me to Whitehead's thought and guided me through many struggles with it. My dissertation adviser at Virginia, Gene Rogers, was a model of openness to novel ideas and an inexhaustible font of information on Barth. More than anyone else, he taught me to be a theologian, and for that he deserves my highest thanks.

Norbert Schedler and Richard Scott, who brought me to the University of Central Arkansas, have earned my appreciation for their encouragement, collegial interest in my esoteric work, and shining example of how to remain engaged and intellectually active while serving students.

For patience and financial support during the dissertation years, and for inspiration and celebration thereafter, I thank my husband, Noel Murray, the best writer I know.

ABBREVIATIONS

The works of Alfred North Whitehead are referred to in the text and end-notes by these abbreviations, followed by the page number:

AI	*Adventures of Ideas*
MT	*Modes of Thought*
PR	*Process and Reality*
RM	*Religion in the Making*
SMW	*Science and the Modern World*

For complete bibliographic information on the editions employed, see the list of sources cited.

Karl Barth's *Church Dogmatics* is cited in chapter 1 (where it is the primary text) by volume, section, and page number, and thereafter by the abbreviation *CD,* followed by volume, section, and page number. For complete bibliographic information, see the list of sources cited.

Introduction

"Oh, how I love Jesus/Because he first loved me," reads a nineteenth-century hymn.[1] The doctrine of election is the theological description of God's love for creation, the divine love that forms the relationship between God and creatures. This infinite and free love precedes and conditions the human response to God—the proper response being represented by the finite gratitude and love expressed in the line quoted above. The term *election* signifies that God's love for creatures is a gracious divine choice, uncompelled by its object, singling out the elected creature for a divine purpose.

The history of the Christian doctrine of election begins with the Hebrew Scriptures' assertion that God chose Israel to be God's special people among all the nations. The Old Testament speaks of a God who has particular purposes for particular individuals, families, and tribes, a God who anoints human beings to carry out special tasks, or for special protection and favor. The New Testament identifies that electing act of God with the work and person of Jesus Christ, the Messiah or Anointed One. Paul uses the language of election in Romans and Ephesians to argue that through faith in Jesus Christ, believers are given a share in his election and become partakers of God's covenant with Israel.

Historically, the discussion of election in Christian theology was often overwhelmed by the problem of predestination and its relationship to human free will. Athanasius and Augustine are among the theologians in the early church who paid special attention to the doctrine. Election achieved its greatest prominence in an influential theological system, however, when the Calvinist branch of the Reformation made predestination and election their bywords in the sixteenth century. Calvin argued for an interpretation of election that elevated God to the position of supreme arbiter of all earthly events and that humbled human beings by viewing

1

them as the objects of an inscrutable and unquestionable divine decree. The Reformed tradition that followed emphasized the life of the elect in faith and the assurance of salvation. It was challenged by Arminius, and later by John Wesley, both of whom contended that God is not the only actor in election but that God is met by the free decision of the creature, which bears responsibility for its own fate.

In the twentieth century, as the neo-orthodox movement in theology became prominent, Karl Barth produced, arguably, the single greatest exposition of the doctrine of election in Christian history. His starting point was Calvinist: the utterly free decision of God. But his method was new: affirming that the distinctions created by God's choice are resolved in the person of Jesus Christ, simultaneously God's eternally elected one and the bearer of the divine rejection deserved by humankind. The result dominates the *Church Dogmatics,* Barth's magisterial work of systematic theology, in a way that no other Reformed doctrine of election had before. Barth's doctrine of election reveals the power of the doctrine as a key to the whole question of God's dealings with creation. Instead of a logic puzzle for theologians anxious to reconcile predestination and free will, election becomes in Barth the framework for the divine plan of salvation, and the first word that Christian theology can speak about Christ.

My attraction to the Reformed doctrine of election rests on three elements shared by the election doctrines of Calvin, Schleiermacher, and Barth. First, election is seen as the basic rubric under which God's relationship with the world can be illuminated. It is bound up with the divine plan for the universe; creation, redemption, and sanctification are further elaborations of God's primordial election. Second, election orients the world toward an end that is divinely ordained. Because election is the precondition for God's further acts toward the world, the goal for humanity that is revealed in God's saving action can be recognized as the end toward which election is directed: eternal life, blessedness, and participation in God's own glory. Finally, election reveals divine grace. God's election is not triggered or compelled by any quality of the creature to which it is directed. Instead, it is founded in God's love and care for undeserving human beings, who recognize God's love first in their own election.

Since theological reflection began in the church, theologians have looked to the best philosophy of their day to provide them with concepts for systematizing and analyzing the Christian witness. Since Christianity believed itself to be the possessor of revelation concerning the ultimate or absolute that philosophy strove to delineate, it was natural and inevitable that Christians should identify the God of Christ with the object of philosophy's quest. As a result of the Enlightenment and the post-Enlightenment investigations into the relativity of various spheres of knowledge, it can no longer be taken for granted that religion and philosophy are attempting to describe the same reality for different purposes. Yet Christian faith still involves basic claims about truth and reality that may very well come laden with metaphysical assumptions, whether recognized or completely unconscious. At the very least, theological disputes over such contentious issues as divine knowledge and human agency are almost always conducted on the common ground of philosophy, where the revelation that is Christian theology's source is outfitted with a framework of theory and tested for coherence and adequacy.

The most basic argument for the relevance of philosophy to theology continues to be the oldest one: that both disciplines have as their goal the description of reality. Theology generally describes reality from the top down, that is, from the ultimate reality of God down to the contingent and perhaps deficient reality of the world. Philosophy does not normally begin by assuming or accepting on authority the reality and nature of God, but instead categorizes human experiences and generalizes from the best explanatory principles discovered there. The issue between them remains: Is it possible for both approaches to arrive at the same conclusion? Is it possible that they may arrive at different, though equally valid, conclusions?

The project on which I am embarking is founded on the belief that philosophy attempts to describe the same reality as theology. As a Christian theologian, I am concerned with the problem of articulating the doctrine of election in a form that addresses the contemporary believer. I believe that metaphysics is not irrelevant to this problem. If theology can harness the insights of philosophy, then theologians will be able to express the Christian faith in terms that ring true to the human being because they are consonant with her deepest intuition of reality.

The clarion call of revelation in Barth's theology is to some extent a reaction against the relativism and uncertainty that plagued twentieth-century science and philosophy. Yet the need for a comprehensive metaphysics that clarifies and systematizes the relationship between the various fields of knowledge remains. The overwhelming importance of scientific knowledge and discovery in contemporary life often results in a conflict for the believer between her faith and the objective facts of empirical investigation. If it is indeed true that the sphere of reality which science explores is not separate from the reality created, ordered, and administered by God, then there should be a way to express the Christian faith in terms that acknowledge and even employ the most potent insights of science and philosophy.

Alfred North Whitehead, a mathematician and philosopher, constructed his "philosophy of organism," now commonly known under the broader term "process philosophy," in order to integrate the discoveries and theories of the physical sciences with a general cosmology. Instead of resisting the seeming erosion of certainty in physics and the elevation of change to a basic principle in biology, Whitehead felt that philosophy needed to embrace these truths and integrate them into a philosophy of becoming, relation, and freedom. Process thought, as systematized in Whitehead's greatest work, *Process and Reality,* attempts to overcome some of the shortcomings Whitehead perceived in the Greek philosophy of Plato and Aristotle by substituting *continua,* or polar unities, for dualistic concepts such as subject-object and mind-body.

The relevance of process thought for the doctrine of election reveals itself in several areas. First, Whitehead conceives God as the active entity that orders reality by limiting possibilities. Election is exactly this kind of selection and preference. Second, the activity of God in Whitehead's system is based upon God's primordial decision to entertain a certain goal for God's self and the world. Election is the description of God's purpose being worked out both in God's life and in cosmic history. Third, God in process thought shares the divine purpose with creatures and utilizes the accomplishments of creatures in luring the world toward greater and greater value. The doctrine of election reveals the divine-human relationship to be concerned with the elevation of creatures, so that creatures can participate in God's activity of saving and sanctifying the world.

The purpose of this work is to construct a doctrine of election utilizing the categories and concepts of process thought, based upon the interpretation of the Christian witness found in the Reformed tradition as exemplified and developed in Barth. The convergences noted above suggest the possibilities inherent in process thought for explicating the doctrine of election in its terms. There are also difficulties in attempting to read Barth in such a way as to make his doctrine of election compatible with a process interpretation. Barth would undoubtedly be hostile to any attempt to integrate a philosophical system with his dogmatics. However, my project is not to construct a process Barthianism, but a version of process that appreciates Barthian thought. In other words, the insights that Barth contributes in his doctrine of election can provide the Christian theological standard toward which the process doctrine of election strives.

Chapter 1 offers an analysis of Barth's doctrine of election in the *Church Dogmatics.* The divine act of initiating relationship and the creaturely act of responding to divine election are explored using Barth's terms and acknowledging Barth's understanding of election's structure and place in theology. Chapter 2 turns to Whitehead's concept of the initial aim, which is the initiation of relationship between God and each individual creature; the chapter provides an introduction to the categories and terms of process philosophy in relation to the interaction between God and the creature. Chapter 3 asks how the expression of election in process terms will reinforce some aspects of the doctrine and necessarily change other aspects that have historically been a part of what Reformed Christianity has asserted therein, drawing some preliminary conclusions regarding the suitability of these concepts for constructing a doctrine of election. Chapter 4 moves from the language of philosophy to the language of philosophical theology. Here the questions of religious adequacy and coherence in the construction of a doctrine of election are considered. This chapter explicates a doctrine of election in the terms of process theology that is consistent, wherever possible, with Barth's insights into Christian theology within the bounds of revelation. Following this constructive work, a brief epilogue considers the application of the doctrine of election, as expressed, to the concerns of Christian life.

The importance of the work here presented is to begin a conversation about the doctrine of election within the community of process thinkers in many fields. Process theology needs to construct religiously adequate doctrines if it is not to remain a merely academic approach to Christianity. That work is still under way in many areas, and the project attempted here would be far easier and far more comprehensive if process theology had already reached a consensus in such areas as Christology and the doctrine of the Trinity. Yet process theology also needs to be open to Christian theology's greatest exponents and to learn from their commitment to the faith. This work cannot wait for further convergence between process theology and more traditional or mainstream theological traditions because it is the condition for further convergence.

A Brief Survey of the Literature

There have been relatively few studies of the relationship between process theology and Reformed theology in general, although many of those that do exist deal with Karl Barth's work. The reason for the dearth of material seems to be the appearance of a mutual antipathy between the two approaches to theology. Process theology's "neoclassical" conception of God, for example, seems to be a redefinition of a classical concept typified by the God of the Reformers: transcendent, absolute, all-determining, and unknowable save through revelation. Since many writers see process theology as defining itself by its opposition to Reformed categories and concepts, the relationship between the two is taken as understood.

This tacit acknowledgment of difference characterizes the major studies on Barth more so than the process literature, which, as a relatively new theological approach, has an interest in finding common ground with established theological schools, or at least in precisely defining the distinctions. Barth himself does not mention process theology or Whitehead, although the two were contemporaries; since his major works were completed before the flowering of process studies in the late fifties, Barth may not have been aware of Whitehead's work. Barthian scholars, as well, devote almost no attention to the relationship between Barth and process thought, which seems on its face irrelevant to Barth's dogmatic enterprise. The exception that proves the rule is Donald G. Bloesch's essay "Process Theology and Reformed Theology," which sees in process theology a sharp contrast to the Reformed approach to the doctrines of God and salvation, and notes that process theologians view Barth as "the main threat at present."[2]

One notable comparison of Barth and Whitehead is Michael Welker's article "Barth's Theology and Process Theology,"[3] which systematically defines and distinguishes the two approaches and examines the possibilities for dialogue. Welker finds that both thinkers criticize classical theism and engage in a search for a new realism; these similarities alone are not productive comparisons, however, since they represent reactions against existing theological approaches rather than constructive methods or concerns. Going deeper into Whitehead's understanding of the roles of metaphysics and theology, Welker asserts that Whitehead seeks a theology that avoids abstraction by focusing on the concrete facts of experience, including the "tremendous fact" of the gospel.[4] For Welker, the most promising similarity between Barth and Whitehead is this focus on the concrete and specific—for Barth, Christ, and for Whitehead, "facts"—rather than the abstract and general. The difference within this similarity, Welker finds, rests in Barth's "dialogical personalism,"[5] which sees the one-to-one encounter as the paradigm of relationship and leads Barth to a hierarchy of power between the divine and creaturely realms, as opposed to Whitehead's complex system of "one-to-many" and "many-to-many" structures.[6] Welker challenges both Barthian and process thinkers to explore whether the commonalities and differences he describes can lead to the enrichment of both schools of thought.

Welker has also been a critic of process thought. In Kenneth Surin's essay "Process Theology," Surin adopts Welker's argument[7] that process theologians are not describing God with their dipolar concept (primordial and consequent), but instead the relationship between heaven and earth.[8] This criticism implies that a "one-world" cosmology that rejects the ontological divide between divinity and nondivinity is untenable for Christian faith. One might counter such an argument by noting the balance of images of divine immanence and divine transcendence in Scripture, and by making the case that the Christian witness does not depend upon a hierarchy in which divine transcendence governs divine immanence. In its consideration of the Christian witness, process theology relies on the normative power of images of the kingdom of God among us.

The significant Barth studies have nothing to say about process theology, either in comparison or contrast to Barth. Accordingly, they are most useful for the present project insofar as they contribute to an understanding of Barth's doctrine of election, especially in those areas that deliver promising insights for the construction of the process doctrine. Hans Küng's *Justification: The Doctrine of Karl Barth and a Catholic Reflection* describes Barth's doctrine of election in two short chapters, "The Eternal Foundation of Justification" and "The Covenant—Prerequisite for Justification."[9] But the questions Küng has for Barth and for Catholic theology in the light of the *Church Dogmatics* are about grace and the incarnation, not about the encounter of election per se. Another Catholic study, Hans Urs von Balthasar's *The Theology of Karl Barth,* likewise offers a summary of Barth's doctrine as the conclusion of von Balthasar's presentation of the Barthian systematic framework (see *"Praedestinatio gemina"*),[10] but von Balthasar unfolds his Catholic interpretation and response in the language of nature and grace rather than the language of election. Both these studies provide Catholic perspectives on the problem of human freedom, an issue related to the doctrine of election especially in light of the process emphasis on creaturely self-determination.

Four Protestant interpretations of Barth prove helpful, to some degree, in understanding Barth preparatory to utilizing his doctrine of election as the inspiration for a constructive effort. G. C. Berkouwer, author of *The Triumph of Grace in the Theology of Karl Barth,* argues that Barth's concept of election cannot be finally described as historical because God's priority and eventual victory override all contingent human freedom and evil; the problem of Barth's concepts of time and eternity dominate the discussion.[11] Robert Jenson, in *God after God: The God of the Past and the Future as Seen in the Work of Karl Barth,* offers a strong reading of the *Church Dogmatics* that argues, in contrast to Berkouwer, that Barth's christocentrism succeeds in producing a doctrine of *particular* and *concrete* election that avoids monism or determinism.[12] Bruce McCormack's Ph.D. dissertation, "A Scholastic of a Higher Order: The Development of Karl Barth's Theology, 1921–1931," although it covers Barth's writings prior to the *Church Dogmatics*, offers a stimulating analysis of the doctrine of predestination in the so-called "Göttingen Dogmatics,"[13] arguing that Barth used a scholastic method in relating his explication to its basis in Reformed dogmatics and confessions.[14] In the expanded and revised version of the dissertation, *Karl Barth's Critically Realistic Dialectical Theology: Its Genesis and Development 1909–1936,* McCormack adds a section on Barth's discovery that God's being is in the divine act of election in Jesus Christ, the basis of the doctrine of election in the *Church Dogmatics*.[15] George Hunsinger examines Barth's concept of the freedom of the divine and human act in great detail in *How to Read Karl Barth: The Shape of His Theology,* and offers a convincing framework of "asymmetry" as a key to Barth's solution of this problem.[16] His chapter "Double Agency as a Test Case" will be cited in the present work. Also worthy of mention is Anthony C. Yu's article "Karl Barth's Doctrine of Election," which summarizes Barth's christocentric approach and criticisms of previous theologians,[17] while raising the question whether Barth's doctrine of God's freedom is in accord with his implicit universalism[18] and historical emphasis.

In the realm of process literature, there are several interesting and important works describing the relationship of process thinkers to Reformed theology and to Barth in particular, although none focus on the doctrine of election specifically, and none go on to use Barth constructively. David Ray Griffin writes about Calvin and Barth in separate chapters in his book *God, Power, and Evil: A Process Theodicy;* both chapters focus on the challenge that the problem of evil poses to the Reformed view of divine omnipotence, as exemplified by Calvin's and Barth's very different approaches.[19] Daniel Day Williams takes on Barth's epistemology in "The Concept of Truth in Karl Barth's Theology."[20] John B. Cobb Jr., who has also written on Calvinism,[21] assesses Barth's theology most extensively in chapter 7 of *Living Options in Protestant Theology.* Here he develops a respectful criticism, arising from his commitment to "a Christian philosophy including or supporting a Christian natural theology,"[22] that Barth fails (albeit brilliantly) to develop a theology of revelation that can stand wholly within the sphere of revelation and not dependent on any commitments that can only be justified by reference to ideas or realities outside that sphere. Cobb also gives a process critique of Barth in two articles, "Barth: An Appreciation from the Enemy Camp,"[23] and "Barth and the Barthians: A Critical Appraisal."[24] The latter article criticizes Barth's legacy as one that excludes rather than includes, that sets up antipathies between various theological perspectives rather than finding common ground.[25] Cobb's theology is itself compared with Barth on the topic of creation, in an article by H. R. Plomp.[26] This is one of many articles and books devoted to a comparison of post-Whiteheadian process thinkers with Reformed traditions.[27]

The primary and secondary literature of process theology contains few references to the doctrine of election. A recent article by Clark M. Williamson, "Reversing the Reversal: Covenant and Election in Jewish and Process Theology,"[28] explores the covenantal reality to which Judaism testifies in its scriptures and history, and argues that process categories best express that reality as established in time between God and creatures. Among the major works of process theology's prominent interpreters, only Daniel Day Williams speaks specifically of election. Williams identifies "election-love" as one of two aspects of the divine love for Israel as presented in the Hebrew Scriptures (the other being "covenant-love" or faithfulness), and concludes that the image of God's suffering reveals that God's election is found in the divine love rather than the divine power. He identifies this insight with Karl Barth when he turns to the analysis of love in the New Testament: "[Barth] finds here his solution of the meaning of election. Love as grasped in the Christian faith is inseparable from the history of Jesus of Nazareth."[29] Clearly influenced by Barth, Williams utilizes the concept of Jesus Christ as "God's Elect Man" in his nontechnical presentation of a process view of the incarnation.[30]

Two writers advance a process interpretation of the doctrine of providence, which is closely related to election. Norman Pittenger wrote on many doctrines and theological subjects from a process perspective, usually with pastoral considerations in mind; his book *God's Way with Men* contains a chapter on divine providence.[31] D. W. D. Shaw's article "Providence and Persuasion" relates Whitehead's redefinition of God's power to the classical concept of divine governance of the world.[32]

Although few process writers have dealt with the doctrine of election, nearly all have something to say about Whitehead's concept of the subjective aim, which will become the basis for the process doctrine of election to be constructed in the present study. Charles Hartshorne is the most prominent and prolific process thinker in the post-Whiteheadian period; however, the difference between Hartshorne's and Whitehead's conceptions of God leads the former in a new direction with regard to the divine-creature relationship. For Hartshorne, God is a series of temporal entities rather than a single nontemporal entity; thus, God has a past and a future, and the election relationship takes on a wholly different shape.[33] Many process theologians draw from both Hartshorne and Whitehead in various proportions, so systematic work in process theology is not clearly and solely Whiteheadian in its concept of God.

One prominent theologian who opts for the Whiteheadian concept of God is John B. Cobb, Jr., whose book *A Christian Natural Theology* is one of the most influential theological statements in the field. Cobb presents a view of the subjective aim that differs slightly in emphasis from Whitehead's in that the initial aim derives to some extent from the entities in the occasion's immediate past as well as from God, so that the occasion chooses among a variety of aims for it, both divine and human.[34] Cobb feels that this solves the problem posed by the immutability and eternality of God's subjective aim in the primordial nature; I will argue, however, that God's primordial and unchanging aim does not constitute a difficulty for a doctrine of election but provides a positive way to speak about divine faithfulness without sacrificing the vitality of the living relationship between God and creatures.

Peter Hamilton's *The Living God and the Modern World* addresses the question of God's relevance to modern science and existential questions by adopting a Whiteheadian view of God's relativity and activity in the natural world. Hamilton presents a view of creaturely freedom in both organic and inorganic nature by coordinating the concepts of the creature's subjective aim and God's subjective aim, in order to relate the order of the universe to God.[35] Bernard Meland is another writer whose theological work has been decisively influenced by process thought; his book *The Reality of Faith* is concerned with the same issues of modernity and human culture as Hamilton's work. With regard to the relationship of God to creatures, the most informative chapters are those on evolution,[36] "the encounter with spirit,"[37] and the exercise of divine power.[38] Schubert Ogden confronts several relevant theological questions in *The Reality of God and Other Essays*, particularly in the title essay,[39] which defends a "neoclassical" theism as the best alternative for presenting a credible gospel to secular human beings. In "What Sense Does It Make to Say, 'God Acts in History'?" Ogden utilizes Bultmann to argue that the actions of creatures can be understood as acts of God, even decisive and revelatory acts of God.[40] Ogden does not use the technical language of subjective aim in these essays, but his presentation is based upon his conviction that the philosophy of Whitehead (through Hartshorne) is the best available "to integrate the cumulative insights of the whole Western philosophical tradition, so as to do justice to the legitimate motives both of classical metaphysics and of the various forms of modern, critical philosophy."[41] His work builds upon the philosophical work of Whitehead and Hartshorne to answer theological questions, not in a systematic or dogmatic context, but certainly as part of a constructive effort in the general field of process thought.

The works of process theology mentioned above do not deal directly with the subject of the current project, and in many cases qualify as second-level reflections on Whitehead, that is, use of Whiteheadian concepts and categories without specific analysis or engagement with the Whiteheadian texts. The existing literature on the relationship between Barth and process theology lays the groundwork for constructive work, such as the current project, through descriptive analysis. In this respect, the relation of these works to the current project is as commentary on the constructive work being attempted here, and as models of how process philosophy may be made useful to Christian theology—no small problem in its own right. It is not surprising that these works barely mention the doctrine of election and do not attempt to elaborate on what a process doctrine of election might look like. In their concern with the relevance of God and Christianity to the modern world, these writers stand in that tradition of nineteenth-century liberal theology carried on by Tillich, Niebuhr, and Bultmann, among others. The doctrine of election—identified as it is with Calvin and Barth, who stand decidedly outside this tradition—has rarely been made the subject of process theology up to this point. By means of a reading of Barth that clarifies his utility for the construction of a process doctrine of election and a reading of Whitehead that finds the metaphysical underpinnings of election in the initial aim, I hope to initiate reflection on election for process thinkers as well as demonstrate to Reformed thinkers how a process perspective illuminates this central doctrine.

CHAPTER ONE

Karl Barth's Doctrine of Election

The most influential doctrine of election since the Reformation is that of Karl Barth, expounded in volume II/2 of his landmark systematic work, *Church Dogmatics.*[1] Its status in contemporary theology is secured by several factors. First, the ascendance of what has been termed neo-orthodoxy in the twentieth century has affected every other theological movement and system. Barth issues a call to return to the true insights of the Reformers while renouncing what he views as the unholy fascination of nineteenth-century liberalism with natural theology. His theological system has therefore become the standard text of neo-orthodoxy, a monument of thought with which critics and followers alike must contend. Second, Barth's method of dialectical theology opened up what he called a "strange new world within the Bible,"[2] bringing to light the alien nature of Scripture and demonstrating that its familiarity obscures the miraculous revelation within. His doctrine of election carries through this scriptural emphasis by treating Christ as the key to understanding election, and furthermore, by treating Christ's election as the key to understanding all scriptural stories of those chosen by God. The reemergence in Barth's work of serious biblical exegesis based on typological interpretation gives his election doctrine a firm foundation in Scripture and diminishes its susceptibility to changes in philosophical or hermeneutical fashion. Whether or not one agrees with all the implications of Barth's discovery of elect pairs in the Old and New Testaments, the seriousness with which Barth treats the biblical witness of election forces his reader into confronting revelation as God's word to and for human beings, and increases the reader's sensitivity to the dangers of substituting human words for divine ones.

Third, and most important as a basis for this study, Barth's doctrine of election claims pride of place in his voluminous system. The author acknowledges it as the central doctrine of Christianity: "The doctrine of election is the sum of the Gospel because of all words that can be said or heard it is the best: that God elects man; that God is for man too the One who loves in freedom."[3] Instead of explaining election through prior stipulation of certain truths about God and human beings, Barth asserts that we come to know the truth about God and ourselves only through election. This emphasis on election as the key to dogmatics is unprecedented, even in Reformed theology, which since Calvin's powerful election doctrine has focused more closely on the doctrine than any other tradition.

It is fitting, then, that the construction of an election doctrine, even in terms of a system of philosophy little known to Barth, take place nonetheless in dialogue with election's greatest contemporary exponent. A careful exploration of Barth's doctrine is a prerequisite for the constructive theologian's understanding of the issues at stake in election, which any election doctrine must address. Barth is a theologian of firm stands and unbending principles, which he applies with remarkable consistency and flexibility, and he argues for his position from the standpoint of internal coherence and agreement with the Christian witness. A doctrine of election constructed with process thought as its metaphysical framework, such as the one proposed in the present work, will take stands on the same issues that sometimes converge with Barth's views and sometimes diverge from them. In order to evaluate the areas of convergence and divergence, it is necessary to conduct a close analysis both of Barth's doctrine in this chapter, and of the process concept of the initial aim—the concept that will become the basis of the election doctrine in process thought—in the next.

The attitude one takes toward Barth's theology determines the use one can make of his concepts and methods. Barth himself develops his theology in dialogue with four centuries of Reformed tradition most closely, and with the entire span of Christian and Jewish thought more generally, and his hermeneutic for reading and appropriating the work of others affects his conclusion. In the larger sense, a theologian would not bother to construct a new expression of Christian doctrine if he did not believe that previous expressions could be improved upon. His exposition, therefore, unfolds in reaction to the work of other theologians to the extent that he finds their expositions lacking. Barth often employs this type of criticism when he is developing a well-recognized and much-discussed aspect of the doctrine, to which a wide range of approaches have been taken in the previous literature. On the other hand, Barth often brings to light relatively unknown Reformed systematic writers, some aspect of whose work he finds especially congenial, and elevates them to the status of forerunners of his own efforts. In addition to these critical and appreciative readings of his predecessors, Barth develops some aspects of his election doctrine by elevating the dialectic seen in other theologians on a given issue to a new, original level. For example, he finds the options available to older writers on the subject of the so-called *Judenfrage,* the question of the continuing existence of Israel after the coming of Christ, to be inadequate for expressing the complexities of the issue in the climate of twentieth-century history. Returning to the Scriptures, he attempts to develop a new foundation for theological reflection on Israel through transcending mutually exclusive options such as supersessionism or two-covenant theory.

The dominant attitude toward past writers that comes across in Barth's writing is aggressive struggle. Barth treats those who are his closest theological partners, such as Calvin and Schleiermacher, with respect, but does not hesitate to point out the areas in which he feels they fall short of theological consistency and adequacy. His work arises out of a deep sense that the theology of the past must be renewed and returned to its source in Christ in order to meet the challenges of the present. So it is natural that he wrestle with his ancestors and assert his thought against theirs where he feels that they fail. How then is it proper for a theologian to approach Barth in turn, to find resources in his thought for the construction of a new doctrine of election? The first disclosure relevant to this question is the theologian's sense of what is lacking in Barth's presentation. My appreciation for Barth's achievement is tempered by my desire that the doctrine of election be placed on a firm philosophical footing. This means that the metaphysical system guiding the theologian's assumptions about divinity, creaturehood, and the relations that obtain between them should be consciously appropriated for the purpose of best explaining election. Barth's attitude toward philosophy is decidedly critical, especially when he feels that it is trespassing in theology's domain. He refuses to grant that a metaphysical system might be placed in the service of dogmatics by guiding its exposition in compatibility with other areas of knowledge because of his commitment to an ontological divide between the divine and nondivine that cannot be overcome except miraculously. Hence, theology must reject any imposed system that seeks to explain the divine realm in the same terms as those applicable to the realm of human experience.

The issue of Barth's attitude toward philosophy will be discussed in detail in the third section of this chapter, in order to introduce his analysis of God's electing act. It is important to note at this point that I take issue with Barth's belief that philosophy is not a useful tool for explicating the doctrine of election. My desire to place election in the context of a metaphysics of relationship results in dissatisfaction with Barth on this matter. However, this point of contention must be placed in the context of the overall attitude toward Barth's work. There would be no purpose to analyzing Barth's doctrine of election if I wished only to reject its premises and outcome. On the contrary, the attempt to construct a new doctrine of election is inspired by Barth's genius and encouraged by his success at bringing election into the forefront of theological discussion. My conviction that Barth is right about the importance of the doctrine of election, and that he gives the doctrine its greatest exposition, fosters an attitude of respect and humility toward his achievement, which guides my interpretation. Barth's understanding of election as the eternal foundation for all God's acts *ad extra* seems to me to be the key to the potential process doctrine of election.

The result of my sympathetic and appreciative reading of Barth, combined with my commitment to process theology as a framework for doing constructive work, is an election doctrine that claims Barth as one of its parents, a result that is no doubt ironic given Barth's distrust of the kind of philosophical theology and natural theology that has been the dominant form of Christian appropriation of Whitehead's work. The very real differences between Barth's mode of thought and the process mode of thought will emerge throughout this work. However, the spirit of this enterprise is a spirit of convergence rather than separation. Despite the distinctions that must be made between their governing assumptions I find similar insights about the doctrine of election emerging from the two systems. The challenge of bringing them together is to show that Barth's insights may be distinguished from his assumptions and that the utilization of process thought as a basis for Barth's central doctrine leads to new insights that are compatible both with the spirit of Barth's exposition and with the Christian witness to truth.

The Centrality of the Election Doctrine

Before delving into Barth's election doctrine proper, we must explore the reasons for his decision to place election at the center of his dogmatics. At first glance, this placement is in line with a general Reformed tradition. Calvin's powerful doctrine of election led to a family tree of Reformed theologians who emphasized election in their systematic presentations. However, the perception that election is central to Reformed thought arises primarily from the fame (or, in some circles, notoriety) achieved by Calvin's chapters on election in the *Institutes of the Christian Religion*. His refusal to moderate the rhetoric of double election has long been the most-discussed aspect of the *Institutes*, but the bold assertion of God's electing will in those chapters does not occur at the most prominent locus in the system.[4] In many ways, Calvin discusses the doctrine of election not so much for its own sake as to make other points that are more important to him. The doctrine of election is largely subsumed by the doctrine of predestination, by which Calvin understands the description of how the elect and non-elect are distinguished in the eternal will of God.[5] Election, then, is an expression of God's absolute sovereignty over creation, which is demonstrated by God's freedom to elect and reject unconditionally and by the creature's complete passivity in election.[6] The moral lesson of the doctrine is humility: Election teaches human beings that they have no power of their own to assert a claim on God or to affect their ultimate fate. Calvin thus urges us to bow before God's inscrutable exercise of power:

> But Scripture, while it requires us to consider this great mystery with so much more reverence and piety, both instructs the godly to a far different attitude and effectively refutes the criminal madness of these men. For Scripture does not speak of predestination with intent to rouse us to boldness that we may try with impious rashness to search out God's unattainable secrets. Rather, its intent is that, humbled and cast down, we may learn to tremble at this judgment and esteem his mercy. It is at this mark that believers aim.[7]

Election's centrality in Calvin, then, is not a matter of position or of the doctrine's theological utility as a basis for other doctrines. Instead, its reputation as Calvin's most important contribution to theology rests on the unusual stress Calvin gives to the doctrine and his unapologetic return to Augustinian formulae of double election.

Barth intends to improve on Calvin by giving the doctrine of election a place in the doctrine of God.[8] His reason is that, since it is through election that human beings come to their experience and knowledge of God, and since that experience and knowledge is of the true God as God really is, then election must precede any other discussion of God's acts toward the world, for it is only through election that such acts appear as works of God.[9] If one begins with the assumption that election refers primarily to God's choosing of individuals for salvation, then the doctrine appears as a part of the doctrine of justification. It addresses the question of why certain individuals are justified while others are not—admittedly, an important question.[10] But Barth understands election to refer primarily to God's choosing of God's own character, revealed in the eternal Son incarnate, and secondarily to the choosing of communities and individual creatures. With this guiding assumption, election appears as part of the doctrine of God because it describes the way God truly is—that is, as God *pro nobis*. It addresses a much larger range of questions than simply the inequality observed in human beings in their relation to God (although it continues to address this question).[11] Election, seen in this light, addresses the question of the relation of the God revealed in God's works *ad extra* to God *in se*. Thus, it addresses the question of who God is.

Barth defines God as "the One who loves in freedom."[12] This phrase might easily be paraphrased as "the One who elects" (first God's self to be Father, Son, and Holy Spirit, and then human beings also to be God's children) because election for Barth is precisely the divine free choice to love. This is the God revealed to us in Jesus Christ. Since Christ is the revelation of the true God, and as such the sole proper subject of Christian theology, Barth seeks the doctrine of election in Christ before all else.[13] By describing election, Barth believes that he can describe Christ, and through Christ, God, and through Christ, human beings. For Barth, therefore, there is no way to exaggerate the importance of the doctrine of election for theology, precisely because God's election is Christ and Christ is the totality of revelation. If Christ is seen as central to election and election therefore becomes theology's concrete basis, there is a greatly reduced danger of going wrong; but if election is shunted off to the side as a part of another doctrine— becoming therefore abstract because Christ is not recognized as the electing God, as if there were any revelation apart from election in Christ—then the pitfalls of theology become much more perilous. Barth regards a christological and central doctrine of election as a prophylactic against the temptations of natural theology on the one hand, and the tyranny of the *deus absconditus* on the other.

In the process of analyzing the doctrine I will have much more to say about Barth's navigation between these extremes, but here it is important to show why election is the corrective to these theological tendencies in Barth's presentation. Natural theology is the human endeavor to find God outside of God's revelation in Jesus Christ. In some senses, of course, it seems to be a legitimate endeavor; since God is the source of everything, there must be traces of the Creator in the creation, accessible even to human reason corrupted by sin. Barth's criticism of natural theology attacks the notion that the human mind can separate any particular thing, either creature or idea, from Jesus Christ and treat it as if it had some separate word to say about God.[14] The doctrine of election tells us that God determined God's self to speak one definitive Word about God's self. That Word is Jesus Christ, and all other words God speaks follow from that Word and are found within it. Human sin is the attempt to speak our own words about God and prefer them to God's Word. So natural theology, to Barth, is the human being's effort to elect God. The truth of election, however, is that God elects God's self for us in Jesus Christ.

The danger of the "hidden God" is the suspicion that the revealed God of Jesus Christ does not have to be the same as God alone with God's self. That is to say, the divine decision to reveal God's self in Christ for the benefit of creatures follows many other decisions—the decision to create and the decision to remedy sin, for example. So before and behind the revelation in Christ, there is a God acting in and for God's self whose counsels are hidden from us and whose decisions we are unable to discern.[15] The doctrine of election is the theological guarantee that in Jesus Christ we are seeing God as God elected God's self to be, not merely in appearance toward us but necessarily in God's self prior to any other divine act *ad extra*. Barth recognizes that the doctrine of the sovereignty of God, if allowed to reign in theology over God's self-revelation, can exercise a kind of tyranny of its own unless we understand that God determines God's self through election:

> [W]e must still ask whether we understand the election aright if we understand it from the very first within the framework of the presumably superior reality of the divine government of the world, as the specific act of this general divine activity. That it is logically convenient to do this is quite evident. But what we must inquire is whether it is in fact correct to do it; whether we ought not rather to understand the divine government of the world in the light of the divine election. . . . May it not be that it is as the electing God that He is the Almighty, and not *vice versa?*[16]

The idea that God's freedom means that we cannot ever be privy to the decisions that guide God's interaction with the world is repudiated by Barth in the name of Jesus Christ.[17] In the Son the hidden God is revealed, so that there is no more God to be revealed, no reserved existence of God kept back from us. God elects God's self to be open to us, and therefore election should take away our fear of God's caprice or unbridled power. If election is first in Christian theology, then we know a God whose grace toward us reaches all the way from God's primordial act through to the limits of history and eternity.

The Act of the Electing God

To analyze Barth's doctrine of election and to facilitate comparison with the process approach, this discussion will proceed under two main headings.

First is the analysis in this section of God as Elector, which identifies Barth's conception of God's agency in election. The next section will look at the creature as elected and will discuss Barth's election anthropology. In that second section, we will be concerned with how Barth understands the response of the creature to God's call. The link between the two sections is Jesus Christ, who in Barth's doctrine occupies (and specifies) both halves of the election relationship, being both the Elector and the elected. Further complicating this scheme is the fact that Christ is not only Elector as God but also as man, and is not only elected as man but also as God! This separation of the doctrine of election into two parts, then, is to some extent natural; Barth writes that "the concept of election has a double reference— to the elector and to the elected."[18] Election is always a relationship with two sides. But it is important to keep in mind throughout the analysis that the divine act of election is not undertaken without an object in mind and without being tailored to that object, since the act is on behalf of that object, and that the creature's response depends upon the divine act and is initiated by that act. The two sides are distinguishable and can be discussed to a certain extent in isolation, but they are inseparable in the reality of election. And even in the discussion, Barth will constantly remind us that Jesus Christ bridges all the gaps.

The Freedom of the Divine Act

The first topic under the Barthian description of any act of God—and especially of election, which is the primordial, defining act of God—is its freedom:

> The doctrine of election is the sum of the Gospel because of all words that can be said or heard it is the best: that God elects man; *that God is for man too the One who loves in freedom.* It is grounded in the knowledge of Jesus Christ because He is both the electing God and elected man in One. It is part of the doctrine of God because originally God's election of man is a predestination not merely of man but of Himself. Its function is to bear basic testimony to eternal, free and unchanging grace as the beginning of all the ways and works of God.[19]

Grace is not grace if it is compelled by some necessity; God is not God unless God is free. Barth here inveighs against those who feel the need to hedge God in with some reason why God cannot do otherwise than elect and save human beings. No praise is due a being who had no choice but to choose—indeed, freedom in the case of election means precisely *freedom of choice*. Here the theologian often finds herself confronting a kind of anthropic principle of election, analogous to the anthropic principle of scientific cosmology. The canonical form of the principle is by the cosmologists Dicke and Carter: "What we can expect to observe must be restricted by the conditions necessary for our presence as observers."[20] This is the paradox that the universe seems to exhibit laws that by coincidence or design are within the very narrow range of values that might support intelligent life, but that we only know this because we, as intelligent life forms, were able to evolve, because the universe in fact supports such an evolution. The anthropic principle of election might be formulated thus: We can have knowledge of God's freedom in election only because God in fact exercised that freedom to elect us. Thus, we find ourselves asserting God's freedom in a sense that almost seems hypothetical, for if God had made another choice, we would not be able to know God or God's freedom to love. The evidence of God's freedom to do otherwise than elect us, in the strictest sense, would be God in fact doing otherwise—but we could not apprehend this evidence, for God would not in that case have revealed God's self to us.

The alternative to asserting God's freedom not to elect, however, is the position, untenable for Barth, of acknowledging some sort of compulsion on God. If God cannot do other than elect, then some extradivine principle actually reigns supreme in the universe. As self-evident as Barth makes this choice seem, there are in fact at least two assumptions that guide his analysis of the situation. First, he assumes that God and creatures inhabit two qualitatively different realities. God's freedom to elect rests on God's existence in a divine reality that is in no way dependent on anything outside itself.[21] Creatures are separated from God by an ontological divide that only God can overcome, because any overcoming of the divide is miraculous and supernatural, not part of the natural order. Second, Barth assumes a kind of anticipatory reality of substances, even particular concrete individuals, in God's realm of eternity, brought into effective existence through election, before or outside of creation. In this way, Barth can talk about a hypothetical influence the realm of creation might exercise over God if God were not the Lord of that realm through election. So the two extradivine realities that Barth denies have any hold over God are (1) a system of metaphysical necessity that holds sway over God and creation alike, and (2) creatures as foreknown or anticipated in God's pretemporal existence.[22] Only if God's freedom over against these two forces is affirmed in theology can the notion of God's freedom have any meaning for Barth.[23]

The danger in theology's need to postulate a hypothetical God who freely decides *not* to elect God's self for creatures lies in the tendency to subordinate God's freedom to God's power at this very point. Barth rejects the position, however natural, that God is powerful, therefore God is free. Does freedom lie in the ability to actualize one among various alternatives, or is it in fact the other way around—that the actualization of the alternative follows the free choice among alternatives? Barth asserts that God is free, therefore God is powerful. Only in this order of things can election become the key doctrine for Christian dogmatics. God's power is manifested in the divine ability to bring about what God has decided to do. God's power is demonstrated in God's bringing to consummation the course on which God embarked in God's primordial self-election. The theologian does not infer God's freedom from the fact that the place, time, and manner in which God exercises God's power is incomprehensible to the human mind. This is tantamount to saying that divine freedom is harnessed to the yoke of divine power and that the revelation of divine power is the reason that God acts freely. On the contrary, Barth states that the revelation of God's freedom is the reason God acts powerfully.

> What makes Him the divine Ruler is the very fact that His rule is determined and limited: self-determined and self-limited, but determined and limited none the less; and not in the sense that His caprice as such constitutes His divine being and therefore the principle of the world government, but in such a way that He has concretely determined and limited Himself after the manner of a true king (and not of a tyrant); in such a way, then, that we can never expect any decisions from God except those which rest upon this concrete determination and limitation of His being, upon this primal decision made in His eternal being; decisions, then, which are always in direct line with this primal decision, and not somewhere to the right or left of it in an infinite sphere.[24]

The theologian observes the freedom of God in the consistency of divine grace, not in its arbitrariness. Divine freedom is not that God acts here and does not act there, or that to human eyes this person is inhabited by divine power and that one is not. Divine freedom is that God elects to act everywhere in the service of the single divine plan for creatures. Divine freedom is that God's electing act is unitary and that all exercises of divine power *ad extra* are in the service of that electing act.[25]

The Relationship between Philosophy and Theology

The polemic against metaphysics that is a recurring feature of the *Church Dogmatics* is part of Barth's attempt to ensure that nothing is given theological priority over divine freedom. To place God in any sort of a system, to make God fit into an overall "worldview," is to limit God's freedom by a factor external to the divine reality. "Theology must begin with Jesus Christ, and not with general principles, however better or, at any rate, more relevant and illuminating, they might appear to be."[26]

> What God does in freedom is in order. And in that it is done in freedom, we can and must perceive and recognize that it is in order without first measuring it by our own conceptions of order and only then recognizing it to be such. It belongs to God that He should teach us what order is.[27]

The building of metaphysical systems that purport to include God is a human limitation on God that refuses to gaze upon God's revelation to find out how God has, in fact, limited God's self. Barth sees two errors at work in metaphysical ideas of God: first, the sin of telling God who God is; second, the sin of telling God what God can do.[28] Both errors arise from the desire of a human being to find out for herself. Both can be corrected by attending to God's revelation of God's self and God's deeds in Jesus Christ.

The outline of the present study demands that we examine this aspect of Barth's thought closely and ask whether he is correct in his assessment of metaphysics. Process theology is based upon a metaphysician's concept of God, derived from the needs of his system. Is this not exactly what Barth rejects? May process theology learn from Barth even as it follows a methodology radically opposed to his own?

In order to provide a provisional answer to this question, to serve until the outlines of process thought have been given in chapter 2, let us look more closely at the two errors Barth condemns in metaphysics. First, the makers of metaphysical systems tell God who God is. Barth writes:

> It must be established at once from the knowledge of God with which we are concerned that everything that is described as "God" on the basis of a free choice cannot possibly be God; and that everything that is declared, on the grounds of this presupposition, to be the knowledge of God cannot have any reality or possibility as a knowledge of God. The knowledge of God with which we are here concerned takes place, not in a free choice, but with a very definite constraint.[29]

I would amend this charge to state that metaphysicians, in beginning their study from "below" (empirical evidence and human reason), can go no further in describing God than to say what function God must perform, given the limitations of creatures. In other words, there are certain essential roles in the universe that evidence and reason tell us creatures cannot fulfill. This is not a proclamation of God based on a free choice; it is forced upon the metaphysician by the structure of reality itself. The metaphysician, in assigning these roles to God, is not yet describing God's being; he is merely stating that since the universe exists, we can infer that conditions are right for its existence and that one of these conditions is the existence and action of a being beyond our own powers.

Given this description of God's necessary function to ensure the continuing existence of the world we experience, the metaphysician might, at this point, go on to infer certain characteristics of God. For example, the eternality of God might be inferred from the need to have the necessary function of this being continue everlastingly, and the omnipotence of God might be inferred from the need for this being to have the power to perform unique and indispensable acts. However, these inferences quickly lose any connection to the Christian God if they are not referred back to the Christian kerygma. Without the use of the norm of Scripture to measure the metaphysician's results, the eternity of God discovered by this functional analysis might be invoked against the temporality of Jesus, or the metaphysician's commitment to omnipotence might lead her to discount God's servanthood in Jesus Christ. Because the metaphysician is led only as far as the *abstract* God in her investigations, not to the *concrete* God in Jesus Christ, Barth's criticism of metaphysics often focuses on the audacity of the metaphysician in using the word *God* to denote what is thus defined:

> When the knowledge of God is under discussion we are not free perhaps to think of Him who in the Bible is called God and Lord, but perhaps equally well to think of some other entity which can similarly be described and proclaimed as "God," and which has in fact been described and proclaimed as "God" somewhere and at some time. We cannot equally well ask about the knowledge of the World-Ground or the World-Soul, the Supreme Good or Supreme Value, the Thing in itself or the Absolute, Destiny or Being or Idea, or even the First Cause as the Unity of Being and Idea, as we can ask about the knowledge of Him who in the Bible is called God and Lord.[30]

Barth's second charge is that those who construct metaphysics commit the sin of telling God what God can do. As I just described, the metaphysician begins by attempting to observe what God has done, in the limited sense of inferring God's action in the world's consistency for which creatures cannot be responsible. Certainly this observation can lead to further speculation, for example, by assuming that the limits of the metaphysician's concept of God are in fact the limits of God's being and action. It could happen that the metaphysician concludes that any action of God that is not systematically verifiable and observable—in short, any action that has a solely religious character—is at best unavailable for thought and at worst nonexistent. If this happens, then Barth's charge is accurately

aimed, for the metaphysician has gone beyond the area of legitimate infer-
ence from the necessity of a certain role-player in the system.

How far can these metaphysical inferences proceed? Admittedly, not far
at all. No characteristic of God that is not required by the evidence of
empirical inquiry can ever be discovered by this method. In other words,
the freedom of God in act can never be inferred from below, since the acts
of God that can be observed from below without any prior assumptions
about God's reality or character are the ones that are necessary to the existence of those observing. What can be described by the metaphysician, in
short, is God in God's secular function. What the metaphysician asserts in
this description, tacitly if not openly, is that the God found in generally
available secular experience must be the same God found in religious experience, even if the knowledge able to be derived from the former is admittedly far less extensive than the knowledge obtained from the latter.
Whitehead makes this assertion explicitly:

> It must not be thought that these non-statistical judgments [of the suitabil-
> ity of actualizing some particular possibility] are in any way religious. They
> lie at a far lower level of experience than do the religious emotions. The sec-
> ularization of the concept of God's functions in the world is at least as urgent
> a requisite of thought as is the secularization of other elements in experience.
> The concept of God is certainly one essential element in religious feeling. But
> the converse is not true; the concept of religious feeling is not an essential ele-
> ment in the concept of God's function in the universe. (PR 207)

The metaphysician's quest to describe the secular function of God is legitimate when the limits of the quest are well understood. These are not arbitrary limits, imposed by theologians to protect their territory. They are
necessary limits imposed by the metaphysician's method. It is interesting that
the metaphysician who calls the entity that performs certain necessary functions in his system "God" is acknowledging the limits by pointing in a direction that would involve a transgression of them. The word *God* is not a
philosophical term; it is a religious term. It is not defined exhaustively by philosophy; rather, without exception, its use involves religious connotations.
When the metaphysician uses this term to indicate the necessary being that
alone can conceivably perform certain necessary functions in his system, then
he indicates by it that the concept of God cannot be limited to the performance of those secular functions. By invoking the name of God, the metaphysician admits that the concept must be filled by religious experience if it
is not to become merely a construct invoked to save the system from collapse.

Barth does not fail to recognize that philosophy has its place. In the
opening pages of his doctrine of creation, he visualizes a philosophical

construction that would do justice to creation "from below," without explicit reference to revelation.[31] Barth asserts that while Christian theology is always marked off from philosophy by the origin, object, and course of its explication of creation as divine benefit, there is no theoretical obstacle to a philosophy of creation that does not remain "stuck either in noetics or at most in ontology,"[32] but reaches "the question of the whence of the universe and provides an answer satisfactory in its own sphere."[33] The hostility to philosophical efforts to describe God's being and activity that characterizes the *Church Dogmatics* is rooted in Barth's commitment to an absolute ontological difference between God and creatures. A "worldview" can never do justice to the divine activity in creation, because one set of concepts cannot encompass both divine and creaturely reality. It is reserved for the divine prerogative to cross the ontological divide, because what is impossible with human beings is possible with God. However, there is room for relative success in the philosophical endeavor to describe the creaturely reality of the universe, with the caveat that the worldview thus constructed must have "the question of the whence of the circle of knowledge and being" as a "boundary and mysterious background."[34] Christian theology cannot deny that the philosophical quest for an answer to the question of creation "is motivated by genuine necessity" and must be accorded "the keenest interest and attention."[35]

What would a successful philosophical description of creation look like? Barth thinks that the most urgent unresolved issue facing philosophy is the adequate understanding of *becoming*:

> The philosophical equivalent for the theological idea of divine creation would have to be at least that of a *pure and basic becoming* underlying and therefore preceding all perception and being. But the world-views normally take their point of departure within the circle of perception and being, subject and object, and are content to describe it according to the relationships determined by a particular view, the variations and differences, progressions and retrogressions, between the individual systems being so great that on the one hand the universe seems to be more like a great thought, and on the other more like a great machine.[36]

This "independent problem of the nature of becoming" has not yet been solved in philosophy, in Barth's estimation.

> It is inadvisable, however, to affirm that from the standpoint of the Christian doctrine of creation this prior question is essentially unanswerable, or to contest in principle the possibility that the independent problem of pure becoming might be seen in undistorted form and positively answered even in a

mythical, philosophical or scientific world-view. . . . [I]t is quite improper for
theology to assume *a priori* an attitude of scepticism.[37]

But Barth assigns one other condition for the success of the hypothetical
philosophy of becoming: It must be able to show "as unequivocally as is the
case in the Christian doctrine of creation that this pure becoming is pure
divine benefit preceding all knowledge and being and underlying all knowledge and being." The becoming thus described "cannot be that of an event
which is neutral in the face of the weal and woe of the evolving and evolved
cosmos." It must match the theology of creation by affirming "that which
becomes" and "that which has become" both alike as "the epitome of divine
benefit." At this very point it will "cease to be a mere world-view" by opening itself up to the "datum of divine revelation," recognizing God as Creator in Jesus Christ.[38]

This passage provides an opening (if a small one) for the pursuit of a *THE POINT*
doctrine of election that appreciates Barth's insights while utilizing the cat- *OF DEBATE*
egories of process theology. Process thought begins with the explication of
creation as pure becoming and relates this world-process to the living,
nontemporal God. The process doctrine of election describes God's provision of an initial aim to each instance of creaturely becoming. This
description establishes God's gracious choice to maximize value through
creation and to achieve the divine aim through the purposeful activity of
creatures. Process thought finds itself open to the Christian kerygma at
this exact point: that God's grace is something revealed in the march of
the universe toward a divine goal but is not something for which a metaphysical reason can be given. Here the limit of metaphysics becomes the
gateway to theology.

In contrast to Barth's hierarchical ordering of theology over philosophy,
Whitehead, as a philosopher, believes that his philosophical endeavor precedes and is the basis for theological endeavors. But he also specifies that
philosophy does not operate in isolation from religious experience, the latter being one genre of experience that metaphysical categories must be certain to cover. The concepts of philosophy receive life through the
concretizing power of religion's emotions, and religious experience
becomes veridical when it is authenticated by a properly constructed metaphysics:

> [Philosophy] attains its chief importance by fusing the two, namely, religion
> and science, into one rational scheme of thought. Religion should connect
> the rational generality of philosophy with the emotions and purposes spring-
> ing out of existence in a particular society, in a particular epoch, and condi-
> tioned by particular antecedents. Religion is the translation of general ideas

> into particular thoughts, particular emotions, and particular purposes; it is
> directed to the end of stretching individual interest beyond its self-defeating
> particularity. Philosophy finds religion, and modifies it; and conversely reli-
> gion is among the data of experience which philosophy must weave into its
> own scheme. Religion is an ultimate craving to infuse into the insistent par-
> ticularity of emotion that non-temporal generality which primarily belongs
> to conceptual thought alone. (PR 15–16)

In accordance with this cooperative but definitely hierarchical relationship between philosophy and religion, Whitehead assigns to religion the task of deepening philosophy's meaning while not straying from its rigor:

> The general history of religious thought, of which the Reformation period is
> a particular instance, is that of the endeavour of mankind to interpret the
> great standard experiences as leading to a more definite knowledge than can
> be derived from a metaphysics which founds itself upon general experience.
> There can be nothing inherently illegitimate in such an attempt. But if we
> attend to the general principles which regulate all endeavours after clear state-
> ment of truth, we must be prepared to amplify, recast, generalize, and adapt,
> so as to absorb into one system all sources of experiences. (RM 149)

There is no doubt that Barth would disagree in the strongest terms with the issues of priority that Whitehead discusses here. However, when White- head notes that philosophy must accept religious experience as a datum rather than treating it as an unverifiable *extra* with which philosophy is not concerned, he places a foot on the beginning of the road that Barth is point- ing out when the latter writes that the philosophy of creation must "become theological at this point, and base itself upon the datum of divine revelation."[39] One may look at the history of process theology and decide, independently of Whitehead's own views on the relationship between rev- elation and philosophy, whether this particular worldview has ceased to base itself upon human experience and reason and has "recognise[d] and confess[ed] creation as benefit because it is the work of God in Jesus Christ."[40] In other words, process theology, if it is to be judged adequate in Barthian terms, must have shed its dependence upon philosophy and really become theology.

A clue to the viability of process theology within Barthian constraints may be found in Whitehead's own assessment of philosophy's ability to perceive and describe God. Aristotle, he writes, found a Prime Mover by following his metaphysical exploration to its limit, but this result is not very religiously productive: "It may be doubted whether any properly general metaphysics can ever, without the illicit introduction of other considera- tions, get much further than Aristotle" (SMW 173). Whitehead recognizes the same issue in his own system: "In the place of Aristotle's God as Prime Mover, we require God as the Principle of Concretion" (SMW 174).[41] The postulation of this entity is necessary for the system, since only such an entity can fulfill certain essential functions. But to call this entity "God" is to recognize that metaphysics cannot tell us everything we want or need to know about it and that something beyond the application of human reason to human experience is required for this further knowledge. Specifically, Whitehead recognizes that the question of what possibilities are in fact actualized—the "why" question of existence's meaning—is a religious question that metaphysics is barred from investigating:

> There is a metaphysical need for a principle of determination, but there can be no metaphysical reason for what is determined. If there were such a reason, there would be no need for any further principle: for metaphysics would already have provided the determination. The general principle of empiricism depends upon the doctrine that there is a principle of concretion which is not discernible by abstract reason. What further can be known about God must be sought in the region of particular experiences and therefore rests on an empirical basis. (SMW 178)

Notice in this passage that Whitehead gives the question of "why" a certain priority over metaphysical investigation, as its basis and limit. The fact that certain possibilities are actualized and others are not is the condition for human discernment of patterns and principles in reality. But metaphysics, precisely because it depends upon this selection, can never give a reason for it. That reason, as far as philosophy is concerned, is hidden in the subjectivity of God. This is the horizon, boundary, or limit that Whitehead perceives for philosophy; it is certainly comparable to Barth's confinement of philosophy within the realm of creation.

If Whitehead and Barth come to a certain amount of unexpected agreement on the issue of what philosophy can accomplish before it must become theology, they remain at odds on the issue of priority. While Barth feels that philosophy must acknowledge the limits placed upon it by its proper sphere, refusing on their account to trespass into the more comprehensive field of theology, Whitehead expresses the opinion that metaphysics, by staying within the limits of reason, can teach theology a lesson about the doctrine of God:

> Among medieval and modern philosophers, anxious to establish the religious significance of God, an unfortunate habit has prevailed of paying to Him metaphysical compliments. He has been conceived as the foundation of the metaphysical situation with its ultimate activity. If this conception be adhered to, there can be no alternative except to discern in Him the origin

> of all evil as well as of all good. He is then the supreme author of the play, and to Him must therefore be ascribed its shortcomings as well as its success. If He be conceived as the supreme ground for limitation, it stands in His very nature to divide the Good from the Evil, and to establish Reason "within her dominions supreme." (SMW 179)

Whitehead cautions philosophers about exalting God so highly, in an effort to give God the power and status needed for God's *religious* function, that as a consequence problems such as theodicy become insurmountable. He believes that the solution is to properly conceive of God's *secular* function first, before considering the needs of religion in the doctrine of God. For Whitehead, this means recognizing that at the heart of reality there is both plurality and unity, a denial of the implicit monism of the view of God as the ground of being. The eternal objects are not created by God; they have within themselves the principle of their eternal existence as possibilities. God's function as their evaluator and elector "divides the Good from the Evil" but does not implicate God in the actualization of less-than-desirable possibilities, since events in the world are self-creating.[42]

By the phrase "metaphysical compliments," Whitehead decries the philosophical urge to push God beyond creaturely reality, into a realm of absolutes and away from the realm of relativity. A proper concept of God would recognize that God's transcendence is no less basic to the divine nature than God's immanence. Whitehead follows his usual rule here of collapsing dualisms into polar pairs, which, instead of being ontologically separate from each other, are in fact dependent upon each other and descriptive of the same reality. Barth tends to reinterpret traditional dualisms as well; for example, he rejects the Calvinist doctrine of double predestination, which opposes a reality of rejection to the reality of election, in favor of an asymmetrical relationship of election with its "shadow side" of rejection.[43] The same strategy of asserting asymmetry works for Barth in many areas, including the issue of theodicy. Evil is not willed by God alongside good but is allowed as a necessary possibility associated with the risk God assumes by choosing creatures for fellowship:

> Without evil as "permitted" in this sense there can be no universe or man, and without the inclusion of this "permission" God's decree would be something other than it actually is. . . . God wills evil only because He wills not to keep to Himself the light of His glory but to let it shine outside Himself, because He wills to ordain man the witness of this glory.[44]

The asymmetry in this case is that of possibility to actuality. Actuality must always be referred ultimately to God, and that means to what is good, while evil has reality primarily as a possibility rather than as an actuality. Barth's asymmetries are expressions of contingent dependence: evil upon good, rejection upon election, creatures upon God. As such, they improve upon previous theological formulations by resisting the tendencies toward dualism and monism alike. Whitehead's polar pairs represent another strategy to accomplish the same improvement: by removing the ontological divide between God and creatures that leads to the pull of dualism on the one hand and monism on the other.

The asymmetry constantly reinforced by Barth is far less evident in Whitehead, but it remains in God's singular function in the universe, which gives God priority over every creature, and in God's singular purpose toward increasing value, which infuses all other creatures with purpose. Election demonstrates clearly that God must be the first actor, but its establishment of a clearly two-sided relationship also requires that monism must be resisted fiercely and fundamentally, that is, at a metaphysical level. It is striking that both of these thinkers, in their contemplation of their respective disciplines' vacillations between dualism and monism, were inspired to search for a third way. For Barth, it appeared in the Chalcedonian christological formulae: The relationship between things that appear to be opposites (good and evil, election and rejection) is governed by the form of the relationship between the divine and human natures in Jesus Christ, that is, union without confusion.[45] For Whitehead, it appeared in the substitution of the category of becoming, self-creation with purpose and in order, for the Aristotelian categories of substance and accident, cause and effect. In both thinkers, the operation of the divine selectivity on God's self and on the world expresses their third way. Both Barth and Whitehead find that the analysis of relationship, especially the relationship between God and creatures, tells the story of reality as such. The present task of defining a doctrine of election in process terms continues the convergence of Barth and Whitehead along the path that they have already marked out.

At this point I have indicated that Barth's openness to philosophy, narrow as it may be, leaves room for Whitehead's project of describing "pure becoming," with its recognition of metaphysics' limits discovered in God's grace. Further, it may be possible for process theologians to argue that they have climbed on Whitehead's method to the point where Barth insists they must listen to divine revelation and allow it to transform their philosophy into theology, and that they have in fact embraced revelation at this very point where limit and mystery appear as the horizon of metaphysical construction. It is sufficient for the task at hand to show that such a conversation between Barth and Whitehead can take place, that despite the appearance of intractable opposition on the issue of the relationship between the task of the philosopher and the task of the theologian, each party acknowledges the legitimacy of the other's quest and perceives the boundaries of both fields. The significant differences that remain on this issue—concerning the priority and utility of philosophy and theology, respectively—remain to be adjudicated. Something can be said about the utility of philosophy by the construction of an election doctrine on a framework of process thought, if that election doctrine turns out to be both faithful to the Christian witness and fruitful of new understanding and insight about the relationship between God and creatures. The next step is to test the theoretical possibilities suggested by Barth and Whitehead in such a construction.

The Act of the Elector toward Jesus Christ

An analysis of Barth's election doctrine must always mention Jesus Christ first. In Barth, Jesus Christ is both the Elector and the elected, since he is both God and human being. So the consideration of God's act of election begins with God's act toward God's self in Christ. In the next section, similarly, the analysis of the response of the elected creature will begin with the response of Jesus Christ.

It is important to keep in mind throughout the discussion of Barth's doctrine that the union of elector and elected in Jesus Christ is not simply equivalent to the union of natures in the sense that the divine nature elects and the human nature is elected. Barth's doctrine hinges on the fact that in Jesus Christ, God elects not only human beings but primarily and previously God's self. Thus, Jesus Christ as God is elected. Interestingly, although far less emphasized in Barth, Jesus Christ as a human being is an elector as well![46] This side of the doctrine will be explored later in this chapter, when the response of the elected creature comes into view. At this point, the topic that precedes all other topics in election is God's election of God's self, which Barth sees revealed in Jesus Christ.

"The election of grace," reads the *Leitsatz* to §33, "is the eternal beginning of all the ways and works of God in Jesus Christ."[47] Before creation or any other work of God *ad extra*, Barth asserts, God *chooses*, once and for all, eternally, taking the first step down a path from which God will not waver. What God chooses is to love not only God's self but also what is not God: "In Jesus Christ God in His free grace determines Himself for sinful man and sinful man for Himself."[48] God's choice is free and unconditioned, and because God is steadfast and faithful, God's primordial choice conditions all subsequent divine acts. In effect, this choice is God's limitation of God's self. It does not diminish God's freedom to proclaim this self-limitation, because God's freedom lies precisely in God's ability to choose God's own destination. The divine self-determination is election because it is the elimination of all other paths that God could have chosen for God's self. God elects God's self to be *for the world,* for what is outside and other than God, and all else follows from this election.[49] In God's election of God's self, all other acts of election can be found, because God's free choice determines God's self for all time, immutable in terms of God's purpose to elect us.[50]

Although we see God's self-election in Jesus Christ, the Son revealing the Father, Barth finds in this primordial act a triune structure:

> In the beginning it was the choice of the Father Himself to establish this covenant with man by giving up His Son for him, that He Himself might become man in the fulfilment of His grace. In the beginning it was also the choice of the Son to be obedient to grace, and therefore to offer up Himself and to become man in order that this covenant might be made a reality. In the beginning it was the resolve of the Holy Spirit that the unity of God, of Father and Son should not be disturbed or rent by this covenant with man, but that it should be made the more glorious, the deity of God, the divinity of His love and freedom, being confirmed and demonstrated by this offering of the Father and this self-offering of the Son.[51]

The choice of God entails the choice of each member of the Trinity. Barth finds the self-determination of God originating in the Father. But the Son and the Holy Spirit choose to enact the roles that the Father has chosen for them: the Son to become incarnate, the Holy Spirit to include human beings in the fellowship of God's inner life. In one sense this means that the Son and the Holy Spirit are elected, but as God they are also possessed of the divine freedom to elect themselves for these tasks and to respond in perfect obedience to the Father.[52]

The triune exposition in this passage is more confessional than theological; Barth's election doctrine proceeds dualistically, for the most part, presenting the elected paired with the rejected. The Holy Spirit is largely absent from the discussion, with the passage cited above an exception, as Barth focuses on Jesus Christ as the object and subject of election. Since subject-object structure is inherently dualistic, it is not surprising that Barth's use of this framework prevents him from developing a truly triune doctrine of election. The passage above suggests that Barth might be able to explicate the Holy Spirit as the unifier of God and creatures in a covenant of election, so that the relationship established by God's act has a character of its own that is *vocational* (i.e., the Spirit calls creatures into the service of God and creates communities that witness to God's glory).[53] A more fully realized role for the Spirit in Barth's doctrine of election might result in a softening—or, more likely, an *Aufhebung*—of the dualism he exhibits throughout the doctrine of election. His dualism causes some discord when he uses it to relegate the synagogue to "the passing form" of election or to justify the inequality between men and women. The tendency to type these pairs makes them abstract symbols of the earthly reality and downplays the role of the Spirit in bringing them into the Trinitarian fellowship as particularities rather than abstract principles. Vocation, as we shall see later in this chapter, connects the call of God and the response of the creature to the *telos* of the universe—that is, with the divine goal graciously extended to the creature to become its goal as well. The biblical model of election is the call to service,[54] and the Holy Spirit is traditionally appointed the work of consummating God's activity, so it is fitting to explicate election and vocation together by bringing the Holy Spirit more fully into the theological structure.[55]

Barth writes, "God in his free grace determines Himself." Here we see Barth returning to the key issue of God's freedom. Theology collapses if God's primordial self-election is not understood as a free act of self-determination and self-limitation. God is not compelled to take on relationships outside God's self:

> God's decision in Jesus Christ is a gracious decision. In making it, God stoops down from above. In it He does something which He has no need to do, which He is not constrained to do. He does something which He alone can constrain Himself, and has in fact constrained Himself, to do.[56]

> Be it noted that this determination of the will of God, this content of predestination, is already grace, for God did not stand in need of any particular ways or works *ad extra*. He had no need of a creation. He might well have been satisfied with the inner glory of His threefold being, His freedom, and His love. The fact that he is not satisfied, but that His inner glory overflows and becomes outward, the fact that He wills the creation, and the man Jesus as the first-born of all creation, is grace, sovereign grace, a condescension inconceivably tender.[57]

The gospel of grace depends, for Barth as for Calvin, on the hypothetical possibility that God might never have created. Because God is God's own object of love, due to the Trinitarian *perichoresis,* the divine reality does not stand in need of anything outside itself. As we have already seen, the definition of freedom that Barth reserves for God is the freedom to be unconstrained by anything except by God's own loving choice. If the world exists alongside God in some relatively independent sense, then God would be obliged to have a relationship outside God's triune self. Barth understands this obligation as a diminution of grace. We must be able to imagine God alone, even if this is an abstraction from the God we know concretely—the God who has decided to be related to us.

If it is necessary for theology to acknowledge the hypothetical possibility of God without creation, however, it is not theologically productive to become enamored of this imaginary alternate history. "We must not be so exact, so clever, so literal, that our doctrine of God remains only a doctrine of God. We must demonstrate its Christian character by avoiding such abstraction."[58] Barth wants to focus our attention on the concrete God, the one with whom we are confronted at every turn in Jesus Christ because there is none other. Although there are two moments at issue in God's revelation, they are not two different moments but distinguishable (yet inseparable) aspects of the same moment. The moment in which human beings specifically encounter God in history is revelation in Jesus Christ. But this moment follows, refines, and temporalizes the first moment, God's eternal self-limitation. It does not contradict that first moment, nor does it redirect that first moment to hide something about God even as God is being revealed. Barth explains that God's self-election is the epistemological condition for revelation, because it defines God's character as this and not that, as Christ and not Satan:

> Therefore the reality of the fulfilment of the true knowledge of God, as the act in which God gives Himself to be known and is known, must always be distinguished from the necessary limitation in which it happens. And the limitation has to be understood as both the means and limit of the fulfilment of the true knowledge of God.[59]

The divine decision to be related to creation, then, imposes a certain limitation upon God's freedom in that it excludes the possibility of God's living without creatures. Barth asserts that the possibilities are even further limited by the specific content of God's decision: to share the divine life with creatures by granting them the honors of autonomy and fellowship. This limitation is "necessary" in the above quotation not logically or metaphysically but only in order for God to condescend to the creature—that "condescension inconceivably tender." It is tender precisely because it is gracious. One can imagine with frightening ease an alternate reality in which God limited God's self in an entirely different way that did not involve that condescension. Theology often consists of reminding ourselves that this alternate reality does not, in fact, exist. In a sense, theological speculation about a God who lives only in and for God's triune existence, although it may be necessary to make a point about grace, is otherwise like speculation about a God who creates a different world with different creatures destined for a different end. It may be entertaining, but it is not Christian theology in the strictest sense, since it is not about the real God who has revealed God's self through Christ.

Election refers properly to the divine act of Jesus Christ. The primordial self-election of God, and therefore all divine election that follows, occurs in, through, and for Jesus Christ.[60] This is the Barthian innovation in the doctrine of election, which to Barth is simply the result of taking the biblical witness seriously but which had never before been carried through with the proper consistency. "It is one of the great puzzles of history that the step which we are taking toward a true form of the electing God and elected man was not taken long ago," he writes after rehearsing the efforts of Augustine, Aquinas, Calvin, and others.[61] By referring all election to Jesus Christ, Barth hopes to avoid the most potent danger of the election doctrine, as evidenced by its development in Calvin into the frightening phrase *decretum absolutum*. That danger is that the incarnation, and the plan of salvation that it presupposes, will be seen as simply one decision of God among many. If it is not the basic decision governing both God and creatures in their relationships, then there is some more fundamental choice in God's character that has nothing to do with us. If divine revelation is simply one act of God among many, then God has decided to reveal God's self for some purpose hidden in God's private counsels. Theology which leaves open the possibility that the God we know is not God as God is for God's self, but only God as God appears to be for us, teaches either implicitly or explicitly a God whose decisions on our behalf can only be more or less arbitrary and temporary:

> If in regard to the decisive factor, the election itself, or the electing God, we cannot fix our gaze and keep it fixed on Jesus Christ, because the electing God is not identical with Christ but behind and above Him, because in the beginning with God we have to reckon with someone or something other than the *houtos* ["the same one"] of Jn. 1:2, a decision of the divine good-pleasure quite unrelated to and not determined by Him, what useful purpose can such an answer serve?[62]

Calvin, committed to a sovereign God whose primordial act of predestining some for heaven and some for hell cannot be questioned, tried to make a virtue of what he saw as necessity by speaking openly of God's absolute decree, like that of a ruler who has the power of life and death over his subjects, who has no responsibility to any principle outside himself, and whom no law governs. Yes, election is seen in Jesus Christ for Calvin, but only as a consequence of a prior decision on God's part of which Christ is the evidence. "All the dubious features of Calvin's doctrine [e.g., double predestination, the *decretum absolutum*] result from the basic failing that in the last analysis he separates God and Jesus Christ, thinking that what was in the beginning with God must be sought elsewhere than in Jesus Christ."[63] Barth seeks to identify that prior decision with Christ, so that we need not merely assert the truth and comprehensiveness of the revelation in Christ as a matter of faith but may rest in the knowledge that God's free being is to beget a Son for us. In this way the doctrine of election both formally conforms to the witness of Scripture and practically gives us the hope and confidence that theologians have longed claimed for it but have rarely been able to explicate:

> Of what avail is it for the Calvinists to protest that as God's decision it is based on grounds which are just and adequate although beyond our comprehension, or for the Lutherans to assist us with the comforting kindness of God towards us? If it is not true that Jesus Christ Himself is for us the electing God, then all these attempts at consolation point us elsewhere than to the Word of God.[64]

Furthermore, for Barth, all God's ways and works spring from the primordial divine decision to be incarnate—that is, to give Jesus Christ to creatures not as a contingent remedy for contingent sin, not as a mere possibility to be actualized in case it is needed, but as a concrete actuality. The ideal does not remain an idea, but becomes real. God's self-limitation, then, is eternally in the form of the creature. God wills to meet the creature as a creature, and it is this primordial decision that both establishes the relationship between God and creature to be of absolute divine importance, and averts the horror of the *decretum absolutum:*

> Must we not say that in His confrontation of the creature, in His relationship with everything which is outside Himself, God is God absolutely in the fact that from all eternity He elects, He decides one way or the other concerning the being and nature of the creature (with all that this involves)? . . . What choice can precede the choice by which God has of Himself chosen to have with Himself in the beginning of all things the Word which is Jesus?[65]

In Christ, Barth sees the incarnate plan of God, the end for which God has predestined the creature already among us. What has been from eternity chosen by God on the creature's behalf—fellowship with God—is enacted in Jesus Christ both to reveal this choice to the chosen ones and to bring it about: "He was also in the beginning with God as 'the first-born of every creature' (Col. 1:15). Himself the plan and decree of God, Himself the divine decision with respect to all creation and its history whose content is already determined."[66]

Does this last phrase mean that Barth finds himself forced to acknowledge divine determinism, the doctrine that either God's foreknowledge or God's active will eternally determines every contingent event? Certainly Barth is emboldened to use the language of predestination that has led many theologians to determinism, because it is a word used in Scripture. He also does not consider the outcome of history to be in doubt; as it was in the beginning, the Alpha of God's primordial decision, so it will be in the end, the Omega of creation's consummation.[67] But the divine decision is to give creatures the honor of a place in the history of God's dealings with the world. God's self-limitation means that God allows creatures the autonomy to make history. Predestination thus does not mean predetermination of every event in the life of the creature. Instead, it means that thanks to the divine election, the creature has a goal for its life that it could not choose for itself if God had not chosen for it in advance: "His decision precedes every creaturely decision. Over against all creaturely self-determination it is pre-determination—*prae-destinatio*."[68] Barth's solution to the problem of divine determinism is not a metaphysical one; it is a dogmatic one. By subordinating the topic of predestination to the topic of election (as in Augustine and Aquinas), he asserts that God's choice is not subdivided into many choices both for and against the creature. These multifaceted aspects of the divine governance of the world are secondary. What is primary is election, in which God decides to be *pro nobis* by deciding to be incarnate. This means that our freedom is elected, our acts are elected, and therefore the doctrine of election itself assures us that we really act in freedom, even as it reminds us that our free acts come after God's act and cannot therefore be in contradiction to God's act:

> The goodness of God's will and work *ad extra* depends upon the fact that in the smallest things as in the greatest God wholly and utterly wills and fulfils and reveals Himself. But He wills and fulfils and reveals Himself not only in Himself but in giving Himself, in willing and recognising the distinct reality of the creature, granting and conceding to it an individual and autonomous place side by side with Himself. . . . To the creature God determined, therefore, to give an individuality and autonomy, not that these gifts should be possessed outside Him, let alone against Him, but for Him, and within His kingdom; not in rivalry with His sovereignty but for its confirming and glorifying.[69]

God "elects man to participation in His own glory"—eschatological glory, yes, but also the glory of the agency that is God's prerogative, the glory of creation, enjoyment, and service.

The issue of human freedom will return later in this chapter, under the topic of the creature's response to divine election. At present we focus on Barth's description of Jesus Christ as the elected God, in preparation for understanding God's act of election toward creatures.

> Between the eternal Godhead of Christ which needs no election and His elected humanity, there is a third possibility. And that is the being of Christ in the beginning with God, the act of the good-pleasure of God by which the fulness of the Godhead is allowed to dwell in Him, the covenant which God made with Himself and which is for that reason eternal, the oath which God sware by Himself in the interests of man.[70]

Christ's priority over all creation is double: as the divine Elector, Christ precedes all creation as God's plan and decree; as the elected human being, Christ is the firstborn of all creation. But primarily and basically, he is elected as God and elects as God, as the condition for his electing as a human being and his election as a human being:

> In so far as He is the electing God, we must obviously—and above all—ascribe to Him the active determination of electing. It is not that He does not elect as man, i.e., elect God in faith. But this election can only follow His prior election, and that means that it follows the divine electing which is the basic and proper determination of His existence.[71]

God's self-election, then, is the true meaning of the doctrine of election for Barth, since it consists of Christ to whom all questions about God's act and being must be referred. Here God determines God's self as the One who loves in freedom, and determines sinful man as the object of divine love. This eternal election is the basis of human faith in God's constancy and is the condition for human existence, freedom, and knowledge.

The Act of the Elector toward Israel and the Church

Although God's self in Jesus Christ is the first place election occurs and comes to light, election also occurs and comes to light, if only secondarily, in the community. Again, Jesus Christ is the revelation of this election as well as the location in which the election takes place, because he is the head of the community. Barth did theology a great service by placing the election of the community before the election of the individual. In this way he reminds Christians that they are part of a body larger than themselves, toward which God exercises God's electing will *in toto*.[72] He also enables theology to utilize the many references in Scripture, Old Testament and New, to God's election of a people. The individualism of the Enlightenment led to an emphasis in nineteenth-century liberal theology on the relationship between God and the human person in her subjective existence. Human existence, Barth reminds us, cannot be considered in isolation from the rest of creation, as if God transacted God's business with us only one by one. Already the doctrine of God's self-election has demonstrated, for Barth, that all of creation is the object of God's unitary act of election. Now Barth considers the further specification and particularization of that act—not yet down to the level of the individual person, but first at the level of the community to which that individual belongs.[73]

The first community that God elects is Israel—first in history and first in God's intention. Jesus Christ is the first member of this community and stands for the entire community, incarnate from all eternity as a particular man, a Jew and heir of the promise to Abraham. In that Jesus Christ is God's act of self-election, however, Barth sees him as the Messiah of Israel for which King David, his ancestor, was a type and predecessor. God's relationship of election with Israel does not begin in history. The Hebrew Scriptures record God's call to Abram to "go from your country and your kindred and your father's house to the land that I will show you," and the divine promise to make of him "a great nation," in Genesis 12:1–2. But Barth asserts that the history of God's determination to choose Israel does not begin here:

> With *Israel's* election in view God has, according to Scripture, acted among men from the beginning of the world in the form of election. And on the basis of Israel's election, in order continually to reveal and attest it, God proceeds to elect men in and from its midst for special appointment, mission and representative function, as exponents and instruments of the mercy in which He has made His people His own.[74]

God's disposition of creation from the beginning of time, and therefore from the beginning of Scripture, demonstrates that Israel is chosen from eternity. And God's revelation in the midst of this community in the person of Jesus Christ demonstrates that Israel is chosen for eternity—that is, that the nation of Israel made up of the descendants of Abraham, Isaac, and Jacob is forever ordained by God to be a special divine instrument, the recipient of a peculiar promise and demand.

For Barth, the story of God's covenant with Israel is also the story of the church, into which Israel's special relationship passes and which becomes the

heir of the promise to Abraham. Where Israel stands over against the nations
in the Old Testament as the elect called out of the world, the church—called
from the nations to be included in the covenant through its head, the King
of the Jews[75]—stands over against Israel, Barth claims, as the elect called out
of the unfaithful nation. Barth's commitment to the contrast between the
elect and rejected leads him to find in Israel the shadow cast by the church.
Katherine Sonderegger writes of Barth's doctrine of Israel:

> The Jews are honored within, and indeed outside the Church, because they
> are the flesh Christ judged, rejected, and condemned. The Messiah, Jesus of
> Nazareth, came first to the Jews because he came out of them. That Jesus
> Christ was born a Jew means that Christians for all time honor the Jews as
> the stiff-necked, disobedient sinners for whom Christ died. Barth, too, raises
> up Israel as a light to the nations, but it is a light that pitilessly exposes the
> Jews as "vessels of wrath" through whose disbelief the Gentiles are spared.[76]

This aspect of Barth's theology remains problematic for theologians con-
cerned with promoting Jewish-Christian dialogue, condemning anti-
Semitism, and taking seriously the eternal covenant between God and
Israel to which the whole Old Testament attests. It must be admitted that
Barth wrestles with the question of supersessionism and the meaning of
Israel's continued existence with the utmost seriousness, and that his affirmation of the eternal covenant is a great advance upon his theological predecessors. But the negative image of Israel that constantly recurs in Barth
remains a stumbling block in his section on communal election.[77]

For the moment, however, I wish to point out a few distinctive features
that Barth finds in the act of God toward the community of Israel insofar
as analysis can divide this act from God's election of the church, keeping
in mind that Barth stresses the unity of these two moments of corporate
election. Notice first that the election of Israel is indeed quite literally corporate, even corporeal;[78] it is God's decision to choose the genetic offspring of a particular man and woman, Abraham and Sarah, for the
purpose of building a nation in which the divine plan will work itself out
with special intensity and from which God's action will resonate into the
rest of the world. Nothing could be further from the general picture of
individual election, in which God deals with each person quite apart from
his race, color, creed, or ancestry—apart, that is to say, from his history,
and considering only his soteriological status—than the first image Scripture gives us of a human being called out from the mass of humanity to
perform a special function. This function is to reproduce and spread the
blessings of God through his seed. God's call to Israel shows that God calls

communities as they are naturally constituted in the creaturely world—
families, societies, and nations. But Barth emphasizes that God is not
bound by the natural boundaries of communities. The Spirit is free to
gather together into a community those who do not naturally belong to
it, and this is in fact the way in which the Gentiles of the church are
brought into the sphere of Israel's election. Conversely, Barth asserts that
God is free to exclude from the promise those who belong to it by nature
but not by the Spirit:

> Some of Israel are, of course, Israel. But not all who are "of Israel" are so in
> the way in which . . . this is to be said of Jesus of Nazareth. Strictly speaking,
> He alone is Israel, and it is only in Him, as His prophets, witnesses, fore-
> runners, that others are as well, those who are specially elected in Him, with
> Him and for His sake. Not one of them is so by nature; not one in virtue of
> his Jewish blood; not one as a self-evident consequence of his membership
> of this people; but each only on the ground of a special election in which the
> election of Israel as such is repeated and established.[79]

God acts toward Israel through individuals within the chosen people
whose actions move the history of the people through the Hebrew Scriptures. But Barth sees Israel as the witness to God's rejection, and the special few—the remnant called out of Israel—are the church already present
in a secret form, the elect in the midst of rejection:

> The existence of the elect in and from Israel does not alter at all the deter-
> mination of Israel as such and as a whole because these elect are exceptions
> which as such do not suspend the rules that Israel has to serve the revelation
> of the divine judgment. . . . And finally, the circle of the elect grows contin-
> ually smaller or at least continually less visible, in the course of Israel's his-
> tory, until it is ultimately reduced to the person of one man, Jesus of
> Nazareth.[80]

Barth interprets the history of Israel in Scripture as a record of the children of Israel as a group, set over against their leaders and prophets, who
are called out of their midst to stand in contrast to them. Moses struggles
with their unbelief during the exodus, and his struggle is a paradigm for the
repeated conflict that Barth sees between the people and those God calls to
lure the people back to the truth. Since these judges, prophets, and kings
are human beings, they sometimes succumb to the same temptations as the
community taken as a whole; they are members of that community, and
when they stray, they do even more harm because they lead others. But the
books of the prophets record God's patience in raising up individuals to
bring the community back again and again. Barth explains that the elec-

tion of the community of Israel involves the election of individuals to guide, reprove, and even discipline the community.

As these members are called out of the community to provide special services to the community by serving God, so Israel is called out of the nations to provide a special service to the world by serving God. Barth depicts Israel as the vehicle for God's grace to all nations through Jesus Christ. Again, the genetic constitution of this election becomes important in the birth of Christ; for Barth, aside from the witness of Israel to God's judgment, Israel's service to God and the world consists most basically in producing this child, with his particular ancestry and his particular bloodline. Jesus Christ is not just any person with an abstract parentage and membership in an abstract nation. Israel's chosenness is revealed in—and in fact for Barth consists of—its distillation into this one specific Israelite.[81]

The nations that exist alongside Israel, however, are chosen in their own right to serve God. Barth sees the election of God manifested in two forms: in the elect, and in those from whom the elect are called. The latter serve God in their contrast to the chosen ones, in standing over against the chosen people as the ground to their figure, as the shadow they cast. Barth is not afraid to call this service rejection, because the Scriptures are not shy to speak of God's wrath and destruction. But Barth does not set up rejection as an independent reality alongside election, as if God's will were bifurcated at this point. The rejected are not outside the sphere of election. They are, in a sense, elected for rejection, chosen to demonstrate this contrast, as Barth interprets Scripture's report that the nations surrounding Israel are raised up by God to punish the chosen people and carry them off to exile.[82] Barth takes this seriously as election, noting at the same time that the wrath of God cannot but be directed at the enemies of those God has chosen. As enemies of Israel, the nations are rejected—but this rejection is elected for them! Barth sees the asymmetrical relationship between election and rejection elucidated here, where election swallows up rejection by fully encompassing its sphere of dependent reality:

> What have the Gentiles to do with Israel's Messiah? Fundamentally and in complete objectivity only what is revealed in the figure of Pontius Pilate. To them He is delivered up by Israel itself to be put to death and after their miscarriage of justice and by their hands He is, in fact, put to death. . . . But for all that it is soon enough for one of them to be able to utter immediately after Jesus' death the first unambiguous confession of faith and sin: "Surely this man was the son of God" (Mk. 15:39). The Gentiles have taken the last step on the long road of Israel's history, and with the confession of the Gentiles it now begins anew. . . . Thus the death of Jesus unites what was divided, the elected and the rejected.[83]

In discussing his doctrine of the election of the church, one should not be distracted by the problems involved from the positive contribution Barth makes in this area. The *Leitsatz* for §34, "The Election of the Community," begins, "The election of grace, as the election of Jesus Christ, is simultaneously the eternal election of the one eternal community of God by the existence of which Jesus Christ is to be attested to the whole world and the whole world summoned to faith in Jesus Christ."[84] Notice that there is only one elect community. Barth reaffirms the unity of God's act of election *ad extra* by connecting it with the unitary act of divine election of God's self in Jesus Christ. It is not the case that the election of Israel was an effort at election gone wrong, replaced and corrected by the election of the church. Barth cannot assert this without giving up the basis of his doctrine of election: its origin in God's election of God's self in Jesus Christ. In Jesus Christ, God elects Israel; in Jesus Christ, God elects the church. Barth makes productive use of Romans 9–11 to explicate the asymmetrical relationship between the two communities. The covenant with Israel is the basis of the covenant with the church; the latter is the "wild olive shoot" grafted onto the tree of Israel "contrary to nature":

> Israel is diminished through the transgression. It is robbed of its lost members. But the full complement of its members is restored at once by the addition of Gentile believers. Thus the Gentile Christians are, in a sense, locum-tenens for those who have dropped out. They dwell in their houses, use their utensils and administer their possessions. But, all the same, they are only locum-tenens; they are only transplanted aliens. . . . If the latter are now where the others used to be, they owe it only to this insertion and therefore indirectly to the others in whose place they have been put.[85]

The church is included in the community of Israel through grace, and the proper response is gratitude toward God and respect toward the "natural" members of the covenant, those born into the divine promise. Both together form "one eternal community of God" for the service of evangelizing the world; both attest to Jesus Christ.

However, the one eternal community of God, for Barth, appears in two forms. Barth finds in Israel the symbol of God's wrath, and in the church the symbol of God's love:

> This one community of God in its form as Israel has to serve the representation of the divine judgment, in its form as the Church the representation of the divine mercy. In its form as Israel it is determined for hearing, and in its form as the Church for believing the promise sent forth to man. To the one elected community of God is given in the one case its passing, and in the other its coming form.[86]

According to Barth, the election of the one community has two aspects; the service for which God calls the community has two divisions; the divine character and act have two representations. Barth asserts that Israel is ordained to be disobedient so that God's judgment may be revealed in it. The service it renders, for Barth, is to serve God's glory by receiving the divine wrath:

> Israel is the people of the Jews which resists its divine election. It is the community of God in so far as this community has to exhibit also the unwillingness, incapacity and unworthiness of man with respect to the love of God directed to him. By delivering up its Messiah, Jesus, to the Romans for crucifixion, Israel attests the justice of the divine judgment on man borne by God Himself. Encountering the fulfilled promise in this way, it remains only its hearer without passing on to faith in it.[87]

The church, on the other hand, is ordained to be forgiven, in Barth's scheme, so that God's mercy may be revealed in it. The service it renders, for Barth, is to serve God's glory by receiving the divine love:

> The Church . . . is the community of God in so far as this community has to set forth to sinful man the good-will, readiness and honour of God. As Jesus Christ the crucified Messiah of Israel shows Himself in His resurrection to be the Lord of the Church, the latter can recognise and confess the divine mercy shown to man. And as it recognises and confesses that the divine Word is in its fulfilment stronger than the contradiction of its hearers, it can believe and keep and do it.[88]

Yet Barth also finds that the church has failed to perform this service as regards its mission to the Jews. Because it has not made the synagogue jealous of its possession of the fulfillment of the promise, the church has become the problematic question; the *Judenfrage* becomes, for a moment at least, the *Christenfrage*.[89] At this point, Barth points to Jesus Christ, in whom rejection and election are revealed together, but for whom rejection is overcome by election:

> These are the two forms of the elected community, the two poles between which its history moves (in a unilateral direction, from here to there), but in such a way that the bow of the one covenant arches over the whole. . . . The antithesis between the two cannot be formulated in exclusive terms. Behind and above the human obduracy characteristic of the Israelite form of the community there stands indeed the divine rejection, but there stands also God's election in which He has determined Himself to take upon Himself the rejection.[90]

Barth maintains that the church possesses not only God's promise, which Israel heard, but also the fulfillment of that promise in Christ and faith in Christ.

The question before us is: How does Barth describe God's act of election toward Israel and the church? First of all, Barth cannot say and will not allow his theology to conclude that God rejects Israel and elects the church. Although the dual determination of Jesus Christ and the implicit dualism he finds in Scripture lead Barth to explicate Israel as a sign of divine rejection and the church as a sign of divine election, the prior, controlling doctrine of God's freedom prevents him from presuming that God in fact finally acts in this way. God is not bound by the instruments God uses to reveal God's self; in God's act, God is free to transcend the limitations of those instruments. Second, Barth asserts that God's act toward Israel and the church is one act of election, the formation of one community for fellowship with God, at the center of which Jesus Christ stands. Finally, God's act of election toward this community calls it to serve God by honoring God's glory and attesting to God's purpose for the entire world. This final observation is the key to understanding Barth's doctrine with respect to Israel and the church. His division of the community into passing and coming forms, into revelations of God's judgment and mercy, reflects his conviction that the community must attest to the whole truth of God. And the riddle of the synagogue for Barth is what purpose it can serve in this tapestry of revelation.[91] Leaving aside for the moment the shortcomings of Barth's understanding of contemporary Judaism's place in God's plan, I want to emphasize that the community is elect in Barth to provide a concrete environment and platform for the service of individuals. The community itself serves God in its very constitution as an actual community, since the survival of a corporate entity over time and space reveals the power of God's life-sustaining and life-giving Spirit. God's election of the community for service points forward to the fulfillment of election in the kingdom of God, when the community of the Spirit will be all-encompassing. To the extent that the Spirit manifests itself in the community today, the community is the present and immanent kingdom of God.

The Act of the Elector toward the Individual

Barth comes to the discussion of individual election per se only after the discussion of Jesus Christ's election and the community's election. This does not mean that the election of the individual is somehow derivative from these, as if God does not act toward individuals but only toward God's self or toward communities. In fact, Barth asserts, there is no election apart from the individual: "It is individuals who are chosen and not the totality of men. And God seeks, calls, blesses, and sanctifies the many, the totality, the natural and historical groups and humanity itself, in and through the individual."[92] The order of discussion results from Barth's understanding that the individual does not possess anything of its own, not even its own existence. The individual is not found divorced from an environment and independent of God. God truly encounters the individual, but not as one suddenly comes upon a stranger. God meets the individual in Jesus Christ, while the individual is still potential, by ordaining a purpose for the creature as such. And God meets the individual in the community by working out the divine purpose through the history of a people, with all the social, cultural, and familial details of that people.

The order of discussion in Barth's doctrine requires him to establish the theological significance of the community for election before defining the individuals that make up the community. Yet he asserts that the election of the community is contingent on the election of its members in their singularity, not the other way around. Barth finds that God's relationship with human beings is most properly and basically the relationship between individuals because of two connected revealed propositions: God is Trinity, and Jesus Christ is One. In this unexpected locus, the doctrine of the Trinity that Barth expounds in *CD* I/1 bears fruit. God in Trinity reveals the nature of relatedness itself by God's self-sufficiency in constituting in God's self both sides of the relation (I-Thou, Father-Son) and the relation that obtains between them (Love, Spirit). "[T]he affinity of the individual to God which makes him the object of His election of grace is based solely on the nature and activity of God as such"[93]—that nature and activity being Trinitarian.

The second proposition, that Jesus Christ is One, makes our individuality a reflection of the singularity of the God-man. Barth makes God's self-revelation in Christ the measure for our self-understanding. We respond to God as "one . . . the bearer of a definite personal name";[94] this recalls to Barth instantly the single hypostasis in Christ (the one person, the one individuality, the one name that identifies the subject of the scriptural narratives). The relationship of this individual to God is identity: Jesus Christ is God. If we take Christ as the prototype by which we are to judge our own individuality, we see that our simultaneous separation from and relation to others is not something defined over against God, as if it is by being creatures that we become individuals. Our individuality is grounded and dependent on God as Trinity, and Jesus Christ reveals that individuality by his unity with God.

In the earlier discussion of the election of Jesus Christ, I focused on Barth's concept of God's self-determination as the basis of all election *ad extra*. Now it is necessary to return to God's election of Jesus Christ to discover Barth's understanding of the divine act toward the human individual. Jesus Christ is, in fact, the true and primary individual. His specificity, his true definition in terms of his personal name, is that he is one with God. God elects Jesus Christ as God, and as a human being. The incarnation confirms for Barth that God elects the human individual in all of his particularity—electing not some abstract person but a real man with ethnicity, personality, needs, and gifts. To generalize Jesus Christ into a symbol of humanity rather than a specific human being is to succumb to the docetic temptation of trying to preserve God's majesty by refusing to let it be sullied by creaturehood, even if God has in fact chosen to express the divine majesty by such condescension. The particularity of Jesus Christ, the human person, represents to Barth the scandal of the Christian faith, the counterintuitive expression of divine freedom that offends human reason. Yet Barth contends that it is precisely in this particularity that God reveals, contrary to what human reason might expect, the election of each individual's uniqueness. The influence of Platonic thought might lead us to assume that our flaws and strengths can be viewed quantitatively, and that if all deficiencies were erased we could arrive at the single perfect ideal of humanity. Divine election does not erase differences and conform individuals to a generic ideal. It embraces the irreducible particularity of the individual creature as it actually is and actually must be, even as it reveals that God does not rank these particularities quantitatively or hierarchically. In Christ there is no male or female, Jew or Gentile, slave or free, not because these differences are leveled in election but because one is not preferred to the other, because God is not bound by the way human beings have construed these differences but is free to turn existing hierarchies on their heads: "He does not choose the free, the wise and the rich. On the contrary, it is He who makes those whom he elects free, wise and rich by electing them."[95]

The elected human being is the recipient of election for a purpose and with a responsibility. God meets the elected one in the form of a promise and a demand. The promise is fellowship with God, already enjoyed for eternity and in history by Jesus Christ:

> [W]hen God elects man for communion with Himself in His eternal election of grace He promotes him to the indestructible position of His child and brother, His intimate and friend. What God is, He wills to be for man also. What belongs to Him He wills to communicate to man also. What He can do is meant to benefit man also. No one and nothing is to be so close to man as He is. No one and nothing is to separate him from Him.[96]

The demand is the faith in that promise and the Lord of that promise, and the obedience in the pursuit of the divine purpose that Jesus Christ exhibited in history and before history: "If we are bidden to hear Him as the Leader, the Disposer and Giver, in that very fact we are all the more bidden to entrust ourselves in faith to His care, to have confidence in what He ordains, to accept and make fruitful His gift."[97]

This promise and demand do not come only to the human being in her individuality. They come first to Jesus Christ, and also to the community that is constituted by the reality of Jesus Christ. For Barth, God's claim upon us is legitimate precisely because God has not claimed us as something other than God's self, but as God's self in Jesus Christ. Our knowledge of God's claim is predicated on God's primordial act of demand upon God's self:

> We move onto solid ground when we seek to learn from this positive attitude [of God's] that which can be learned concerning the knowledge and reality of God, considering Him and conceiving of Him in the constant light of His revelation and all His works. . . . God lays upon us the obligation of this attitude because first of all He lays it upon Himself.[98]

Here the demand of God is seen in the light of covenant partnership. Barth asserts that God could claim our obedience in the guise of a tyrant, for we are God's creatures and completely dependent upon God's provision of existence and environment for us. God could claim our obedience in the name of the absolute divine freedom that sets the limits that, from the point of view of relative freedom, must always be arbitrary. But for Barth, the word *God* in the two sentences above does not denote the God that actually exists, but a hypothetical God; not God as God has concretely determined God's self to be, but God as we might imagine God: "It is not, however, an abstract freedom as such, but the freedom of the One who loves in freedom. It is He Himself, and not an essence of the freedom of choice, or of free choice, who is the divine Subject of the electing which takes place at this point."[99] The claim that the true, living God exercises over creatures is the claim of a covenant-maker who becomes a covenant partner. The covenant-maker dictates the terms by which both partners abide. By entering into a covenant, both partners do not become equal; one partner dictates while the other receives. But the dictating partner binds himself to his own terms and condescends to treat the other as an equal in this relationship. In the case of the covenant between God and the human being, the ontological inequality is not erased but is made of no account. God condescends to humanity to the extent that God fulfills the covenant in God's own person.

What is the content of the claim and promise that come to the individual? Barth sees them as revelation—that is, their content is God for us, which is God's very self. The frightening aspect of the law-gospel dichotomy in many theologies, especially those of Luther and the Reformed thinkers whom Luther influenced, is that the promise and demand that God delivers to human beings are not essentially connected to God's self, but seem to be the result of some contingent decision of God. If God can make two covenants with humanity, even if the two are compatible, then there is some hidden divine plan behind those covenants. If Barth is compelled to say that the content of the law is different from the content of the gospel, then the single truth of God remains unrevealed. Instead, Barth can only say that God's mercy is the same as God's righteousness, that the election that comes to us as demand and promise is one election with one content and one message: God as God has determined God's self to be in the company of creatures.

> The righteousness of the divine mercy which has offered itself and bestowed itself on elected man requires of him only that he should be, and conduct himself as, one to whom this offer and gift has been made. Whoever and whatever he may be, he has heard the Word of God. The Word of God lives with his very self. Therefore he may in turn live with it and by it. This is the meaning and substance of the Law. It demands of man this appropriate action, this response, this subsequent motion of his lips and heart.[100]

The demand is that we live as individuals graciously drawn into the relationship of the Trinity, as brothers of Christ bound to the Father by the Spirit. The promise is that we are indeed those individuals.

The salient feature of Barth's doctrine of individual election is the density and scope of his scriptural exegesis, in which he presents a parade of biblical figures matched in pairs representing election and rejection. The pair of Israel-church presented in §34 becomes specific in the concrete details of Isaac and Ishmael, Jacob and Esau, Saul and David, and so on. In the next section, under the topic of the human response to election, I will briefly discuss an example of Barth's use of these pairs. Under the heading of God's act toward the individual, a few points may be noted. First, the election of the individual is for service. Each elect figure is given a certain task to perform, as ordinary as parenting children or as extraordinary as unifying a kingdom. The foil that each rejected figure provides to this election for service is that the rejected figure could have performed the service, may even try to perform it or to keep the elected figure from the task, but fails because God has ordained only one, and it is not the rejected one. Second, the identity of the elect and rejected may change, suggesting that

God's constancy in election is not the simple matter of divine immutability. Saul, for example, is God's anointed king but becomes the rejected foil for David. Third, the rejected serve God along with the elect; through the tragic witness of their failed efforts to elect themselves, they witness to the reality of the electing God. Finally, Barth emphasizes through his recitations of this very tragedy that the efforts and worthiness of the individuals involved has nothing to do with their service to God as either elect or rejected. God disposes of these individuals in matched and ordered pairs according to the divine need for service and witness, not according to human standards of fairness. When we reach the topic of the individual's response to God, these observations will reemerge in more detail.

The Response of the Elected

Given Barth's commitment to the description of an asymmetrical relationship between God and creatures, it is understandable that he gives more attention and emphasis to God's act of election than to the creature's response. As we shall see in the following discussion, Barth understands the latter as to some extent immaterial to the discussion. Theology as a human activity does properly have, secondarily, the human being as its subject; Calvin prefaces the *Institutes* by saying that "true and sound wisdom consists of two parts: the knowledge of God and of ourselves."[101] Barth is convinced, along with Calvin, that the knowledge of God leads to the true knowledge of the human being. Therefore, the former always precedes and informs the latter, and the latter points not to itself but backward and onward to its source and destiny in God. But Barth also applies this order of priority to the respective acts of God and the human being, so that the divine act precedes and conditions the human act, while the human act cannot be other than what God determines for it.

What then are the consequences of this asymmetrical priority for the freedom of the elected one? Barth transcends the dilemma of opposing absolute divine freedom to relative human freedom by treating Jesus Christ as the elected one first and foremost. Since Jesus Christ is the elected God as well as the elected (and electing) human being, he exercises the absolute freedom of God in his love and obedience to God's election. The elected human being's act is enabled by God's prior free act and empowered by Jesus Christ's free response. This exercise of freedom on the part of the human being is not something natural to human existence as such, in the sense that we seek to claim freedom as a right and possession of our own.

It is grace. Barth sees in the gift of cooperative agency given to creatures the honor and grace of God, which cannot be expected, claimed, or called down on the basis of the creature's reality:

> But the sovereignty which was to be confirmed and glorified was the sovereignty of His love, which did not will to exercise mechanical force, to move the immobile from without, to rule over puppets and slaves, but willed rather to triumph in faithful servants and friends, not in their overthrow, but in their obedience, in their own free decision for Him. The purpose and meaning of the eternal divine election of grace consists in the fact that the one who is elected from all eternity can and does elect God in return.[102]

Strictly speaking, the exercise of human freedom is miraculous, because there is no metaphysical connection between God's realm of freedom and the creature's realm of dependence.[103]

Barth is interested in the details of the creature's response to election because these details provide the conflict in the story of election and drive the story forward to its resolution. But the resolution takes place on God's terms and not the creature's. If the conflict of the creature's free response is necessary for the story to move forward, the priority and sovereignty of God's determining act is necessary for the story to begin and end. Barth maintains that the same divine act of election starts and completes the story of the relationship between God and creatures, and that therefore the act of the creature insofar as it sets itself up against that divine act, as another act for another purpose in another direction, does not bring about the creature's desired result, but God's desired result as revealed in divine election:

> What man does with his negative act can only be the admittedly real and evil and fatal recollection and reproduction of that which has been removed from him; but for all its wickedness and disastrous results this negative act as such can never be other than impotent. Man can do it and persist in it. He can become a sinner and place himself within the shadow of divine judgment which his powerless representation of the man rejected by God is unable to escape. He does all this. But he cannot reverse or change the eternal decision of God—by which He regards, considers and wills man, not in his isolation over against Him, but in His Son Jesus.[104]

Hence, the description of the response of the creature in Barth's doctrine of election is not the description of an independent reality that changes the world on its own terms. The creature does change its world, but on God's terms. Barth defines creaturely freedom as the ability to do God's will, and therefore finds it expressed only in the gracious and divinely powered relationship established in election. The creature does not have the freedom to damn itself, because the creature's freedom is not to oppose God but to accept God.

The discussion of the response of the elect proceeds in the same order as that of the previous section. First, the response of Jesus Christ, the paradigm and firstfruits of election, provides the setting for all creaturely response. Second, the response of the community, in its two forms as Israel and the church, will be revisited briefly; it has already been a topic of the previous section since Barth defines and conceptualizes these two forms of community in terms of God's determination of their response. Finally, and most pertinently for the present project, the response of the individual creature becomes apparent through the revelation of Scripture.

The Response of Jesus Christ to Election

In the previous discussion of Jesus Christ as elector, one aspect of Jesus Christ as elected could not be avoided because it forms the basis for Barth's entire doctrine of election. That aspect is Jesus Christ as elected God, the self-determined God who limits God's self in freedom to elevate human beings into the Trinitarian fellowship of love. Barth recognizes a second aspect: Jesus Christ as elected human being. Here Barth points out to his readers their first glimpse of themselves in the doctrine of election. As we are met by the electing God, so also was Jesus Christ in his historical, concrete, incarnate existence. More properly, Barth would say that as Jesus Christ the man encountered God, so we encounter God, following Jesus Christ's lead and having been given a setting for the encounter in his election.

Jesus Christ's response to election as a human being cannot be reduced simply to a model that human beings are encouraged to emulate. Such a simplification would leave out the "in" and "through" Christ of Ephesians: "just as he chose us *in Christ* before the foundation of the world" (1:4), "he destined us for adoption as his children *through Jesus Christ*" (1:5). Barth asserts that Jesus Christ responds to his election by becoming what he is elected to be: the unique man who, in unique unity with God, enables the election of all the human beings for whom unity with God is an impossibility:

> What we have to consider in the elected man Jesus is, then, the destiny of human nature, its exaltation to fellowship with God, and the manner of its participation in this exaltation by the free grace of God. But more, it is in this man that the exaltation itself is revealed and proclaimed. For with His decree concerning this man, God decreed too this man should be the cause and the instrument of our exaltation.[105]

Jesus Christ responds to election as human beings cannot. He responds to the offer of fellowship with God by accepting and claiming the destiny that God has chosen for every human being on behalf of every human being. Barth denies that human beings as such, apart from Christ, have the possibility of claiming that destiny even if it were offered to them. The offer itself is Jesus Christ, and its acceptance is Jesus Christ. The entire transaction takes place in this single concrete human being; therefore, for the rest of humanity, election is already offered and accepted. Barth expounds Scripture only in this light, because all individual instances of election to which Scripture attests explicitly or implicitly point to Christ as their source, either as a future or a past necessary condition:

> We ask then: When it is a question of the understanding and exposition of what the Bible calls predestination or election, why and on what authority are we suddenly to formulate a statement which leaves out all mention of Jesus Christ? As presented to us in the Bible, what can the election be at all, and what can it mean, if it is divorced from the name and person to which the whole content of the Bible refers as to the exhaustive self-revelation of God, here with the forward look of expectation and there with the backward look of recollection?[106]

Jesus Christ's freedom as elected man is expressed by Barth through the relentless use of the *communicatio idiomatum,* the rule for Christian speaking that allows divine attributes to be predicated of Jesus Christ as man, and human attributes to be predicated of Jesus Christ as God. As a human being, Jesus Christ exercises lordship proper to God; as God, Jesus Christ serves as human beings should. Barth certainly understands that the response of Jesus Christ the human being to God's election is obedience, but obedience is primordially attributable to God, in the divine self-election. God's example, not a human being's example, provides the reason obedience can be expected of human beings:

> The truly astonishing feature about the person of Jesus Christ is this, that here is a man who not only testified to God's rule by His Word and deeds. In the last analysis all the prophets had done that. Jesus did that, too, but in doing it He did more. He actually claimed and exercised lordship, even the lordship of God.[107]

God's will to create and honor human beings is expressed in the one concrete individual who acts as the created and honored human being. Then the obedience of that individual bears fruit in the way that the attempted works of sinful human beings never can, because the latter inevitably try to elect themselves rather than God.[108] In the following passage, Barth describes God's self-election in terms of humanity, but only the God-man can fulfill this particular divine self-determination. Without Jesus Christ as the object of God's act of election, no human being could lay hold of the destiny prescribed for her:

> God's eternal will is man: . . . man in a state of utter and most abject responsibility over against God, who even in this responsibility, even in the acknowledgement of the absolute pre-eminence of God Himself, is and becomes an individual and autonomous, and in the sphere of creation a sovereign being, and as such the image of God. God's eternal will is the act of prayer (in which confidence in self gives way before confidence in God). This act is the birth of a genuine human self-awareness, in which knowledge and action can and must be attempted; in which there drops away any fear of what is above or beside or below man of what might assault or threaten him; in which man becomes heir to a legitimate and necessary and therefore an effective and triumphant claim; in which man may rule in that he is willing to serve.[109]

Barth mentions prayer as the essential human act because it is the only possible human initiative (using that word relatively, of course) in the relationship between God and human beings. Only because God has reached out to us and brought us into the divine fellowship may we address our own words to God. Through election we are empowered to speak as human beings to our Creator. So any words of her own that the human being speaks are in fact due to the initiative of God. But the true human prayer is the human election of God, the human being speaking not her own words but God's Word. And Barth is able to point to the Word of God himself, Jesus Christ, in prayer before God, as the form in which all true human acts participate.

In one of Jesus Christ's prayers we find him petitioning the Father: "for you all things are possible; remove this cup from me; yet, not what I want, but what you want" (Mark 14:36). The cup that Jesus is about to drink, according to Barth, is the rejection appropriate to sinful human beings, which God graciously takes upon God's self rather than imputing it to those who deserve it. The rejection of Jesus Christ is not due to anything Christ is or does as a human being. His response to God's election is perfect, but the service for which Christ is elected is rejection, so his perfect obedience leads him to become the rejected one: "And being found in human form, he humbled himself and became obedient to the point of death—even death on a cross" (Phil. 2:7b–8). Barth acknowledges, with Schleiermacher,[110] that if the believer is forced to postulate concrete human beings, fellow creatures, whom God rejects while electing others, then the doctrine of election cannot be anything other than a *decretum absolutum*.

The division of creation into elected and rejected camps certainly does not occur according to the merit of the creature or its response to God's call, since this Pelagian doctrine would violate the prior understanding of God's absolute freedom, which must govern election. If such a division is demanded by theology, it must be a secret without reason except in God's hidden counsels. But Barth contends that theology does not necessitate such a division in the human race, because in Jesus Christ rejection has been united with election, revealing to us the unity of creation under the single, free divine decree of election:

> If in the face of the divine predestination we are believing and obedient and thankful, if we have a right understanding of its mystery, we shall never find there the decreed rejection either of ourselves or of any other man. This is not because we did not deserve rejection, but because God did not will it, because God willed the rejection of His Son in our stead.[111]

Because Jesus Christ was obedient in becoming the one and only divinely rejected one, his perfect response reveals to us that rejection has no independent reality but always appears in the service of election. Jesus Christ allowed himself to be rejected so that in him we all might be elected. For that reason, Barth informs us, our freedom is to elect God and others, never to reject God and others. Who can reject what God has elected, that is, God's self and all creation?

> The believer cannot possibly recognize in the unbelief of others a final fact. How can he even establish it with any certainty as their unbelief? . . . But the believer cannot possibly confront the unbeliever with the suspicion that the latter is perhaps rejected. For he knows who has borne the merited and inevitable rejection of the godless, his own above all. How can he possibly regard others as perhaps rejected merely because he thinks he knows their unbelief and therefore their godlessness? If he does, what becomes of his own faith? What of his own election? We cannot—essentially—believe against unbelievers but only for them; in their place, and as we address to them the promise which is for them also.[112]

In Jesus Christ's response to rejection, Barth sees the divine demand placed upon human beings in their election, to believe in God's all-inclusive mercy and Jesus Christ's sufficiency for all.

The Response of the Community to Election

Given that Jesus Christ is the concrete elected and rejected one, beside whom there is no other, how does Barth's division of the community into rejected and elected forms, represented by Israel and the church, reflect the responses of these communities to God's call? Barth maintains that both the obedience and disobedience of the elect serve God's purpose as revealed in Christ. The response of the community is an attempt to determine itself eternally, but God reserves to God's self the determination of the elect. Hence, our question becomes: How does the elected community, in obedience and disobedience to its election, testify to the concrete reality of election in Jesus Christ?

The discussion of the response of the community to election is a discussion of events in history. Certainly, Jesus Christ's response to election is also historical insofar as it is enacted in time and space, in a specific human person. But for Barth the historical event of Jesus Christ is the revelation of the extrahistorical event of God's election of God's self. In Jesus Christ, the asymmetry between the divine reality and the creaturely reality is resolved in favor of a divine unity, not a creaturely one; the human nature of Jesus Christ exists in the person of the Logos. When Barth comes to the response of the community assembled from creatures, he reminds us that the history of human response to God is not to be treated as an equal reality to God's election simply because it is the reality in which we live and from which our reflection on revelation begins. God's self-determination in favor of creaturely reality enables history and the autonomy of creatures, which cannot then take off in their own direction, but can only serve God's election. God has determined God's self for relationship with another outside of God's self, and this means that there is a creaturely history to election: "The life of this relationship cannot, therefore, be one-sided. Even if God has a powerful advantage over man, it is still necessarily two-sided, and its mystery must be thought of as the mystery of the human decision as well as the divine."[113] But just as Jesus Christ's history is grounded in the Son's primordial obedience to the Father, reenacting and revealing that mutual election, the history of Israel and the church is grounded in God's eternal purpose for creation, which is not derailed or nullified by any human response:

> The glory and the life of all this history are God's. Certainly it is a history between God and man. Certainly there takes place within it a twofold human decision [sin and prayer]. But this decision takes place in such a way as to form, not the second point in an ellipse, but the circumference around the one central point of which it is the repetition and confirmation. . . . In this history there is, of course, cooperation between God and man, but not of a kind which does not owe its origin entirely to the working of God. This history is a triumph only for God's grace and therefore for God's sovereignty.[114]

The community revolves around the central point of God's decision, and this motion does not involve any tangents based on the decisions of its members who are or are not in accord with God's decision. Nor does Barth assert that the decision of the community as a whole, which is not collective or quantitative but organic, can alter the circle. The historical response of Israel and the church to God cannot do otherwise than testify to God's single election.

Barth finds the evidence of Israel's disobedience in the Hebrew Scriptures and in the continuing existence of a Jewish community that is not part of the church. According to Barth, the obstinacy of Israel as recorded by its own historians and prophets has historical consequences: the tyranny of evil rulers, exile into foreign lands (even the loss of the tribes of Israel), the fading away of their distinctiveness, and the forgetting of their election. But Barth does not consider that disobedience irredeemable, since the Hebrew Scriptures also offer ample evidence of God's patience and repeated forgiveness. Barth maintains that for its sins, Israel is chosen out of all of history to stand for disobedience, relegated to the representation of the form of divine rejection. This sin is for Barth the failure of Israel to recognize and acknowledge their Messiah, sent expressly to lead them into God's fellowship:

> Precisely at this decisive point [Israel] listens inattentively and inaccurately. It hears the promise and lives with it as if its content were not God's mercy but were still God's judgment upon all men, as if it called on man to provide himself the presuppositions for its fulfilment by requiring this provision. It thinks that it can and ought to put itself into the right relationship to God. Through sheer zealous activity it fails to hear and do the one thing it would have to do if it heard willingly. It thus places itself in a vacuum. It besmirches its honour at the very moment when, if only it would believe, it would at last shine out. It jeopardizes by its failure the existence of the one community of God which cannot do without it.[115]

Israel's negative response to divine election, according to Barth, means that it lingers on as opposition to God even when God's self-revelation, directed at and realized within the chosen people, has become a historical reality: "What happens . . . is that it resists its election at the very moment when the promise given with it passes into fulfilment."[116]

The community's positive response to divine election is represented by the church, and it is in terms of the church that Barth phrases his condemnation of Israel. The proper response to election is to recognize in Jesus Christ the Messiah of Israel as well as the Savior of the Gentiles. This openness to revelation (enabled by Jesus Christ as the one who not only embod-

ies the gracious condescension of God but also conveys it to human beings)
provokes a response of faith:

> The attitude which confronts the true Messiah, which is therefore worthy of
> elected man and does justice to the electing God, can only be the faith of the
> heart in the presence of the completed self-demonstration of God. It can only
> be trust in the pure deed of God (promised and enacted) which consists in
> the resurrection of Jesus from the dead.[117]

The church is a community formed on the basis that the promise to Israel
has been fulfilled. By contrast, Israel in its present form as the synagogue is
a community that persists in the erroneous notion that the promise has yet
to be fulfilled. Barth charges Israel with the sin of attempting to dictate to
God a human timetable of salvation—of not believing the gospel they hear
of the Messiah's coming but preferring to wait for a Messiah of their own
choosing. The evidence of this sin is their refusal to join the church and
form the single community of God; Barth even finds this evidence but-
tressed by such historical events as the destruction of the temple in 70 C.E.,
a divine sign that specifically Jewish worship has ended:

> Israel refuses to join in the confession of the Church, refuses to enter upon
> its service in the one elected community of God. Israel forms and upholds
> the Synagogue (even though the conclusion of its history is confirmed by the
> fall of Jerusalem). It acts as if it had still another special determination and
> future beside and without the Church.[118]

Barth claims that the disobedience that frustrated and saddened Paul
continues to the present day, and is in fact ordained by God to serve a revelatory purpose. In other words, Israel's disobedience to its election, for
Barth, does not mean that it ceases to serve God's purpose:

> But God does not wait until Israel is obedient before employing it in His ser-
> vice. This is settled and completed in and with the election as such, so that
> Israel cannot in any way evade it, whether it is obedient or disobedient. God
> does not make the purpose He has with Israel dependent on Israel's attitude
> to it. The situation is rather that Israel's attitude is itself dependent on God's
> purpose with it. Whatever the attitude, it necessarily takes place in the course
> of the fulfilment of the service assigned to and required of Israel in and with
> its election.[119]

Barth here asserts that the negative response of the elect does not exclude
that individual or community from the service of God; it does mean that
the service provided is involuntary. The elect who resists her election does
not want to testify to God's mercy or judgment, but cannot escape the

sphere of service that includes all creaturely reality. The negative response of the elect is turned by God into positive witness, transformed into a contribution to the kingdom, despite the adverse will of the elect that directed her decision—impotently—toward a sphere of reality not ruled by God but by the creature. Such a decision is in the final analysis a fantasy directed at an imaginary world. Failure to conform to God's purpose means that Israel, in Barth's view, pursues a purpose that she imagines God has authorized in the empowering covenant, but that in fact is an illusion because it is inconsistent with God's purpose as determined in the divine self-election in Jesus Christ:

> [Israel] lacked the relevant relationship to the meaning and goal of its special mission and endowment. What it lacked was that it did not want to rely on the promise, on the mercy of God, but on itself, on its own willing and running to bring about the fulfilment of what was promised. Therefore, having all, it lacked all. It lacked all just because there was no lack of human purpose at the point where nothing but submissive recognition of the divine purpose could be adequate to what it had, to the Law.[120]

Barth's view of Israel's disobedience provides the model for the negative response to election by the individual, a model that could not appear in his theology until this point because although Jesus Christ is the rejected human being, he is not the disobedient human being. The model of disobedience presented here is the substitution of our own purposes and our own powers of obtaining them for God's purpose and power. The Barthian model, then, presupposes that this disobedience cannot reach its goal of being real disobedience, because God's purpose and power always precede, condition, and govern our own, bringing our disobedience into the divine service as surely and potently as the most reverent human worship.

The Response of the Individual to Election

Barth is on firmer ground historically and empirically when he speaks about the obedience and disobedience of individual human beings than when he generalizes about the status of ongoing communities. While it is difficult to make a case that Israel is the concrete representation of disobedience in history (and similarly that the church is the concrete representation of obedience) except scripturally and theologically, the evidence for the various responses of individuals to election is clear in the present day. Individuals are not all related to God in the same way. Some believe, and some do not; in terms of election, some respond with faith, and some do not. Having already established from revelation that election appears with rejection as its dependent shadow, Barth might be expected, then, to base his description of the response of the individual human being on the empirical evidence of contemporary human beings who stand in various relationships to God. The theological procedure of Barth's predecessors in the Calvinist tradition was most often to begin with the existence of believers and nonbelievers and the biblical witness to predestination, and from these facts to draw conclusions about the response of individuals to election.

Instead, Barth at this point returns to the Bible to discover the freedom of the human response. We have already seen that the human power to respond to God—to elect God—is, strictly speaking, Christ's power imputed to us and not a human power as such. The response of the elected and rejected pairs of individuals that Barth discovers in Scripture always points to Jesus Christ, typologically. In order to maintain the christological focus of the doctrine, Barth does not attempt to find the theological principles of human response to God's act in the coexistence of believers and unbelievers in the present day. For Barth, anthropology as well as theology begins with Jesus Christ. What is unified in Christ is found in the types of Scripture, separated into various individuals but connected in the narratives that bring individuals together.[121] Therefore, the principles that govern the human response to God are to be found first in the revelation of Scripture rather than in empirical objectification of ourselves.

Barth's twinning of elected and rejected characters in the biblical witness is intended to show that human history reveals God's election in Jesus Christ in its details as well as in its structure:

> Both [characters] attest always the covenant which comprehends both, whose power is neither based upon the faithfulness of the elect nor to be destroyed by the faithfulness of the rejected, whose fulfilment is indeed proclaimed by the blessing heaped upon the elect but also announced, and therefore not denied but made the subject of a new promise, by the curse heaped upon the rejected. . . . It is for this reason that the elect and the rejected, in spite of the greatest dissimilarities, can see that in many respects they are only too similar. It is not merely that in spite of the variety of their functions they operate together. On the contrary, they can exchange their functions.[122]

The dominant Old Testament pair, Saul and David, demonstrates some of the important conclusions Barth draws from this method about God's use of human beings as revelatory agents and the consequences of human acts. Saul is an example of a character who exchanges his function of being God's elected king of Israel with David. "When Samuel saw Saul, the LORD told him, 'Here is the man of whom I spoke to you. He it is who shall rule over my people'" (1 Sam. 9:17). Yet when Saul spares the king and cattle of the

Amalekites against God's express instructions, the Lord tells Samuel: "I regret that I made Saul king" (1 Sam. 15:11). "Now the spirit of the LORD departed from Saul, and an evil spirit from the LORD tormented him" (1 Sam. 16:14). Instead, Samuel is instructed to anoint the youngest son of Jesse, "and the spirit of the LORD came mightily upon David from that day forward" (1 Sam. 16:13).

Barth contends that Saul is elected to serve God by being cut off from God's kingdom, even as he leads the kingdom of Israel. Whatever the dimensions of his personal sin, which seems to the Old Testament reader to be far less grievous than that of David, God chooses Saul to express the divine judgment upon the sin of the people:

> No gross, no blatant personal sin of Saul is needed to exhibit this negative aspect of the grace of the kingdom willed and created by God. All that needs to be seen is that he is just the person and ideal which the nation has foolishly imagined, and can only imagine, as its king. And it is this which is made evident in the double sinning [of Saul] which is microscopic to human eyes, but gigantic and absolutely decisive in God's eyes. Saul himself will sacrifice. Saul himself will represent the reconciliation between God and His people. Saul himself will furnish the conditions for a prosperous national existence in the presence of its enemies, and therefore for its peaceful life in the promised land.[123]

Saul's function as sacrifice, like the slain goat in the scapegoat ritual of Leviticus 16, is for Barth a symbol of God's mercy. Saul may well rage against the departure of God's spirit from him, but Barth urges us to rejoice in the sacrifice and death that Jesus Christ shows us is the service of the elect: "Let us gratefully know ourselves to be elect in the picture of the first goat of Lev. 16—grateful that we are accepted to sacrifice ourselves, grateful that we may suffer the saving judgment of the wrath of God, which is the wrath of His love, as only the elect can do!"[124] Saul is elected to represent the divine judgment and to participate in the kingship of Jesus Christ over humanity's disobedience:

> Saul is therefore legitimately and in all seriousness among the prophets. He and the Samarian kings who follow him, even while they are allowed to fall, do not fall out of the hand of God. In all the frightful blossoming of their sin, which is much more the sin of their people than their personal sin, and in all the terrible darkness of the divine wrath under which their government stands, they prophesy and exhibit the King who, himself innocent, has interposed himself as a Leader and Representative at the head of all sinful men, and between them and God. . . . Who but the Son of God can be the King of men in this terrible function?[125]

The disobedience of the human being to divine election, revealed in Saul's sin but even more clearly in the people's desire for a king, is the misguided desire to assert human individuality by pitting oneself against God, as if acceptance and obedience lead to the loss of individuality rather than to its consummation. Deciding that human individuality requires the possibility or actuality of isolation from God,[126] the disobedient human being subjects herself to the dangerous illusion that autonomy can define itself against God's power rather than on the basis of God's power. It is only an illusion, however; the power of the human being does not include the capacity to reject herself or to exclude herself from the scope of the divine purpose:

> What man can do with his negative act can only be the admittedly real and evil and fatal recollection and reproduction of that which has been removed from him; but for all its wickedness and disastrous results this negative act as such can never be other than impotent. Man can do it and persist in it. He can become a sinner and place himself within the shadow of divine judgment which his powerless representation of the man rejected by God is unable to escape. He does all this. But he cannot reverse or change the eternal decision of God—by which He regards, considers and wills man, not in his isolation over against Him, but in His Son Jesus.[127]

This understanding of election, grounded in God's primordial and unchanging decision to be God *pro nobis* and consummated in God's patient and creative utilization of the creature's free act, will be useful in conceiving of the electing God in process theology, which sees divine purpose in primordiality and divine inclusion of the world's actualities ordered toward that purpose in the consequent nature.

David succeeds Saul as the Lord's anointed, and Barth sees in his election the continuation of a prominent Old Testament theme: the divine upsetting of human hierarchies. Rather than choosing the eldest son, God chooses David from the sheep fields, the youngest son. This is consistent with the string of Old Testament reversals of elder and younger, such as Israel's blessing of Joseph's sons Ephraim and Manasseh. God is free from human conventions in God's electing choice—even to the extent that God is free to preserve the rejected one, graciously including him in the covenant:

> The tradition could not be clearer as to the continually operative principle of the distinguishing choice; the freedom with which this choice cuts across and contradicts all distinctions that are humanly regulated or planned on the basis of human predilections, and the relativity of the distinctions actually made; the fact that those who are cut off, who are not distinguished by actual

choice, are not on that account utterly rejected, but do in their own way remain in a positive relation to the covenant of God.[128]

David is elected to be the foundation of the eternal throne of Israel, but God's election is not based upon David's merits as a human being. In fact, David's sin of murdering Uriah and stealing his wife Bathsheba is far more seriously treated in the biblical narrative than are Saul's sins. Barth does not see David's distinction from Saul in David's response to election, but in God's act of election. The elect and the rejected are similar in their humanity, their sinfulness, and even in their service to God; to look at Saul's ordination by God is to see David, and to look at David's sin is to see Saul. Barth understands this merger of the pictures of elect and rejected in his pairs to demonstrate that God has indeed chosen *sinful* humanity for fellowship with God's self:

> For if the proper and positive character of this picture—as seen from its subject Jesus Christ—unquestionably places before our eyes the meaning and power of the divine election itself, and the glory of God's grace in the person of the king of Israel introduced by Himself, we are reminded by the negative aspect—which, although it is crowded out by the positive, is not denied but is specifically mentioned and can still be seen—who it is that God has chosen, and what kind of a people it is whose King is so great and glorious. We are reminded that it is composed of lost sinners who are justified and saved by Him. . . . We cannot forget the rejected king in the elect. We cannot forget Saul in David and Solomon.[129]

David's response then is not simple obedience. Yet he serves God as the elected one, just as Saul serves God as the rejected one.

The obedient human being finds his individuality in the divine predestination of his life event. In his acceptance of the divine vocation, the obedient human being responds to God's call by finding in the divine purpose for all creation the unique divine purpose for himself and himself alone. The obedient human being responds by replacing his vision of human power with the autonomy given graciously to humanity through God's self-determination, and determines himself to serve God with that gracious power alone. But we have already seen that David represents this response of obedience only fitfully, and that God's election is revealed in God's maintenance of the relationship of election despite David's disobedience. For Barth, there is only one obedient human being in the true sense, and that is Jesus Christ. Thus, the *Leitsatz* to §35, "The Election of the Individual," does not mention the election of the God-fearing human being but only that of the godless human being, for all humanity without Christ is godless, isolated, and rejected, but with Christ is transformed:

> The witness of the community to every individual consists in this: that the choice of the godless man is void; that he belongs eternally to Jesus Christ and therefore is not rejected, but elected by God; that the rejection which he deserves on account of his perverse choice is borne and cancelled by Jesus Christ; and that he is appointed to eternal life with God as the basis of the righteous divine decision.[130]

Barth's examination of the minute details of biblical characters and stories raises the question: How is the human response to election compatible with God's active determination of history? Barth speaks of God's action in history in terms of God's life; that is, it is in the events of history that God is revealed as the living God, God's plans are revealed as living plans and not dead letters, and God's purpose is still being worked out. One of the horrors of predestination, for some, is that everything that matters has already been determined outside of time, reducing history to a rote recitation of a fixed text:

> On the basis of a doctrine of God which was pagan rather than Christian, [traditional teaching] thought of predestination as an isolated and given enactment which God had decreed from all eternity and which to some extent pledged and committed even God Himself in time. Because of His immutability, even God could not alter this enactment once it had been determined.[131]

But Barth maintains that God's freedom as the ruler of creation is not to be conceived of as more restricted than that of a human ruler, who applies the letter of his decree with a living will. Furthermore, the decree of the human ruler "can always be corrected or suspended or replaced by another decree," and "sooner or later it will actually be corrected or suspended or replaced in this way."[132] For Barth, this correction is a positive characteristic of a living decree and not a reflection of the imperfection of the original decree, so that the appearance of change in God's dealings with the world in history is not an illusion but the reflection of God's living will:

> We must remember however—and in so doing we part company with the older teaching—that God's decree is a living decree, a decree that is infinitely more living than any decree of man. It is the letter of God in the beginning in virtue of the fact that this letter is determined and posited with all the constancy, faithfulness and the dependability of God Himself, enjoying an authority and power greater than that of the letter of any possible human law. But it is also spirit and life in a way impossible for even the very best of the written laws of man as best expounded or applied.[133]

God's decision is not for God alone but also for us. In its encounter with creation, God's will issues into events.[134] And these events find not only their unity but their individuality in their reference to the eternal Word of God.[135] The decree of God is expressed in creation, becoming actual not only in God's eternal Trinitarian being but also in the realm of creatures. It is reiteration but not mere repetition, for the concrete creaturehood of God is the result of God's primordial decision, the condition for the consummation in which creatures are sanctified for fellowship with God. History then is not a superfluous theatrical production for Barth, because predestination is not a pretemporal event that freezes history into a preset pattern, as if it were finished before time begins, but "a work which still takes place in all its fulness today."[136] Barth expands upon this concept of the living God's involvement in history by commenting on the "activist theory" of Peter Barth, which attempts to take seriously biblical language indicating God's thought and action engaged with human beings. This does not mean that one can thoughtlessly apply the concept of change to God in the same way it applies to history, but it means that the "activist" God "reserves to Himself the freedom to put forth His own superior power in unforeseen and astonishing developments."[137] If the unity of history is seen in God's unitary act of election in Jesus Christ, Barth contends that predestination cannot conflict with God's activity in history because Jesus Christ is both God's decree and historical event:

> Once we see this point it is settled that predestination does not antedate time, and all that is in it, in the form of a letter, which, limited in this way, can mean only a dead letter. Predestination precedes time as a living act in the Spirit similar to the cloud which went before Israel in the wilderness. It is settled, then, that predestination did indeed happen in the bosom of God before all time, but that for this very reason, it happens and happens again before every moment of time.[138]

With this potent idea of continual, active predestination through the Holy Spirit, Barth arrives at a concept of election that can no longer be restricted to a primordial determination of each individual's eternal status. Each moment of time has a role to play in the divine purpose. Each event is predestined, that is, given by God a destination to which God brings it willingly or unwillingly. "Predestination is man made usable to God by the Holy Spirit."[139] This predestination has the character of the divine promise and demand: God's expectation for the elected creature is always before it like the cloud before Israel, to lead it with the reassurance that God is in this path, but the same expectation marks off this path from all other paths and serves as a warning to those who would prefer not to follow. God leads, but cannot be eluded. God's predestination frees us to serve the divine purpose by revealing the divine purpose where we live:

> The sovereignty of God and of God's good pleasure consists in the fact that it is a sovereignty which orders history, the content of God's eternal will. We must think of that eternal and self-ordered will as the will of the living God, a progressive and constantly renewed act of the Spirit. But in so doing we must also think of it as law, as a letter which can neither be reinterpreted nor replaced.[140]

The standard set by God's predestination of every event and every creature is not a matter for human freedom, but only for divine freedom. God's unceasing action in history is the divine purpose fitted to the actualities of the creaturely realm, giving not only a general direction to history but also a specific vocation for every individual within history.

The response of the human being to God's act of election is the free act of the creature made possible by God's gracious sharing of the divine freedom and purpose. It may be positive or negative—the acceptance of vocation along with the power to serve God in the chosen role, or the rejection of that role in favor of the (illusory) human power to choose another. The difference between these responses is not in their outcome, for God's freedom and power enables the use of both belief and unbelief to bring about the divine kingdom. Rather, the difference rests in the graciously given ability of human beings to attain true knowledge of God and themselves, in the difference between a correct (revealed) understanding of human individuality and an incorrect one. If a person thinks of her individuality as something proper and intrinsic to herself as a human being, she defines herself over against others: I am not you, or him, or God, or anyone else but myself. But Barth notes that God's individuality is not defined negatively, over against that which is not God, but positively, as the One who loves in freedom. Only through the revelation of Jesus Christ can I learn that my negative definition of my individuality over against God is incorrect, for Jesus Christ, the true individual, *is* God. Jesus Christ has exploded the absolute distinction between God and human beings, so that my definition of individuality can only be the result of ignorance. God defines the individuality of each human being by God's act of election, by the fact that God chooses each of us individually to be included in the divine fellowship:

> Thus, the divine election of individuals does not consist in the enigma of that individuality and solitude, nor in that which distinguishes them as this or that person. On the contrary, the mystery of the special name, of the individuality and the solitude of any one person, consists in his divine election.

> It is the individuality and solitude of God which constitutes the elect indi-
> vidual, and to which he owes the particularity of his name. Because and as
> God is this One, they—the elect—are this or that person.[141]

The Vocation of the Elected Human Being

The analysis of Barth's doctrine of election would not be complete without
due consideration of his concept of the divinely given vocation, which he
discusses in *CD* IV/3. The vocation given to each human being is to serve
God and thereby to enter into the divine fellowship. The service ordained
for each human being is to reveal God's Word, as we have observed in
Barth's depiction of the service of the elect in the last section. God's grace
makes human beings useful and enables the human fulfillment of vocation
in faith and gratitude:

> Defined very generally, this [event of vocation] is the event in which man is
> set and instituted in actual fellowship with Jesus Christ, namely, in the ser-
> vice of His prophecy, in the *ministerium Verbi divini*, of the Word of recon-
> ciliation, and therefore in the service of God and his fellow-men. Even more
> generally, one might say that it is the event in which the grace (*charis*) of God
> which justifies man before Him and sanctifies him for Him find its counter-
> part in the gratitude (*eucharistia*) of man.[142]

Notice how closely the concept of vocation is related to the event of election as it is enacted in history. God's decision to establish humanity in the
divine fellowship leads directly to the gift of that actual destination to each
individual. Here Barth shows election leading to the human role of God's
servant and steward, divine power having been bestowed upon the individual to fulfill that role. The idea of divine election for service, which
forms a recurring motif in Barth's doctrine of election, finds a positive
counterpart in the human acceptance of vocation, which enables the recipient of election to respond with worthy service.

Barth does not directly identify election with vocation. Instead, he
claims that "election is the basis of vocation,"[143] echoing the *Leitsatz* of
§32:

> [Vocation] has as the seed and root of its historical reality, truth and cer-
> tainty the absolutely prevenient "history" which as the *opus Trinitatis inter-
> num ad extra* is in God himself the eternal beginning of all His ways and
> works, namely, the election of grace of the God who loves in freedom, and
> is free in love, in which the Son, thereto ordained by the Father and obe-
> dient to the Father, has elected Himself for sinful man and sinful man for
> himself.[144]

The distinction lies in the sphere of reality proper to each event. Election is a decision and occurrence proper to the divine reality, preceding all human response. But vocation, as Barth defines it, is the elevation of the human decision and response, which takes place in creaturely reality, into the true service of God, which takes place in the harmony of the divine kingdom. Here the asymmetry of election, where Barth conceives of God's act as the first and last word in a two-sided yet unequal relationship, gives way to the bilateral meeting between covenant partners that is always the goal of election but cannot be its presupposed reality. Vocation appears in Barth's dogmatics in an eschatological context; it is a foretaste of the fellowship for which human beings are ultimately destined. It precedes the discussion of the mission of the community of God for the world and the discussion of the Christian life of hope. While the doctrine of election brings the sinful and powerless, yet elected, human being into focus, the doctrine of vocation sees within that elected human being the divinely given power to serve and to witness.

Barth describes vocation in the *Leitsatz* to §71 as the result of the efficient power of God's Word, manifested in the human recipient as knowledge, faith, and service:

> The Word of the living Jesus Christ is the creative call by which He awakens man to an active knowledge of the truth and then receives him into the new standing of the Christian, namely, into a particular fellowship with Himself, thrusting him as His afflicted but well-equipped witness into the service of His prophetic work.[145]

The call of vocation is creative because it is the birth of the new human being with a new life's journey to a new destination. It puts the human being in touch with God's purpose and ordering of the world. This knowledge is not only cognitive content but also the divine illumination that makes the human being Christian by changing her completely.[146] The human being is called to serve as a witness to the living God, to the One who has determined God's self to love and have communion with creation,[147] by participating in Jesus Christ's prophetic function of calling the world to repentance. By fulfilling her vocation, the human being fosters and aids that call, and therefore works alongside the Holy Spirit in gathering the community of God.

Barth's doctrine of vocation focuses upon the Christian who exists in the world yet is called for the special service of witness, which constitutes him as a Christian. This particular recipient of vocation is afflicted because he is "called to be a Christian, and even as a Christian he is still man and therefore exposed to human suffering."[148] Yet as a Christian and the bearer of this vocation, he is given the power of God's Word in its divine fullness:

> [T]he vocation of man takes place in such a way that for the called it neces-
> sarily carries with it a supremely personal endowment and equipment. The
> Word of God goes forth indeed to all men, for Jesus Christ who speaks it is
> the Head of all men, and what he declares, the gracious act of God accom-
> plished in Him, has taken place for all men, for the whole world. In the event
> of the vocation of His witnesses, however, it comes to these men in such a
> way that they enjoy a special liberation, namely, that it is given to them to
> receive it, its content disclosing itself to them and they themselves being
> opened to its content.[149]

If Barth discusses the vocation of the believer here, this does not mean that the rejected (as opposed to the elect) or the godless (as opposed to the God-fearing) lack a vocation. Barth would have us remember that no one can claim any distinction on the basis of her belief or her calling from the general mass of humanity, for the designations *elect, rejected, God-fearing,* and *godless* refer most strictly only to Jesus Christ, in whom God elects all. As the shadow of rejection is banished by the light of Christ, so the voca-tion of the non-Christian is illuminated by that same light: "Not in and of himself, but in Jesus Christ as the eternal beginning of all God's ways and works, no man is rejected, but all are elected in Him to their justification, their sanctification and also their vocation."[150] The Christian witness is not to the glory of the Christian's own call, but to the glory of Jesus Christ in whom all are called and whom all serve:

> [The Christian] is directed in his knowledge constantly to put himself where
> non-Christians are in their ignorance, clinging not only to his Jesus Christ
> but to the Jesus Christ whose work has taken place for all and whose Word
> is addressed to all, by whose call all are ordained to be called instead of
> uncalled, and therefore, whether it is heard or not, the situation of every man
> is altered. It is in relation to Him that non-Christians and Christians, for all
> their differences, are what they are, namely, men who have their calling only
> before them on the one side, and men who have it both behind them and
> before them on the other.[151]

In his concept of vocation, Barth transcends the differences between the elect and the rejected by specifying that the elect are called to participate in the enlargement of God's kingdom to include the rejected. The witness of the elect to God's character becomes the active witness of the elect human agent in her Christian work to God's activity in gathering together elect and rejected into one community.

Conclusion

The preceding survey of Barth's doctrine of election has been necessarily brief. I have presented the framework and method that Barth utilizes to explicate the doctrine, noting its major strengths and weaknesses. My analysis has the purpose of highlighting the areas in which Barth and process theology may be fruitfully compared and contrasted. Before moving on to an analysis of Whitehead's concept of the initial aim, let us review the concepts and ideas discovered in Barth's doctrine of election that will become important in the construction of the process doctrine of election.

1. The conflict between metaphysics and theology is quite pronounced in the *Church Dogmatics*. Since process theology has its roots in Whitehead's "philosophy of organism," a metaphysical system, the task of allowing Barth to inform constructive work in Christian process theology is made all the more arduous by Barth's explicit animosity to any worldview or cosmology that attempts to consolidate theories of creation and divinity. It is striking, however, that when Barth mentions the type of philosophy called for by the Christian doctrine of creation, he specifies the unsolved problem of continual becoming—exactly the problem that process thought was designed to address.

   Barth's warning against theology "from below," however, must not be set aside in the discussion to come. The Christian kerygma must be the standard against which the insights derived from process philosophy, about God and creatures alike, are judged, if the doctrine of election that results is to be Christian.

2. The doctrine of election is the theological description of God's initiative in meeting creatures. Barth emphasizes God's absolute freedom in the divine act of election. But this freedom is not an abstract characteristic of God that can be seen only in the incomprehensibility of the divine act. It is expressed in the concreteness and definiteness of God's self-determination and self-limitation. Election most properly refers to the divine order established by God's decision to be for creatures, which, far from being mysterious and hidden from creatures, is concretely present in both the divine and creaturely realm as Jesus Christ. Barth's language of limitation and concreteness through the divine self-election is remarkably consonant with Whitehead's vision of God as principle of concretion and the source of order. Barth finds God's freedom nowhere else than in the divine love and grace; the doctrine of election expresses God's

free exercise of divine power in God's gracious inclusion of creatures
in the divine purpose.

3. The election of communities has a prominent place in Barth. Much
attention has been paid to the problems raised by Barth's concepts of
Israel as "rejected" and the church as "elected" forms of the community, and I have mentioned a few of the difficulties involved. In the
conversation between Barth and Whitehead, however, Barth's concept of a corporate relationship between the community and God has
the positive implication of allowing for real election at a different level
of complexity and organization than the human being. Process theology conceives of atomic individual entities that comprise societies
with their own emergent individuality. Election takes place all along
the continuum of organization, from the simplest actual entity to the
most complex society. Barth's concept of the election of the community has the possibility of being used as a model for understanding
the relationship to God of various levels of social organization in
process thought.

4. Barth's emphasis on the reality of primordial divine election, that is,
God's eternal self-determination, is balanced by his insistence on the
reality and consequence of the historical enactment of election in the
creaturely realm. The doctrine of election does not render history
irrelevant, but invests history with divine purpose. God's activity in
human history does not merely repeat intra-Trinitarian activity, but
re-presents it in such a way as to make the divine reality a creaturely
actuality. Process thought, similarly, proposes that God is actual only
with God's consequent nature, that is, with the history of God's activity in enacting the divine purpose. Both systems of thought are aimed
at eliminating the possibility of thinking about an inactive and therefore abstract God.

5. The freedom of creatures is not in any way comparable to the freedom of God in Barth's doctrine of election. Yet it is true freedom,
thanks to God's gracious act in honoring creatures with agency. The
divine determination to bring creatures into fellowship with God
means that creatures are given the ability to work with God toward
the divine goal, participating in the freedom to act that is the proper
arena of God alone. Process thought conceives of the freedom of the
nondivine entity in a much stronger sense than does Barth; the freedom of self-determination is something every actual entity, from God
to the tiniest puff of existence in space, possesses by virtue of its actuality. Yet process thought agrees with Barth that the creature is impo-

tent unless divinely empowered; the exercise of self-determination depends on God's provision of an aim for the creature as well as on God's fostering of an environment in which the creature's choice bears fruit.

6. Barth expresses God's sharing of the divine purpose with creatures in terms of the vocation of the elected human being to serve as a witness to the divine reality. The notion of vocation and purpose will be of great importance in the construction of a process doctrine of election. Election is not merely a matter of the eternal salvation of the creature for Barth; it also brings the creature into the sphere of revelation and enrolls it in the service of God. This service may be conscious or unconscious; the creature may resist, but it cannot by its own decision dismiss itself from this service. Process thought understands election to be the imparting of the divine purpose to creatures in the form of an initial aim given to each individual, on which the decision of the individual operates. Again, the creature, while subject of its own decision about its service to the divine purpose, does not make the final determination of its place in God's plan. Its act is redeemed and transformed by God's patient evocation of the best from the world.

7. This summary of Barth's contribution to the project at hand would not be complete without a consideration of Barth's christological focus in his doctrine of election. Christian process theology is not yet prepared to take full advantage of the leadership and innovation of Barth on this point. Its doctrines of the Trinity and Christology have not advanced far enough to enable the doctrine of election to be founded upon them as Barth does. But Christian process theology should not fail to take note of Barth's ability to solve the problems plaguing the doctrine of election with his creative and consistent use of Christology. Especially important in this regard is the utilization of the biblical passages regarding election, which in the New Testament involve explicit reference to Christ as the author and mediator of election. The Christian doctrine of election should be based upon the biblical witness to election in its Old Testament and New Testament forms, and should express the unity of election throughout God's dealings with creatures in Scripture. If at this stage in its development, Christian process theology cannot do justice to Barth's christological method, this does not mean that it should not do its best to be Christian while learning from Barth how to refer to Christ as the complete revelation of God's self-election as well as the election of creatures.

CHAPTER TWO

Whitehead's Concept of the Initial Aim

The doctrine of election deserves to hold a central place in theology because it expresses the fundamental relationship between God and creatures. Before creation, God made a choice in favor of those to come—those who are not God. God determined God's self on behalf of creatures, orienting God's self toward the goal of bringing creatures into fellowship with the divine life. This is the mysterious love to which Christianity bears witness, revealed in the story of Jesus Christ.

One aspect of God's being that the doctrine of election makes clear is that God is in relationship. Far from a lonely divine existence that excludes real communion with others, God chooses to establish a relationship with every creature. So the Christian faith witnesses that the divine life is ordered in such a way that it is open to others, giving and receiving in a relationship of love. Expressed in this way, it is clear that any doctrine of election must give an account of the establishment of this relationship: its origins in the divine self-determination, the resulting act of divine giving to every creature, the creature's response, and God's receipt of that creaturely act. In other words, the doctrine of election is framed in terms of a philosophical or theological system that analyzes the nature of a divine-human relationship.[1]

If this is true, why are so many doctrines of election based on the assertion that one cannot speak of a fundamental, universal, metaphysical relationship between God and human beings? In fact, the power and centrality of Reformed doctrines of election come from their insistence that the establishment of this relationship is unprecedented and miraculous. The communion between the divine and the other-than-divine that election has as its goal is not a state that creatures may naturally expect. It is beyond their powers as creatures to bring about. Only by virtue of the gracious intervention of God do we even know that a relationship between God and ourselves obtains. The positing of this metaphysical gulf between God and creatures, rather than the metaphysical basis for relationship mentioned above, ensures that Reformed Christians remember election as gratuitous, unconditioned, and unmerited.

This type of doctrine serves well the didactic purpose of teaching God's freedom and grace. When it comes to describing the relationship that is in fact established through election, however, it is less effective. Since, in this conception, the relationship is impossible by creaturely lights and only possible through God's omnipotence and free choice, it is best described by metaphor and paradox. A strict metaphysical systemization becomes more difficult since this event, the divine reaching out to the nondivine, is indescribable in terms of the system's categories and normal limits. Even the fact that such a reaching out has occurred, as evidenced in the relationship between God and human beings that election establishes, does not diminish the ontic gulf. The exception proves the rule in the case of Emil Brunner. Brunner argued, for example, that the existence of a relationship between God and humanity reveals that the possibility of the relationship has always existed—that a "point of contact" for the divine exists at least potentially in human nature. That idea provoked a strong response from Karl Barth, who denied that any potential for communion with God exists in humanity before God unilaterally and miraculously brings human beings into relationship.[2] From that controversy it is clear that the development of a metaphysical system that describes and systematizes divine relationships with creatures is not welcome in all theologies.

On the one hand, the lack of such a descriptive system has severely limited what can be said about the divine-human relationship in these theologies. A metaphysical description of the relationship that characterizes the meeting-place of God and creatures would be an aid in constructing a fruitful doctrine of election, one that is able to account for the divine act and response as well as the creature's act and response in the establishment of the relationship. On the other hand, theologies that accept the idea of divine-human relationships too easily—without the adoption of a philosophical framework that makes the idea not only intelligible but also religiously significant—have tended to lack a strong election doctrine. There seems to be little point in expounding the wonder of God's divine choice to be a God *pro nobis* if Christians have already assumed that very point in theology, interpretation of the Scriptures, and moral theory. To make God accessible to human thinking and seeking may accomplish the goal of rendering God relevant to human lives, but it may also make the divine choice seem superfluous. If God is the type of God who is related to us, then the divine nature must be "set up" for relations with us, and the question of divine choice is moot. If human nature is similarly open to relationship with God, natural theology becomes possible, even warranted, and election retreats further into the background, since in this scenario, human beings are the active agents, choosing to seek God rather than vice versa.

Election requires that the electing God be open to relationship with creatures but still be the initiator of any relationship that occurs. One way to accomplish this goal is to develop the doctrine in a metaphysical framework that regards relatedness as fundamental to any type of existence. In process theology, God does not represent an exception to the metaphysical rule that no entity is an island. Rather, God exemplifies to absolute perfection the relatedness that is characteristic of every entity. From the point of view of the divine life, God's primordial and consequent natures in process theology impart a universal order to, and include that order in, the achievements of all creatures. From the point of view of creaturely life, God establishes the relationship between the creature and God by imparting a unique purpose for each creature's life.

The concept of the initial aim in Whitehead's writings provides a metaphysical description of how election works. In its emphasis on God's *essentially* relational nature, it moves away from election doctrines that deny any "predisposition" for God to be related to human beings, reserving that fact of relatedness for God's contingent choice. However, by providing a general description of the relationships that obtain between God and other actual entities, it avoids the difficulty in speaking about election that results from a total qualitative separation between divine and creaturely existence. Through the concept of the initial aim, process theology is able to codify and systematize the fact of every entity's relationship to God, without being hampered by an overriding theological agenda that hopes to use the doctrine of election to illustrate God's freedom or sovereignty. Calvin, for example, used the doctrine as a way to teach humility before God's inapproachable and unquestionable decree. Barth balances God's freedom with the fact of God's love bestowed freely in election. The latter approach deals not primarily with the possibility of election as one among many acts God might have chosen, but with its historical reality, and finds in the fact of election a revelation of the loving character of God: "Its function is to bear basic testimony to eternal, free and unchanging grace as the beginning of all the ways and works of God."[3] Barth thus inspires the process doctrine, which aims to describe this divine character in terms of its relation to creatures. The aspects of the divine nature that the process doctrine of election wishes to illustrate are love, compassion, resourcefulness, omniscience, and creative freedom. It does not take extensive argument to reconcile these attributes of God to the portrait of the giver of the initial aim found in Whitehead. The term *election* is an apt theological description for the metaphysical process of aim-giving, aim-receiving, aim-modifying, and aim-achieving by each actual occasion.

The Initial Aim in Whitehead's Process Philosophy

The description of Whitehead's concept of the initial aim given here is specifically directed at the use of this idea for the development of a process doctrine of election. I shall begin by analyzing the divine act, starting with the envisagement of the eternal objects, then narrowing the focus to the individual aims given to creatures. The creature then responds by modifying the initial aim (that is, choosing a goal for itself from the graded possibilities God offers) and actualizing novel possibilities. Finally, its achievement of value is received by God and ordered into the divine consequent nature. The second half of this chapter will consider the initial aim as election, demonstrating how this Whiteheadian concept corresponds to election. The initial aim, as a fundamental part of the process system, also involves metaphysical assumptions that pose difficulties for some aspects of the traditional and influential doctrines of election, especially the well-known doctrine of the Reformed or Calvinist tradition. The ideas that a process doctrine of election must deny or redefine are discussed in chapter 3. These parameters look forward to the construction of a process doctrine of election, using the idea of the initial aim as the basis for theological discussion of divine election.

God's Subjective Aim

The process that results in the gift of the initial aim to each creature begins with God's primordial self-determination. It is important to remember, throughout the discussion of Whitehead's ideas, that in process thought God is one actual entity among the many actual entities that make up the universe. God is treated as not differing absolutely from the other actual entities; the divine entity's special functions and attributes result from God's eternality and primordiality, which make possible the ongoing temporality and historicity of creatures. Because of the metaphysical unity of God and creatures, certain features of reality are exemplified in both the divine realm and in the world—in the divine realm conclusively and in the world inconclusively.[4] This should not be interpreted to mean that the world is any less real than God. Rather, it means that while both God and creatures participate in the same metaphysical categories, God's process of becoming defines and extends over all applications of those categories, while other actual entities participate in some part of the system of reality.

A fine example of this principle is the subjective aim of God, which is the sine qua non for the resulting subjective aims of creatures. The subjective aim of an actual entity is the goal of self-ordering toward which the entity aims in the process of its own becoming. This goal acts as a final cause, luring the entity toward its satisfaction as an object of desire. God is unique among actual entities because only God provides God's own subjective aim. All other actual entities—all creatures—derive their initial aim, which they modify into their subjective aim, from God.

To understand God's subjective aim, it is necessary to understand what function God performs in Whitehead's system. God is the source of order for the universe; God originates order by grading the eternal objects in God's subjective aim from the most desirable possibilities to the least desirable, and God mediates order for the world by providing graded aims to creatures. Whitehead recognized that the evolution of complexity and the progress toward greater value that he saw in the world would be impossible without some primordial order. This universal value system, as it were, allows for the limitation of possibilities that is essential for actuality. An actual occasion does not have the possibility of being and doing anything it pleases. Rather, its options are limited, and hence made achievable, by an orderly inheritance from its past. This system of orderly transmission from the past into the present makes possible the maintenance of multilevel organisms in which simple systems are combined and built up into a complex unity. Without the inheritance of form and purpose from the immediate past, the functioning of each system could not be maintained and the whole could not exist—in which case, of course, the separate systems would cease to exist as well. Thus, an order that pertains to all entities is necessary to conserve the existence and the value created by each entity, by ensuring that it can be passed on as a dominant force in the becoming of subsequent entities.

On the other hand, Whitehead also understood that order was necessary not only for conservation of value but for the creation of increased value as well. The novelty that is relevant to each entity must be made available to that entity as a possibility for its process of becoming. Without an ordering of as-yet-unrealized possibilities in terms of both their desirability and their relationship to the entity that is able to choose to actualize them, the potential for novelty in the world is greatly decreased, since entities cannot lay hold of the possibilities that can become real possibilities for them. This ordering of possibilities is what Whitehead calls the primordial nature of God; it is one pole of the dipolar divine nature, the other being the consequent nature. Speaking of the premordial nature as a "superject," that is, as a finished and effective decision, Whitehead writes:

> Such a primordial superject of creativity achieves, in its unity of satisfaction, the complete conceptual valuation of all eternal objects on which creative order depends. It is the conceptual adjustment of all appetites in the form of aversions and adversions. It constitutes the meaning of relevance. Its status as an actual efficient fact is recognized by terming it the "primordial nature of God." (PR 32)

God's primordial nature is God's self-determination, which is the condition for the existence of the world, and for the existence of value and purpose in the world.

According to Whitehead's concept of the dipolar divine nature, God determines God's self not primarily in terms of attributes, but in terms of purpose. The ordering of the eternal objects (Whitehead's term for possibilities, or what Plato calls the Ideas) is goal-oriented rather than arbitrary. God's goal is to maximize value, defined by Whitehead in aesthetic terms as intensity of feeling, involving harmony and contrast.[5] Thus, the eternal objects are ordered to favor the possibilities that, when actualized, will increase value. The resulting order is God's subjective aim—the goal God entertains for the divine becoming. Apart from God's action, the eternal objects have no unity but are simply a random set of possibilities. It requires the presence of an actual entity capable of complete envisagement of the realm of eternal objects, namely God, to give them a determined, ordered unity, and hence to render them relevant to individual creatures, as Whitehead explains:

> The conceptual feelings, which compose his primordial nature, exemplify in their subjective forms their mutual sensitivity and their subjective unity of subjective aim. These subjective forms are valuations determining the relative relevance of eternal objects for each occasion of actuality. (PR 344)

How specific is this divine aim? Under the rules of the process system, it is not possible to regard God's subjective aim as a version of divine determinism. While God's general goal remains constant, the specific possibilities best actualized in particular situations may change depending on the free actions of creatures. In fact, Whitehead considers it necessary that the subjective aim order the eternal objects in such a way that all possible states of affairs in the world will have a specific goal:

> The "primordial nature" of God is the concrescence of a unity of conceptual feelings, including among their data all eternal objects. The concrescence is directed by the subjective aim, that the subjective form of the feelings shall be such as to constitute the eternal objects into relevant lures of feeling severally appropriate for *all realizable basic conditions*. (PR 87–88, italics mine)

So God's subjective aim is flexible enough to react to the changing world situation, but constant in its underlying drive toward maximum value. This notion of a fundamental purposefulness in God, which is reflected in the purposes passed on to creatures, places Whitehead's philosophy in a realist camp. Truth and value are not simply abstractions; they are located in an actual entity, namely, the divine actual entity. And they become efficient facts for the world through the purposeful activity of God in aiming at an ideal and providing an ideal as a goal for creatures. Thus, process philosophy avoids relativism by postulating a subjective aim for God that precedes and informs all creaturely aims.[6]

Calling God's primordial nature an "efficient fact" in the context of Whitehead's system has a special meaning. The primordial nature is made up of conceptual prehensions—prehensions of possibilities, not actualities. According to what Whitehead terms "the ontological principle," only actual entities can be reasons.[7] This means that if we seek a reason, we are looking for an actual entity. In the case of the coming-to-be of actual occasions in the world, for example, if we inquire about the reason why the actual occasion is what it is, the answer lies in the universe of other actual occasions that the concrescent occasion prehends. Each actual occasion "feels," or is directly affected by, the other actual occasions in its environment (to be precise, in its immediate past, since causality only occurs over some duration of time). In turn, each actual occasion is felt by, or affects, some future actual occasion in the creation of the world to come.[8] Those data from the environment cause the occasion that is coming to be; they are immanent in the concrescent occasion, or in other words, they compose that occasion. While this description of an occasion's becoming will be elaborated below, it illustrates the Whiteheadian terminology being used. To be an "efficient fact" means nothing less than to contribute to the becoming of an entity or entities by acting as a datum.

God's primordial nature not only acts as a datum for the creaturely occasions in the world, providing them with a structured value system and relevant possibilities and ideals; it also acts as an efficient fact in God's own becoming. It is the satisfaction or consummation toward which God orders all the actualities that come to be in the world process. The primordial nature is the final cause that directs the ongoing inclusion of the created world in God's self, in the consequent nature. I will return to this theme below, when discussing the consequent nature in detail, but here it is sufficient to note that the primordial nature does not represent a side of God that is aloof, ineffective, and hidden from the world. Instead, it is God's eternal decision to be God for the world, bringing the world into the divine fellowship.

The issue of God's decision and therefore the divine responsibility for what occurs as a result of that decision brings up an unresolved debate within process thought. Does God establish the metaphysical structure of reality as well as abide within it? If God establishes the metaphysical categories by God's primordial decision, then God is responsible for the situation in which value is obtained at the risk of destruction, and thus ultimate responsibility for evil can once again be laid at God's feet. If God does not establish the metaphysical categories, however, there is a "greater" reality than God. Whitehead is not clear on this matter, leaving room for the issue of Plato's *Timaeus* to arise in the process realm.

JESUS?

One possible answer to this question is that God only establishes the contingencies of *this* cosmos, and the metaphysical categories are necessary in *any* cosmos. Another is that God establishes the metaphysical categories in a free decision that has no alternatives. This latter solution, while preserving God's omnipotence in a way more consonant with Christian tradition, does not seem to square very well with the precise way in which Whitehead uses the word "decision." If there is no cutting-off of alternatives, then for Whitehead no decision has occurred. The first solution is also more in the spirit of Whitehead's discussion of God's activity in response to evil: God minimizes its effect, but the responsibility clearly is found in the decisions of the nondivine actual entities.

In this scenario, God could still be held responsible for the decision to risk evil in pursuit of value. Presumably, in many cosmological alternatives under the necessary metaphysical conditions, evil would either not be a risk or would be a much-reduced one. So the *possibility* of the evil we experience can still be laid at God's doorstep, but not its *actuality*, for which the buck stops with the free decisions of creatures. The metaphysical situation requires this tradeoff: Freedom to create value entails the freedom to destroy value. For Whitehead, the very meaning of freedom requires there to be alternatives. So the second proposed solution to the dilemma, in which God's decision is a free choice in a set of possibilities containing precisely one member, is internally inconsistent with Whitehead's terminology, and the metaphysical categories must be considered necessary.

To return to the main thread of the discussion: The division of God into two natures, primordial and consequent, is of course an analytical tool. It allows us to show both God's similarity to all other actual entities, which like God are dipolar, and the unique attributes of God that become clear due to God's unique function in the metaphysical system. For example, while creatures begin their concrescence with the physical pole, or data, and move toward the mental pole, or satisfaction, God alone begins with the mental pole and moves toward the physical pole.[9] God begins with the divine satisfaction in the ordering of eternal objects, and the divine process consists of the accumulation of data in the consequent nature. Whitehead is careful to show that the two natures of God complement each other to present a complete picture of the divine nature.

> Thus, when we make a distinction of reason, and consider God in the abstraction of a primordial actuality, we must ascribe to him neither fulness of feeling, nor consciousness. He is that unconditioned actuality of conceptual feeling at the base of things; so that, by reason of this primordial actuality, there is an order in the relevance of eternal objects to the process of creation. (PR 344)

Notice that this description of God's primordial nature as incomplete and unconscious is an abstract distinction. It does not describe God as such, but only a mode of God's functioning, a phase of God's process. Elsewhere, Whitehead famously remarks, "To sum up: God's 'primordial nature' is abstracted from his commerce with particulars. . . . It is God in abstraction, alone with himself. As such it is a mere factor in God, deficient in actuality" (PR 34). At first this picture of the primordial nature as "deficient in actuality" appears to contradict the ontological principle. How can something that is not an actual entity be a reason, an "efficient fact"? Here Whitehead buys into the Aristotelian distinction between efficient and final causes. While God's mental pole cannot be an efficient cause, like the "physical" data from actual occasions that have become objective facts for their heirs in the world, it can be a final cause, in the sense of a goal toward which entities direct their striving. It can even be a final cause for God's activity. While all other actual entities derive this final cause initially from God, God is the sole actual entity that derives its aim from no source other than itself. This is a teleological way of stating that God is *causa sui*. The balance between teleological explanations for reality, and explanations in which the cause precedes and produces the effect, marks the process system consistently. Whitehead's realization that final causes are effective in the universe alongside efficient causes, and that both must be operative to sufficiently describe reality, leads him to postulate the dipolar nature of actual entities.

To sum up, the concept of God's primordial nature describes God's self-determination to be oriented in a particular way toward an aesthetic goal. This goal is consistent over time since it is determined by God in God's nontemporal actuality; however, it does not determine specific events in the temporal flow, which are left up to the decisions of other actual entities. These creaturely decisions take place in relative independence from God, conditioned by but not determined by God. God's subjective aim, which consists of God's ordering of the eternal objects in terms of their desirability, gives the universe a fundamental system of ideals and values. God's self-constitution in terms of order and purpose enables the world's progress, which can only occur through the infusion of order and purpose by God in relationship to the world. The primordial nature is the basis of the process assertion that God is effective in the world's history, as George Allen explains:

> If it is asserted that God acts in history, then the claim is being made that God is caught up in the structures of purposefulness. Such divine involvement should, I suggest, be seen as twofold. First, to believe that God acts in history is to assert that the aims, values, and methods of an individual's activity are influenced by the divine presence. . . . Second, one claims that the divine reality itself considers certain things valuable, entertains ideal ends, and engages in behavior aimed at the actualization of those ends.[10]

As Allen suggests, the next step in discussing God's action in the world is to describe how God's purposes become our purposes. This leads us to the presentation of relevant possibilities for the creature in its initial aim.

God's Gift of the Initial Aim

One stage of concrescence, or the becoming of an actual occasion, is its physical prehensions of the occasions in its immediate past. "Prehension" is Whitehead's technical term for what he also calls "feeling," meaning the way one entity becomes related to another.[11] The prehending occasion takes in the data from its environment, and is the active subject; the prehended occasion has finished its process of becoming and is objective data, the passive side of the relationship. In an important sense, the prehended data constitute the prehending occasion. But in another sense, the prehending occasion is more than its data. A mere collection of data does not constitute an occasion because it does not exhibit the order that is inherent in subjectivity. The prehending occasion feels each datum in a specific way, and this constitutes its individuality.

Since all order originates in God, as we have seen, the story of the emerging individuality of each actual occasion is the story of how that occasion receives order from God. To analyze this process, one long quotation from Whitehead can serve as an encapsulated introduction:

> According to the ontological principle, there is nothing which floats into the world from nowhere. Everything in the actual world is referable to some actual entity. It is either transmitted from an actual entity in the past or belongs to the subjective aim of the actual entity to whose concrescence it belongs. This subjective aim is both an example and a limitation of the ontological principle. It is an example, in that the principle is here applied to the immediacy of concrescent fact. The subject completes itself during the process of concrescence by a self-criticism of its own incomplete phases. In another sense the subjective aim limits the ontological principle by its own autonomy. But the initial stage of the aim is an endowment which the subject inherits from the inevitable ordering of things, conceptually realized in the nature of God. The immediacy of the concrescent subject is constituted by its living aim at its own self-constitution. Thus the initial stage of the aim is rooted in the nature of God, and its completion depends on the self-causation of the subject-superject. (PR 244)

Notice first that Whitehead sees two basic types of reasons for the concrescence of each actual occasion: other actual entities that provide data for the concrescing occasion, and the concrescing occasion itself, which determines its own subjective aim. This is how Whitehead manages to tread a middle path between scientific determinism and philosophical voluntarism. An occasion is constituted by the data that it receives from its past, but it is able to add value to those data by organizing them in terms of a "personal" purpose. Each occasion aims toward a certain unified reality in its own satisfaction, which is then presented as a datum for occasions to come. Not only does this analysis represent a *via media* between determinism and voluntarism but also between monism and pluralism, two poles between which the universe is constantly oscillating. As Whitehead puts it in a famous aphorism, "The many become one, and are increased by one" (PR 21).

How does the divine endowment to creatures fit into this scheme of causality? God figures in both types of reasons. First, since God is an actual entity, God is a source of data for concrescence just as other actual entities are. Unlike other creatures from which the concrescent occasion receives data, however, God is not in the past; the divine actual entity is nontemporal.[12] This means that God (in the primordial nature) is the unchanging fact prehended by all other actual occasions, and accounts for the consistency of purpose that enables the universe to progress toward a goal.[13] The data that God provides are God's conceptual valuations of the eternal objects. This is similar to the data derived from other actual occasions in that they are part of the concrescent occasion's physical pole, from which concrescence begins; although the data received are conceptual, they are prehended via the physical prehension of the actual entity prehending the eternal objects, in what Whitehead terms a hybrid physical prehension:

> A "physical feeling" is here defined to be a feeling of another actuality. If the other actuality be objectified by its conceptual feelings, the physical feeling of the subject in question is termed "hybrid." Thus the primary phase [of the concrescent process] is a hybrid physical feeling of God, in respect to God's conceptual feeling which is immediately relevant to the universe "given" for that concrescence. There is then . . . a derived conceptual feeling which reproduces for the subject the data and valuation of God's conceptual feeling. (PR 225)

The hybrid physical prehension also enables the concrescent occasion to include as data the conceptual feelings of other actual occasions than God. In this way, God is no different from other actual entities in the emerging occasion's universe. God differs from God's fellow actual entities in respect to the completeness of the divine conceptual valuation and in the immediate divine presence to each actual occasion. Only in the data derived from God does the actual occasion receive a complete system of ideals and values, which gives an initial (aesthetic) order to all the data of the physically prehended universe.

We see then that God serves as data for the concrescent occasion alongside the other actual entities in that occasion's universe, with the differences being that the divine data are nontemporal (hence, not strictly in the occasion's past) and complete in God's envisagement of the eternal objects. The other source of causation for the occasion's concrescence is the subjective aim, by which the occasion exercises its own decision over its own becoming. God is also active in this reason for concrescence, namely, as its initiator. The decision-making capability of the occasion cannot create its own standards for differentiation, distinction, and preference. It must accept, reject, and react to a standard given to it. Thus, Whitehead sees God as the source of the initial aim, which becomes the subjective aim through the free decision of the concrescent occasion. This is the same inheritance of God's conceptual feelings via a hybrid physical prehension, only now we are not considering it as data for the physical pole but as the initiation of the mental pole. The wider context of the preceding quotation shows how the two aspects are united:

> Each temporal entity, in one sense, originates from its mental pole, analogously to God himself. It derives from God its basic conceptual aim, relevant to its actual world, yet with indeterminations awaiting its own decisions. . . . There is then . . . a derived conceptual feeling which reproduces for the subject the data and valuation of God's conceptual feeling. This conceptual feeling is the initial conceptual aim referred to in the preceding statement. In this sense, God can be termed the creator of each temporal actual entity. (PR 224–25)

So far we have identified God's part in the network of causes that enable the concrescence of a new actual occasion. It is now possible to describe more completely the divine conceptual valuation passed to each occasion, which Whitehead calls the initial aim. The long quotation that began this section called it "an endowment which the subject inherits from the inevitable ordering of things, conceptually realized in the nature of God" (PR 244). If one were to generalize about all initial aims given to actual occasions, one might say that the initial aim is the presentation of ideals. By communicating to the occasion what God values, God sets up a contrast between what is and what might be. This disparity can be in itself creative if it initiates movement in a particular direction toward unrealized possibilities. Cobb and Griffin describe the presentation of ideals in terms of a human recipient:

> Our experience is organized in terms of purposes and memories inherited from our past. This route of inheritance determines our sense of self-identity through time. There is, however, in all our experiences also the divine presence and agency, the initial aim, the principle of creative transformation. This aim is what would be best in each moment in terms of a wider view of the consequences than we ordinarily take. There is a tension between oneself and one's experience of what ideally would be, between what one is and the rightness in things that one dimly discerns. Hence the divine presence is experienced as an other, sometimes recognized as gracious, often felt as judge.[14]

The feeling of contrast is not necessarily conscious, since it occurs in all occasions from the most basic up through the most complex. Cobb and Griffin, however, are showing that the disparity created by the presence of the divine ideal is also the basis of a religious sense.

An ideal can be very general or very specific, and process thought allows for the experience of God's valuation at both a general and a specific level. At high levels of consciousness and reflective thought, actual occasions can use their general apprehension of God's value system to examine hypotheticals and compare alternatives. If the initial aim were solely a general value system, however, the divine reality would be deistic, inactive, content to show a broad path and leave it to individuals to work out the specifics. In fact, to allow for the maximum creative advance, the initial aim is maximally specific—unique to each actual occasion. Again, if one were to generalize about all initial aims, one might say that the uniqueness of each is due at its most basic level to the unique spatiotemporal position of the occasion that entertains it. No two occasions can occupy the same position in space and time; this is the basic metaphysical reason why each occasion receives a different initial aim. The initial aim provides each occasion with a role to play, a role that no other entity can fulfill because no other entity has exactly the same set of possibilities and relationships inherent in its given position.[15] When God provides each occasion with a unique role, God is initiating each occasion's self-identity.[16] For the purpose of discussing election, the important concept to be derived from this uniqueness is that the initial aim is *relevant* to each occasion. Election, in this view, is not simply a change in the entity's ontological status, prescribed from an eternity that is immune to the temporal vagaries of the world. It is a call that comes to each individual where that individual lives. Because the initial aim is relevant to the situation of the emerging occasion, election really takes place within the contingencies of history.

The term *relevance* appears over and over again as Whitehead discusses the advent of God's primordial nature in the world process. It is intended to balance the doctrine of the primordial nature with the picture of God as affected by and responsive to the world. If God's primordial nature were the only agent in the giving of the initial aim (leaving aside the "deficiently actual" character of that nature, which precludes its being an efficient cause without the corresponding physical pole), then each occasion would receive the same initial aim. The eternal ordering of possibilities, after all, cannot be affected by individual circumstances. The occasion would be left to its own devices in figuring out where it fits into this grand scheme of value and purpose. With the participation of the consequent nature, however, the initial aim can be made relevant to each unique situation, because in the consequent nature the occurrences of the world become part of God's self, ordered and redirected toward God's satisfaction. This "taking account" of the world is absolutely necessary in a nondeterministic cosmology if God is to be thought of as an effective agent. God acts in history, according to the Christian faith; therefore God knows, works within, and uses the contingent circumstances of history.

The idea of relevance in the initial aim is a bridge between the primordial grading of eternal objects in God's subjective aim and the particular "viable possibilities" of history. By "viable possibilities" I mean the potential events that really can be actualized at any particular time. Obviously this is only a tiny subset of the vast range of logically possible events. The selection and grading of those real possibilities for each moment of time is a matter that is dependent upon the eternal grading of the primordial nature,[17] but is equally dependent on the inclusion of the world in the consequent nature. Whitehead explains this creative infusion of eternity into actuality as metaphysically necessary for the transition from one occasion to the next:

> Thus the transition of the creativity from an actual world to the correlate novel concrescence is conditioned by the relevance of God's all-embracing conceptual valuation to the particular possibilities of transmission from the actual world, and by its relevance to the various possibilities of initial subjective form available for the initial feelings. (PR 244)

Elsewhere, Whitehead is even more explicit regarding how what is not yet, the merely possible, becomes a causal factor in the realm of actuality through the advent of eternal objects in the world process:

> This abrupt[18] synthesis of eternal objects in each occasion is the inclusion in actuality of the analytical character of the realm of eternality. . . . This graded envisagement is how the actual includes what (in one sense) is not-being as a positive factor in its own achievement. It is the source of error, of truth, of art, of ethics, and of religion. By it, fact is confronted with alternatives. (SMW 176–77)

The differentiation between what is actual and what is potential is a key element in the creative advance. But not all potentialities are equally close to actuality. By themselves, actual occasions do not have the scope of awareness to judge which potentialities are realizable and which, when realized, will result in progress toward God's aesthetic goal. Only God's prehension of eternal objects is a complete valuation of the entire infinite realm, therefore only by prehending God can an emerging occasion internalize the finite range of real possibilities for its becoming, along with God's assessment of the relative value of these possibilities.[19] Recall that for Whitehead, the value of any possibility is aesthetic; therefore, progress is measured by the capacity of the world as a whole for enjoyment, defined by intensity of experience. The relevance of the possibilities given to actual occasions has to do both with their continuity with the past and with their contrast with the past.

> The birth of a new aesthetic experience depends on the maintenance of two principles by the creative purpose: 1. The novel consequent [ideal forms] must be graded in relevance so as to preserve some identity of character with the ground. 2. The novel consequent must be graded in relevance so as to preserve some contrast with the ground in respect to that same identity of character. (RM 115)

If identity is not maintained, then there can be no aesthetic progress because complexity cannot be built up in an evolutionary process. If there is no contrast, conversely, there can be no aesthetic progress because novelty has not entered into the evolutionary process. Therefore, the relevance of an eternal object to a concrescent occasion involves both continuity and contrast.

The selection of *which* eternal objects will have ingression into the world and become productive of the actuality of a concrescent occasion is the work of God, and forms the specific, unique content of the initial aim given to each creature. We have already seen that there is a limitation of possibilities by the fact of an occasion's time and place; not all possibilities are actualizable by all occasions. But there must be a further selection even among the possibilities that are viable for a certain occasion. If all viable possibilities are equal to the occasion, then once again progress is thwarted because forward motion and retrograde motion cannot be distinguished from one another. The further selection of *preference* is necessary so that there is a direction to history.[20] The relevance of the eternal objects to the concrescent occasion, then, is dependent on God's valuation of them in terms of God's aesthetic goal, while at the same time it is dependent on the facts of the world. Both these factors inform the question of what really possible outcome is most desirable in every present moment. The moment itself must be taken into account, having been brought about by all the history of all actual occasions up to its very brink. The next moment is anticipated, as it will be formed by the moment that is now at hand. The actual past and the anticipated future collide in causing the present moment. And God is the coordinator of these causes, forming the present by passing to the occasion the desire to be a step from a past that cannot now be changed to a future that is not yet determined.[21] This step requires the limitless envisagement of possibility in God's primordial nature as well as the limitless and constantly increasing inclusion of actuality in God's consequent nature. So Whitehead can write about the relevance of possibilities to the concrescent occasion:

> There can thus be an intuition of an intrinsic suitability of some definite outcome from a presupposed situation. There will be nothing statistical in this

suitability. It depends upon the fundamental graduation of appetitions which lies at the base of things, and which solves all indeterminations of transition. (PR 207)

Without an actual entity—God—as the mediator between past and future, this suitability would be merely statistical, an expression of the blind forces of probability alone. Because the mediator is an actual entity rather than simply a metaphysical or mathematical principle applied indiscriminately to all existence, there exists a discrimination among possibilities for the present, born of an unchanging purpose entertained by a purposeful being. God is not simply a conduit that facilitates the conversion of possibility into actuality, or a necessary stage along the assembly line for the construction of reality. God's urging of the world toward the creation of value, through the gift of the initial aim, makes divinity more than a metaphysical factor. The final pages of *Process and Reality*, with their poetic descriptions of God's activity and nature, are not an aberration in Whitehead:

> He is the lure for feeling, the eternal urge of desire. His particular relevance to each creative act, as it arises from its own conditioned standpoint in the world, constitutes him the initial "object of desire" establishing the initial phase of each subjective aim. (PR 344)

Because God embodies a goal for the world and enables the world to reach that goal, the name "God," expressing the object of religion and the one worthy of worship, appropriately applies to Whitehead's concept.

[handwritten margin note: WHAT'S THE DIFFERENCE?]

From Initial Aim to Subjective Aim

So far I have been discussing God's gift of the initial aim to each occasion. This aim is "initial" because it is the beginning of purpose in the occasion, not its end. The initial aim cannot be the final determination of the emerging entity because Whitehead fears that if it is, divine determinism has reappeared. Instead, Whitehead writes that each occasion "derives from God its basic conceptual aim, relevant to its actual world, yet with indeterminations awaiting its own decisions" (PR 224). "The subject completes itself during the process of concrescence by a self-criticism of its own incomplete phases" (PR 244). Whitehead insists on a description of the actual occasion as self-creating,[22] and his system assumes that the decision of a free subject to constitute itself as it chooses, within the limitations imposed upon it by the structure of necessity, is inviolable. This self-creation begins with the creature's adaptation of the initial aim into the subjective aim.[23]

What is the relationship of the initial aim to the subjective aim? To what extent does the former determine the latter? In some places, Whitehead seems to indicate that the initial aim is less specific than the subjective aim: there are, he writes, "indeterminations awaiting [the occasion's] own decisions" (PR 224). It is at least clear in *Process and Reality* that Whitehead reserves for each creature the opportunity to determine itself in contrast to its inheritance from the world and from God, as well as in continuity with that inheritance. There is always a "subjective valuation" by the concrescent occasion of data from the world and from God that autonomously "modifies the subjective forms throughout the whole range of feeling in that concrescence and thereby guide the integrations" (PR 245). We are most aware of this ability to reevaluate and transcend one's inheritance in living individuals that both endure and change over time; the ingression of "novel conceptual feeling" that informs the valuation of data allows the individual to change based on its own decisions.

However, the example of living individuals is not necessarily the canonical instance of autonomy in Whitehead. Most actual occasions we encounter—in nonliving nature, for example—have "negligible autonomous energy," meaning that the input of the concrescent subject into the process of its own self-creation is minimal. For most intents and purposes, the factor of decision in these occasions can be ignored, and they can be considered macroscopically as instances of pure cause and effect.

> [T]he subject merely receives the physical feelings, confirms their valuation according to the "order" of that epoch, and transmits by reason of its own objective immortality. Its own flash of autonomous individual experience is negligible for the science which is tracing transmissions up to the conscious experience of a final observer. (PR 245)

In other words, for occasions that occur in the circumstances of empty space, or in enduring objects like a rock, the patterns of the past are simply repeated with virtual identity, again and again. A kind of Newtonian attitude toward these nonliving occasions can prevail, so that their self-creative aspect is understood as so minimal that it does not result in any observable effect. Notice that even here, Whitehead maintains that a self-creative process is still occurring in these concrescences—namely, the occasion "confirms" the prior valuations, thus repeating the ordering of data that it inherited from its direct ancestor. Even though no appreciable change has occurred, the occasion has still individualized itself by this decision. Even though its options for doing otherwise are severely limited, we still understand through the science of physics and relativity that there *are* other options, however remote and improbable;[24] therefore, the decision of the occasion is nonetheless real and effective.

With the understanding, then, that the translation of initial aim into subjective aim refers to enduring objects that change by their own decision as well as those that remain relatively unchanged, it is my contention that when Whitehead speaks of the "indeterminations" which await the occasion's own creativity, he does not mean that the initial aim is merely a general purpose, which awaits the creature's creativity to add specific individual goals. On the contrary, Whitehead repeatedly affirms the specificity of the initial aim: "The initial aim is the best for that *impasse*" (PR 244); "There is not just one ideal 'order' that all actual entities should attain and fail to attain. In each case there is an ideal peculiar to each actual entity" (PR 84); "[God's] *particular* relevance to each creative act, as it arises from its own conditioned standpoint in the world, constitutes him the initial 'object of desire' establishing the initial phase of each subjective aim" (PR 344, italics mine). "The basic conceptual feeling suffers simplification in the successive phases of the concrescence. It starts with conditioned alternatives, and by successive decisions is reduced to coherence" (PR 224). If the modification by the creature is a simplification among alternatives, then the original aim provided by God must be a complex of specific alternatives, not a vague general direction. It is within the power of God, as described by process categories, to deliver to each occasion a specific aim, since God both entertains an aim for the entire universal process and is aware of the situation of each occasion in that process. But process categories, specifically what Whitehead calls the "Category of Freedom and Determination," also stipulate that it is *not* within the power of God to determine everything about the concrescence of the actual occasion: "This category can be condensed into the formula, that in each concrescence whatever is determinable is determined, but that there is always a remainder for the decision of the subject-superject of that concrescence" (PR 27–28). Therefore, the initial aim is maximally specific in presenting graded alternatives for the present, but it does not determine the response of the creature to this specific aim. God's particular providence and the creature's free decision in self-creation are both preserved.

To recap what we have learned so far about the origin of purpose, which also constitutes the origin of each occasion of experience: The initial aim is derived from God and presents to the concrescent occasion the primordial divine valuation of possibility, made relevant to the particular situation in time and space of the emerging entity. This aim is the initiation of the relationship between God and the creature, a relationship conditioned both by

God, who gives the emerging entity a determinate standpoint in relation to its inherited data and an initial direction toward its own becoming, and also by the creature, whose specific, contingent historical situation determines what aim is relevant for it. In the next phase,[25] the occasion transforms the initial aim into the subjective aim by its own decision regarding how it will feel its data. This phase is the response of the individual creature to the relationship established by God. The data that the subjective aim grades in terms of desirability are the physical prehensions of the emerging occasion's immediate past. Whitehead puts the relationship of God, world, and free subject in this scheme:

> If we prefer the phraseology, we can say that God and the actual world jointly constitute the character of the creativity for the initial phase of the novel concrescence. The subject, thus constituted, is the autonomous master of its own concrescence into subject-superject. (PR 245)

The phrase "subject-superject," which has appeared in several quotations, now requires a more detailed definition. We have begun discussing the actual occasion as a subject that is the master of its own self-creation, an agent of decisions that affect itself in its own becoming. This is the meaning of the modification of the initial aim into the subjective aim. When Whitehead refers to the entity as both subject and superject, he is indicating that the decision of a concrescent entity does not only affect itself but also the entire lineage of entities that will arise in its wake. In its final satisfaction, when the subjectivity of the occasion ceases and it achieves immortality as an object for the prehensions of others, the occasion "hurls itself beyond itself" into the future. This role of the occasion, after its subjective death, is a factor in what the occasion aims toward during its becoming.[26] The aim is not only toward what it will make of its present, but toward what it will leave as an inheritance for the future. Whitehead writes, "But the 'satisfaction' is the 'superject' rather than the 'substance' or 'subject.' It closes up the entity; and yet is the superject adding its character to the creativity whereby there is a becoming of entities superseding the one in question" (PR 84). As we have seen, God's aim is at maximum value, defined as intensity of experience. Similarly, a creature aims at its own intensity of experience primarily in its emerging present, but it also aims to leave that value for its future: "The subjective aim, whereby there is origination of conceptual feeling, is at intensity of feeling (a) in the immediate subject, and (b) in the *relevant* future" (PR 27). The subjective aim, then, is not simply a private matter of the subject's own experience, but reflects the subject-superject's public existence after its subjectivity has ended. The purpose that a creature entertains, along with its relative success in achieving that purpose, continues to act as a cause for the world at large after the creature's death.

The question of the occasion's freedom to become what it chooses to become dominates the discussion of this phase in the concrescence. One of the features of Whitehead's philosophy of organism is its attempt to mediate two models of the universe: a deterministic model and a voluntaristic model. The deterministic model maintains that freedom is illusory since every effect is fully determined by one or more prior causes, while the voluntaristic model maintains that living creatures have the power to make decisions that produce immediate, real effects. Whitehead advocates a middle way that acknowledges that many effects are determined by the past, but asserts that complete determinism is metaphysically impossible because of the irreducible freedom of every occasion of experience to determine for itself how it feels the data from the past:

> The concrescence of each individual actual entity is internally determined and is externally free. This category can be condensed into the formula, that in each concrescence whatever is determinable is determined, but that there is always a remainder for the decision of the subject-superject of that concrescence. This subject-superject is the universe in that synthesis, and beyond it there is nonentity. This final decision is the reaction of the unity of the whole to its own internal determination. This reaction is the final modification of emotion, appreciation, and purpose. But the decision of the whole arises out of the determination of the parts, so as to be strictly relevant to it. (PR 27–28)

Whitehead locates the freedom of each entity in its inalienable ability to interpret the data it receives in terms of purpose. The occasion feels the data in a certain subjective form that is the form of its own individuality. Granted, that individuality is not the sole creation of the occasion; only God is *causa sui* in the sense of producing God's own individual aim that determines God's self. Although God can be termed the first cause of the individual's creation, God is not a sufficient cause for the emergence of a free individual because individuality can only result from the (conditioned) decision of the subject itself. "An actual entity feels as it does feel in order to be the actual entity which it is," writes Whitehead. "In this way an actual entity satisfies Spinoza's notion of substance: it is *causa sui*. . . . All actual entities share with God this characteristic of self-causation" (PR 222).

Related to the concept of individual freedom is the problem of how novelty enters the world. Freedom, in the sense in which Whitehead wants to use the word, would be meaningless if there were not real alternatives on

which decision could act. And, as far as the freedom to fulfill individual
purposes and make progress toward a goal is concerned, it is not enough to
choose among alternatives that have been actualized in the past. Emerging
occasions may decide to actualize an unrealized possibility in a clear
demonstration of their freedom to break from the past. Novelty might have
been explained simply by the unique configurations of data that each occasion embodies, and this is one kind of novelty mentioned in *Process and
Reality*.[27] But Whitehead thinks (along with Plato) that, as envisaged by
God, unrealized possibilities have a kind of real efficacy, though not the
efficacy of *actual* entities—rather, they are a kind of *potential* entity, what
Whitehead calls an eternal object.

It takes the intervention of two actual entities to make an eternal object
productive of actuality: (1) God, whose primordial conceptual prehension
of the eternal object both gives an initial value to it and makes it available
to the concrescent occasion, and (2) the concrescent occasion, which
chooses to make the eternal object part of its final satisfaction. Whitehead
writes, "Thus an originality in the temporal world is conditioned, though
not determined, by an initial subjective aim supplied by the ground of all
order and of all originality" (PR 108). The "originality" in this case is the
actual occasion in its process of becoming, the basic instance of novelty in
the world, since each actual occasion is a new creation, unique in its position in the "extensive continuum"[28] and in its "actual world."[29] The advent
of an eternal object in the world is not deterministic even though the eternal object is felt through a prehension of God, who has a certain subjective
feeling toward the eternal object. In a hybrid physical prehension, the occasion *physically* prehends God's *conceptual* prehension of the eternal object,
and this is the mode of ingression for the initial aim. But the concrescent
occasion is not bound to feel the eternal object in the same way God feels
it: "But the two conceptual feelings in the two subjects may have different
subjective forms" (PR 246). In other words, God is needed as a reason for
the influx of novelty into the world, since only actual entities can be reasons and eternal objects are not in themselves actual. But although the
divine valuation of eternal objects is the beginning of purpose and novelty
in the world, it is not the whole story of purpose or novelty. The activity of
actual occasions embodying creativity makes novel and hitherto unrealized
possibilities actual, and it does so by virtue of the occasion's unique, self-
determined subjective decisions concerning those possibilities.

To return to the first quotation in the previous paragraph, the role of
God in the influx of novelty is as both "the ground of all order and of all
originality" (PR 108). God is the ground of all order as the principle of lim-

itation or concretion. Limitation does not mean a decrease in freedom; on the contrary, it is necessary for the operation of freedom. Whitehead correctly understands that freedom implies definite choices that have been limited by outside agencies, not an abstract ability to move in any of an infinite number of directions:

> But there is no such fact as absolute freedom; every actual entity possesses only such freedom as is inherent in the primary phase "given" by its standpoint of relativity to its actual universe. Freedom, givenness, potentiality, are notions which presuppose each other and limit each other. (PR 133)

God is the principle of concretion in that "he is that actual entity from which each temporal concrescence receives that initial aim from which its self-causation starts" (PR 244); in other words, without God's limitation of the realm of eternal objects by the divine provision of relevant possibilities, nothing concrete can ever arise. The fact that decisions are possible in our world implies that there is a primordial decision, or limitation, enabling all subsequent decisions.[30] The ground of order, then, is also the ground of originality, since without order, nothing new can arise. This is God as the mediator between potentiality and actuality:

> The things which are temporal arise by their participation in the things which are eternal. The two sets are mediated by a thing which combines the actuality of what is temporal with the timelessness of what is potential. This final entity is the divine element in the world, by which the barren inefficient disjunction of abstract potentialities obtains primordially the efficient conjunction of ideal realization. . . . By reason of the actuality of this primordial valuation of pure potentials, each eternal object has a definite effective relevance to each concrescent process. Apart from such orderings, there would be a complete disjunction of eternal objects unrealized in the temporal world. Novelty would be meaningless, and inconceivable. (PR 40)

It appears at first glance that God's role as ground of order and originality refers to the primordial nature. Notice, however, that both these roles presuppose the existence of the consequent nature. If God did not take into account the actuality of the world's entities, in their freedom to determine themselves, the primordial ordering would quickly become meaningless as world history diverged from the ideal. And the possibilities offered to each entity must have actuality as a background in order to be relevant for the entity's historical situation, as we have already seen.[31]

When describing God's role in the production of novelty, there is a temptation to overlook the equally essential role played by the creature. For example, this summary statement of the influx of novelty into the world shows a tendency to make God the sole creator of novelty: "White-head's more fundamental account then is that God, the primordial actual entity which prehends the eternal objects, is the source of the initial sub-jective aim which produces novelty in actual occasions."[32] But the initial aim given by God remains a set of mere possibilities until, by the decision of the creature, one or more of those possibilities are actualized. God knows both potentialities and actualities (in the divine primordial and consequent natures, respectively), but God only knows actualities as actual *conditionally* upon the decision of the creature. To put it in Stephen C. Pepper's words, "God in his primordial status does not know when an original idea will become actualized until the favorable occasion occurs which takes it in."[33]

The freedom of actual occasions to produce novelty entails a true deci-sion between viable alternatives. This means that there are times when an occasion chooses to actualize a possibility that is not the best for that par-ticular moment in history. Novelty in and of itself is not a good; only nov-elty that is properly situated in time, so that it can become productive of greater intensity, is good. A possibility brought about before its time may actually be destructive, as Whitehead notes:

> A new actuality may appear in the wrong society, amid which its claims to efficacy act mainly as inhibitions. Then a weary task is set for creative func-tion, by an epoch of new creations to remove the inhibition. Insistence on birth at the wrong season is the trick of evil. In other words, the novel fact may throw back, inhibit, and delay. But the advance, when it does arrive, will be richer in content, more fully conditioned, and more stable. For in its objective efficacy an actual entity can only inhibit by reason of its alternative positive contribution. (PR 223)

This illustrates another aspect of novelty: its exclusion of alternatives. Once a possibility is actualized, all other possibilities for that moment are cut off. A path is chosen in the present, and the immediate future occasion will find itself on that path, with its choices constrained by the past deci-sion. If the alternatives for a concrescent occasion were not graded in God's gift of the initial aim, novelty would always arise willy-nilly in this fashion, with entities moving erratically in no particular general direction of progress or regress. With God's contribution of order and limitation, there is a directionality to history that transcends the entropic direction of time for matter and energy. God aims that history be characterized by a steady increase in value. This increase is dependent, however, on the actions of free creatures to choose the better alternative for their own concrescence. Still, even when occasions choose a worse alternative, and the actualization of out-of-place novelty results in a destructive setback to God's plan, all hope of future progress is not lost. The destruction is minimized, and new construction can even be made on its foundation. God uses whatever actuality comes about in the world, whether it is the best that could be or somewhat less than the best. The quotation above shows that even a novelty which appears at the wrong time will lend greater value to eventual progress, although that progress will be slower in appearing. Elsewhere, Whitehead claims that God's role in dealing with destructive actuality is itself destructive: to so minimize its impact that the actual occasion itself is made trivial in the final satisfaction:

> This function of God is analogous to the remorseless working of things in Greek and in Buddhist thought. The initial aim is the best for that *impasse*. But if the best be bad, then the ruthlessness of God can be personified as *Atè*, the goddess of mischief. The chaff is burnt. What is inexorable in God, is valuation as an aim towards "order"; and "order" means "society permissive of actualities with patterned intensity of feeling arising from adjusted contrasts." (PR 244)

Whitehead here imagines a situation where an actual occasion finds itself unable to contribute any value to God's final satisfaction. Whether or not such occasions occur is possibly a matter for faith rather than for metaphysics. Yet there is an inescapably religious dimension to the idea that a creature might be asked to sacrifice itself for the greater good. At every moment, reality finds itself at an impasse that can only be resolved by the decisions of free entities. Might not some entities be called upon to decide to annihilate themselves, as it were, in terms of their future effectiveness, so that the next entity to arise will not be bound as tightly by past mistakes? What is contrary to the general religious idea of martyrdom in this scenario is that the sacrifice is made to put an end to an unproductive line of actuality rather than to open up new possibilities. After all, the martyred saints were presumed in early Christianity to have everlasting effectiveness as mediators in heaven after their death on earth, and their sacrifice was not to be forgotten, but to be retold over and over as a model and inspiration. This is obviously not what Whitehead has in mind. His sacrificial occasion fulfills its aim only to be dismissed into triviality so that progress can occur in another direction. "The chaff is burnt," he writes, calling to mind the harsh aspect of Jesus' parables wherein judgment elevates some but correspondingly casts out others. Until a further discussion of the initial aim as judgment below, it is enough to say here that Whitehead is recognizing a valid possibility in his metaphysical system: that in certain situations there may be no increase in value possible, and that the best for that situation is to cut it off without progeny, so that future occasions are not bound to reenact its sterility.

Satisfaction \WHAT IS IT?

The decision of the occasion to enact its own subjective aim leads directly to the final phase of the concrescence: the satisfaction. The satisfaction is the unification of all the occasion's prehensions into one complex unity, ordered according to the subjective aim. It is the "becoming actual" of the entity in the sense that the entity now is one definite thing, able to act as an efficient cause for other entities. The following is Whitehead's definition:

> The final phase in the process of concrescence, constituting an actual entity, is one complex, fully determinate feeling. This final phase is termed the "satisfaction." It is fully determinate (a) as to its genesis, (b) as to its objective character for the transcendent creativity, and (c) as to its prehension—positive or negative—of every item in its universe. (PR 25–26)

Whereas the objective data of the entity's actual world act as efficient causes toward the satisfaction, the subjective aim is the final cause. Upon attainment, the becoming of the occasion ends, along with its subjectivity. As a determinate satisfaction, it is now an object to be prehended as data for the concrescences of future occasions. Its subjective character is no more, but its superjective character remains. Whitehead summarizes the process:

> The "objectifications" of the actual entities in the actual world, relative to a definite actual entity, constitute the efficient causes out of which *that* actual entity arises; the "subjective aim" at "satisfaction" constitutes the final cause, or lure, whereby there is determinate concrescence; and that attained "satisfaction" remains as an element in the content of creative purpose. (PR 87)

The satisfaction phase has two aspects with respect to election. First, the satisfaction reveals the dual character of the purpose given to each entity, to become something for itself and for others. Each initial aim is a goal not only for the private completion of the occasion to which it is given but also for subsequent public life of that occasion. In other words, inherent in every specific, momentary purpose for the present are larger purposes for the immediate future:

> This double aim—at the *immediate* present and the *relevant* future—is less divided than appears on the surface. For the determination of the *relevant* future, and the *anticipatory* feeling respecting provision for its grade of inten-

sity, are elements affecting the immediate complex of feeling. The greater part of morality hinges on the determination of relevance in the future. The relevant future consists of those elements in the anticipated future which are felt with effective intensity by the present subject by reason of the real potentiality for them to be derived from itself. (PR 27)

Every contemplation of a private aim, then, involves some consideration of how the attainment of that aim will affect the future. At higher levels of consciousness, that consideration becomes moral reasoning. We have already seen that the subjective aim acts as a final cause, a lure for the concrescence of the occasion. This aim is not only at a satisfaction that unifies the data and achieves the goal of the present occasion but is also one that takes a step forward in the creative advance so that occasions in the immediate future have the advantage of a better starting point and a more valuable inheritance. There is a nested order to purposes; the most basic are the private goals of individuals, but these feed into larger aims for the future, immediate and more remote, and finally into God's eschatological purpose for the universe. At a conscious or unconscious level, all these purposes are entertained by creatures thanks to their prehension of God's subjective aim.

The second aspect of the satisfaction that has to do with election is its assumption into God's consequent nature. Above, under the heading of novelty, we discussed the difference between God's knowledge of possibilities and God's knowledge of actualities. The satisfaction of an actual occasion is the full actuality of that occasion, and it is this phase—the occasion as a unified, definitive whole—that achieves what Whitehead calls "objective immortality" in its status as efficient cause for the future, and in the consequent nature of God.[34]

To fully consider how the satisfaction of each creature becomes part of the divine nature, it is necessary to understand how Whitehead has inverted the usual hierarchy of concerns in this area. The continuous change observed and experienced in the world led philosophers and theologians for centuries, following Plato and Aristotle, to search for a realm of changelessness in which this flux would be grounded.[35] If the world represents change, then the divine must embody immutability. Movement, for them, implied an Unmoved Mover. Hence, God was seen philosophically as a refuge of permanence, while the world was seen as coming to be and passing away. Whitehead prefers to see the problem as more complex: Permanence and fluency require each other, and neither can be reduced to a principle that stands over against some other independent principle and that could conceivably explain all phenomena without recourse to its opposite.[36] The question then becomes: How are permanence and fluency characteristic of God, and how are they characteristic of the world? White-head states the "double problem":

> The first half of the problem concerns the completion of God's primordial nature by the derivation of his consequent nature from the temporal world. The second half of the problem concerns the completion of each fluent actual occasion by its function of objective immortality, devoid of "perpetual perishing," that is to say, "everlasting." (PR 347)

In Whitehead's system, the notion of satisfaction answers the religious and philosophical longing for permanence, without sacrificing the combination of change and changelessness that is characteristic of both God and the world. The actual occasion attains a state of changelessness, or objective immortality, in its satisfaction, which becomes a stubborn matter of fact for all other entities, including God. And God orders all temporal satisfactions in the divine nontemporal satisfaction, affording them a place in the perfect order of the *eschaton:*

> The problems of the fluency of God and of the everlastingness of passing experience are solved by the same factor in the universe. This factor is the temporal world perfected by its reception and its reformation, as a fulfilment of the primordial appetition which is the basis of all order. In this way God is completed by the individual, fluent satisfactions of finite fact, and the temporal occasions are completed by their everlasting union with their transformed selves, purged into conformation with the eternal order which is the final absolute "wisdom." (PR 347)[37]

The consequent nature, in other words, is a real concrescence, putting the divine subjective stamp on the data of temporal satisfactions, feeling them in a way that is uniquely God's way—that is, feeling them with divine love. The process that begins with God's providence of the initial aim ends with God's sanctification of the occasion's contribution to the whole.[38]

Does this type of "everlastingness" conform to the Christian message when the latter speaks of "eternal life"? Whitehead leaves open the question of whether the subjectivity of conscious beings might continue after death.[39] What is certain in his system is that God experiences the lives of creatures completely and intimately:

> The perfection of God's subjective aim, derived from the completeness of his primordial nature, issues into the character of his consequent nature. In it there is no loss, no obstruction. The world is felt in a unison of immediacy. The property of combining creative advance with the retention of mutual immediacy is what in the previous section is meant by the term "everlasting." (PR 345–46)

Thus, the immortality achieved by each entity in its satisfaction is not diluted over time, as the present moves ever forward and away from the moment of the entity's satisfaction. It remains fresh, not in the "memory" of God, but in the immediate divine experience; it remains effective as a factor in the ever growing unity of God's ordered consequent nature.

Satisfaction is a concept that plays a crucial role in Whitehead's system. As it marks the "death" of each occasion in terms of its subjectivity, and the necessary condition for the possibility of another occasion arising, it reinforces the reality of "the many"—the plurality of actual entities that Whitehead insists upon as a stubborn fact of experience. At the same time, however, as it refers to the unification of disparate pieces of data into a single, unique whole, the idea of satisfaction reinforces the simultaneous reality of "the one"—the order imposed on the many by each occasion of experience to form a single subjective identity. God's subjective aim toward satisfaction plays a special role in this interplay of many and one in process thought, for it is in God's consequent nature, wherein the divine subjectivity imposes order upon every fact of the world, that truth is located. It would be impossible to refer to truth or fact if there were not an actual entity that embodied these abstractions and gave them actuality. Only by the inclusion of the world, complete and without loss, in God's consequent nature, and by God's valuation of the world's various aspects, can there be a perspective to which we refer as "truth" in an actuality with the power to determine other actualities:

> The truth itself is nothing else than how the composite natures of the organic actualities of the world obtain adequate representation in the divine nature. Such representations compose the "consequent nature" of God, which evolves in its relationship to the evolving world without derogation to the eternal completion of its primordial conceptual nature. In this way the "ontological principle" is maintained—*since there can be no determinate truth, correlating impartially the partial experiences of many actual entities, apart from the one actual entity to which it can be referred.* (PR 12–13, italics mine)

In God, truth is made an objective unity out of the plural experiences of creatures. The initial aim given to each occasion has the force of ultimate truth behind it, not simply in God's primordial ideal for the world but in the actual world that has come to pass, however it deviates from this ideal. The initial aim strives for a goal that is reachable because it derives from a God who knows the world both as it is and as it should be.

The Initial Aim as Election

Having given a description of the concept of the initial aim, its source in the divine nature, and its function in the concrescence of actual occasions, we are ready to consider in what ways this concept resembles the Christian doctrine of election. This discussion is a preliminary ground-clearing for the constructive work to be undertaken in chapter 4. Here we are concerned with the convergence of a fundamental notion in the Christian message, along with its elaboration in doctrine throughout Jewish and Christian history, and a metaphysical description of the basic nature and origin of purpose in the world. The two are not automatically identical; it requires some effort of comparison and contrast to show that they may be seen as the religious aspect and the metaphysical aspect of the same phenomenon. I shall begin by considering four aspects of the initial aim that express the religious significance of election: as the establishment of the God-creature relationship, as goal for the creature, as providential governance of the world, and as revelation of grace. The next step is to discuss concepts that have often been connected with the doctrine of election in Christian tradition but that are incompatible with process metaphysics and therefore must be denied in a process doctrine of election. Finally, I shall elaborate the aspects of election that process theology redefines, thanks to its metaphysical emphases.

The Initial Aim as the Establishment of a Relationship between God and Creatures

One of the most puzzling aspects of process theology to those who hold a more traditional theism is the metaphysical parity of God and the world. A God without *some* world—without an other to provide data for the divine consequent nature—is inconceivable in process thought, because without a consequent nature God would be "deficiently actual." This leads to a denial of creation *ex nihilo*, since that doctrine presumes that God did in fact exist "before" time, without any world, and conceivably could have decided not to bring any world into being. Whitehead regards the traditional doctrine of creation as a tragic outcome of the synthesis of Aristotelian and Christian thought:

> The notion of God as the "unmoved mover" is derived from Aristotle, at least so far as Western thought is concerned. The notion of God as "eminently real" is a favourite doctrine of Christian theology. The combination of the two into the doctrine of an aboriginal, eminently real, transcendent creator,

at whose fiat the world came into being, and whose imposed will it obeys, is
the fallacy which has infused tragedy into the histories of Christianity and of
Mahometanism. (PR 342)

This difference between traditional Christian theism and process theology will be discussed in greater detail below, when we come to the question
of what aspects of previous election doctrines must be denied in a process
doctrine. At this point, the question under discussion is the nature of the
God-creature relationship in process theology. The creature has a status in
process thought that cannot be accurately described by Schleiermacher's
famous phrase "absolute dependence." Dependence still characterizes the
relationship, but it is *mutual* dependence, and it is balanced by mutual
independence in the sense that both sides of the relationship cause each
other as well as causing themselves.

We have already seen that the initial aim is the first phase of the concrescence of the actual occasion; for that reason, it is often identified with
the Christian doctrine of creation.[40] This identification does not necessarily conflict with my argument that the initial aim is the moment of election for each occasion, since the doctrines of creation and election are
closely connected. It seems natural to think about creation as the first act
of God that affects creatures, since creatures did not exist before God created them. However, although creation is the first act of God toward creatures considered temporally, election is the first act of God toward creatures
considered in order of logical priority. God's primordial decision to be a
God who relates to creatures is logically prior to any other act regarding
creatures. This primordial self-determination of God to be "for us" is the
foundation of election *ad extra*. In this decision, God chooses the realm of
creatures for relationship with the divine and chooses to constitute God's
self for relationship with the realm of creatures.[41] Creation, redemption,
and sanctification all follow from this primordial election of God's self and
of potential creatures. In some forms of the election doctrine, the election
of individual creatures also takes place before any creatures are created.
Whether through simple foreknowledge or an actual deterministic divine
will, the creatures that will come to be are chosen specifically in God's eternal act of election.

How does process theology modify this picture of election and creation,
since in the process system God does not exist "before" or without a world?
The primordial election cannot, therefore, occur "before" the existence of
any creature, since God is never without a world of creatures. What has
been changed in the process system of thought is the meaning of the distinction between what is temporal and what is eternal or everlasting. In

traditional theism, based on Platonic or Aristotelian categories, the eternal is seen as beyond the temporal; transcending the changeability of time and history is the changelessness of the eternal, identified with the divine. In process theism, the eternal is immanent in the temporal, and the temporal is immanent in the everlasting. God's changeless primordial nature enters the world continuously through initial aims given to creatures, and the temporal occasions enter God's everlasting, ever growing consequent nature through God's inclusion of the world. Each transcends the other; neither is metaphysically preferred.

The priority of election over creation in process theology refers not to the election of individual creatures, as it does in those forms of Christian doctrine that regard foreknowledge or predetermination of future individuals as either possible or even metaphysically necessary. It refers to God's self-determination in the divine ordering of eternal objects and the divine subjective aim. Here, in the primordial nature, God constitutes God's self for the purpose of increasing value in the universe through the encouragement of complexity and diversity in creaturely experience. Whatever creatures exist in whatever numbers or forms, this divine drive is unchanging. God's election of God's self results in God's election of individual creatures through the provision of initial aims; this subsequent election of occasions, societies, nexus, and perhaps even human communities is directed toward the fulfillment of God's own subjective aim by giving purposes to creatures that, if actualized, advance God's goal for the universe.

Thus, the election of specific individuals, in process theology, is indeed identical to their creation. No genre of primordial election of individuals is possible in this system because both foreknowledge and divine determinism have been metaphysically ruled out of court. God certainly knows occasions before they arise as *possible* individuals, but God cannot know them or their decisions of feeling, by which they are constituted, as *actual* until they begin their process of becoming objective facts in their concrescence. Aims are not given to abstractions; they are given to real individuals because only actual occasions have the power to become efficient causes for the future.[42] Only real individuals can effect change in the world; hence, the enjoyment of purposefulness is only appropriate to actual occasions (and individual, personally ordered societies made up of actual occasions). Similarly, the concept of a God whose will determines every detail of history is foreign to process theology. The decisions of actual occasions among the viable possibilities open to them determine the future of the world, and this determination cannot be usurped by any will, however powerful. Election, then, comes to real individuals as they arise. It cannot be otherwise, since the answer to the question of what actualities will come into being is unforeseeable and unable to be determined by any agency except that of the immediately preceding world of actual occasions.

However, the election of individuals that occurs in history is presupposed by God's self-election, which occurs in the eternal, divine primordial nature. Without this determinate ordering of eternal objects, the purposes that are given to occasions in history would be random and contradictory. More importantly for our understanding of God's nature through God's act, election is revealed as the key to understanding the relationship between God and creatures. Not only is the relationship between God and each individual occasion established through a unique act of election, but the universal form of all relationships between God and creatures is established in eternity by God's primordial act of will—electing God's self to work toward maximum value through the accomplishments of creatures. The changelessness of God's purpose means that no creature arises before, after, or outside the divine plan for the universe. That plan, in the form of God's primordial valuation of all possibilities, encompasses every occasion that could ever arise.[43] The infinitely smaller subset of occasions that do become actual are evaluated, in turn, on the basis of the subjective aims that they in fact adopt and fulfill; therefore, the election that initiates the relationship perseveres through the concrescence and is fulfilled in God's ordering of actualities in the divine consequent nature.

Whitehead's innovation in the arena of the metaphysical description of relationships is to see, not separate beings connected in a merely external fashion, but entities that are constituted by their internal objectification of other entities. This is the doctrine of internal relations, which stipulates that the relationships that are effective in the concrescence of an actual occasion are the result of an objectification of one entity by another, "the principle that the 'power' of one actual entity on the other is simply how the former is objectified in the constitution of the other" (PR 58). There are two types of this objectification, which occurs in every prehension of a concrescence. Other actual entities are related to a present occasion through "'causal objectification,' [in which] what is felt *subjectively* by the objectified actual entity is transmitted *objectively* to the concrescent actualities which supersede it." Eternal objects are related to the concrescence through "'presentational objectification,' [in which] the relational eternal objects fall into two sets, one set contributed by the 'extensive' perspective of the perceived from the position of the perceiver, and the other set by the antecedent concrescent phases of the perceiver" (PR 58). This second type of internal relation is the relation of possibilities to the concrescent

occasion; first, the occasion prehends the possibilities as envisioned by God
or by another occasion, then it modifies those possibilities through conceptual prehensions of its own. These are internal relations, again, because
they have determinative power for the occasion that entertains them:
"Every actual entity is what it is, and is with its definite status in the universe, determined by its internal relations to other actual entities" (PR 59).
External relations, on the other hand, are those that are the result of simultaneous existence in a nexus or an "extensive continuum" but do not have
an effect on the entities so related.[44] In a more general sense, any relationship that can be divided into the individuals so related has an element of
externality, because this is the basis of an atomistic view of entities: Even as
they are related, they are separate.[45] By means of this polar character of
internal and external relationships, wherein one does not exclude the other
but rather presupposes the other, Whitehead intends to debunk the exclusive emphasis on external relations in much Western philosophy, while at
the same time resisting a collapse into monism as a consequence of the
boundaries between things being broken down. Both "the many" and "the
one" are characteristic of the universe; "the many" describes the irreducible
atomic character of actual occasions, while "the one" describes the unification of the world in each occasion through internal relations. The relationship with God is internal in the sense that it is effective in each
concrescence and is an ordered component of each satisfaction, but it is
external in the sense that the occasion and God remain separate entities.
Whitehead's doctrine of God has been called "panentheistic" for this reason. God is in every moment of experience, but every moment of experience is not identical with God. Conversely, the world is constitutive of
God's consequent nature but is not identical to that nature, since God's
decision with regard to the world orders the "raw data" to make them effective as a divine, unified reality.

The Initial Aim as Goal for the Creature

The relationship that is established, both in God's primordial self-election
and in the giving of initial aims to individual creatures, is characterized by
purpose. Whitehead, in calling the gift of the initial aim God's act of creation, identifies creation with purposive action: God's purpose in providing graded possibilities to the occasion is to further God's own goals in the
universe, and the occasion's purpose in modifying the initial aim is to
become a unique center of intensity of feeling—to become actual. Both the
data from without and the decision from within are described in terms of

purpose. Whitehead stipulates that the occasion has a dual character as subject-superject. It is something for itself (thanks to a private goal for its own subjectivity), and it is something for others (thanks to a concern for what data it will leave for future prehending occasions). The initial aim has this same dual character: It urges the occasion toward maximum intensity in its own actuality, while at the same time it identifies the best possible legacy to be left by the occasion for its descendants.

As we have already seen, the two "aims" of the initial aim are not always identical, and Whitehead suggests that a compromise is sometimes necessary to diminish subjective intensity in favor of a better future outcome. Whitehead is somewhat enigmatic on this point, as the passage quoted above that identifies this function of God with Atè, the goddess of mischief, shows. He elaborates in another passage:

> No element in fact is ineffectual: thus the struggle with evil is a process of building up a mode of utilization by the provision of intermediate elements introducing a complex structure of harmony. The triviality in some initial reconstruction of order expresses the fact that actualities are being produced, which, trivial in their own proper character of immediate "ends," are proper "means" for the emergence of a world at once lucid, and intrinsically of immediate worth. (PR 340–41)

A clear example of Whitehead's point is the problem of complexity: If the aim of every occasion were at the kind of consciousness characteristic of the human soul, then no occasion would ever achieve such consciousness for the lack of a body to support them, a biosphere in which to live, and so on.[46] An entire range of aims for an entire range of grades of occasions, from the subjectively trivial to the subjectively complex, is necessary to sustain a world in which the maximum complexity and hence maximum intensity can be achieved.[47] This speaks to my point that the aim at what is best for the private experience of the occasion is not always the same as what is best for the universe at large, and that God must balance these goals in the initial aim given to each occasion.

The passage continues, however, in another vein:

> The evil of the world is that those elements which are translucent so far as transmission is concerned, in themselves are of slight weight; and that those elements with individual weight, by their discord, impose upon vivid immediacy the obligation that it fade into night. (PR 341)

The trade-off is that occasions that have only trivial experiences themselves can transmit their pattern of feelings to their descendants with very little change or loss, while occasions with complex, intense experiences have correspondingly greater possibilities to reject the pattern of their predecessors and therefore reverse the gains that have been made. The experience of the high-grade occasion often does not live on in its heirs. With greater complexity comes not only greater possibilities for aesthetic achievement but also greater risk for failure—for the production of an aesthetic vacuum. God's self-determination in the primordial nature is to take that risk by encouraging the evolution of complex creatures, instead of settling for the sure but minimal intensity of low-grade occasions. "Thus," Whitehead writes, "if there is to be progress beyond limited ideals, the course of history by way of escape must venture along the borders of chaos in its substitution of higher for lower types of order" (PR 111).

Election, in Christian theology, has not always been discussed in terms of goal-directed behavior. Although there is strong scriptural warrant to speak of a "call" to perform some task for God, from the Hebrew Scriptures through the New Testament, the language of election moved away from this vocational meaning under the influence of Greek metaphysics, which sought to minimize God's direct involvement in the flux of history and valued protology, the cult of origins, over eschatology. An ontological understanding of election developed, which emphasized the eternal destiny of the individual as determined by God once for all, reflecting the overriding importance of the question of salvation and the fear of death. Election was divorced from history and placed in the realm of God's primordial decision, and the response of creatures to this decision was deemed irrelevant thanks to the doctrine of God's effectual call and irresistible grace. No longer were creatures called to do or be something in God's service; their situation in the world was immaterial, and only their situation in eternity mattered. For Reformed theologians, the Arminian controversy resulted in a primary concern to avoid Pelagianism. If human beings cannot do anything to affect their eternal salvation, *and* if individual salvation is the chief or sole result of election, then it follows that no human act is significant in connection with election. Yet within this primary emphasis on eternal, ontological election, there remained areas in which Christian theology acknowledged a divine call to a historical vocation. The ordination of clergy in most branches of the church depends heavily on an understanding of a divine call that must be answered by human action.

According to the process doctrine of election being developed here, such calls to special missions are simply the conscious and religious form of a call that is received by every creature. God transmits the relevant part of the divine aim to each occasion, which then has the opportunity to respond in order to become what God wills, or to become what it itself wills. The initial aim, considered as election, is not at all the simple determination of eternal status, elect or reprobate, that the doctrine became when God's sovereignty and immutability were the attributes that governed it. It is fundamentally the passing into the world of the divine purpose, which becomes effective as it is accepted and enacted by creatures. The initial aim is the election of each occasion to play a role in the creation of value and the harmonization of the universe, by the gift of a specific purpose that links the possible achievement of that occasion to the advancement of God's unchanging goal:

> God is that function in the world by reason of which our purposes are directed to ends which in our own consciousness are impartial as to our own interests. He is that element in life in virtue of which judgment stretches beyond facts of existence to values of existence. He is that element in virtue of which our purposes extend beyond values for ourselves to values for others. He is that element in virtue of which the attainment of such a value for others transforms itself into value for ourselves. (RM 158)

In this passage, God is the mediator between the purpose of the subject and the purpose of the superject, as I have already discussed. Only by conforming to a plan that encompasses all entities can the occasion as superject become maximally effective. Only in God can cross-purposes straighten and converge, both in the gift of the initial aim and in the ordering of actualities according to God's subjective aim. This coordination of purpose is the meaning of election, for it is God's call to each occasion to be for God, for itself, and for others. When the occasion accepts that goal, it responds positively to God's election. When it rejects that goal in favor of a goal for itself alone, dismissing its superjective nature, it responds negatively to God's election—and yet, the election is nonetheless real. The initial aim is still a factor in the occasion's concrescence, albeit prehended as a negative against which the occasion defines itself. More important, the fulfillment of election in God's ordering of actualities in the consequent nature is not thwarted by the occasion's decision. A different actuality than was preferred is known by God in the consequent nature, and Whitehead recognizes that with the greater decision-making power of consciousness has come a greater rejection of God's initial aim. Human history, and specifically religious history, teaches him that explicit recognition of God's purposes for us, even God's moral purposes, has not always led to greater fulfillment of those purposes:

> Indeed history, down to the present day, is a melancholy record of the horrors which can attend religion: human sacrifice, and in particular the slaughter of

children, cannibalism, sensual orgies, abject superstition, hatred as between races, the maintenance of degrading customs, hysteria, bigotry, can all be laid at its charge. Religion is the last refuge of human savagery. The uncritical association of religion with goodness is directly negatived by plain facts. Religion can be, and has been, the main instrument for progress. But if we survey the whole race, we must pronounce that generally it has not been so: "Many are called, but few are chosen." (RM 37–38)

Is election the calling, or the choosing? This particular text has been used to prove that all are not elect, even though God wills to save all. Process theology cannot make an absolute distinction between call and choice; as a matter of fact, it is difficult for any theology to account for a call without a choice. The initial aim is a call to make a contribution toward universal progress, but this call entails God's choice of that particular occasion to make that particular contribution. In addition, God reaffirms the divine choosing of each occasion in the consequent nature. The notions of choice and vocation are inextricably connected in the concept of the initial aim: God's choice of the divine subjective aim, which is the foundation of all creaturely purposes; God's choice of each occasion to fulfill one particular purpose in harmony with the divine goal; the occasion's choice in responding to the initial aim; and the occasion's accomplishment, incorporated into the order of God's consequent nature.

The Initial Aim as Providential Governance of the World

The doctrine of providence traditionally encompasses three concepts: *gubernatio,* or divine governance; *conservatio,* or divine sustenance; and *concursus,* or divine working with creatures. The concepts that seem, on their face, to be most compatible with process metaphysics are *conservatio* and *concursus.* God's continual upholding of creation—*conservatio*—describes the constant involvement of the divine actual entity in the world process. Without God's activity as the principle of limitation, creativity would stagnate and new occasions could not arise. *Concursus* refers to the immanence of God's purpose and God's will in every creature. The divine element of purpose is the necessary starting point for the emergence of creaturely purposes and creaturely accomplishments.

Gubernatio, which has been utilized by many Christian theologians to support a version of divine determinism, seems an unlikely candidate for reinterpretation in process terms. The idea of God's governance of the world is connected in many theologies to God's sovereignty as an absolute ruler. Unlike earthly rulers, the perfect king would be able to ordain everything in the kingdom according to the king's will. Whitehead considers this concept of God's sovereignty to be the result of a mistaken, unsophisticated theory of God:

> This worship of glory arising from power is not only dangerous; it arises from a barbaric conception of God. I suppose that even the world itself could not contain the bones of those slaughtered because of men intoxicated by its attraction. . . . The glorification of power has broken more hearts than it has healed. (RM 55)

Its mistake is evident in the life of Christ, which Whitehead considers to reveal not voluntary abdication of power, or *kenosis*, but the true nature of God's agency:

> The life of Christ is not an exhibition of over-ruling power. Its glory is for those who can discern it, and not for the world. Its power lies in its absence of force. It has the decisiveness of a supreme ideal, and that is why the history of the world divides at this point in time. (RM 57)

The ideal is not merely a goal for creatures that God can and does violate at will because it is not a divine ideal. God and creatures do not dwell in separate realms of reality; so what is an ideal for creatures is also an ideal that God embodies. That ideal is not force. It is patience, creativity, and the power of persuasion. Whitehead does not deny the reality of force as an element of the world process, but he identifies it with the physical determination of cause and effect, a type of power that does not exhaust all power in the universe:

> The sheer force of things lies in the intermediate physical process: this is the energy of physical production. God's rôle is not the combat of productive force with productive force, of destructive force with destructive force; it lies in the patient operation of the overpowering rationality of his conceptual harmonization. He does not create the world, he saves it; or, more accurately, he is the poet of the world, with tender patience leading it by his vision of truth, beauty, and goodness. (PR 346)

What type of governance is this exercise of persuasive power? Emphatically not the type of governance by which God ordains and directs all actions, corporeal or mental, toward an end instituted by God's self—if by "ordains and directs" one means "exhaustively determines."[48] The actions of actual occasions cannot be finally determined by any power other than the occasion's own power of self-determination, although as we have seen, low-grade occasions exhibit a trivial level of this self-determination and are, for our practical purposes, fully determined by their inheritance. The theology that regards *gubernatio* as full determination of all aspects of the world commits the mistake of treating all occasions as if they were low-grade occasions, as if the causes that impinge on an occasion produce effects on a one-to-one ratio. On the contrary, the variety of levels of agency found in actual occasions increases the *indeterminacy* present in the world process, allowing for novelty and creative advance (as well as unfortunate setback). This indeterminacy is resolved through the decisions of creatures, conditioned by God's intention and persuasion. Whitehead, as a scientist, is fully in agreement with the basic mechanism of cause and effect; his dissent from the deterministic model is that the occasion in which the transaction takes place exerts its own power on it:

> The novel actual entity, which is the effect, is the reproduction of the many actual entities of the past. But in this reproduction there is abstraction from their various totalities of feeling. . . . This abstractive "objectification" is rendered possible by reason of the "divisible" character of the satisfactions of actual entities. By reason of this "divisible" character causation is the transfer of a feeling, and not of a total satisfaction. The other feelings are dismissed by negative prehensions, owing to their lack of compliance with categoreal demands. (PR 238)

In other words, every reproduction involves a transmission from one subjectivity to another, and therefore involves some change, so that the resulting satisfaction is never identical to a past satisfaction, but is unique to that entity. The change is negligible in low-grade occasions where Newtonian rules of cause and effect still hold true in a macroscopic analysis, but can become very significant in high-grade occasions with greater decision-making power due to their complexity and wide range of relevant possibilities. Whereas low-grade concrescences can be more or less adequately described in terms of "simple physical feelings,"[49] high-grade occasions exhibit more complex metaphysical categories:

> It is evident that adversion and aversion, and also the Category of Transmutation,[50] only have importance in the case of high-grade organisms. They constitute the first step towards intellectual mentality, though in themselves they do not amount to consciousness. But an actual entity which includes these operations must have an important intensity of conceptual feelings able to mask and fuse the simple physical feelings. (PR 254)[51]

The fact that the *potential* for decision regarding its data is inherent in every occasion of experience makes a deterministic interpretation of *gubernatio* impossible in the process system. In addition, no absolute distinction can be drawn between occasions that determine their own fates and those whose fates are determined by outside agencies, because all occasions are to some extent self-determining, even if that extent is vanishingly small to any outside observer. Process theology, then, cannot advocate an intermediate theory of *gubernatio* in which God ordains the course of inanimate matter or nonconscious life, while allowing human beings to direct their own lives, either through divine self-limitation or metaphysical necessity. The freedom that negates the deterministic view of *gubernatio* extends at least in minimal presence, if not in discernable effect, to every instance of actuality in the universe.

How then can process theology redefine *gubernatio* to conform to its metaphysical presuppositions? God governs the world in a way that is much closer to the ideal for a human ruler,[52] that is, not through the use of force but through patience and persuasion, so that the will of God is not opposed to the will of God's creatures, but the will of the creatures is lovingly brought into accord with the will of God:

> Such order as we find in nature is never force—it presents itself as the one harmonious adjustment of complex detail. Evil is the brute motive force of fragmentary purpose, disregarding the eternal vision. Evil is overruling, retarding, hurting. The power of God is the worship He inspires. (SMW 192)

This relationship may be rightly termed "governance" because God aims at a goal and works in all actual occasions to reach that goal, which is the best outcome for both governor and governed. Only God can be said to govern, even though creaturely decisions are effective and God is not the *sole* determining factor in those decisions.[53] Only God shapes the initial aims of occasions toward a single unchanging goal, only God orders the satisfaction of occasions into an everlasting order, and only God is active in every moment of existence to bring about creative advance. "What is inexorable in God," says Whitehead, "is valuation as an aim towards 'order'; and 'order' means 'society permissive of actualities with patterned intensity of feeling arising from adjusted contrasts'" (PR 244). This is the essence of a process interpretation of *gubernatio*. There is an inexorable divine drive toward a determined goal for God and world considered as a single system, but the result of this drive is a society of many actualities with governance over their own creation, unified by God's governance of the whole.

Because the initial aim is bound up with the concept of God's overall goal for the universe, this reinterpretation of *gubernatio* as a part of providence is necessary in a process doctrine of election. God does not merely conserve and work alongside creatures; the notion of an overall goal toward which the world is directed cannot be divorced from *conservatio* and *concursus* in process thought, because purpose is the key to understanding process metaphysics. Specifically, the fact that God has purposes that God works out through creatures is assented to both in the deterministic view of *gubernatio* and in the process view. The difference is that determinism sees a divine will that cannot be thwarted, while process sees a divine patience that cannot be exhausted:

> The universe includes a threefold creative act composed of (i) the one infinite conceptual realization, (ii) the multiple solidarity of free physical realizations in the temporal world, (iii) the ultimate unity of the multiplicity of actual fact with the primordial conceptual fact. If we conceive the first term and the last term in their unity over against the intermediate multiple freedom of physical realizations in the temporal world, we conceive of the patience of God, tenderly saving the turmoil of the intermediate world by the completion of his own nature. (PR 346)

With this redefinition of *gubernatio,* we are equipped to unpack the following statement, on the final page of *Process and Reality,* in terms of a process understanding of providence: "The action of the fourth phase is the love of God for the world. It is the particular providence for particular occasions" (PR 351). The "fourth phase" is the consequent nature of God passing "into the temporal world according to its gradation of relevance to the various concrescent occasions" (PR 350); "the perfected actuality passes back into the temporal world, and qualifies this world so that each temporal actuality includes it as an immediate fact of relevant experience" (PR 351). We have already spoken of this phase as the influence of the consequent nature—God's ordering of the world's actualities according to the divine subjective aim—upon the initial aims given to creatures.

The sense in which process theology can affirm *conservatio* and *concursus* is more straightforward and requires less redefinition than the notion of *gubernatio*. God preserves and sustains the world in every moment of time; this is the meaning of *conservatio*. God provides the means for each occasion to begin its concrescence, establishing the link between abstract possibilities and concrete actualities.[54] God is also the originator and transmitter of the order without which no progress is possible.[55] Finally, God as the embodiment of truth in the consequent nature "recycles" the reality of the world back into the creative process in order to provide the possibilities that are viable for each contingent historical moment.[56] Without an actual entity to perform this function of limitation and concretion, the world would be stagnant, and a world that is not in process is impossible in Whitehead's system because permanence and flux can never exist without each other. *Concursus* refers to the way in which God "runs along with" each entity; in traditional theology, it is the cooperative act by which God works through secondary causes, without negating by divine ultimate causality the reality of creaturely causes.[57] The process metaphysics accepts the Aristotelian idea that events can be attributed to more than one cause, and utilizes the scheme of efficient and final causes.[58] It differs from Aristotle, and the Thomistic tradition of theology based on Aristotle, in its insistence that each entity transcends its causes, including God, by its own self-causing decision.[59] However, *concursus* as the notion that God works through temporal occasions to produce effects is certainly maintained in process theology with its strong emphasis on God as persuader, or "lure for feeling":

> He is the lure for feeling, the eternal urge of desire. His particular relevance to each creative act, as it arises from its own conditioned standpoint in the world, constitutes him the initial "object of desire" establishing the initial phase of each subjective aim. (PR 344)

So each initial aim involves *gubernatio*—its direction toward God's goal for the universe and its provision of the means to fulfill that goal in each moment; *conservatio*—its initiation of the new concrescence, its providence of the order without which nothing new can arise, and its synthesis of the totality of reality into the possibilities for that particular contingent moment; and *concursus*—its presentation of alternatives for a decision that only the creature can make but without the presentation of which no decision would be possible. In these ways, the initial aim is the vehicle for God's providential governance of the world.

The Initial Aim as Revelation of Grace

The fourth way in which the initial aim can be seen as God's election is in its role of revealing God's grace toward the world. This final observation marks the first time our discussion has ventured from the primarily metaphysical realm, in which God is seen in terms of God's function in the world process, and into the primarily religious realm, in which God is seen as our spiritual progenitor, savior, and object of worship. Whitehead's aim is to unify the ideas of religion and metaphysics; therefore, although the word "grace" has an almost exclusively religious connotation, the concept of grace is present in the doctrine of the initial aim even in the strictly secular realm of metaphysical explanation. The particular subjective aim that God entertains and toward which God's actions are

PROCESS
GRACE

directed is a contingent, not a necessary matter; the fact that this subjective aim involves the cooperation of creatures to create value is the result of God's free choice, and could have been otherwise.

The attribution of *choice* to God in the divine self-determination must be clarified further. In process thought, there is no already existing substance called "God" that subsequently makes a choice to elect. To assert this is to fall into the substance-accident dualism that Whitehead rejects. God *is* the primordial nature that is ordered toward the goal of maximizing value through creatures. But in saying this, process thought means to say exactly what Barth means to say by the concept of God's self-election: God *is* God only in this way, only in the divine love for creatures. The theological talk of a God prior to or outside of this self-election, however instructive as a hypothetical, is merely abstract, and the guarantee of this is that Jesus Christ, the Word of the God who loves in freedom, is not a Word spoken upon due consideration and with the possibility that God might speak one or another Word. God constitutes God's self in God's Word, so that God, eternally and temporally (or primordially and consequently), *is* for us. For Barth, speaking of God as "a Subject which can and does elect, a Subject which is furnished, of course, with supereminent divine attributes, but which differs from other such subjects only by the fact that in its election it is absolutely free," is "a temptation" that leads to the sterile harshness of the *decretum absolutum*. Instead, God must be spoken of as God is, that is, as Father, Son, and Holy Spirit; so that God is never without God's Word:

> This choice was in the beginning. As the subject and object of this choice, Jesus Christ was at the beginning. He was not at the beginning of God, for God indeed has no beginning. But He was at the beginning of all things, at the beginning of God's dealings with the reality which is distinct from Himself. Jesus Christ was the choice or election of God in respect of this reality. He was the election of God's grace as directed towards man. He was the election of God's covenant with man.[60]

Barth gives process theology an example of how to speak of the divine self-determination without falling into substance-accident dualism. The language of choice may imply that dualism for the reader, but Barth specifically rules it out. Similarly, the process language of decision in speaking of the concrescence of the actual occasion implies that there is some concrete, already-determined thing making a decision; yet Whitehead is clear that the occasion is not a determined objective fact until it has completed its self-creation and ended its becoming. There is a rule in both process thought and Barthian thought, then, that the language of self-determination does not imply a substance-accident metaphysics. In accordance with Barth's example, I make bold to speak of God's *choice* to be primordial in the way God actually is primordial, on the grounds that God's ordering of eternal objects toward the divine subjective aim is a free and unconditioned self-determination, self-constitution, and self-election. Although the terminology suggests a substance-accident scheme in which God somehow exists prior to or outside of this choice, neither Barth nor process theology intends this implication. Both systems conceive of God existing in and only in the act of the divine self-determination.[61]

God's empowerment of creatures to reach subsidiary goals in harmony with the divine goal produces a benefit to the creatures themselves, as they enjoy their own consummations. God enables this enjoyment by encouraging the evolution of ever more complex creatures, with ever increasing capacity for the creation of value. Divine grace can be observed and experienced in the progress of evolution, biologically, sociologically, and culturally.[62] All this progress is a consequence of God's self-determination alone, not of any metaphysical principle that is above or outside of God. Along with the greater possibility for an increase in value, this decision in God's primordial nature involves a correspondingly greater risk that God's purposes may be thwarted, since the potential for greater value creation requires a greater range of viable possibilities for the decision of the creature; this increase in the number and variety of ways freedom can express itself carries along with it the chance that more creatures will choose badly. At any moment, creatures may choose to merely preserve the values of the past rather than take the risk of moving forward, and in fact this powerful desire is found in the longing for permanence, the conservative impulse:[63]

> The world is thus faced by the paradox that, at least in its higher actualities, it craves for novelty and yet is haunted by terror at the loss of the past, with its familiarities and its loved one. . . . Yet the culminating fact of conscious, rational life refuses to conceive itself as a transient enjoyment, transiently useful. (PR 340)

As we have already seen, Whitehead regards the tendency to appeal to God as an unchanging refuge from change as indicative of this retreat from risky novelty into comfortable stability. But God is not simply the guarantee of safety, although in the eternal purpose of the primordial nature and the everlasting order of the consequent nature, God is certainly that. "The worship of God is not a rule of safety—it is an adventure of the spirit, a flight after the unattainable" (SMW 192). It is God's grace in the initial aim gradually, with infinite patience, to bring the unattainable within reach.

Grace is revealed in the initial aim in three fundamental areas. First, the overall progress of the entire world is attributable to God's primordial self-determination to be a God who is gracious toward the world, whatever that world might turn out to be: "[God's] unity of conceptual operations is a free creative act, untrammeled by reference to any particular course of things. . . . His conceptual actuality at once exemplifies and establishes the categoreal conditions" (PR 344). Every initial aim derives from this primordial nature of God, and is what it is by virtue of God's election of God's self to be and act for others. This divine self-determination is the original act of grace, since it is presupposed by every subsequent gracious act of God.[64] The second type of revelation occurs in God's steering of the world toward the actualization of particular purposes. No specific goal is inherent in the primordial nature, only the general goal of increasing value: "The *particularities* of the actual world presuppose *it* [the primordial nature], while *it* merely presupposes the *general* metaphysical character of creative advance, of which it is the primordial exemplification" (PR 344). The sure way of maintaining and moderately increasing value is simply by encouraging the becoming of low-grade occasions, trivial puffs of existence that achieve their own unity but transmit little because they are not involved in any nexus or society. This scheme would only increase value slowly, arithmetically, over the history of the world by the expansion of God's consequent nature to include all these occasions; but if God had ordered the eternal objects toward this end, the risk of reversal and destruction would have been greatly reduced. However, God's grace is revealed by God's choice of a different method for increasing value: the evolution of complex creatures that can experience levels of intensity many orders of magnitude greater than the simple, singular low-grade occasion—with the accompanying risk of reversal and destruction that comes from the greater scope for creaturely decisions. Having chosen this path for the world, God refines the general divine aim at increasing value into particular aims toward the achievement of particular events and conditions for further advance in the world, based on the qualifications of creativity in the decisions of actual occasions. So the attainment of particular stages in the history of the world, its societies, and its institutions is due to the grace of God and the cooperative working of many initial aims.

The final revelation of grace is in the possibilities given to each individual occasion to become a creator of value in itself and a transmitter of value for others. There is for each creature the possibility of selfishly hoarding value, of refusing to consider the immediate future. There is also the possibility of complete selflessness, of sacrificing what one might have become in the hope that future generations (or even God) might have the glory. The doctrine of the initial aim considers both these options less than ideal, as emphatically not God's will for the individual. The progress of the world depends on the achievements of individuals, and these are both private, in the individual's subjective character, and public, in the individual's super-jective character. The initial aim provides a route for becoming that allows individual excellence as well as social progress, and this balancing of the world's good in favor of creatures individually and corporately is a revelation of God's grace.

What links together these forms of revelation found in the initial aim is the idea that grace is primarily to be seen in the adventure of the world's upward progress into ever greater value, even when no physical form of existence is permanent. Whitehead explains this vision of divine grace in the final pages of *Religion in the Making:*

> The universe shows us two aspects: on the one side it is physically wasting, on the other side it is spiritually ascending. It is thus passing with a slowness, inconceivable in our measures of time, to new creative conditions, amid which the physical world, as we at present know it, will be represented by a ripple barely to be distinguished from non-entity. The present type of order in the world has arisen from an unimaginable past, and it will find its grave in an unimaginable future. There remain the inexhaustible realm of abstract forms, and creativity, with its shifting character ever determined afresh by its own creatures, and God, upon whose wisdom all forms of order depend. (RM 159–160)

Conclusion

In this chapter I have set forth the basic principles of process thought as they relate to the concept of the initial aim. Whitehead's explanation of the initial aim begins with the primordial nature of God, which can be seen as divine self-election or self-determination. The subjective aim entertained by God is the basis of the initial aim given to each actual occasion, but the source of God's own subjective aim is God's self. God orders the eternal objects by the value God assigns to each possibility in God's primordial nature. In the midst of the world process, God then presents to each occasion the graded set of possibilities relevant to that occasion's time and place, ordered according to God's aim for that occasion and for the world. This is the initial aim, which initiates the process of concrescence for the individual occasion. The occasion's response to this aim prehended from God is its own decision regarding that aim, choosing among the set of possibilities and transforming the initial aim into the subjective aim by the exercise of its own inalienable freedom. Through this process, novelty enters the world as occasions aim to actualize possibilities that have never been actualized before. The occasion's final satisfaction is its fulfillment of its subjective aim, the end of its subjectivity, and the beginning of its objective immortality. This final actuality is then included in God's consequent nature, along with all actualities, where it is ordered according to God's subjective aim.

CHAPTER THREE

Convergence and Divergence

What Process Theology Affirms and Denies

In the course of arguing that the process system is amenable to the formulation of a doctrine of election, it is necessary to address specifically how this reformulation will differ from the doctrines of election that have framed the discussion historically. The strongest, most vital understanding of election in Christian theological history is the doctrine of the Reformed church, which gives election a central place in dogmatics. In the following discussion, Barth, Calvin, and Schleiermacher are cited as representatives of different aspects of the Reformed understanding of election. Because of the famous emphasis on election in the theologies of Calvin and Barth, the philosophical and metaphysical assumptions that govern the Reformed system are closely associated with the doctrine of election. While affirming that process theology can give its assent to the essential content of the election doctrine, I recognize that the systematic framework in which their doctrines are promulgated contains elements that are unfavorable to process theology. To ferret out the essence of the Christian message about election, then, as far as possible, I propose to identify those problematic elements while indicating why the process doctrine of election does not depend on them. Although the Reformed doctrine of election has been the most visible and central election doctrine in Christian discourse since the Reformation, and has served to remind us that election is a crucial factor in any complete theology, it is not necessary to accept this particular doctrine along with all its accompanying assumptions in order to have any doctrine of election at all. The process doctrine must deny, or radically redefine, certain key ideas in that accompanying framework and offer convincing alternatives based on its own metaphysical understanding.

What Process Theology Denies about Election

Radical Divine Aseity

Reformed dogmatics maintains that only a God who has no need for the world—who would have been no less complete and perfect existing alone throughout eternity—can act with true freedom in God's voluntary relations with the world that God contingently created. The gratuity of election is interpreted to mean that even the existence of creatures to be elected cannot be postulated a priori. For God's election to be truly an act of grace, God must not be moved to elect by any necessarily existing creation.

The understanding of aseity in the Reformed doctrine is that God exists by God's own power as the only necessary being. But this implies, for Reformed thinkers, the idea that God could, and prior to creation did, exist without a world, because God cannot be put in such a position that God depends upon the world. Process thought can affirm the first, limited meaning of aseity, since the process system maintains that God alone among entities provides God's own initial aim, and so exists through God's own power alone, whereas all other entities exist through their own power and God's power. Furthermore, any particular world does not exist necessarily, but *some* world must be. However, especially in the Reformed discussions of creation's gratuity, aseity has come to be identified with the notion of a God who hypothetically might have chosen not to create; a God who is solitary is a metaphysical possibility for Reformed thought, while process thought, with its concept of God as primordial and consequent, asserts that God depends upon the world just as the world depends upon God.

As we have already seen, process thought can concur with the idea that election has a logical priority over all God's other works toward the world (creation, redemption, and sanctification), since all these works presuppose a primordial determination to be a God for creatures. This is the side of election that is located in God's primordial nature, where the possibility of increased value in the universe through the agency of complex creatures is chosen by God to be part of the divine subjective aim.

Where process thought cannot concur is in the hypothetical postulation of a God without a world. Whitehead makes this point at some length in section 5 of the final chapter of *Process and Reality*.[1] The primordial nature is "abstracted from his commerce with particulars. . . . It is God in abstraction, *alone with himself.* As such it is a mere factor in God, deficient in actuality" (PR 34, italics mine). The consequent nature is required for God to be an actual entity, just as a physical pole in addition to the mental pole is required for every actual occasion; and the consequent nature requires a world to be its object. The freedom of God's electing and creating acts remains undisturbed by this metaphysical change, since any particular world chosen and brought into being by God is contingent. Even if God does not have the metaphysical possibility of radical solitude, the God of process thought is self-actualizing in ways that differ qualitatively from creatures. Alone among actual entities, God provides God's own initial aim (the divine self-election, which is the ground of all creaturely election), and primordially *is* that initial aim. In this sense, only God has the power to exist through God's self, without deriving that power from others. Yet the primordial concept of God is "deficient," that is, not fully actual and therefore not effective, without a consequent nature. It is the position of process thought that God necessarily creates, but that the creation of any *particular* world gives God contingent properties (as the contingencies of the world are included in the consequent nature), since God is necessarily affected by the particular world brought into being and therefore depends upon that particular world.

The biblical witness that "God is love" has forced theology to admit that an impassible divine being, absolutely without social relationship, cannot be a fully adequate description of the God to whom Christ bore witness. The Trinity has allowed theologians to ascribe sociality and therefore love to God in God's self, enabling them to maintain that God does not need a world to be a loving God. Even if God (understood in either a Trinitarian or unitarian sense) is taken to be a society of actual entities,[2] process theology would still have to maintain the necessary existence of some world outside of God's self, for the reason that the term "God" would then describe the society, and the consequent nature of this society would still require, for its own actuality, that actual occasions come into being as "matters of fact."[3] In a dialogue with Wolfhart Pannenberg, Daniel Day Williams argues that process thought gains much more than it gives up when it denies the radical aseity of God:

> Pannenberg is quite right in saying that process thought sees a certain inevitable plurality in being. The reason for this from the process point of view is that if God is love he must have a world to love, to act upon, and respond to. The creatures in that world must have their measure of freedom, creativity, and unique value if they are real things and not just mechanical expressions of a prearranged plan.[4]

What is gained is the possibility of regarding the world as ultimately real and consequential; what is lost is a God who lacks a dependent relationship

to anything outside God's self. Process thought argues that Christianity has
never postulated a God without dependence, except in theory. A loving God
is always dependent on the objects of God's love, since love entails responsiveness and openness toward the love object. A God without any relationships of dependence is not a loving God, and therefore is not the God of the
Christian witness. Barth argues against the hypothetical solitary God by
affirming that election does not testify to a God who only goes so far and
no further, who reserves reality and freedom jealously to God's self and
avoids the complexities and complications of creatures. The God of election
is the God of dependent love that, unlike the dependent love of finite creatures, is victorious over the hate or indifference of its object.[5]

Absolute Divine Sovereignty

The Reformed tradition's insistence on God's absolute sovereignty is related
to its concern for radical aseity just discussed; both doctrines aim to ensure
God's freedom to save humankind, in opposition to any notion of compulsion. If God does not control all events, the reasoning goes, then something beyond God's power can threaten our ultimate destiny. Combined
with the classical doctrines of God's omnipotence and omniscience, this
insistence on sovereignty can result in thoroughgoing determinism. With
regard to the doctrine of election, this determinism takes the form of predestination: the proposition that God not only knows in advance all the
details of each individual life but also has caused all these details, through
them bringing the individual to a predetermined end.

The Reformed tradition does not deny human freedom, but it asserts
that whatever human beings do with their freedom cannot run counter to
the will of God. Calvin attempts to absolve God of blame for sin even as
he maintains that the fall of humanity is predestined:

> Where you hear God's glory mentioned, think of his justice. For whatever
> deserves praise must be just. Accordingly, man falls according as God's prov-
> idence ordains, but he falls by his own fault. A little before, the Lord had
> declared that "everything that he had made . . . was exceedingly good" [Gen.
> 1:31]. Whence, then, comes that wickedness to man, that he should fall away
> from his God? Lest we should think that it comes from creation, God had
> put his stamp of approval on what had come forth from himself. By his own
> evil intention, then, man corrupted the pure nature he had received from the
> Lord; and by his fall he drew all his posterity with him into destruction.
> Accordingly, we should contemplate the evident cause of condemnation in
> the corrupt nature of humanity—which is closer to us—rather than seek a
> hidden and utterly incomprehensible cause in God's predestination.[6]

Schleiermacher, while devoting more attention to the idea of human freedom, finds that God's predetermination of events is not in opposition to the creatures' conscious exercise of their own freedom, since God temporally governs the world in accordance with the eternal divine will:

> How our proposition is in harmony with the consciousness of freedom has already been shown, and in that inference it might also have been stated thus: that the manner and time of each individual's regeneration is determined by what is peculiar to his own inner life, that is, his freedom. . . . Primarily, then, the kingdom of grace or of the Son is absolutely one in origin with the kingdom of omniscient omnipotence, or of the Father; and since the whole government of the world is, like the world itself, eternal in God, nothing happens in the kingdom of grace without divine fore-ordination.[7]

But if human freedom cannot be exercised with regard to grace, as for example when a person dies before hearing the gospel, Schleiermacher must unhappily conclude that this is also God's will:

> Thus obviously it is the divine government of the world which appoints that many—whether few or many really makes no difference, since their attitude toward the proffer of divine grace is in any case the same—die unregenerate simply because the course of their life is run. . . . We cannot therefore resist the conclusion that if God had not willed this definitely and unconditionally, He would have either established a different order of nature for human life, or a different way of salvation for the human spirit.[8]

Barth's view is the most nuanced of the Reformed thinkers and the closest to the process view, using "predestination" and "predetermination" to refer to the drawing of all events, whether in accordance with the immediate will of God or not, to a victorious consummation where every No becomes a Yes. Predestination is not temporal but eschatological. The human freedom that opposes God has no final actuality or effect:

> Therefore even in the past, present and future godlessness of the elect the rejected himself exists only as the object of that evil, dangerous, but powerless representation—in such a way that he is denied from the very outset by his election (the election of Jesus Christ), and is now denied in practice too by his faith in Jesus Christ, being exposed and discredited as a liar. . . . The faith of the elect is the recognition of the supremacy of the elect Jesus Christ in the face of the rejected—the very rejected to whom the godlessness even of the elect seems daily to give substance and actuality. The faith of the elect (his faith in the election of Jesus Christ) denies the actuality and asserts the passing of the existence of the rejected. It is faith therefore—together with Jesus Christ—which marks the limit of the shadow, and even in the godlessness of others, the rejected cannot exist except in this shadow-form.[9]

A God who possesses sole power to bring about every event is unknown in process theology, let alone a God who controls every detail of every event. One of the reasons process thought and Reformed thought have been seen as opposites is that the process conception of a persuasive divine agency acting in cooperation with effective human agency seems to be a direct reaction against this very concept.[10] The contrast is indeed a sharp one, especially when Calvin is taken as the norm on the Reformed idea of divine sovereignty. In process thought, because of the indeterminacy of the future, shaped by the decisions of actual occasions, foreknowledge is impossible. Similarly, because of the freedom of those actual occasions, the future cannot be determined in advance. Thus, predestination is ruled out in the strong Calvinist sense of the term by the metaphysical system of process thought, which maintains that creatures transcend God in their free self-creation, just as God transcends creatures in the divine concrescence of the consequent nature. This position is similar to Barth's eschatological pre-destination: God brings the world to consummation *despite* the ability of creatures to oppose the divine purpose in history.

Total Lack of Human Power

If God exercises absolute and sole power over human history, then it is difficult for theology to leave creatures room to exercise decisive power over their own lives, much less over the course of world history. The theological reasoning behind this abrogation of power is to ensure that human beings do not make the mistake of thinking that they have done anything to effect their own salvation—that they recognize it is entirely God's act from beginning to end. The doctrine of election is, in itself, often used to bolster this concept. Election is a movement initiated by God and directed at creatures; the structure of this act seems to render God purely active and the creature purely receptive. Reformed theology recognizes that human freedom must be *enabled* rather than disabled by election; the third Canon of Dort asserts that the regenerating work of the Holy Spirit is needed to enable the human being to will the good, which he is totally unable to do on his own.[11] Schleiermacher manages to develop this idea into a theology of sanctification. Yet Reformed theology, apart from Barth, has had difficulty doing justice to their recognition that election underlies human freedom rather than undermining it.

The distinction between God's act and the creature's receptivity describes the first phase of election in a process framework, but it does not fully describe the relationship that is established between God and actual occasions. All actual occasions have some measure of freedom to determine themselves—the amount and quality of that freedom being dependent on the complexity of the organism and its environment—and this freedom is inalienable. It cannot be usurped by any other agency, including God. Certainly the initial aim is first formulated by God alone, as an ordering of the possibilities open to that particular entity at that particular junction of space-time. This act of God enables the advent of God's vision of order and value into the world. But the creature is involved in every step of election that succeeds this initial presentation. It is the creature that prehends the initial aim offered by God, incorporating it (along with the God whose vision it is) into the data from its own past. It is the creature that modifies the initial aim based on its own subjective "feeling" for the data. It is the creature that either largely conforms to God's goal for the immediate future, or rejects that aim in favor of subjective self-interest. And it is the creature that transforms its modified subjective aim into actuality. The unique role of divine creativity in this process comes at its beginning and at its end: Without the entrance of possibility relevant to the occasion's situation, neither order nor novelty is possible, and without God's consequent ordering of completed actualities according to God's own subjective aim, the increase in value that results from historical and evolutionary progress is impossible. Thus, a process doctrine of election consists not only in the act of God that initiates and redeems the relationship but also in the acts of creatures that incorporate God's purposes into their lives and turn them into temporal facts.

Ultimate Atemporality of Election

The final distinction to be drawn between the Reformed doctrine and the process doctrine concerns the former's locating of the electing act solely in eternity. Again, the reason for the Reformed insistence on this point is to protect God's unilateral action from any influence by contingent creaturely reality. The cause of election was to be found in God's self alone, thus preserving the freedom of God from any necessity.

We have already seen how process theology seeks to balance God's primordial nature (the "eternal, unchangeable" pole of divinity) with an understanding of God's consequent nature, which is responsive to temporal actualities. In this case, process asserts that election has, in addition to its eternal component, an equally important historical component. To be actual and therefore to be effective in the world, election cannot be only a primordial determination in the divine nature. It must enter the lives of

creatures and become a factor in the history of creatures. In addition, given
the indeterminate future described above, the content provided by God in
the act of election cannot be independent of the contingent history of the
world. Because what is given in election is a goal, a purpose, a vocation, it
must be relevant to the historical situation of the receiving entity. Hence,
it is dependent on what has actually transpired, which is not knowable until
it has happened. The content of the initial aim is contingent. This analysis
of election's historicity seems to provide a better fit with the biblical witness than what Wolfhart Pannenberg calls the "abstract notion" that
became the classical Christian form of the doctrine.[12] The biblical concept
of election "refers to a historical event as constitutive for being chosen. And
it assigns a mission to the elected one that relates him to a more comprehensive context of God's design in history."[13] Process thought can respond
to the authenticity of this vision of election more fully than can the classical doctrine.

Reinterpretation of Election by Process Theology

The preceding section listed ideas that are commonly associated with election—due to the influence of Reformed dogmatics on the discussion of
election—but that a process doctrine of election cannot affirm because they
clash with the basic tenets of process theology. Now, as a final preparatory
step to the construction of a process doctrine of election, let us consider the
ways in which process theology reinterprets election. Every formulation of
the doctrine has a certain specific intent—to highlight aspects of the doctrine of God, anthropology, or soteriology that are considered important
in the overall system. Process theology is designed to highlight relativity,
freedom, and purpose as real and effective characteristics of the entire universe, including God and the world. The doctrine of election in a process
system will reflect these overriding concerns and therefore will differ in
emphasis from orthodox formulations of the doctrine. A process doctrine
of election reinterprets the Christian message about God's choice of creatures in three areas: the election of nonhuman creatures, the idea of vocation, and the historicity of election.

Election of Nonhuman Creatures

Human beings do not have the special or exclusive status in process metaphysics that they have enjoyed in many systems. Until the Enlightenment,

religious and philosophical cosmologies alike agreed that human beings are qualitatively different from other creatures in the plant, animal, and non-living realms. The Hebrew Scriptures, for example, state that humanity is a special, separate creation in God's own image and likeness,[14] given special privileges and responsibilities toward the rest of the world.[15] Most Christian theologies followed suit until the advent of scientific evidence of the close evolutionary kinship between human beings and other animals. In the twentieth century, feminist and ecological theologies took the lead in asserting that the restriction of God's special care and salvific activity to human beings perpetuates a patriarchal, egotistical, and "speciesist" attitude that is untenable in light of contemporary knowledge.

Process thought is designed to complement and enrich the knowledge gained through science; it asserts that science and religion do not operate in separate spheres of reality, but describe the same cosmic order.[16] Therefore, compelling scientific ideas such as the theories of evolution and relativity, which explain large amounts of empirical data, are important to process thought as elements of experience that the system must coordinate and of which it must take account. It is fair to say that, based on his conviction that science provides crucial knowledge that can be taken as clues to the nature of reality, Whitehead engineers his metaphysical system to include these concepts as basic ideas. The ideas of relatedness and progress that recur in process thought reflect the fundamental importance of Einstein's and Darwin's insights, and therefore of scientific insights in general, in Whitehead's system.

In the case of evolution, which is germane to the current point regarding the status of nonhuman creatures, process thought disagrees with some evolutionists' interpretation of Darwin's theory, while accepting the theory itself as descriptive of biological processes. At the same time, process thought disagrees with certain religious movements that refuse to accept the theory of evolution on the grounds that it is a denial of divine creation. What some scientists have deduced from Darwin's theory is the same interpretive scheme rejected by creationists: a blind materialism that reduces nature to a complex mechanism and completely relativizes any notion of progress. Whitehead argues that, properly understood, evolution need not be seen materialistically:

> By a blindness which is almost judicial as being a penalty affixed to hasty, superficial thinking, many religious thinkers opposed the new doctrine; although, in truth, a thoroughgoing evolutionary philosophy is inconsistent with materialism. . . . Evolution, on the materialistic theory, is reduced to the role of being another word for the description of the changes of the external

> relations between portions of matter. There is nothing to evolve, because one
> set of external relations is as good as any other set of external relations. There
> can merely be change, purposeless and unprogressive. But the whole point of
> the modern doctrine is the evolution of the complex organisms from the
> antecedent states of less complex organisms. The doctrine thus cries aloud
> for a conception of organism as fundamental for nature. It also requires an
> underlying activity—a substantial activity—expressing itself in individual
> embodiments, and evolving in achievements of organism. (SMW 107)

Both the materialistic evolutionists and the creationists have misinter-
preted the theory. While it is true that the theory by itself does not explain
progress, it does not exist in isolation. Together with a theory of organism,
as Whitehead envisions it, evolution describes the progress that we in fact
observe in the world.[17]

One reason for the creationists' religious revolt against the theory of evolution is evolution's insistence on the kinship between human beings and
other animals. Slogans and songs ridiculing human descent from "mon-
keys" are a staple of antievolutionary rhetoric. The notion of human beings
evolving from a primate ancestor threatens the special status on which
humanity has prided itself in both religion and philosophy. It suggests that
other animals have the potential, through evolutionary development, for
intelligence, artistic creativity, even spirituality; it calls into question
human utilization of other animals for service, products, and entertain-
ment. If, unlike the creationists, we accept evolution's description of
human origins and therefore recognize a kinship with nonhuman nature,
what are the consequences for the doctrine of election?

The discussion of the initial aim in chapter 2 refers almost exclusively to
"actual occasions" as the recipients of the aim, rather than human beings.
This is consistent with Whitehead's insistence that purpose characterizes
the universe not only in its enclaves of consciousness but also in all its con-
stituent events. The word *decision,* used to describe the activity of an occasion choosing its subjective aim, refers in ordinary usage to a conscious
experience. Whitehead extends its usage to refer to any actual entity,
whether or not it meets prior definitions of "life" and whether or not it is
aware of its activity. The distinction between living things and dead nature
is done away; "experience," "decision," and "life" are now words that apply
to every real thing that can be pointed to in the universe, from the human
soul to the most trivial puff of existence in empty space: "The doctrine that
I am maintaining is that neither physical nature nor life can be understood
unless we fuse them together as essential factors in the composition of
'really real' things whose interconnections and individual characters con-

stitute the universe" (MT 150).[18] The primary object of election, then, is this "really real" thing, the actual occasion. Actual occasions are the building blocks of living beings as well as what we think of as dead matter.

The process doctrine of election recognizes that God's purpose for the world involves specific purposes for every element of the world. As we have seen, Whitehead asserts that all entities, from subatomic particles to human souls, are characterized by the purposes they entertain. God is the origin of every purpose through God's provision of the initial aim. Therefore, when we consider the initial aim as election, we may say that God elects all actual occasions, which includes every moment of individual experience in the universe. This universality of God's electing action does not mean that God gives the same sort of purposes to all occasions or in general deals with all occasions in the same manner. There is a difference in quality between the experience of a low-grade occasion and that of a high-grade occasion. As I discussed in the second and third sections of the last chapter, the initial aims for low-grade occasions involve few possibilities for change, while the aims for high-grade occasions may present many varieties of graded possibilities. High-grade occasions, such as the presiding occasions in living societies and complex organisms, are on the cutting edge of evolutionary progress, representing the world's most potent opportunities for increasing value. But the supporting world of low-grade occasions, such as cells and molecules, has not been left behind; it remains essential not only as the environment for higher organisms but also as a creator of value on its own level. God's election of every occasion of every grade indicates that every occasion has fundamental, inherent value in itself, as subject, along with its instrumental value for others, as a finished decision or superject. The most important consequence of process theology's extension of election to nonhuman and even nonliving entities is the promotion of an ecological worldview, in which the experience of all types of creatures is recognized as inherently valuable. If we see nonhuman nature as a realm where creatures respond to God's election and make decisions with regard to God's purposes, we will be more inclined to promote the preservation of nature in order to maximize its possibilities for the creation of value and the fulfillment of God's purposes.

Scriptural warrant for the election of nonhuman creatures can be found by reinterpreting some of the most troublesome stories of the Old and New Testaments: those that depict God working directly through animals and other natural elements. Scientific sensibilities have long been offended by scriptural passages that seem fanciful or legendary, such as the story of Balaam's talking ass in Numbers,[19] the plagues of insects and frogs in Exodus,[20] and even Elisha's bears in 2 Kings.[21] Attempts to describe biblical miracles in terms of the processes of natural science have generally ignored those involving higher animals as obviously mythological. While the plagues of insects and frogs in Egypt can be traced back to the biological cycles characteristic of the region, and the parting of the Red Sea can be attributed to wind events or shallow water, a talking pack animal is simply a unique event that has so far gone unobserved in scientific history and seems to be ruled out by all accepted zoological knowledge.

Process theology accepts the legitimacy and value of the scientific quest for understanding, and builds upon the knowledge obtained by scientific methods. It is logical, therefore, for process theologians to accept the scientific study of the Scriptures as well, including the identification of mythological traditions within the Scriptures (of which the story of Balaam's ass is representative). However, to label a story as mythic or prescientific does not mean that it should be discarded, or interpreted as a strictly symbolic or moral tale. Process theology, in its understanding of the election of the nonhuman world, can recover another layer of truth from these stories, one that illuminates a neglected facet of the scriptural worldview.

The key can be found in the story of Elisha's bears. Unlike the plagues, this story does not lend itself to scientific explanation; unlike Balaam's talking ass, it is not simply implausible as a description of events. Didactically useless in an age when scaring children into right behavior is not accepted pedagogy, it seems to be simply a curiosity of Scripture. And even more than the others, its implications are morally troubling. Delving more deeply into why the story's message seems suspect reveals that not only does it speak of a vindictive prophet who uses his connection with divinity for various magician's tricks, and the punishment of dismemberment for children's insults, but it also speaks of a God who uses animals as tools. To Descartes, who believed that animals were machines without the sensations of pain or pleasure, this implication would not be cause for alarm. After all, human beings train animals to do their will; God, with perfect and immediate control over their minds and behavior, is simply the supreme animal trainer. But for those of us who have become convinced of our close kinship with animals, to the extent that we see ourselves as having a nature in common with animals, it is unsettling to think that God could make animals into robots. If them, then why not us? Or perhaps God does sometimes manipulate a person's will, as in the case of Pharaoh's hardened heart. If this is the message of Scripture, then the consequences for human free will and responsibility are dire indeed. Does God merely allow us to exercise free will but in fact is able to take control of our wills at any time? If so, then why doesn't God stop certain people from doing certain things?

The argument over human freedom and moral action is joined, as it has been over the centuries, and we are no closer to a satisfying answer.

Consider a process interpretation of the story of Elisha's bears, however. The bears are autonomous creatures, not mere instruments of either Elisha or God. Like human beings, they may be in God's will or out of it, responding in obedience and cooperation to God's aim for them or rejecting that aim. The story is shaded by the biblical author's interpretation of their actions: The bears are exacting God's judgment on the disrespectful children. It illustrates the danger of interpreting all events in the world as direct expressions of God's will—God is held responsible for all sorts of reprehensible acts, since God controls nature as the operator controls the machine. But if nature is full of autonomous creatures that are not bound by God's election but free to respond to it with their own creativity, then so-called natural evil cannot be attributed to God's will. The message of Elisha's bears, along with many similar stories in Scripture, is that God elects human and nonhuman creatures alike to fulfill divine purposes;[22] not every act of every creature, however, represents the carrying out of a divine purpose, since creaturely acts can express the creature's freedom to pursue its own aims as well as to pursue God's aim for it. The Psalms are an excellent scriptural resource for the process view of nature, since they often portray all parts of nature responding to God's grace with free praise: "Let heaven and earth praise him, the seas and everything that moves in them" (69:34); "Then shall all the trees of the forest sing for joy before the LORD; for he is coming, for he is coming to judge the earth" (96:12b–13a); "Let the sea roar, and all that fills it; the world and those who live in it. Let the floods clap their hands; let the hills sing together for joy" (98:7–8). This worldview can be used to reinterpret those portions of Scripture in which nature seems to be seen mechanically.[23]

Election as Vocation

The identification of the gift of initial aim as the basic divine act of election means that election becomes a doctrine about God's purposes for the world. Process theology has a fundamental interest in becoming rather than being. Election, like the other doctrines of process theology, is concerned with what an actual occasion *becomes,* its choice of aim for itself and its achievement of that aim, rather than with what it *is,* its unchanging ontological status or substance. Indeed, it considers substance or being to be something of a metaphysical illusion. There is no unchanging ground on which the figure of change moves. Instead, there are only moments of

becoming and the transition between those moments. The great organizing principle of this world of becoming is purpose, and the coordination
among purposes that is found in the world, that enables the world to
progress, is the result of God's purposes communicated to individual occasions. What I have identified as election, then, is the divine gift of vocation
to creatures.

Election has not always been concerned with vocation in Christian theology. As the Greek conception of divinity came to dominate Christian
thought, first through Platonism and Neoplatonism and then through
Aristotelianism, the notion of a God who needed human beings to help
carry out divine plans became untenable. The omnipotent, omniscient,
atemporal, immutable God is not the giver of vocation, because this God
does not have aims that depend on the actions of human beings. Hence,
the doctrine of election moved away from its consequences in creaturely
life, and became, by the Reformation, a pretemporal decision by God in
which the ontological status of all human beings is fixed. Barth leads
Reformed theology back toward an understanding of the service of the elect
by identifying them as witnesses to God, specifically sent into the world to
participate in Jesus Christ's apostolate of grace, existing not only for themselves and God but for others as well:

> The elect is, therefore, one who stands in the service and commission of the
> gracious God. As a result of his election, he is summoned by the operation
> of the Holy Spirit. His election as it has taken place in Jesus Christ can be
> declared to him. By faith he can appropriate the promise given. But if this is
> the case, it is not merely his private calling but also and as such his official
> calling. . . . He is elected in order to break forth with his weak voice, but with
> all his voice, into the rejoicing which has its source in the divine election of
> grace, and courses through all God's creation, accompanying all His works
> and ways. This is his determination, and it is his duty and obligation to do
> this. If he does not, he necessarily compromises and denies his election.[24]

In process theology, there is no election without vocation. The idea of
an election that makes no difference in the creature's life—that merely
moves its cosmic counter from the "damned by right" column to the "saved
by grace" column without requiring any knowledge or response on its
part—is alien to the process conception. Once again, this is an area in
which many of the scriptural touchpoints for election can be reinterpreted
and recovered. The many models of election found in the Hebrew Scriptures are unquestionably based on the fundamental idea that God elects
individuals for service. Abraham was chosen by God not only to father a
race—something he might have done without ever having been aware of a

divine mandate to do so—but first to "go forth from your country and your kindred and your father's house to the land that I will show you" (Gen. 12:1). This response to God's call is the condition for the covenant between God and Abraham, consistently repeated in Scripture, that God will bless Abraham and make him a great nation (Gen. 12:2; 13:14–17; 15:5–6; 17:4–21; 22:15–18). Certainly the story of Abraham represents a model of election that is less dependent upon the individual accomplishment of the elected one and more upon the unique placement in time and space of the elected one, which enables him to fulfill God's purpose. H. H. Rowley, in his book-length survey *The Biblical Doctrine of Election,* writes:

> One of the consequences of the very constitution of human society is that a man may bless or curse not alone himself, but those who are associated with him and those who come after him. By the very fact of his exaltation of character, and the tradition of that exaltation which he passed on to his descendents, Abraham was a blessing. No man lives to himself alone, and no man can tower above the level of his contemporaries without blessing others.[25]

The service for which Abraham was elected is not something any other person could have accomplished, yet it did not rest primarily on Abraham's efforts to be of service but on his character. Yet obedience to God's will is no small service; and the story of Abraham's sacrifice of Isaac clearly indicates that his obedience is the goal toward which God's call to him aims. The angel tells him, "By myself I have sworn, says the LORD: *Because* you have done this, and have not withheld your son, your only son, I will indeed bless you, and I will make your offspring as numerous as the stars of heaven and as the sand that is on the seashore" (Gen. 22:16–17). Rowley's point, however, that Abraham was called to bless others through his existence and progeny, is well taken in a process understanding of vocation. Our service is in what we become as subjects—the value we add to the world through our own experiences—and in the legacy we leave as superjects.

Further biblical examples of election point more clearly to a specific task the elected one must perform—in other words, to the creation by the elected one of a condition for future progress. The election of Moses to lead the Hebrew people out of Egypt sets the standard for election-for-service in the Pentateuch.[26] Moses several times questions his fitness for the service to which he is called, but God reassures him that he will be equipped for the task.[27] The fact that Moses' full election is contingent on his fulfillment of the task set to him is indicated by God's refusal to allow him to die and be buried in the promised land.[28] The election of Moses is a call to perform a certain service, and Moses' relationship with God changes over time according to how faithfully that service is performed. This model is also demonstrated by the election of Saul to be king of Israel.[29] After Saul failed to obey God's command to utterly destroy the Amalekites, God withdraws Saul's election because of his failure at the task set him: "The word of the LORD came to Samuel: 'I regret that I made Saul king, for he has turned back from following me, and has not carried out my commands'" (1 Sam. 15:10). In his place, God elects David.[30] God's covenant with David, that Israel would always have a king from his house,[31] is not broken through David's sin with Bathsheba, although that sin results in the death of their child;[32] his sin of taking a census results in three days' pestilence,[33] but does not nullify the election.

The final model of election in the Hebrew Scriptures is the prophetic call. Once again, this is unmistakably a call to perform a service, namely, to carry the word of God to a designated audience. The service may involve more than simple preaching, as Hosea found when he was ordered to marry a prostitute.[34] The call cannot be avoided by running away, as Jonah found in his mission to Nineveh.[35] Moreover, the call requires a response: "Then I heard the voice of the Lord saying, 'Whom shall I send, and who will go for us?' And I said, 'Here am I; send me!'" (Isa. 6:8). Among the prophets whose messages are recorded in the prophetic books of the Old Testament, none lost their election through their failure to fulfill the terms of their service. But the fact that some prophets received the call and did not respond with faithful obedience is borne out by the histories of "false prophets," who do not speak the true words of the Lord.[36] In the case of the prophet, the priest, and the king, God gives the elected one a mission to others. In fact, that mission is the very same as the election itself—initiated by God, but with an essential element of human response.[37] Rowley writes of the "false prophets": "This is not to deny the reality of his election, or to suggest that it is *his* election of the vocation of prophet which makes him a prophet. He is a prophet because he is chosen of God, and responds to the choice."[38]

There are at least two clear paradigms of election in the Gospels. Jesus himself is identified as the Messiah, the "anointed one" or chosen one of Israel. The term goes back to 1 Samuel 10:1 and connects Jesus with the kingly tradition.[39] The service the Christ was to perform, according to Jewish expectation, was the salvation of Israel; according to Christian understanding, the service that Jesus renders in response to his election is the salvation of the world. As part of this service, Jesus called disciples; discipleship and apostleship form the second major model of election in the

New Testament.[40] The disciples are called out of their various occupations to serve Jesus by learning from him, caring for him, and eventually proclaiming his message.[41] Paul is the apostle called last, and spiritually rather than physically: "He fell to the ground and heard a voice saying to him, 'Saul, Saul, why do you persecute me?' He asked, 'Who are you, Lord?' The reply came, 'I am Jesus, whom you are persecuting. But get up and enter the city, and you will be told what you are to do'" (Acts 9:4–6). "But the Lord said to [Ananias], 'Go, for he is an instrument whom I have chosen to bring my name before Gentiles and kings and before the people of Israel; I myself will show him how much he must suffer for the sake of my name'" (9:15–16). Paul uses election in a way analogous to its use in the Old Testament referring to the progeny of Abraham, Isaac, and Jacob. The elect are the new Israel, the "remnant chosen by grace" (Rom. 11:5), the branch grafted into the tree of the children of Abraham (11:17–22). In other words, election in the seminal passages of Romans 9–11 is corporate; the election of Jesus Christ entails a corporate election of those whom God has adopted as sons in the same sense that the election of Abraham entailed a corporate election of the nation that would spring from his loins. Yet it is not unconditional, just as the election of Israelites as a body is not unconditional:

> They [i.e., the original branches] were broken off because of their unbelief, but you stand only through faith. So do not become proud, but stand in awe. For if God did not spare the natural branches, perhaps he will not spare you. Note then the kindness and the severity of God: severity toward those who have fallen, but God's kindness toward you, provided you continue in his kindness; otherwise you also will be cut off. (Rom. 11:20b–22)

Paul implies that just as God elected the children of Israel to be faithful covenant partners, God elects the church for service—to be a "vessel of mercy" (Rom. 9:23, RSV), a useful tool in God's hand.

One further permutation of biblical election is worth noting under this heading. The elected one, called for service, need not be aware of her role in God's plan. In the Hebrew Scriptures, various individuals and nations are spoken of as instruments of God's will, even though they do not know God personally and consciously. Pharaoh's hardness of heart allowed God to demonstrate his power in bringing the Israelites out of Egypt.[42] The Scriptures also speak of God's specific election of various pagan nations to punish Israel for its disobedience.[43] These passages indicate that God uses the acts of those who are not religious believers or even particularly moral. Need we go so far as to say that God calls nations to war and urges them to wage death and destruction? As in the example of Elisha's bears, this is a case when we deny the interpretation placed on the event by the biblical writers, while affirming a certain aspect of the worldview behind that interpretation. There may be times when, as Whitehead admits, the best for that situation may be bad, and God's role is to urge self-destruction in order to limit wider future destruction. In general, however, the message to be drawn from God's election of unwitting participants in the divine plan is twofold: first, that all actual occasions have a relationship of election with God and a role to play in the attainment of God's aim, whether or not the occasion is aware of the relationship or the aim; second, that God is able to turn even the destructive, rebellious acts of free creatures to the divine purpose, through God's patient drawing-out of the best consequences from whatever situation arises. Does this mean that all acts are equal in relation to God's will, since God can turn any creaturely act to the divine purpose? Not at all—God's subjective aim still provides an eternal standard against which all creaturely responses may be measured, as Rowley affirms:

> If God could integrate into His purpose acts which sprang from indifference to His will, that was the mark of His greatness. . . . It is but that God chooses the free acts of men to execute His will. Sometimes it is the unwitting service which the pursuit of human purposes may render, and the praise or blame it earns depends on whether its character makes it harmonious with the will of God or whether He has to bend what is alien to His will to serve His purposes.[44]

Although the creature, even in the realm of creatures with self-consciousness, may not know that God is the one to whom it is responding, the response still involves that creature in the relationship of election, initiated by God's call. These two biblical aspects of election, of God's people as they know themselves and of the nations or the Gentiles in their relative ignorance of God, are unified in the *content* of the vocation given to both groups, as Pannenberg points out:

> The tension between a particularistic and a more universalistic interpretation of God's election of Israel has been effective from this point on through Jewish history. In the light of the New Testament this ambiguity is clarified in favor of a more universalistic intention. The particularism of the love of God for the elected one is to be related to the more comprehensive horizon of God's love for all mankind. The chosen one, then, is assigned a function for that wider context. He is elected in order to serve as God's agent in relation to a more comprehensive object of God's love. Therefore the chosen one belongs to God precisely in serving God's greater purpose in the world.[45]

The process focus on vocation, and hence on election for service, represents a reinterpretation of the Christian doctrine of election, especially as it developed in the Reformation. The greater the theological focus on God's sovereignty, immutability, and impassibility, the more likely election is seen as election to salvation, with no response required on the part of the elected individual. By contrast, process theology sees the response of the creature as essential to election. This is consistent with the idea of vocation, or election for service, which presumes that the elected one plays the indispensable role of accepting the service and carrying it out. As we have already seen, however, if all creatures are the objects of God's election, then election cannot be tied to a conscious acceptance and response of the creature, since not all creatures are capable of conscious, reflective decision. Whitehead does believe, however, that all creatures are capable of *response*—to their environment and to the task of self-creation. The election of God in process theology is the gift of a potential accomplishment; it takes the creativity of the creature, responding to election, to accomplish the task set for it.

Election in History

The final concept that must be reinterpreted under the process view of election is its relationship to time and eternity. Already this has been considered in its negative aspect in the last section, when I noted that the atemporality of election found in the Reformed doctrine must be denied under process theology. The concept of election's historicity is closely related to its vocational content, just discussed. If election takes place entirely in prehistory, in God's eternal decision, and has nothing to do with the contingencies of time, then it need not be concerned with vocation for contingent creatures; the outcome of God's decision would merely await enactment, without any need for the creature's response and involvement. If, however, God's eternal decision concerns a purpose for the world rather than its specific historical details, then the assignment of specific aims to creatures can only take place in response to contingent events that cannot be known ahead of time, and the cooperation of creatures in achieving universal aims is necessary for progress.

Process theology denies that the future can be determined in advance, due to the irreducible freedom of creatures to create themselves, and therefore to create actuality, by their own conditioned decisions. Therefore, election means something other than the predetermination of the fates of creatures. In the last section I argued that election in process theology means the assignment of vocations to each actual occasion. Due to the indeterminacy of the future and the contingency of historical events, a meaningful vocation for each occasion can only be determined by God's knowledge of what has actually transpired in the world, in the divine consequent nature. The election of each occasion, then, occurs as that occasion arises, and depends on the particular situation that obtains at that moment.

This historical aspect of election is dominant in process theology, but there is still an eternal aspect that cannot be ignored. If election were merely historical, there would be no coordination of the vocations given to each occasion. The unity of election—its expression of a single divine aim toward which all creatures' initial aims are directed—is dependent on God's primordial nature. God entertains God's own subjective aim based on the divine valuation of eternal objects. I have spoken of this as God's self-election, the primordial and eternal decision to be God aiming at the increase of value through the creativity of creatures. This eternal aspect of election gives consistent direction to the specific instances of historical election toward creatures.

The important distinction to be drawn in this reinterpretation is that process thought's historical focus must deny determinism while affirming God's unchanging purpose for the world. That this purpose is subtle, many-faceted, and flexible is a matter of observation. The gradual evolution of complex creatures from simple ones requires that God deal with an ever increasing possibility that God's immediate purposes will be thwarted. Complex creatures governed by high-grade occasions have many more possibilities on which to exercise their freedom of choice. The probability that such occasions will choose to actualize a possibility for their own becoming that is less than optimal, in view of God's purpose for the world and the specific election-for-service of each occasion, is quite high. But this risk is justified, for the overall world process and God's guiding purpose, by the vastly greater value that can result from the activity of high-grade occasions. However, when occasions do "go wrong" by choosing a path that deviates from the ideal presented in the initial aim, all is not irretrievably lost. God's patience is the divine turning of creaturely missteps into new paths of creativity and value. Since God's purpose is unchanging, God is able to use whatever happens in actuality toward the divine subjective aim; perhaps a detour is required, perhaps a less-than-direct path must be taken, but even if the route history takes is indirect, the goal is never out of sight.

The importance of metaphysics in this process is that the world in microcosm and macrocosm consistently exemplifies certain rules. Whitehead indicates that these rules are part of God's self-determination in the primordial nature.[46] These rules are made effective at every point in the process, both within the concrescence of a single entity and within the life of an enduring society. God's consistency in translating God's subjective aim into specific initial aims for creatures ensures that coordination of aims across the lines dividing the simple from the complex can occur. The complex, then, can gradually be built up from simple components, while the simple components continue to have their own aims and own experiences and create their own value, apart from their subordination in function to the complexity of which they are a part. Election holds this many-layered world together by balancing the purposes of occasions as simultaneously subjects and superjects, as values unto themselves and values to be transmitted to others. And God's primordial self-election, in the choice of divine subjective aim, is the one purpose that holds together the "many" of the historical election of creatures, by providing a single overriding goal toward which all other purposes are auxiliary. This goal is not specific in every detail, but is general enough to allow for modification and even surprise in the final outcome. The goal entertained by God in the primordial nature, in other words, does not negate or render unnecessary or repetitive the playing-out of historical actuality. One might compare it to a blueprint before a house is built. The house is not reducible to the blueprint; the existence of a blueprint does not mean that the house is now superfluous. A house serves an entirely different function from a blueprint, and yet a blueprint is necessary if the house is to be built in the proper order. The blueprint is the idea, the ordered set of eternal possibilities; the house is the actual world that emerges from the application of these possibilities to real agents and materials. To extend the analogy even further, blueprints are modified in response to problems and opportunities that arise in the course of building. It may not be proper to attribute to God the same kind of changing of one's mind that occurs when houses are built to the specifications of human beings, since God's purpose is eternal, but it seems entirely proper to say that when a builder makes a mistake, God can alter the plans so that the house continues to be built and need not be abandoned.

If election's historical component is deemed as significant as its eternal component, then Christian theology must take seriously the experience of the creatures caught in the flow of history, in which they encounter their election. Process theology redefines election to emphasize the experience of creatures and the unique historical situation that their election reflects. In a process system, as we have already seen, eternity is not a refuge from the vagaries of time and change.[47] It is not an assurance that the future is already determined, but it does guarantee that God's purpose is unwavering.

Eternity without time is dead and unproductive; time without eternity is directionless and chaotic. Instead of fleeing our temporal existence with a theological overemphasis on eternity, process theology seeks to reclaim the value of existence in time, with its constant flux, by affirming the role of creatures in advancing the world's progress. A commitment to history in the process doctrine of election elevates the contribution of the elected one to a position complementary to the contribution of the electing God. At the very least, it indicates that God takes the contingencies of history into account when calling creatures for service. If historical election is taken even more seriously, it asserts that the response of the creature cannot be separated from the divine call when election is discussed, for the free act of the creature in response to the election of God creates history itself. God responds to history in shaping the specific aims offered to creatures, and a creature responds to the eternal divine aim as embodied in its own initial aim by making history in its self-determination.

Conclusion

To associate the concept of the initial aim in process philosophy with the doctrine of election in the Jewish and Christian traditions, I have discussed four ways in which the concepts describe the same idea. First, the initial aim establishes a relationship between the creature and God, initiated by God but including both partners in reciprocal give-and-take. The initial aim provides a goal for the creature, involving it in a teleological structure. God governs the world through the divine providence of the initial aim, cooperating with creatures and preserving the continuing world process. Finally, God's grace is revealed in the providence of the initial aim, as creatures are graciously included in the divine purpose for the world.

The differences between process theology, which aims to revise theologies based on older metaphysical systems, and the traditional assumptions that have governed Christian theology, result in a doctrine of election that must deny certain aspects of the most influential election doctrines in the history of Christian thought. Reformed theology, for example, uses the doctrine of election to emphasize the sovereignty of God, particularly God's radical aseity, which includes divine self-sufficiency and impassibility. Process theology asserts that although God is *a se* in a unique sense because God provides God's own initial aim, some world and God are co-eternal and codependent. Hence, the role of the creature in election will be much more important than it is in a theology that sees contingent, temporal reality as less significant than divine reality. Also denied are the omnipotence and omniscience of God where those attributes are defined as "power to determine the decisions of free creatures" and "knowledge of future contingencies." Process metaphysics is incompatible with the notion of human powerlessness in the face of the electing God, since the act of the free creature transcends any would-be determinative causes. And the idea of an election that is essentially atemporal is also foreign to process theology, because the circumstances of history condition the content of the aims given to creatures, and those circumstances cannot be determined ahead of time.

Along with these premises that must be denied, I have identified three ideas that process theology adopts from biblical theology and Christian theology but redefines in accordance with its metaphysical assumptions. Election cannot be limited to the human race, or even to what we consider living beings, under the process system, since all actual occasions from high-grade to low-grade receive aims from God upon which they exercise some degree of self-determination. Election as vocation means that creatures are not elected to an end toward which they contribute no act or work, but instead are elected for service, in order to advance the world process toward God's subjective aim. Finally, election in history affirms the consequential and effective nature of contingent world events and asserts that God operates through a history that cannot be determined but that can be directed through the divine gift of purpose. In chapter 4, I shall lay out the systematic elements of a process doctrine of election, drawing upon the assumptions and parameters established in this chapter.

CHAPTER FOUR

The Process Doctrine of Election

God's Call and the Creature's Response

Having introduced both the history of the doctrine of election and the fundamentals of the process idea of initial aim, I will now proceed to propose a process doctrine of election. In chapter 2 I argued that process theology's emphasis on relationship and reciprocity must result in a doctrine of election that describes and interprets not only the electing act of God but also the creature's response. The concern in that chapter was the explanation of process philosophy's categories and assumptions about God, actual occasions, and the initial aim; it was followed by categorization of the process doctrine's necessary parameters in comparison and contrast to the historically significant Reformed doctrine. In this chapter, I shall return to the discussion of God's act of election and our response, addressing them from the point of view of constructing a doctrine, based on the process ideas, that is religiously adequate and in agreement with the Christian message as expressed in Scripture and tradition. Specifically religious considerations were also present in chapters 2 and 3, especially when the character and activity of God were at issue. But process philosophy, as found in Whitehead's writings, primarily describes God's secular function—that is, God as an indispensable part of the world process quite apart from the knowledge or worship of conscious creatures. Process theology is an extension of these ideas to formulate doctrines for describing and utilizing belief in the religious sphere of human activity. This chapter is a proposed doctrine of election for a process theology based on Whitehead's philosophy.

The first section discusses the divine act of election, including the involvement of the primordial and consequent natures of God, the effect of world history, and the transformation of divine purpose into creaturely purpose. By way of transition into the next section, the discussion ends with a proposal for how process theology might interpret the activity of the Trinity in election. The creature's response to the divine initiative of election is the topic of the next section. Topics include the relationship of the creature to God, the reception of vocation, the creature's free decision regarding its aim, and its final actualization of its aim. The religious ideas of redemption, sanctification, and immortality receive interpretation here. The chapter ends with concluding remarks on the adequacy of the doctrine constructed. I consider some additional aspects of the religious dimension of the process doctrine of election—such as its contribution to the human existential debate, the idea of "special election" that comes to the few rather than to all, and the gift of religious vocation—in the epilogue.

The Divine Act

It is impossible to analyze any act or attribute of God in a process framework without taking into account both the primordial and the consequent natures. However, to discuss each nature separately is to run the risk of seeming to separate what cannot, in reality, be divided. Certainly the two natures of God are divisible for purposes of analysis. But both religion and philosophy, if they strive to apply themselves to real experience, require that what is divided in analysis be reunified in the description of the world as it really is. Therefore, although the two natures must to some extent be considered separately if we are to understand the role of the eternal versus the temporal, the unchanging versus the ever changing, the one versus the many in the divine act of election, it is necessary to keep in mind that only one actual entity is being described, of a single mind and purpose, all of whose acts are unified in their direction toward the divine goal.

In the same way, it is to some extent artificial to separate the discussion of election into two parts, one for the divine initiator and one for the creaturely respondent. However, like the division of God's nature into primordial and consequent aspects, the separation is a natural way of showing that the doctrine of election can be approached from these two points of view. There are two centers of experience involved, and two free acts of decision. The artificiality of the distinction arises from the fact that the two experiences condition each other—indeed, the experiences of creatures are constitutive of God in God's consequent nature, and prehensions of other entities (including God) are constitutive of the initial phase of each concrescent actual occasion. This is the nature of analysis in process philosophy: Since relationships are central to the process that creates new generations of individuals, the analysis of any aspect of that process means separating it from the relationships that make it what it is. With this in mind, and constantly reminding ourselves of the essential unity that stands above the analysands being separated, we can proceed to consider election from the divine perspective.

Election's Origin in the Primordial Nature

Although the election of individual creatures is a historical phenomenon, the roots of election are found in the primordial nature of God, which is eternal and unchanging. The primordial nature consists of God's definitive valuation of all eternal objects, which provides God with God's own subjective aim. This ordering of possibilities determines God's goal for the universe and establishes the order of nature the world process follows. The election of individual creatures depends on this divine act of valuation because election involves the transmission of purposes from God to creatures, and God's purposes are established in the primordial nature. But the primordial nature is not only the foundation and prerequisite of election but is in fact a divine act of election in its own right—God's election of God's self.[1]

Although this concept of divine self-election has already been introduced in chapters 1 and 2, its constructive contribution to the doctrine of election in a process context deserves further elaboration. According to the concept of divinity inherited from Greek philosophy, God has certain necessary attributes (not only "necessary" in the sense that without these attributes the being in question would not be God, but also *logically* necessary in the sense that a being with these attributes must exist, according to proofs such as Anselm's ontological proof of God's existence). God has no choice but to possess attributes such as omnipotence and omniscience, for example, although God may voluntarily restrict God's exercise of these powers. Since the essence of election is choice, the meaning of God's self-election is not that God chooses to be omnipotent, or to have any other necessary attributes; only God can choose to be God, so this is a tautology.

God's choice, rather, is to be a God who chooses to fulfill the divine subjective aim through the creativity of creatures. God's aim to maximize value does not bind God to any specific course of action in pursuit of that goal. One sure way to maintain the level of value in the universe is not to risk losing value through the destructive activity of creatures that have inherent freedom of choice. Otherwise, only simple creatures might be fostered, which have limited options and hence cannot do much damage. But God has chosen to encourage the evolution of high levels of complexity, diversity, and even consciousness in the world. This strategy can lead to the creation of unique value through the vastly increased level of freedom of choice, but it can also result in wrong choices by the creatures that destroy value already achieved, prevent other creatures from achieving their goals and hence suppress the creation of value, and reverse the progress made by creatures as a whole toward God's aim.[2]

Nonetheless, God in the primordial nature determined God's self to pursue the latter path. By doing so, God set the stage for all election of individuals by electing the realm of creatures as a whole to be cocreators of value. The dignity thus afforded creatures is a share of God's honor as creator; we have been elected in God's determination of the universal order to cooperate with divine persuasion in advancing the world process—in bringing about the kingdom of God. Reformed theology, most notably that of Karl Barth, makes a similar point about God's election of God's self to be God for creatures by pointing to the incarnation as evidence of God's primordial choice to bring human beings into fellowship with divinity. God elects God's self in the form of a human being, Jesus Christ, signaling both God's condescension to the human situation and humanity's elevation into the divine life.[3] This choice to be God for others is not based on any circumstance foreseen in the world; it is inherent in the Trinitarian structure of self-giving love among the Father, Son, and Holy Spirit.[4]

The issues of Trinity and incarnation are discussed later in this chapter. At this point, it is important to comment on Barth's concept of God's self-election by noting how the process concept differs. The similarity is that both Barth and process theology see God determining God's self to be oriented toward God's creation in a way that is not necessary but purely gracious. However, process theology does not single out humankind as the sole or even primary object of God's grace. God's decision in favor of creaturehood means that God gives of God's self to every actual occasion, ranging from a single electron to a plant cell to the human soul. The divine self-election does favor human consciousness in the sense that God urges the world process toward the evolution of conscious beings. However, process philosophy does not assert that there is anything ultimate or final about humanity—neither as the predetermined end to the evolutionary process, nor as its highest and best product. God may well intend for some further refinement of creativity to supplant humanity; it is by no means an assumption of process philosophy or the science that informs it that human beings are at the top of the evolutionary ladder. God's self-election encompasses God's purpose for relationship with all sorts of occasions, from the simplest to the most complex, and beyond occasions themselves, to the societies and structures that foster them and within which they operate. The divine self-election, therefore, cannot be conclusively identified with the incarnation, since the former's implications are not limited to its effects on God's relationship with individual human beings. The incarnation may be an example of the kind of self-revelation to creatures that results from the divine self-election, but it cannot be said to be the only or even the primary example.

Another difference between Barth's concept and the process concept is that Barth develops his idea of divine self-election under the assumption that divine sovereignty requires an absolute difference between God's being and creaturely being. This ontological gulf is a factor in Calvin's insistence on double predestination, which assumes that God brings creatures to various ends regardless of their willing or acting, since the power to determine history and eternity rests entirely on the divine side. Process theology rejects the Calvinist view of divine determinism because its metaphysical categories preclude both the exercise of coercion on the decision of any free entity and foreknowledge of the future.[5] Therefore, a divine self-election that involves predetermination of the structure of history and predestination of individuals is unknown to process theology. Instead, God's choice to be God for creatures is a decision to entertain an unwavering purpose to foster and encourage the creation of value through creatures. The details of the fulfillment of that purpose await actualization by creatures themselves and cannot be foreordained, but God redeems each actuality by ordering it toward the divine purpose in the consequent nature.[6] Therefore, in process thought, God's primordial decision is a goal for history rather than a finished vision of history.

The larger point, that Barth postulates an absolute distinction between divinity and humanity that is overcome only by God's omnipotence in the incarnation, is also impossible for process theology to affirm. God and creatures both exemplify the metaphysical categories applicable to actual entities; the difference between them is in God's *perfect* exemplification of a dipolar nature, relatedness, and so forth. We have already noted some differences or exceptions that Whitehead allows to enable God to fulfill God's unique function in the system: the everlasting nature of God's concrescence, the immediate and total inclusion of actuality in the consequent nature, the provision of God's own subjective aim. These distinctions between God and creatures are not absolute, however; the two sides of the election relationship are the same type of entity—both are involved in the process of becoming and both are purposeful. Hence, the type of sovereignty that Barth attributes to God in God's self-election, by which God overcomes a gulf that creatures could never cross, is not a characteristic of the process God. Indeed, the creature in a sense does cross the gulf between divinity and creaturehood to claim its own election—it is the actual occasion that prehends the initial aim by its own act. But God's act of providing that aim is something creatures could never do for themselves, by reason of their incomplete vision of eternal possibilities. Only God, who starts the divine concrescence from the mental pole and hence enjoys a complete and ordered envisagement of all potentials, can elect creatures for the specific task that will advance God's subjective aim. In other words, it is only through God's self-election that election of creatures becomes possible—and this statement is congruent with Barth's claim even while its metaphysical framework differs.

Daniel Day Williams sums up the process interpretation of God's self-election:

> [T]he way in which God can act on other things is categorically determined by the metaphysical order constituted by his primordial nature, and which he does not violate. It would be meaningless to speak of his violating his own essence. This means that God acts upon other things by objectifying his being for them so that he can be prehended by them. God acts by being felt by his creatures, and in this process he enters into the constitution of their successive moments of experience.[7]

This is a description of the act of election taking the primordial nature as abstracted from God's unitary nature. If taken alone, it seems to indicate that the primordial nature is God's being or God's divine nature, the passive object of others' actions, while the consequent nature is God's agency, the active entity. Such a description hardly squares with Whitehead's integrated understanding of dipolar divinity—in which the primordial nature is in fact an efficient creator of actuality and the consequent nature is receptive of the world's actuality—and the abstraction detracts from our understanding of God's electing act. Whitehead calls the primordial nature "free" and "unconscious," and the consequent nature "determined" and "conscious."[8] These matched pairs do not square with the easy division of God's nature into passive and active sides. Both natures express God's self-determination to be God for creatures, although this decision originates in the ordering of possibilities that comprises the primordial nature, as God's concrescence itself "originates" in the primordial nature. This means simply that God's primordial nature, including the divine self-election, is unchanging, constant, ever an efficient fact for the world. But the consequent nature expresses the divine self-election as it orders contingent actuality in accordance with that unchanging purpose. Rather than minimizing the creaturely impact on the creation of value for the universe, the consequent nature maximizes it and, through its passing back into the world in a new generation of initial aims, fosters ever greater creaturely participation. So both natures express God's self-election, and both natures participate in the act of electing each individual in the world.

The Effect of Creatures on Election

Election occurs in history and takes account of the reality and consequence of each individual's historical situation, as well as the possible positive and negative effects of that individual on the future. Election, in other words, has to do not only with eternal verities of purpose and value but also with contingent historical events. This is inevitable in the process framework: What is being elected is not "beings" per se—Aristotelian substances with a fundamental identity underlying an ephemeral string of accidents—but *events themselves*. The actual occasion is "the limiting type of an event with only one member," says Whitehead;[9] this locution is used to indicate that the primary elected individuals are not things that change over time, but the momentary, unmoving instances of becoming that cumulatively make up history.[10] Since each of these actual occasions has created in itself an ordering of its actual world, each event provides an objectified fact to which later events have access. This is the accumulation of history, which at every moment is complete but which moves forward every moment to include another generation of events. An event is "a definite fact with a date" (PR 230); its election occurs prior to its becoming definite and seeks to influence what sort of definiteness it will express. Election is not only *in* history, it is *of* history.

Given this relation, then, what nondivine factors affect the content and act of divine election? First, the reality of creaturely agency means that the events taken into account by God—the world situation—are not determined by any one power or cause. The world situation is the result of the free acts of free creatures, which are the creators of history. The agency of creatures has often been seen in philosophy as an idea that must be reconciled to the power of God by argument. In other words, there appears to be an immediate and apparent conflict between the premises "God is omnipotent" and "Creatures are free agents." Process theology proposes that there is no conflict, because the absolute power of God does not and cannot include coercive power over the decisions of free creatures. If the power to determine the free decision of a creature is metaphysically ruled out, then it is no slander on God's omnipotence to say that God cannot do this. What God's self-election to be God for creatures does accomplish is the imposition of order upon the world, in which creatures have a choice between viable possibilities, and in which the evolutionary growth in complexity of creatures affords them ever greater numbers of viable possibilities among which to choose. In other words, God cannot abrogate the freedom of creatures, but it is God's gracious decision to enhance that freedom and use its results to build a world of maximal value.[11] Regarding the relationship between creaturely freedom and divine power, one introduction to process thought proposes:

> It is because God exercises power upon us, persuasive power, that a space is opened up for us within which we are free. If there were no God, there would be no freedom, and the future would not be open to be shaped by human decision. The future is open and we are free because of God. The power to open the future and give us freedom is a greater power than the supposed power of absolute control, for a power effective over free beings is a far greater power than what would be involved in the manipulation of robots.[12]

Therefore, since the primordial divine self-election is in favor of this cooperative, persuasive relationship between God and creatures, God's election of individuals must be sensitive to the particular conditions that arise from the activity of free creatures. It also must be tailored to the possible positive accomplishments of the elected one so as to maximize the value that this one can create—or, as Whitehead notes, to minimize the damage done if the elected one is not in a position to accomplish any good.

The indeterminacy of the future is another factor that influences the election God offers to creatures. The future cannot be foreseen or predetermined in exact detail, as a result of the fact that actual occasions are free to create their own future, as just discussed. A creature's inalienable freedom means that no matter how completely the causes impinging on its action are known, there is always a "black box" aspect of the occasion's concrescence into which not even God can see. This is metaphysically guaranteed in process theology by the solitude of the actual occasion in its concrescence. All the data that constitute the initial phase of the concrescence are in the occasion's past.[13] Contemporaries do not prehend each other.[14] So once the data are gathered, their ordering by the concrescent occasion is absolutely unconditioned by anything existing concurrently with the occasion and outside the occasion. God's influence on the concrescent occasion is in its prehension of the initial aim as a scheme for ordering its data; but God waits along with the rest of the world to find out what subjective aim the occasion actualizes. This is a real difference from classical theology, which does not recognize any zone of absolute privacy for the creature.

The future is unknowable as actual simply because there is nothing actual about it. It is purely potential, and therefore God, who knows all potentials, knows the future as potential.[15] Creatures know the future as potential as well; the anticipation of the future is an important influence on creatures.[16] The greater the ability of the creature to weigh alternatives and visualize consequences, the greater the influence the future has upon the creature's present. But until one of the myriad possibilities is actualized in the present, the future remains only potential. God's knowledge of it is complete, since God's envisagement of all possibilities is complete, while creaturely knowledge of it is incomplete. Due to God's complete knowledge of future potentials, the initial aim given to each creature is far more comprehensive than a hypothetical aim based on the creature's own knowledge. But even God's complete knowledge does not include definitive knowledge of what will in fact happen. Therefore, divine election does not take for granted its own success. Because the future is created by creatures as they actualize their private subjective aims, God must account for its indeterminacy in the act of election.

The final way in which nondivine reality affects election is in the consequent nature of God. The world in all its contingency is included in God, and in every moment God's ordered vision of actuality is given back to the world:

> The problems of the fluency of God and of the everlastingness of passing experience are solved by the same factor in the universe. This factor is the temporal world perfected by its reception and its reformation, as a fulfillment of the primordial appetition which is the basis of all order. In this way God is completed by the individual, fluent satisfactions of finite fact, and the temporal occasions are completed by their everlasting union with their transformed selves, purged into conformation with the eternal order which is the final absolute "wisdom." (PR 347)

When we speak of God's taking the contingencies of history into account, we are speaking of the combined action of the consequent nature, through which God includes the reality of the world, and the primordial nature, through whose eternal order the events of history are judged and evaluated. The initial aim given to each occasion is an ordering of possibilities based not only on the eternal ordering of the primordial nature but also on the contingent events that make up the world situation. God gives to each creature a vision of what and where it is, along with a vision of what it can be. In fact, these two components of the initial aim are inseparable in process theology. An individual is nothing more or less than what it makes itself, just as it is nothing more or less than its location and legacy. To become the creator of greatest value, a creature must appropriate the best of its inheritance, reject misleading data, and project its impact on its future. For this activity, the prehension of God's consequent nature is essential. Apart from the divine ordering, both primordial and consequent, there is no direction or meaning to history; the creature's prehension of that order gives it a definite place in history and a role to fulfill in its continuation. It is clear from the involvement of the consequent nature in election that the relationship that is initiated is between the creature and a God who is relevant to the world, a God who is concrete and active: "The consequent nature acts by being prehended, *felt* by the creatures. This means that not only the primordial structure but the concrete being of God in his relation to the world is communicated to the creature."[17]

God as Principle of Concretion

The order in God's primordial nature, when it is transmitted to the world in the divine act of election, functions as the "principle of concretion," to use Whitehead's phrase. By this I mean that God's electing activity consists of ordering competing possibilities in order to offer a coherent view of what might be actual. Not all sets of possibilities are actualizable; the selection of certain possibilities entails the concurrent selection of other possibilities that are compatible with the first group, while a third group of possibilities is eliminated because of its incompatibility with the selected options. Whitehead contends that only through the ideal valuation in God's primordial nature is the world's reality able to exhibit any order. As we have already seen, the order that is characteristic of the universe as we know it is a necessary condition for the maintenance and further evolution of complexity. God's function as principle of concretion enables this order by presenting, in the initial aim, possibilities that are evaluated not only according to their desirability but also according to their relevance to the existing situation:

> The order of the world is no accident. There is nothing actual which could be actual without some measure of order. The religious insight is the grasp of this truth: That the order of the world, the depth of reality of the world, the value of the world in its whole and in its parts, the beauty of the world, the zest of life, the peace of life, and the mastery of evil, are all bound together—not accidentally, but by reason of this truth: that the universe exhibits a creativity with infinite freedom, and a realm of forms with infinite possibilities; but that this creativity and these forms are together impotent to achieve actuality apart from the completed ideal harmony; which is God. (RM 119–120)

There is also a sense in which this function of God is not only adjunct to election but is a form of election itself—an election of possibilities rather than actual entities. The primordial nature represents the divine self-election to be God for creatures, and as such also represents the election of a goal for the entire universal process: the world, God, and the world as included in God. Pursuant to that goal, God chooses certain possibilities as most desirable for achieving the divine purpose. As the world moves through time, God's choice of what possibility is best actualized for each occasion moves from the general aims, which are relatively constant—the grand schemes of historical movement—to the specific focus on the moment immediately at hand. This is a choice among possibilities, a limiting action that rejects certain possibilities as counterproductive and selects others as optimal. Daniel Day Williams interprets Whitehead: "In *Process and Reality* he identifies the principle of concretion with God's function as providing for every occasion that 'initial aim' from which it takes its rise. That is, there must be an order of participation in an actual world with a definite presentation of this order before there can be a new occasion."[18] The initial aim—the election of actual entities—is dependent on God's election of potentials, in the primordial nature as the divine subjective aim, and in God's concrete act as the formulation of individual initial aims.

The reader will notice that for the first time in the discussion of the process doctrine of election, the issue of rejection has been raised. The rejection of potentials, metaphysically speaking, is necessary if there is to be any actuality. Because both sides of an antithesis are simultaneously potentials, it is clear that not all potentials can be simultaneously actualized, since only one of the two antithetical possibilities can be actual at any one time. Therefore, the selection of any possibility entails the rejection of its opposite; practically speaking, it also entails the rejection of an entire world of associated possibilities that are rendered practically impossible by the actualization of the selected eternal object. In this realm, at least, rejection must exist alongside election. The question remains whether actual occasions as they concresce are like possibilities in this way, such that the election of one entails the rejection of another or others. This issue must be considered when the ideas of redemption and salvation are discussed in the next section.

The point to be made at this time is that God's activity as the principle of concretion is twofold: first, the divine election of certain possibilities as most desirable (along with the corresponding rejection of other possibilities as incompatible with the divine purpose), and second, the divine election of concrete individuals through an offering of initial aim. This second

aspect is the passage of possibility from the eternal realm of God's envisagement into the temporal realm of concrescent creatures—the movement
from possibility to actuality. Neither divine function can be dispensed with
in process metaphysics since the orderly coming-to-be of actual occasions
depends on the primordial order of possibilities and, conversely, the
ordered possibilities remain simply potential, not actual, until they are
selected and concretely enacted by actual entities. Both aspects can be seen
as election: The first is broadly encompassed under God's self-election but
also involves a consequent election of potentials, while the second is the
historical election of individuals, which has been the primary topic of the
doctrine of election.

Coordination of Divine Aim and Creatures' Aims

The content of election is conditioned by God's subjective aim to maximize value in the universe. By this I mean that God does not elect creatures
simply in themselves, but primarily in order that they might become something. This is perfectly in keeping with the metaphysical assumptions that
govern the process doctrine of election. In an important sense, there is no
"being" in a simple state of existence for God to elect.[19] Each creature is in
the process of becoming itself when God provides its initial aim. This aim
directs the creature toward a certain optimal outcome for its concrescence—optimal not only with regard to the creature's contribution to the
accomplishment of God's subjective aim but also with regard to the creature's own private enjoyment. The initial aim represents a balance between
these two goals, the macroscopic and the microscopic. If God were not
inclined to consider the enjoyment of creatures in the gift of their initial
aims, then it is possible that increasing freedom of choice and consciousness in evolution would not be a part of the divine plan. As we have seen,
however, God's self-election in the primordial nature determines God's self
to foster the becoming of creatures with a high capacity for the enjoyment
of their own value creation.

This strategy of coordination between God's aim and the aim of creatures involves a balance between the private life of creatures as they concresce in solitude, and their public life as superjects. The former is the
domain of the creature's own aesthetic feeling; the latter is the value they
pass on to the world after their own life has ended. In the achievement of
the divine subjective aim, only the legacy of the creature's immortal satisfaction counts. One can imagine a world order in which creatures leave a
positive, progressive legacy more uniformly than is the case in our world;

however, according to the process view of the risks and rewards of freedom, this hypothetical world would not be a place in which creatures enjoyed themselves at the highest possible levels. John B. Cobb Jr. and David Ray Griffin write:

> On the basis of the positive correlations among these first four dimensions of experience, we see that the development of beings with the capacity to enjoy significant values, and to contribute significant values to those beyond themselves, necessarily meant the development of beings with the capacity to undergo significant suffering, and to contribute significantly to the suffering of others beyond themselves. The good cannot be had without the possibility of the bad. To escape triviality necessarily means to risk discord.[20]

In other words, both sides of the balanced aims are put at risk through God's strategy of fostering the creation of value through creatures. God's subjective aim may suffer setbacks due to the free actions of creatures that are able to choose possibilities for their actualization that do not conform to God's will; at the same time, the ability of creatures to aim at the highest good may suffer because of the destructive legacy they inherit or the impoverished opportunities of the actual world they inhabit. This is the price paid for the rich tapestry of aesthetic enjoyment that is possible in our world.

The rub in all this talk of aims and achievement is the freedom of creatures to choose their own aim from the ordered set of possibilities they prehend in God. For conscious creatures such as human beings, the balancing of divine aims and creaturely aims has a direct effect on behavior. On the one hand, there is an ultimate standard of value, a goal for all of history, an aesthetic and moral lure that tugs at all of us. On the other, there is the moment-by-moment decision making that refers in some way to that standard, yet cannot be reduced to a simple appeal to that standard. The second aim differs from the first because it not only refers to an action that moves world history toward the kingdom of God, but to the becoming of our own character through acts that, once performed, are an irrevocable part of us. Our freedom may be used to sacrifice ourselves for the greater good of the world, and there may be times when this is indeed the greatest legacy of good that we can leave. However, more often our freedom is used in self-creation through our decisions. This aim of self-creation does involve as a component the anticipation of the future consequences of our decisions on others, as well as on ourselves. As our gaze widens, we can see the effect of our decision on groups of people around us—on our community, culture, and world—and the question of absolute standards that we believe to govern all behavior becomes more crucial. Process ethics

might be described as a continuum from self-interest to abstract moral reasoning, or perhaps as the former nested inside the latter, as the initial aim
given to creatures is nested compatibly inside the subjective aim of God.
Cobb and Griffin write:

> Although the initial aim derived from God is not perfectly fulfilled, it is not
> ineffective. Because of God's presence in us in this form, "our purposes
> extend beyond value for ourselves to value for others" (RM 152). Because of
> God we experience unrealized ideals; and adventure, morality, and religion
> all result from this. We are dimly aware of a rightness in things "attained or
> missed, with more or less completeness of attainment or omission" (RM 60-
> 61). But we have seen that this rightness does not lend itself to a single for-
> mulation of the right way to live or act. What is right for one occasion is not
> right for another. Indeed, the aim for each occasion differs.[21]

The aim given in election is effective in two ways. First, it connects the
creature with the divine aim, which is eternal and unchanging, and gives
the creature a standard against which its eventual decision of self-creation
will be measured. As Cobb and Griffin put it, we are aware, however dimly,
of a purpose that our lives should serve for others. Second, the initial aim
effects the beginning of private aesthetic enjoyment. The standard given is
not only God's, not only a moral imperative tuned to the greatest good for
the greatest number; it is our tool for engineering intensity of feeling for
ourselves. Private aims and public aims can be satisfied at the same time if
both find their source in God; this is one of process theology's core tenets.
Election, in which God coordinates the vocations given to creatures with
each other and with the divine aim, is the instrument for transforming this
balance of aims into a balance of actual achievements, which advances the
world's progress toward the end ordained for it in God's primordial nature.

The Completion of Election in God's Consequent Nature

Earlier in this chapter, I spoke of election as originating in God's primordial
nature, adding the caveat that the natures cannot be spoken of as separate
agents with their own peculiar operations. The same applies to the consideration of the completion of the act of election, which may primarily be
thought of in terms of the consequent nature but which cannot be reduced
to an act of the consequent nature or the continuing process of the consequent nature. The completion of election is God's ordering of finished actualities in the consequent nature according to the divine subjective aim. Just
as potentials are evaluated and ordered in the primordial nature, so that God
includes all eternal objects, actualities are evaluated and ordered in the con-

sequent nature, so that God includes all actual occasions. The involvement of the primordial nature in this activity is, of course, that the primordial valuation of possibilities provides the rubric for the ordering of actualities. It is according to what is valued as potential that what is actual is judged.

The completion of election in God's consequent nature has three theological aspects. First, it is the continual growth of the all-inclusive kingdom of God, and as such it has an eschatological aspect. Second, it is the tender care of God that nothing be lost, and as such it has a soteriological aspect. Finally, it is the final word of God upon the works of every creature, and as such it is judgment.

Eschatology. As eschatology, the consequent nature is prehended by every emerging creature as a deification of the world in which it finds itself and as an ideal for the world that will survive it. The consequent nature is never static or finished. It is always reaching forward for the next moment, always oriented toward the future. God orders the satisfactions of actual occasions not into a bounded and finished work of art but into a progressive, expanding whole. The divine vision of the world looks beyond what is to what might become of what is. And so the kingdom of God, the eschatological realm, is constantly immanent in the world by virtue of election. If we did not receive, in whatever part is comprehensible to us, God's vision for the future, then our election to service would be meaningless; we would not be servants of God but cogs in an arbitrary machine designed for some purpose beyond our ken. However, the consequent nature is present to us as evidence of our concrete progress toward the eternal *telos.* The goal given to a creature in its initial aim is the next step in the formation of God's self, the inclusion of the world in the consequent nature, all ordered toward that step that now this creature, at this moment, can take.

In what sense is this eschatological aspect of the consequent nature an operative cause in the act of election? Daniel Day Williams writes:

> The consequent nature acts by being concretely apprehended in feeling in such a way that God's specific response to the world becomes a constitutive function in the world. Here there is a specific divine causality. It should be remarked that this assertion in no way denies the operation of all the other actual entities in the world as causes. God's causality is exercised in, through and with all other causes operating. There is no demand here to factor out what God is adding to the stream of events apart from those events. But there is the assignment of specific functions to God's causality. These include the presentation to the creature of a supremely adequate center of feeling through which the meaning of every occasion is received into and transformed by the divine experience, and this is concretely known by the creatures in such a way as to qualify their experiences.[22]

God is not only known as supremely purposeful in the primordial nature; here God is known as *supremely related,* supremely creative in ordering the divine feelings into a coherent, consistent, productive whole. Our election is qualified by the fact that God reveals God's response to the world prior to our response to God. It is through the divine relatedness that we learn how to be related; it is through the divine response to creatures that we learn how, as creatures, to respond to God. The perfection of God's response to the world is eschatological in that it provides us with a supreme example of responsiveness, responsibility, and creativity, and in that its ongoing and fluid perfection in all circumstances lures the world toward its own mode of perfect response. Eschatology is not merely the purging of what is evil from the world as it is; it is also the fostering of new modes of creativity and value. And in God's response to the world, in the consequent nature, we also find an openness to what is new. Again, God's inclusion of novel occasions and actualities into God's self is not blind acceptance, or celebration of the new simply because it is new. God's consequent nature is a model and a lure for creatures in its valuation of novelty and in the limits it places on the conditions in which novelty is productive.[23] This is an apt description of election: a call to produce something new in the world, under the rubric of God's overall purpose. Every creature receives a call with some eschatological component—a promise that the creature's service to God places it in the center of God's will and on the path to God's kingdom. That desire to bring about a better future is the eschatological desire that informs our response to God's call.

Soteriology. The consequent nature can also be seen as the salvation of the individual creatures, which thereby are included in God. Salvation here would mean the bringing of creatures into fellowship with God, their elevation from their original state to kinship with divinity. From the discussion in chapter 3, it will be evident that process thought has no concept of original sin, or of a generic state of human fallenness from which all human beings, by virtue of nothing more than their membership in the human race, need to be redeemed. Creatures indeed take part in a fallen nature, more or less uniformly, to the extent that corrupted social institutions and a polluted environment cannot help but affect the becoming of new occasions. Such pervasive evil persists over countless generations and penetrates into every corner of the world, thanks in large part to the ingenuity of conscious and intelligent creatures in spreading their unenlightened self-interest, to the suppression of the freedom of others, human and nonhuman alike. An important aspect of human sin, then, in process theology, is the disintegration of common purpose among the one and the many, a narrow

view of self-interest in which creatures fail to take account of the possibilities for bettering their world by leaving a positive legacy for the next generation. In election, God makes the first move toward saving creatures by
providing them with purposes that balance their best interests with the
progress of the universe toward God's goal. The completion of this move
in God's consequent nature is God's acceptance of the creature's accomplishment for inclusion in God's self. Here God accomplishes the divine
purpose to save the creature by bringing its satisfaction into the order of
God's own consequent self.

Are all creatures saved? Process theology certainly asserts universal fellowship with God. Every creature has a relationship with God that initiates
its own becoming, and the satisfaction achieved by every creature becomes
part of God's consequent nature. Using the definition of salvation we
adopted above for process theology, then, all creatures are saved. This does
not mean that all creatures achieve goals that advance God's plan; as we
have seen, the freedom of creatures to determine their own subjective aim
from the initial aim given by God means that the aim achieved in the creature's satisfaction is not always God's will, and may at times be directly
counter to that will. However, the history of the world is still directed by
God's providential governance at God's aesthetic goal, regardless of the
detours and redirection and unexpected twists in the path toward that goal
necessitated by the actions of free creatures. Every creature's accomplishment (or failure) is included in the consequent nature as a part of that man-
ifold, infinitely complex path toward God's goal, ordered in such a way as
to give it a definite place in the history of God's creative action toward the
world and the world's creative response to God. Universal salvation in
process theology does not mean a general acceptance of whatever occurs, a
general indifference toward the specifics of individual lives, an undifferen-
tiated inclusion. The inclusion of God's consequent nature is very specific.
It is the saving of even the worst creaturely purposes by God's infinite
patience in turning them to their best result—even if the best that can be
done is destruction. In this way, election for service is fulfilled in the salvation of the service rendered. Norman Pittenger writes (of the action of the
Holy Spirit):

> It is tragically true that people are often very seriously misguided and mis-
> taken in their grasp of what is right and good, beautiful and just. And almost
> inevitably, because of their human finite understanding, they fail to see the
> full reality of the goals after which they strive. Equally plain is the fact that
> people are prone perversely or carelessly to ignore the plain facts; nobody but
> a blind fool could think that things are otherwise in this world. Yet even then,

in that very imperfection and failure and distortion, the Holy Spirit is working—he is taking whatever good has been seen and done, correcting subtly
whatever error or evil has been present, and making everything serve in the
long run toward the accomplishment of the divine purpose in the creative
advance which we call the world.[24]

The consequent nature not only saves the creature in the sense of preserving its satisfaction in God's everlasting life, it also brings that satisfaction into the light of God's creativity. While a creature's purpose is finite,
and therefore can be irreversibly thwarted, God's purpose is infinite, and
can find a way around any setback. It is the conviction of the process doctrine of election—which, like all election doctrines, is intended to be a
word of hope—that our election to service finds its fulfillment (and our salvation) far beyond our limited understanding of our place in God's purpose and far beyond our limited power to bring about God's kingdom. God
puts our accomplishments to work in producing a new world every
moment, luring creatures like ourselves on to greater things, and even what
seems to be forgotten by the world is everlastingly a part of God's consequent nature, oriented toward the divine purpose.

Judgment. The disparity among creatures with regard to the extent to
which they fulfill God's purposes for them, however, brings us to the final
aspect of the consequent nature's completion of election: the divine judgment pronounced on each satisfaction in God's ordering of actualities.
Here the process doctrine of election is honed to its sharpest edge.
Reformed dogmatics has contrasted the category of judgment with that of
mercy, thanks at least in part to Luther's law-gospel dichotomy, which
influenced the entire Reformation. Calvin holds that the judgment to
which human beings are subject outside of Christ, of which the Old Testament is a witness, is revealed in the reprobate, while the mercy effected
by Christ's sacrifice is revealed in the elect.[25] In their zeal to celebrate the
gospel of grace and repudiate the law of works, the Reformers tend to deny
that what a person does has any bearing at all on the person's relationship
with God. This emphasis represents their attempt to correct what they saw
as the previous tradition's overreliance on ritual actions as a way of maintaining the relationship between human and divine realities. Its positive
side is the realization that this relationship is not dependent on the human
person's consciousness of it or even desire for it. Karl Barth, for example,
analyzes one of Schleiermacher's sermons as follows:

We have gathered here, the preacher concludes, in order that the Savior may
come among us. He has not come to judge the world—for there is nothing
more to judge where his peace reigns—but to save the world [Jn. 3:17]. "In

the peace of the Lord are enclosed all the good things which attract us as objects of our striving both in the inner spiritual life and also in outer public life. Therefore may his peace be with us!"[26]

But the Reformed doctrine also has a negative side, when measured against the witness of Scripture and the Christian message. It does not give the proper place to divine judgment even of the elect, which is attested to not only in the Old Testament but also in the Gospels and of course in the book of Revelation.[27] No, separation from the law does not mean eternal separation from God. But neither does a relationship with God mean that deeds are unimportant. The process doctrine of election is linked to vocation, which means that God elects us and brings us into relationship with God in order to perform some deed. Our accomplishments, then, are measured by the task that is given us. Works are not an indifferent component of the creature's relationship to God in process theology—indeed, they cannot be ignored for the simple reason that a creature is nothing more than what it has decided to *do* in its own self-creation. God's relationship is not with a basic substance that then has accidental adventures that do not affect the creature per se. It is with the event, with the deed itself, which *is* the entity.

The completion of election in the consequent nature is judgment because it is the final evaluation of what the creature becomes. God judges us according to what we do as compared to what we had the opportunity to do. This is judgment against an ideal, which is contained in the primordial nature and the initial aim derived from the primordial nature. "Thus the creativity with a purpose issues into the mental creature conscious of an ideal. Also God, as conditioning the creativity with his harmony of apprehension, issues into the mental creature as moral judgment according to a perfection of ideals" (RM 119). Judgment is not against an arbitrary ideal or one unknown to the creature; God's standard of value in the primordial nature, as well as the specific divine plan for each creature, is a part of that creature's prehended data. The law is written on our hearts.

What are the consequences for transgressing that law? In the worst imaginable case, the ordering of a creature's satisfaction in the consequent nature would diminish to insignificance that creature's impact on the future. "The initial aim is the best for that *impasse*. But if the best be bad, then the ruthlessness of God can be personified as *Atè*, the goddess of mischief. The chaff is burnt" (PR 244). But thanks to God's infinite patience, even those events that seem utterly destructive and evil can be brought into the stream of God's purpose. There is still judgment against these creatures for their decision to act against God's will, but there is no annihilation, no ultimate rejection. Every creature becomes part of the consequent nature—whether valued high or low—and thus election is fulfilled even in judgment. God's grace is active to redeem even the most rebellious deed by integrating it into the harmonious divine vision of actuality.

The process doctrine of election here strikes a balance between law and gospel by asserting that there can be judgment without absolute rejection. The biblical concept of election for service describes a relationship with God that can be altered by the rebellion of the elected individual or group. The rebellion, however, does not break the relationship to the extent that God's choice is rendered invalid and ineffective. The chosen one remains the chosen one even when he runs from his election, as in the story of Jonah, and the job remains to be done. The notion of covenant, which governs many of the examples of election found in the Hebrew Scriptures, is a reciprocal contract. The chosen one agrees to a responsibility when she enters into the covenant, and judgment of her performance is to be expected. Pannenberg writes:

> The inherent dangers in any claim to chosenness are obvious. They are essentially the same as in the history of ancient Israel—pride, exclusivism, presumptuous security, and contempt of possible or even impending judgment. But these dangers do not render the claim to chosenness illegitimate. *They are taken care of by the category of judgment.* By its claim to chosenness a group places itself under God's judgment in a specific way because it pledges itself to the will and purpose of God in history. Thus it makes itself accountable to the terms of God's covenant.[28]

Process theology goes beyond the conscious and volitional covenants described in the Old Testament in asserting that all creatures, conscious or not, have a relationship with God. What is important in the nonhuman case is that the creature is possessed of God's primordial standard of value and assessment of the world situation, and that this prehension of God informs the creature's free decision. The category of judgment simply means that election imbues each creature with responsibility, and that the creature will be held responsible for its use of its resources.

God's Redefined Attributes in Election

All doctrines of election arise from certain definite conceptions of God's character and attributes. "Perfect Being" theology, which arose from the Greek philosophical conception of divinity, has dominated most Christian theologians' conceptions of God's attributes. God is understood to exemplify all perfections—perfect knowledge, for example, or perfect power. Process theologians have seen their metaphysical assumptions as a challenge to this norm. Perfect Being theology, they maintain, is incompatible with the Christian message because it renders God responsible for evil, or eliminates the possibility of Christ suffering in his divine nature. Various traditional attributes of God, therefore, have been redefined in process theology so that the concept of God is coherent both within the set of metaphysical assumptions that characterizes process thought, and within the testimony of Scripture, both Old and New Testaments.

The doctrine of election is directly concerned with four of God's attributes. First, immutability and impassibility are replaced in the process conception of God with the concepts of God's dipolar nature and omnipassibility; then, omnipotence and omniscience are redefined in accordance with the metaphysical limitations on power and knowledge in process thought.

Immutability

Immutability as an attribute of God has its biblical origins in the psalms that speak of God's steadfast love and characterize God as a rock or a fortress against which the variability of the world cannot prevail.[29] God's constancy is contrasted with the changeability of creatures and the natural world. Unlike human beings, God is faithful in God's promises: "O give thanks to the LORD, for he is good; for his steadfast love endures forever" (Ps. 107:1); "The LORD has sworn and will not change his mind" (Ps. 110:4a). As the early church absorbed Greek influences, a concept of immutability based more on logic was added to this idea of faithfulness and trustworthiness. If God is perfect, the reasoning ran, then God cannot change, since the only change possible would be to something less than perfect. Perfection is a state with but a single aspect; there cannot be more than one way to be a perfect being, or the possibility is opened up for there to be more than one perfect being. According to the ontological proof, there is only one perfect being. Therefore, God does not change. For the doctrine of election, the original biblical idea of steadfastness and faithfulness remained the primary reason for maintaining a doctrine of God as immutable. A changeless God does not take back election, but bestows it once for all upon certain individuals, who are then everlastingly made citizens of God's kingdom. Salvation is put upon a sure foundation, since God cannot swerve from God's purpose to save creatures.

Process theology challenges the validity of a changeless conception of God on both scriptural and logical grounds. The witness of the Old Testament, especially, is of a God who moves through time with creatures, who observes the occurrences of the world and reacts to them, who even alters the divine plan for achieving God's purpose based on the actions of creatures. All this testimony must be dismissed as pretheological myth, or as a misunderstanding of the religious experience of the Israelites, if the doctrine of God's immutability is to be maintained. An alternate explanation, that God allowed God's self to *appear* to change for didactic reasons, or to fit divine revelation to the capacities of its recipients, places us in the position of maintaining that God did not truly reveal God's self in the Old Testament, or that God deliberately deceived the Hebrew people regarding God's nature. Process theologians maintain that a redefinition of the doctrine of immutability, so that it refers to God's aim (the primordial nature) rather than God's being, allows the integrity of Scripture to speak for itself under a new set of assumptions about divinity.

On philosophical grounds, process thinkers argue that the notion of a changeless God has never fit comfortably into the structure of a Christian metaphysics. At the very least, if God knows the world's actuality, God's knowledge must be changing as world history moves from future possibility to present actuality to past actuality (assuming, as process theology does, that there are no future actualities to be known). The Christian kerygma asserts a fundamental moment in the history of divine-creature relations when God became human. To say that no change took place in God's life due to the incarnation is to carry divine timelessness to a point where it becomes almost unintelligible. The Gospels attest to the breaking of the bond between Father and Son at Calvary; is there no change in the divine life there? The more seriously Christians take the notion of a relationship between human beings and God—and this notion is basic to Christian practice as well as theology—the harder it becomes to maintain a concept of divine immutability in practice or in doctrine.

Of course, the doctrine of divine immutability was not taken wholesale from Greek philosophical thought into Christian thought without reason. A God who does not waver or stray is a trustworthy God, one whose determination to save human beings is not a passing fancy but an eternal characteristic. However, the contrast between God's faithfulness and human fickleness is not the only contrast that was being drawn when the absolutes of Greek thought were appropriated for use in Christian theology. The perfection of God was understood not simply as a quantitative limit on human traits—as if a human being who could be conceived to know everything, for example, would be omniscient and thus similar to God. Perfect divine attributes are not based on or defined by the human trait in question. Instead, God in God's perfect knowledge is, in this very characteristic, qualitatively other than ourselves. Human nature is to be imperfect, divine nature is to be perfect, and never the twain shall meet. Kathryn Tanner writes that the use of immutability language in speaking about God expresses God's otherness:

> Immutability would be chosen, similarly, not to suggest that God is at rest rather than in motion, or that God is fixed and simply opposed to change— God as the transcendent source of being is presumably beyond the contrasts by which finite beings are distinguished and differentiated. This choice would indicate, as the contrary terms could not, that all our language, supposing as it does a world in process, is inappropriate.[30]

Process theology takes issue with this choice because it imposes an absolute and unbridgeable distinction between the divine realm and the realm we inhabit. This dualistic mode of thought goes far beyond what is needed to guarantee God's power to save us. In extreme forms it jeopardizes that very power by implying that God cannot share such human experiences as change, suffering, loss, and joy. The more radical the separation, the harder it becomes to harmonize theology with the witness of Scripture, which documents repeated and intimate communion between the divine and human realms, including that ultimate example of communion, the incarnation.

In suggesting that God is in process along with the world, process theology advocates a univocal use of language. God is an entity like ourselves metaphysically, therefore God shares all our experiences "from the inside," as it were, not simply through observation or imagination but in perfect empathy. However, to locate God and creatures in the same realm is not to suggest that what we observe in our lives is exactly attributable to God. Process theology holds that change, for example, is not a feature of individual actual entities, which simply achieve satisfaction and then perish. Change happens *between* entities, in the process of transition; it becomes evident in the differences between an entity and its descendants. Since God in Whitehead's thought is a single entity, not a society or series of entities, it is not precise to attribute change to God. More accurately, we should say that God *becomes* or *grows*. God's knowledge of actualities is always increasing, as actual entities come to be, while God's knowledge of possibilities remains fixed. The consequent nature grows as it includes every facet of the world's process.

The issue of language is central to the redefinition of God's attributes in the process doctrine of election. Tanner notes that we call God immutable to indicate that the language we use to talk about the world flux is inappropriate to talk about the divine. Whitehead often speaks of the unavoidable inaccuracy of language in talking about any metaphysical truth, whether in regard to God or to nature. The language that needs to be reformed, in his view, is the language used to talk about ourselves. In order to see our world as it really is, to unite the microscopic and macroscopic realities in one order, we must recognize that many of the "facts" we acknowledge in our speech as assumptions are simply heuristics or shortcuts for thought, not true representations of reality at all. Recall that Whitehead repudiated the common assumption, reflected in our forms of speech (subject-predicate syntax), that the world is composed of basic things (substances) to which things happen and properties adhere in a nonessential fashion (accidents). The philosophy this grammar assumes is untenable, according to Whitehead.

If we speak accurately about ourselves, we will by extension begin to speak accurately about God, since divine and creaturely reality is the same. As composite creatures, societies made up of many levels of actual entities, each with its own experiences, it is merely shorthand to speak of ourselves in the singular, as if a single identity were undergoing all our experiences. Process thought seeks to awaken us to a vision of ourselves as myriad processes, conscious and unconscious, in a historical continuity and present cooperation that gives cohesion to our individuality. That individuality undergoes change because we are societies, as are nearly all the other creatures we encounter and experience. Hence, change is a universally observed feature of our reality. But when we recognize that the entities that make up the most basic level of reality do not undergo change but simply become themselves and perish, we begin to understand that God, likewise, is not changing, but becoming. God does differ from other actual entities in that God's becoming is everlasting, without perishing. The categories of immutability and mutability, however—the choice that the tradition has given us concerning the divine and creaturely realms—represent a false dichotomy. It is not the case that everything observed in the world is negated in God, but it is the case that God transcends the world eternally, just as every actual entity transcends its world during the moment of its concrescence. With the redefinition of God's attributes that process postulates, that transcendence is characterized as growth in perfection.

Because the Reformed tradition emphasizes God's sovereignty to guarantee the divine election, the classical attributes play an important role in Reformed theology. These emblems of perfection demonstrate God's otherness. Where human beings are the problem, God is the solution; therefore, what is true of human beings is not true of God, and vice versa.

Process theology's repudiation of many of these attributes, and its redefinition of others, is seen by many Reformed thinkers as the exact opposite of their theology—as, indeed, its mortal enemy. Consider this quotation from Donald G. Bloesch:

> Reformed theology insists that in Jesus Christ God took upon himself the burden of the world's afflictions, the penalty for human sin. It is not God who needs to be changed (as the process thinkers contend) but fallen humankind, and this change is enacted not through the will to creativity but through the mystery of supernatural regeneration. The hope of humanity rests not on our cooperation with the power of creative transformation but instead on a divine intervention in human history that happened in the past and will happen once more when Jesus Christ comes again to bring in the kingdom that shall have no end.[31]

The implication is that process theology has done away with immutability because it contends that a static God is somehow imperfect. It is not the case that process thought considers immutability less perfect than mutability—as if God "needed" to change. Instead, process thought maintains that God is a part of process, and along with other entities in process, God continually becomes. Whatever does not become, is dead; God, since God becomes, lives and includes all things. Reformed theology, as Bloesch implies, sees our existence in process as a problem to be solved, and sees God's immutability in a realm of changeless eternity as the solution. Process theology operates from a different viewpoint: the processes of becoming and change in which we live are not problems. In fact, these structures represent the opportunity to create ourselves and our world. God, as ultimately creative, is involved in these structures, but not as their prisoner—rather, as their perfectly adept master.

The conflict between process theology and Reformed theology on this point clearly relates to the Arminian-Calvinist controversies. Although Arminians did not see the immutability of God as an issue in the election doctrine, their insistence on the involvement of human beings in their own election is the true source of the wrath that Bloesch directs at process theologians. After all, if humans are to have something to do with their election, then there is some connection between human and divine on this point. God is no longer removed, other, independent; the qualitative distinction has been compromised. Albert C. Outler puts the conflict succinctly:

> Both parties professed a common belief in the authority of Scripture; both were equally agreed on the doctrine of justification by faith alone. The

Calvinists preferred to measure God's sovereignty by his freedom *from* the
world; the "Arminians," by his victorious involvement *in* it. One side saw salvation threatened by "free will"; the other saw God's character defamed by
"reprobation."[32]

Process theology stands in exactly the same relationship to Reformed
theology. When the battle is joined over the doctrine of election, the attributes of God quickly become the battleground. Note in Outler's phrases
how both sides of the controversy take their sides based on what they perceive to be the essence of God: for the Calvinists, unconditioned divine
freedom and power; for the Arminians, love for the world. Process theologians agree with the Arminian perception of God's essential nature as
love, expressed in God's omnipassibility. It is, finally, the conviction that
a relationship involves an effect on both sides that leads process to insist
that God is not immutable in the classical sense. The effect of the world
on God is that God ever increases in knowledge and scope, and that God's
methods for achieving the divine purpose depend on a world situation
that is not predetermined.

There is, of course, a sense in which God is immutable, and that is in
the primordial nature. What God has determined for God's self—the
divine purpose and valuation—does not change or grow. Because God
knows and orders all possibilities, it is impossible for this pole of the divine
nature to become anything more than what it is eternally. The pool of possibilities, of eternal objects, does not change, increase, or lessen. The
changelessness of the primordial nature is the guarantee of God's constancy
that Reformed theology finds in the doctrine of immutability. Because
God's purpose is set in God's self-election, it can never be altered whatever
the vagaries of history, however far from this purpose the world strays. And
because God determines God's self to be for creatures, to allot them a share
in achieving the divine purpose, we can be assured that we are elected to be
a part of the kingdom. The primordial nature is the rock of steadfast love
that will not be moved.

But the primordial nature by itself is dead. It can have no effect on the
world by itself. Its eternal, changeless purpose must be enacted and completed in the consequent nature. Above, I called the primordial nature the
"rock of steadfast love." Love, however, is an act, not an eternal state. It is
not the act of either of the natures working alone, just as no act of God proceeds from either of the natures working alone. Any act of God is the result
of God's *eternal* purpose taking shape *in history*. As the Arminians understood, love is the reason that the classical notions of God's perfection must
be modified in light of the gospel. Love is not static; it grows to encompass

the entire world as that world grows, and it grows to include each individual entity as that entity grows. Election is the revelation of God's love, so the process doctrine of election must insist that the doctrine of immutability be restricted to God's eternal purpose to love creatures. That love itself is neither mutable nor immutable, but beyond those categories; election love *becomes,* as the entities in the world become to receive it.

Impassibility

Closely related to immutability is impassibility, the second divine attribute to be redefined by process theology. God's impassibility expresses the divine immunity to suffering; more broadly, it means that God is not a "patient" as well as being an agent. God acts, but is not affected by any outside force. Again, this divine attribute is taken from the Greek idea of what imperfections in the world a perfect being would not experience. Suffering, or being buffeted by forces beyond one's control, is a feature of creaturely experience that reflects the creature's imperfection. A perfect being would control the inputs as well as the outputs of its experience. Nothing could affect such a being, because to be affected is to be under the control of another, and the perfect being controls all. Impassibility then is dependent upon an interpretation of omnipotence that asserts divine determinism.

The attribute of omnipotence, and process theology's redefinition thereof, will be discussed below. Impassibility, as a part of the Christian doctrine of God, has rarely been explicitly connected with omnipotence in theological discussion and therefore has not been seen as affected by objections raised to a classical view of omnipotence. Instead, the problems that theologians have with impassibility have to do with the scriptural witness and the integrity of the incarnation. Scripture certainly speaks of God as if God were affected by the world. God is said to see events in the world, feel emotions regarding those events, and make decisions based on what is seen.[33] Christologically speaking, the discussion of the meaning of Jesus' suffering on the cross has been accompanied by debate over whether the divine nature of the Son suffered also and over whether the Father suffered along with the Son (patripassionism). It appears, to take the debates simply as an indication of what is problematic theologically, that the doctrine of impassibility makes a rough fit with the biblical doctrine of God and the biblical doctrine of the passion, which proclaims that Christ's suffering is redemptive.

Once again, process theology proposes to take the dichotomy of passible/impassible, imperfect/perfect, and transcend it by understanding

perfection in a different way. For Greek philosophy and the Christian theologians influenced by it, perfection meant an existence separate from the
world of imperfection, unable to be infected by the finitude and fallibility
of the world. But process thought proposes to place God and creatures in
the same realm. Therefore, perfection is the absolute of the same categories
we find exemplified in our own experiences. Everything in our experience
is influenced and affected by other things; in fact, this relational understanding of the world is the very basis of process thought. Nothing happens
without relationship, without one thing affecting another; nothing comes
to be, nothing progresses, no goals are attained, no decisions are made,
without passibility. How is God the perfect exemplar of this relatedness?
God is *omnipassible*—affected by everything.[34] Only God has immediate
and direct relationships with every entity as it comes to be. Only God has
immediate and direct relationships with every eternal object. And due to
this absolute inclusive relatedness, only God can enact God's purpose in
every entity, order every possibility toward that purpose, and order every
actuality according to its contribution toward that purpose. If we see election as the establishment of a relationship, then, only an omnipassible God
can elect. Clark Williamson relates God's perfect sociality to the notion of
the covenant:

> Also, as internally related, bonded, to all others, God is the only one who
> knows all others and who takes all others into account, the one to whom all
> others matters, who bestows upon their fleeting days abiding worth. God is
> the chief exemplification of the metaphysical principles and therefore
> supremely free, primordially self-determining and *causa sui*. God is the rea-
> son for the decisions that God makes. Thus, the metaphors of process
> thought (appealing for the imaginative leap that they require) articulate a
> view of the divine mystery that gives voice to God's covenanting grace on the
> very points that are important: a covenantly God must be personal, social,
> and free, not an "it."[35]

Put this way, it begins to sound as if the doctrine of impassibility should
have prevented Christian theology from explicating election or covenant.
Of course, it has not. However, it has shaped the theological use of the ideas
of election and covenant, pushing them into a primordial predetermination by God, downplaying or eliminating any idea that a *reciprocal* relationship is established, in which the creaturely partner has any effect at all
upon the relationship. Election, in this view, is either the unconditioned
manipulation of creation by the sovereign God, or the divine overcoming
of God's own impassibility, by opening God's self to relationship outside
the divine Trinity. Yet even given this definition, it is difficult for any the-

ologian holding to divine impassibility to say that God's placing of God's self in fellowship with creatures means that creatures affect God; this seems to give creatures power over God that God could not (or should not, given God's character) grant them.

Since process theologians see God's character differently, they also see the relationship that is established in election differently. God is no longer seen as impassible, but omnipassible. Therefore, God is affected by all occasions in the world. For election, this means that the relationship that God initiates through the initial aim is fully reciprocal; God affects the emerging entity, and the entity (as fully actual) in turn affects God. It should be noted that the issue of priority in election is firmly decided in favor of God under the process metaphysical framework. God causes *before* God is caused. This priority is logical as well as temporal. Logically, God's gift of the initial aim is prior to any acts or decisions of the emerging occasion; it sets the conditions under which those acts take place. The concrescence of the occasion does not take place over time, but its satisfaction marks the end of its quantum of existence, and upon its satisfaction it becomes *past*, immutable and unable to be further affected. It is this satisfaction that then affects God, as it affects all the other entities that prehend it. Since this satisfaction is in God's past when it becomes effective in God's consequent nature, the effect of the creature on God always takes place *after* the effect of God on the creature.

One further issue must be mentioned under the heading of process theology's redefinition of impassibility. The dipolar nature of God means that God must always be affected; there must always be some world that God includes in the consequent nature. The conecessity of God and some world (no particular world is necessary) was mentioned in chapter 2 when I discussed process theology's denial of radical divine solitude. If the universe is defined in relational terms, then there can never be only one actual entity. Actual entities are formed by their relationships, so a multiplicity must always exist. The notion of God as essentially social is not the invention of process theology by any means. It has been recognized by theologians from many philosophical and doctrinal standpoints that if the statement "God is love" is taken seriously as a definition of the eternal divine character, then there must always exist some love object for God. Robert W. Jenson, among others, suggests that in the classical doctrine of God, the Trinity fulfills this requirement that God always have another to love.[36] In the Trinity, God contains God's own other, and love flows mutually among the Father, Son, and Holy Spirit. But process theology is heterodox on the subject of the Trinity in most of its expressions. God is either a single eternally concrescent actual entity (Whitehead) or a temporally ordered series of actual entities (Hartshorne). God is not a concurrently existing society of entities. (A consideration of the possible nature of the Trinity in process theology, along with a discussion of the relationship of the triune persons to election, occurs in the next section.) Therefore, God's sociality cannot be satisfied by God's self; God's love requires an object that is not God, namely, a world. Daniel Day Williams writes (in response to Wolfhart Pannenberg):

> Pannenberg is quite right in saying that process thought sees a certain inevitable plurality in being. The reason for this from the process point of view is that if God is love he must have a world to love, to act upon, and respond to. The creatures in that world must have their measure of freedom, creativity, and unique value if they are real things and not just mechanical expressions of a prearranged plan.[37]

Here Williams adds to the positive theological value of omnipassibility by asserting that it guarantees the reality of creatures over against the reality of God, and protects the world from being seen either as merely part of God (monism or pantheism) or as devoid of intrinsic power or value. For election, this means that creaturely reality has consequences. God does elect God's self first, but in electing creatures God is not simply repeating that primordial self-election. God elects real creatures in their own individuality, and accepts the reality of those creatures into God's self—a reality created by the creatures themselves, conditioned by but not determined by any outside agency. Election establishes a reciprocal relationship in which creatures are affected by God and in turn affect God. A creature's effectiveness is its creation of value for itself and for others—ultimately and everlastingly for God, who orders that accomplishment according to God's own unified vision of reality.

Omnipotence and Omniscience

I have chosen to discuss these two attributes together because process theology redefines both of them in terms of one theological problem: divine determinism. Whether the world is determined by God's sovereign power or by God's foreknowledge of contingent events, the classical attributes attest to a worldview in which creaturely freedom is utterly transcended by divinity.[38] Thanks to this predetermination—before history, of all history's contingencies—God is never surprised by what happens; God need not "look and see" what happens, since God either chooses specifically that it happen or knows in advance of its happening. Most important, the freedom we feel as creatures to form our own future is to a greater or lesser extent illusory, since that future is either determined or known in all its detail by God.

The involvement of all actual entities in the overall structure of "creativity" is a well-known tenet of Whitehead's philosophy. It is intended to counter exactly the sort of quantitative apportionment of power and knowledge that is often on display in interpretations of God's omnipotence and omniscience. By involving both God and creatures in the same metaphysical framework, process theologians hope to show that both express the same features of the cosmic process. God may be creative to a much greater *extent* than creatures can be, given God's everlasting lifespan and penetration into all areas of the universe, but creatures are creative in exactly the same way as God, to their finite capacities. So God's omnipotence does not mean that God possesses all power to the exclusion of any creature's possession of power. Instead, it means that whatever power creatures possess is possessed by God in its fullness. More accurate than the language of wielding power in the discussion of omnipotence is the language of expressing creativity by actualizing possibilities. God has access to all possibilities, and provides each concrescent entity with the possibilities relevant to its own time and place. The actual occasion, then, has immediate access to those possibilities that are actualizable in its moment. The creature's power is to actualize its choice of possibilities by ordering itself according to its subjective aim. God's power is to shape the entire world process toward the actualization of certain possibilities, the most highly valued in the divine subjective aim. In every respect, God's ability is the same as the creature's, yet on a cosmic scale: God can aim at the far future as well as the next moment, and God can organize all past actuality into the self-ordering, the unity, of the consequent nature.

Omnipotence is redefined in process theology in two ways. First, the notion of what it means for God to act, or exercise power, is redefined.[39] The greatest conceivable power is not the power of coercion—the ability to forcefully manipulate matter and spirit to achieve the desired result unilaterally. Process theology regards the greatest conceivable power to be the power of *persuasion*—the ability to enlist other free entities in one's cause and obtain their cooperation.[40] Through this power the world, composed of free actual occasions, is moved toward a goal that both creatures and God share. Through this power freedom and creativity is harnessed to produce the greatest possible value—value that would be immeasurably diluted if its production arose from mechanical, forceful, determinative means, because value arises from the *experiences* of creatures that are immortalized in their accomplishments. To Whitehead, this redefinition of power as persuasion rather than force is the key insight of Christianity, which was threatened when the Gospels' message was combined with the more ancient vision of God as an "oriental despot":[41]

> Whitehead's two theses about the significance of Christianity are, first, that Christianity as expressed in the initial testimony of the Gospels understands that the salvation of the world lies in the triumph of persuasion over force; and second, that this insight was lost when Christian dogma degraded its vision of the divine persuasion by combining the concepts derived from Semitic religion of God as omnipotent will with the Unmoved Mover of Aristotle[42] and the Neo-Platonic conception of God as the eminently real, thus producing a conception of God as world ruler which contradicts the ethical sensitivity affirmed by the Gospel itself.[43]

Second, the logic of power is redefined. Coercion, in the sense of determining the actions of an entity, is ruled out by defining the metaphysical system in such a way as to eliminate this possibility. God cannot dictate the free act of a creature not because of any self-limitation, but because such dictation is impossible. Each actual occasion is free in its own self-determination to choose between the available alternatives, however broad or narrow this choice might be, and this freedom is ultimately secure from violation by any other entity, including God. If omnipotence is defined as the ability to do everything that is logically possible, then it is no limitation on omnipotence to say that God cannot do something which is impossible.

Omniscience undergoes the same sort of logical redefinition. God knows all that is possible as possible, and all that is actual as actual. Creatures, on the other hand, know a limited subset of what is possible and a limited subset of what is actual, based on what has been passed down from ancestors and what has been experienced directly. God's knowledge is comprehensive—it expands with the expansion of actuality in the consequent nature, and is eternally infinite in its vision of possibility in the primordial nature. The process concept of temporal movement, however, stipulates that the future is only possible, not yet actual. Therefore, God knows the future only in the form of its possibilities, not in the form of a predetermined actuality. Granted, God knows precisely how great or how small that possibility is—up to the point of certainty for events where the necessary and sufficient conditions for their occurrence have already been fulfilled but the effect has not yet occurred. Nevertheless, no matter how inevitable an event in the future given the powerful causes in the present massing to bring it about, God only knows that event as a possibility until it happens.

Conversely, many events—especially in a world of creatures with high levels of decision-making power and free creative energy—are not foreseeable or inevitable in the simple cause-and-effect, Newtonian way we think of inevitable. Whether a certain possibility will be enacted or remain merely possible depends, in many cases, on the action of a free actual occasion, alone and supremely powerful in the domain of its own concrescence. The process redefinition of omniscience does not impugn God's knowledge; it merely categorizes it in such a way that foreknowledge of the future in determinate detail is impossible. Hence, another barrier to a deterministic world is erected in process metaphysics.

Furthermore, as we have already noted, even under the classical definition of omniscience, God's knowledge of the world implies that the world affects God. Omniscience is in this sense opposed to impassibility in its strictest sense. Unless God absolutely determines everything that happens, so that the impact of the actual world upon God's knowledge adds nothing to the knowledge God primordially possesses about what the actual world will be, omniscience implies that God is changed by the world. At the very least, the notion of a God completely independent of the world is contradicted by omniscience; the knower is dependent upon the thing known. Of course, God's independence from the world is a hypothetical notion in Christianity, since God has chosen to be involved with the world; the hypothetical situation being invoked is that God would still be omniscient even if there had been no creation. The point of the redefinition is that there *is* a world for God to know. Therefore, unless we are to resort to divine determinism, God's knowledge of that world involves a certain logical dependence on the world. Process theology's redefinition of omniscience does not give up any part of the meaning of the term, just as the redefinition of omnipotence maintains both the sense of "all" and the sense of "powerful." The process theologian fervently affirms God's complete knowledge, while making certain assumptions about what is knowable that differ from previous assumptions. The doctrine of omniscience is closer to the core of Perfect Being theology than the doctrine of impassibility. Therefore, process redefines impassibility far more radically, and brings it into harmony with omniscience.

What is the impact of these redefinitions on the doctrine of election? The chief result is the denial of divine determinism and the affirmation of a reciprocal relationship between God and creatures, in which both parties affect and are affected. Divine determinism must be overturned in doctrine before a true concept of creaturely freedom can emerge, and before the notion of the free creature's responsibility can be taken seriously. Although my exposition of process theology's tenets has been selective, it should be clear that one of process theology's aims is the restoration of dignity, responsibility, and power to the creature. Whether this can be done without diminishing God's holiness and worthiness of worship is a topic on which process theology has been criticized.

Election is a key doctrine for this debate. A properly formed doctrine of election correctly places God in the role of initiator and creature in the role of respondent. By doing so, however, it also unifies the two sides into one relationship. The process doctrine of election utilizes the redefinition of God's attributes to show that the relationship is not dictated or controlled solely by the divine participant. However, an overemphasis on this point may leave the impression that God comes to creatures as a supplicant, begging for the favor of their aid, metaphysically prevented from exercising divine power. Framing the relationship in terms of election helps to correct this misapprehension. God's self-election to foster the creativity of creatures and accept their contributions toward the divine aim demonstrates the priority of grace in the election relationship. God's vision of possibilities in the primordial nature, given relevance by the knowledge of the world in the consequent nature, fosters both order and novelty in the emerging creature. Without this foundational act of God, the act of election, the creature could not exist. Because God is the sine qua non of the world process and each individual component of it, the divine partner always takes precedence in election. It is God who first chooses us. But our response is not divorced from or irrelevant to divine election. The creature chooses in response to—perhaps in defiance of—the divine choice. Thanks to God's self-election, creatures with high levels of power to choose and vast realms of alternatives have come to be. Especially for them, election means the opportunity to accept a divine challenge, contribute to the present and coming kingdom of God, and enjoy participating in the victory of the divine will in that moment. God's election does not flow into a void, swallowed up by unchangeable history or unalterable fate. It is election for service—and the creatures elected have the power to serve, along with the inevitable shadow side of that power; the power to rebel. The process doctrine of election constantly reiterates both the gracious initiative of God and the creative response of creatures to provide a full portrait of a properly ordered, reciprocal relationship.

The Trinity in Election

I mentioned in the last section that for theologians concerned to ensure that sociality is part of God's character, the Trinity has historically been the first line of argument. Neatly and logically, the doctrine of the triune God has been suggested as a way out of the dilemma that comes from the juxtaposition of the scriptural definition of God as love and the philosophical definition of God as perfectly complete within God's self, needing no other. A God who consists of three persons is able to love and be loved completely within the Godhead; from this it follows that creation is gratuitous, and that creatures have no independent standing before God, but rather exist in absolute dependence.

It is worth remembering, however, that the doctrine of the Trinity did not originate as a way to get out of the dilemma of a loving yet (hypothetically) solitary God. The doctrine was formulated, slowly and painfully, in the early centuries of Christian theological reflection as a way to do justice in the structures of thought to the witness of the gospel. The claim that Jesus is the Son of God seems to be central to the Christian kerygma, articulated in the Gospels (especially John) and, more fully, in the Pauline writings. How does this square with the radical monotheism that marks the Hebrew Scriptures and sets them apart so definitively from the religious expressions of contemporary cultures? The struggle at Nicaea to define the relationship of Jesus Christ and the one he called Father, and later, at Chalcedon, the relationship of these two to the Holy Spirit of which Acts and Paul's letters constantly speak was certainly a debate in part over God as God is *in se;* this is what the church fathers were explicitly talking about. But the terms of the dialogue were framed by the story of God as God is *pro nobis*; that is, the story of the gospel. The doctrine of the Trinity that resulted from these controversies was not intended to lock God's essential sociality away within God's self and shield God from the necessity to love creatures. Its primary duty—and the primary duty of any theory of the Trinity a theologian articulates—is to faithfully interpret the Christian witness.

The following brief discussion of election and the Trinity is necessarily a preliminary and incomplete proposal. Since I am interested in articulating a doctrine of election rather than constructing a fully formed Trinitarian doctrine, the discussion is intended to be neither comprehensive nor definitive on the latter subject. Those interested in election from the point of view of traditions without a doctrine of the Trinity may skip over this section without losing anything essential to the main argument. But since Barth's doctrine of election, which is my model and standard, actively refers to and makes use of a Trinitarian framework, I provide a brief sketch of what type of Trinitarian thinking the process doctrine of election might entail.

Already it has been emphasized in many different contexts that God is a single actual entity in Whitehead's system.[44] This precludes many visions of the Trinity, including any view that takes "person" to mean "center of consciousness." The separation between the persons of the Trinity in process theology can only be the distinction between different aspects of God's everlasting concrescence.[45] One scheme for distinguishing the Trinity in Whitehead's system is to regard the primordial nature as the Father, the eternal objects as the Son, and the consequent nature as the Spirit. In the following discussion, I will be using this scheme to discuss the particular contribution of each person of the Godhead to election.[46] It should be borne in mind throughout this section of the chapter that any process Trinity should exemplify the dogmatic motto that the works of the Trinity are not divided *ad extra*.[47] That is, all persons of the Trinity are at work in every act of God. My insistence throughout this work that the primordial nature or consequent nature does nothing alone but instead that God, possessor of a dipolar nature, is the agent behind all of God's acts, is the process version of this motto.

Before discussing the contribution of each member of the Trinity to election, a few more comments about the nature of this proposed process Trinity are in order. Although I just made the statement that God is a single actual entity and therefore the Trinity cannot be seen as a society in Whitehead's term, the essential sociality of God is on display in the process Trinity—not as a closed society within the Godhead, but in the fact that each person involves a specific relationship to an other or others. The primordial nature (Father) is defined by its relationship of order and purpose to the unity of the eternal objects (Son). The unity of the eternal objects, likewise, is defined by its relationship to the primordial nature (Father), which makes it effective in the world. And the consequent nature (Spirit) is defined by its relationship to the primordial nature, which gives it order; the eternal objects, toward which the consequent nature is ordered as its future; and the world of actual occasions, which is included and ordered toward God's aim. The primordial nature and the eternal objects flow into each other, and the consequent nature opens to the world, to give the former relevance and to accept the world into God's self. It is beyond the scope of this study to give a detailed defense or description of this proposal.[48] The following discussion will, however, demonstrate how this vision of the Trinity can be used to elaborate God's action in election.

The Father: God's Primordial Nature

The role of the Father in the Trinity is to represent the source of all things, the fount of divinity, the "ultimate determining source of cause," as Norman Pittenger puts it.[49] The Father is the aspect of God that is the eternal and endless resource for God and the world. As the origin of God's unchanging purpose for God's self and the world of creatures, the Father is immutable. But these attributes of eternality and immutability do not make the Father into a symbol of what cannot be known about God, or how God differs from creatures. God's dipolar nature is the same as that of creatures: a mental pole (God's primordial nature, from which the concrescence begins) and a physical pole (God's consequent nature). Creatures also have an immutable aspect of their natures, but for them it is the physical pole, the data from the past that impinge upon the present concrescence. For creatures, the mental pole is formed out of that data and is the novel, original legacy left for future generations.

The terms used to describe the Father—primordial, eternal, immutable—have a connotation of depth and mystery. It is easy to form the impression that when we speak of the Father we are speaking of the God behind Christ, the God on whose face human beings cannot gaze, the God who spoke to Job out of the whirlwind: "Shall a faultfinder contend with the Almighty? Anyone who argues with God must respond" (Job 40:2). In short, classical theology tends to see the Father as the *deus absconditus,* the God whose ways are hidden from us but justified by God's divinity and absolute sovereignty. Even though the hidden God is, properly, the Trinity *ad intra* as opposed to the revelation *ad extra,* there is a tendency to appropriate what is inscrutable in God to the Father as the divine person not directly involved with creatures, unlike Christ and the Holy Spirit. Here is where we are asked to cease questioning. The process conception of the Father does greater justice to the proper intention of classical theology by consistently opposing this notion of a division between God's revelation of God's self in Christ and God's true self, as should be evident from the fact that the process Trinity speaks of one entity rather than three. There is no room for duplicity in this one God; what the primordial nature purposes, thus are the eternal objects ordered, and thus is the consequent nature brought about. The one entity God is being described, and this God is not of two minds.

Pierre Maury writes:

> Often, moved by the adoration of the divine majesty, the great predestinarian doctors—especially Calvin—have exalted the mystery of the *absolute decree.* But why have they turned it into a mystery as impenetrable as night, the secret of an opaque God? God does not live and act in the obscurity of eternal darkness, but in light—"unapproachable," yes, but light! Darkness

and night are, in the Bible, the abode of the Devil, in which he plans and
prepares his "works of darkness." If there is any tyrannical power that would
victimize man, it is he, not the Father, "who hath delivered us from the power
of darkness" (Col. 1:13), and "hath called [us] out of darkness into his mar-
vellous light" (1 Pet. 2:9).[50]

This is the spirit of the process doctrine of the Father, whose eternal purpose is not hidden from us but evident in the direction of history and the
joy and desire of God's creatures. The emphasis is not on the sovereignty
of God, where divinity is revealed in God's immunity from our questions
and standards, but on the love of God, where divinity is revealed as God's
doing what God has eternally purposed to do—namely, guide the world
into ever greater experiences of enjoyment.

Maury's metaphor of darkness and light clearly has an epistemological
connotation; God does not hinder or block our knowledge of God. But it
also applies to God's actions. Since God works out God's purpose through
persuasion directed at the free acts of creatures, and since that purpose is
unchanging in its drive toward increasing value, the kingdom of God is not
a mysterious end of history but a constantly emerging presence in the
world. The goal is always in sight, present to every creature through the initial aim. God does not work in secret, but in the light. The Father, the primordial nature, embodies that goal toward which all creation is ordered:
"God is that function in the world by reason of which our purposes are
directed to ends which in our own consciousness are impartial as to our
own interests" (RM 158). The Father loves us by giving us direction, in
order that we may make the most out of our lives for others and for ourselves. This goal, evident in every occasion in the world, is the purely giving love of the Father, expressed and made effective in the election of
creatures.

The Son: The Eternal Forms

The eternal forms are a part of God in their unity and order, given by the
Father. In this way process theology can truly say that the Son is begotten
of the Father. It is natural for process theologians to identify the eternal
forms, in their God-given order and unity, with the Son because of the
long-standing Johannine identification of Christ with the Word, the *logos*.
The Son is the order that enables creativity to express itself. The Son is the
unity of the infinite realm of possibility that enables the embodiment of
the Father's eternal purpose in creatures and hence enables the actualization of progress toward the kingdom of God.

When we speak of the Son, we must speak of the incarnation. The Son is our pathway to the complete knowledge of God, since it is through Christ that God has revealed God's self. A complete process Christology is, once again, beyond the scope of this study.[51] However, this is the place to indicate the role of the Son in election, which is revealed in Christ. Calvin, following Augustine, called Christ "the clearest mirror of free election that we who are among the members may not be troubled about it," indicating that God's election of Christ is the paradigm case for divine election of creatures. The first didactic point to be drawn from Christ's election by Calvin is "that he was not made Son of God by righteous living but was freely given such honor so that he might afterward share his gifts with others."[52] Certainly this is a lesson from which process thinkers can learn. Election is not given to creatures with regard to what they have accomplished, but with regard to what they have the opportunity to accomplish. Christ's election was for service: to reveal God to the world through his life, teaching, death, and rebirth. Jesus Christ reveals God to creatures by bringing pure possibility—the Father's perfect plan—to life as a real human being. The Son, the ordered realm of eternal objects, embodies God's choice of an ultimate goal for the world. Through the Holy Spirit, these perfect possibilities became actual in the man Jesus. And in Christ, we see exactly what God chooses for human life, we see precisely God's values, and we see the perfect obedience of a creature to his election.

It is relatively easy for process theology to articulate an "exemplar Christology," with Christ as the perfect model for us to follow. But this is only one facet of the Christian witness. To be faithful to the gospel and to be faithful to the full power of the doctrine of election, process theology must be able to speak of our election "in" and "through" Christ. In other words, the power of Christ is not merely a paradigm in the past to be accessed by those lucky enough to be told the story, but a force that can reach across time and space to gather together all creatures. Paul writes to the Ephesians:

> Blessed be the God and Father of our Lord Jesus Christ, who has blessed us in Christ with every spiritual blessing in the heavenly places, just as *he chose us in Christ* before the foundation of the world to be holy and blameless before him in love. He destined us for adoption as his children *through Jesus Christ,* according to the good pleasure of his will, to the praise of his glorious grace that he freely bestowed on us in the Beloved. . . . He has made known to us the mystery of his will, according to his good pleasure that he set forth in Christ, as a plan for the fullness of time, to gather up all things in him, things in heaven and things on earth. In Christ we have also obtained an inheritance, having been destined according to the purpose of him who accomplishes all things according to his counsel and will, so that we, who

were the first to set our hope on Christ, might live for the praise of his glory.
(Eph. 1:3–6, 9–12)

This remarkable passage explicates election (1) as an act of the Father
through the Son, (2) which reveals to us God's plan, (3) so that we might
live holy lives for God's glory. Here is revelation of purpose, grace for living, and election for service united in the figure of Christ. The Son, understood as the unity of eternal objects in God's vision, is the primary divine
location of election ("*in* Christ") because the Son is the medium in whom
God elects God's self. God constitutes God's self to be for creatures by
ordering the eternal objects in order to value creaturely contributions. Jesus
Christ, the incarnate Son, becomes the primary creaturely location of election because he responds to God's presentation of possibilities perfectly,
with the full power to actualize God's plan for that crucial historical
moment. The primacy of Christ in election in the divine nature is the eternal selection of possibilities to be actualized; the primacy of Christ in election in the human nature is the actualization of those possibilities. Indeed,
God (the Father) chooses that set of possibilities not as a wish for a potential state, but *so that it might become incarnate* (actualized). Hence, there is
an eternal aspect to the incarnate Son, at least in the sense that God's
unchanging plan in God's self-election was that the Son should become a
creature.

This brief description of how we may speak of our election "in Christ"
must be complemented by an explanation of election "*through* Christ."
The Ephesians passage uses the phrase to indicate the adoption of creatures into the divine family: We are made children of God through Christ.
More generally, the preposition "through" indicates that some act or quality of Christ has enabled our election and that in our election we partake
of Christ's power. Possibilities qua possibilities are only effective as final
causes; this is the power of the initial aim given to each creature in election. Therefore, the ordered set of eternal objects that is the offspring of
the Father in the process Trinity has the power of a lure given to each creature. But the incarnate Christ is that set of possibilities made actual, and
an actuality has the effectiveness of an efficient cause. By coming into contact with the Christian kerygma, which mediates the efficient power of
Christ by presenting the story of Jesus and the Christian interpretation of
that story, the incarnate Christ becomes our ancestor, an efficient cause
upon our own becoming. For creatures without the opportunity or capacity for knowledge of Christ, the Christ event still functions as an efficient
cause because the incarnation of God's plan in purity and perfection has

changed the world irrevocably. Not only did Christ demonstrate that the possibility of complete obedience and world-changing creativity was viable for us, but he also made viable a set of possibilities that required for their actualization this singular historic event. Every creature that comes to be in the world made possible by the incarnate Son has been touched by Christ's power. Each election to service is made possible by the service of the elected Son, both in the immanent Trinity as the locus of God's self-election, and in the economic Trinity as the God-man.

Christ's role in election is bound up with his function as the complete revelation of God. Clark Williamson writes:

> Process theology has to affirm two things: first, the mode of God's action upon the world is always the same. The way God acts in Christ is disclosive of how God acts everywhere and anywhere. This follows from the strictly universal character of God's agency. Second, God's particular grace for special occasions, the initial aims around which each actual entity arises, is always in higher-grade occasions at the kind of possibility that will enhance both the occasion's ability to be sensitive to its environment, to be more adequately related to, and aware of, those around, and to overcome exclusivism and dichotomies in its experience.[53]

This passage acknowledges that process theology, if it is to be Christian theology, must take Christ to be the revelation of how God acts (for our purposes, in the act of election). Williamson's second point, however, can also be expressed in terms of Christ. Our election to the highest value of experience for ourselves and for others, that "particular grace for special occasions," is not outside of Christ or beside Christ or beyond Christ. It is in and through Christ, whose actualization of the highest possibilities for himself has made possible that election, that these particular aims are given to us in election. It is in and through Christ, who as God aims at God's own satisfaction and yet as God and human aims at our concurrent enjoyment and cooperation, that we are elected to participate in the kingdom of God, which is coming (acting as our aim and final cause) and is already here (in Christ's perfect embodiment of it). Yes, Christ reveals to us the Son, true God, the ordered eternal objects, and through them the Father who gives them order, but revelation is not the sole function of the incarnate Son. Not only our knowledge but all the conditions under which we come to be are affected by Christ's power.

The Son is also our judge. It is God's vision of the perfect possibility for us against which we are measured. Pierre Maury asks how God's choice in election is compatible with the Christian message of the God of love:

> We seek to know if it is compatible with God's being God that he should
> choose between his creatures, and thus that he should have favorites at the
> expense of others to whom he does not give preferential treatment. And we
> find ourselves in yet another classic impasse: God is not just if he does not
> treat everyone in the same way, if he does not respect the rights of man, which
> are the same for all; or in other words: what is the signification of rejection,
> of damnation, in the doctrine of a God of love?[54]

This is the question that has dogged the Reformed doctrine of election
since Calvin. That one should be chosen and another rejected without any
grounds but God's good pleasure is difficult to see as good news, despite
Calvin's insistence that in the doctrine of election is found our greatest
comfort.[55] The process doctrine of election is not founded on God's sovereignty or on God's ability to do as God pleases. It is founded on God's love,
that God who did not have to choose us, did choose us. The category of
judgment, which is part of any scripturally based Christology, is not a negation of universal election. It is a warning that rejection comes even to those
who are elect if the elect do not fulfill their service. All creatures are judged
by Christ, the incarnation of God's plan. Once our becoming has ended,
our accomplishment is set up against the standard Christ embodies. Our
failure to meet that standard does not negate our election, but it does mean
that we have not done all we could to bring the kingdom into being. Our
place in God's everlasting consequent nature is determined by what we have
done; it is judgment tempered by the mercy of God's including us and making the best of what we have done. To answer Maury's question from the
perspective of a process doctrine of election predicated on Christ's judgment, then, the significance of rejection in the doctrine of a God of love is
that our deeds matter to God and to our fellow creatures. But love transforms even our most rebellious deeds into a part of God's plan. We are
called to imitate Christ, but if we cannot become perfectly obedient as
Christ was, that does not mean our efforts to follow Christ were all in vain.
Thanks to our election, primordially in God's eternal decision to be for
creatures, historically in the actualization of forms given in the initial aim,
and consequentially in God's acceptance and ordering of the world's actualities, judgment, real as it is, is swallowed up in love.

The Holy Spirit: The Consequent Nature

Because process theology postulates a necessary relationship between God
and some world, its doctrine of the Trinity must include not only an immanent Trinity but an economic Trinity as well. Under a theology that con-

siders creation unnecessary, the economic Trinity is a contingent feature of God. But process theology balances its picture of God *pro se* with an equally essential picture of God *pro nobis*. Some economic Trinity must be a part of any conceivable process Trinitarianism, although God's relations with the world need not have been the same as they, in fact, are.

Thus far, in speaking of the Father and Son, I have been describing primarily God's relationship with God's self. The primordial nature of God consists of God's ordering of the eternal objects, and the realm of eternal objects so ordered is what I have equated with the second person of the Trinity. These two aspects of divinity are each defined in terms of the other, just as the Father is defined by generation of the Son, and the Son is defined by having been generated by the Father. Even here, of course, process theology sees God defined by God's decision to be related to a complex world of creatures. It is this self-election that determines both the subjective aim God holds in the primordial nature and the selective valuation of the eternal objects that leads to their unity. Hence, even the two persons of the Trinity whose relationship is primarily defined in terms of each other are also open to the world.

However, the third person of the Trinity is primarily defined by God's acceptance of the world, enabling of its progress, and transformation of its failures into God's victory. In the process Trinity proposed here, the Holy Spirit is identified with the process concept of God's consequent nature. The consequent nature is God's receptivity toward the world, involvement in the world process, and continual assurance of order in the world through mediation between its historical, contingent actualities and God's eternal purpose.[56] Without this explicit connection between God and the world, it would be impossible to say that God acts toward the world, since it is from the consequent nature that the relevance of each initial aim given to creatures is determined. Because the Spirit moves in the world, however, God's love extends specifically to every creature in its individuality and particularity. Every actual occasion is taken up into the consequent nature to be ordered according to God's valuation and unified into the whole of history.

The Spirit's work in election, if we are asked to analyze its contribution in abstraction from the one electing act of God, is twofold. First, the consequent nature is included in the emerging occasion's prehension of God. This means that God's ordering of the world *in anticipation* of the concrescent occasion's contribution toward the plan of history is part of the gift of election to that occasion. The creature's assurance of election even before performing its own service comes from the fact that all previous actualities have been valued *toward* the possibilities of the one moment this particular creature represents. Second, after the creature has reached its satisfaction and has accepted or rejected the aim offered it in election, it is taken up into the consequent nature in the fulfillment of its election. The promise of a place in God's kingdom, which the original feeling of the consequent nature promised, is fulfilled. Once again, as I have emphasized in the previous discussion of judgment, all places in God's kingdom are not equal. There is a value placed on what the creature has accomplished, and this value may be vanishingly small if God's judgment is harsh. But thanks to the inclusive love the Spirit spreads abroad, no one is left out. On the consequent nature's role in election, Williamson writes:

> As such, God offers us the past with our perspective on it, our freedom and agency, the possibility of efficacy upon the future, and the promise that we count with God who everlastingly presides over the world with a tender care that nothing be lost. This God is the same one with whom all others also count and is the God of a quite singular promise and demand: the promise is that our life is grounded in God's free and gracious action toward us and that its final meaning is found in and only in God's consequent love of us; the demand is that, because God also loves all others, so must we exercise love and justice (justice being the social form of love) toward them.[57]

The Holy Spirit is the mediator of God's "promise that we count with God." It is the consequent nature that provides evidence that all creatures count with God, and provides the structure of history that ensures that our lives will contribute to the ongoing progress of the world. The promise and demand of which Williamson speaks both come to us through the Holy Spirit, whose presence in and with the world is the sign and guarantor of God's grace in the divine decision to be God for us, and whose orientation toward the future and preservation of the past informs us of the values toward which God lures us. The Holy Spirit enables our positive response to God by providing the conditions under which that response is effective in God and in the world.

Daniel Day Williams's analysis of how the consequent nature acts includes this statement: "The feelings which enter into the constitution of our being are transformed through awareness of their reception in the consequent nature of God."[58] Whitehead's version of this statement reads: "The power of God is the worship he inspires" (SMW 276). In other words, since it matters to God what we make of ourselves, it therefore matters to us. Without the consequent nature of God to give our lives that meaning, it would be impossible for us to manufacture meaning for ourselves. One aspect of that meaning is the fact that in the consequent nature, our experiences are everlastingly preserved as an integrated part of the entire world process. Not only are we remembered in all our individuality, but we are also included in the structure of God's kingdom. What we do matters to God in the immediacy of our experience and in the ongoing ramifications of our actuality. It is our awareness of this gracious inclusion—our sense of the presence of the Spirit—that is the evidence of God's power in our lives. Whitehead's statement about worship applies to every member of the Trinity and to God as a whole: Our worship is inspired by God's self-determination in the primordial nature, by God's ordering of the eternal objects (which provides our model and value system), and by God's inclusion of the world and ordering of its actualities toward the divine aim in the consequent nature. All three aspects of divinity, Father, Son, and Holy Spirit, are expressions of grace toward us. This grace inspires our response.

The Response of the Creature

In the previous section, I discussed at some length the electing act of God. At various points in that discussion, I emphasized that God's act is never without a response from the act's object, the creature as it emerges in its private process of becoming. Now we come to consider that response. Before I begin, I will reiterate two points that should be kept in mind throughout. First, although process theology affirms the freedom and autonomy of the creature in its response, the creature's act is still a *response*—it depends upon the initial act of election that can only come from God. Therefore, God's electing act always retains its priority. Second, and related to the first point, the creature's response cannot be effective in creating progress unless it is received into God and transformed in the consequent nature. Through the prehension by a new generation of entities of the consequent nature, the "stubborn fact" of that response is given context and is made part of the divine plan. Therefore, God's electing act always is necessary to complete the creature's response.

The analysis of the creature's response to election has been less prominent than the consideration of God's act in the history of Reformed theology. Although election is the foundational doctrine for the meeting of God and creatures, its theological expression has focused almost exclusively on the divine act. This is understandable in light of the development of the doctrine, from Augustine through Calvin and Barth, toward a celebration of God's sovereign prerogative to elect whomever God chooses. In such a context, there is no point to a theological description of the response of the elected one, because that response has no effect. It is irrelevant to an analysis of election's outcome.

Alongside this line of election theology, there has developed an intermittent theological tradition that takes seriously the response of the elected creature—either as an effective component in the overall picture of election, or as an important outcome of God's act. This line of thought begins as a response to Calvinism in the work of James Arminius and John Wesley, and continues as an implicit criticism of Reformed thought from within in the work of Schleiermacher. The former were adamant in their insistence that a human being is elected because of faith, or at the very least in foreknowledge of faith; in other words, something is required of the elected one. Election is not an arbitrary exercise of grace but a partnership between God and human beings. Schleiermacher believed that election has certain observable consequences in the elected one, namely, that a Christian consciousness would begin to grow in him. On this basis, Schleiermacher's explication of election is that God elects a person to be sanctified, a process that is not indifferent as to the conditions of that person's earthly life and the progress made toward holiness during life. Karl Barth's uncompromising emphasis on God's sovereignty in election is matched by his serious consideration of the consequences of election upon human beings. In his lengthy and detailed discussion of election in the lives of biblical figures, in both Old and New Testaments, Barth demonstrates a concern with the existential experience of election while insisting on God's absolute priority and freedom in God's act toward human beings.

Process theology has more in common with the theological tradition that believes the response of the creature has a place in the doctrine than with the stricter Calvinist tradition whose main concern was the battle against Pelagianism. However, it is misleading to assume that the process doctrine of election will be a simple Arminian doctrine, based upon process theology's insistence on the free will and decision-making power of creatures. While the anthropology that informs Arminianism and Wesleyanism is clearly sympathetic to process theology's metaphysical assumptions, the implicit universalism of Barth, which proclaims that God's electing power can transform human rebellion as well as human obedience into the service of God's plan, is closer to the spirit of the process doctrine of election. The creature's response is effective in the ongoing creation of the future, and it is likewise effective in the everlasting concrescence of God's consequent nature. But it is God's power to accept and order that response as part of the divine plan that culminates and closes the process doctrine of election.

The creature's response to God's initiative is not the last word; instead, God is the alpha and omega of election. It should be kept in mind during the following discussion of the role of the creature in election that God's redemption frames every creaturely act.

The Common Relationship of All Creatures with God

The primary task of the theologian in formulating a doctrine of election is to describe the relationship between the elector and the elected. This task involves a metaphysical description of the two sides of the relationship and an analysis of the establishment of relations between them. Since relationship is at the heart of process thought, the description of the relation between all creatures and God involves basic process concepts and categories. In chapter 2, I discussed these concepts extensively in describing the metaphysical mechanisms of relation in process thought; specifically, I discussed how process treats the relation of God and creature as a special case of relationship, which nevertheless exemplifies the general properties of all relations. Many doctrines of election that are based on the assumption of an absolute and qualitative difference between divine reality and creaturely reality must treat the divine-creature relationship as sui generis, unlike any other relationship found in the world. The process doctrine of election handles a description of the special aspects of the divine-creature relationship without having to construct unique metaphysical categories to cover this case or postulate a miraculous divine transcendence of general metaphysical limits.

All creatures share the property of being related to God. This is true in any theology that has God as creator, and creatures, therefore, as dependent upon the relationship of creator to those created. In the last chapter, I noted that process theology does not accept the orthodox doctrine of *creatio ex nihilo,* in which the relationship between a set of creatures and God is contingent because God need not have created. God's sociality, which nature God shares with every actual entity, requires that God always coexist with *some* world. However, the relationship between any particular creature and God is contingent, because no particular creature is necessary as God is necessary. Thus, the graciousness of God's creation, redemption, and sanctification of this world is maintained in process theology. Every actual occasion is, before its concrescence begins, a potential occasion that might or might not be actualized. Therefore, in speaking of the relationship between God and individual creatures, the dependent relationship between creator and creature holds true.

As I explained in chapter 2, dogmatically speaking, the doctrine of creation can be considered an outgrowth or consequence of the doctrine of election. God's primordial choice to favor creatures with the dignity of becoming cocreators of value logically precedes all other divine acts toward creatures, including their creation. Logically prior to any creature's becoming, God determined God's self to a course of fostering and nurturing creatures. Thus, all creatures are elected potentially in God's self-election. But the doctrine of election does not only treat God's election of creatures as a general class, as if a generic relationship that applies to all creatures is the only relationship between divine and creaturely reality. The Christian witness acknowledges both the election of specific groups (the children of Abraham) and the election of individuals (prophets, disciples). The process doctrine of election, then, cannot be content with establishing that some relationship always obtains between God and creatures. It must describe and account for the particular, unique relationships that occur between God and particular, unique individuals.

Clark Williamson argues that process thought's fundamental reliance on relationships as a way of explaining experiences makes it the best system in which to formulate a doctrine of election:

> The question whether process thought can adequately articulate the covenantly reality seems to be stood on its head: Can any other position articulate the covenant adequately? No other theology speaks coherently of the all-encompassing divine mystery as "the" person in the strict sense of the term, nor works out a comprehensive theory of internal and external relations of which God is the eminent or perfect case. That is, God is externally related to all other individuals as their creator, the one by knowing whom all the others are enabled to come into being, graciously empowered to become and, at the same time, commanded to attain and contribute, the highest relevant possibility available to them. God is the one person known by all others, to which knowledge their very being attests (although it is quite clear that they/we do not all or always know God *as* God).[59]

This passage argues that process theology articulates election better than theologies based on other philosophical systems because process theology has a relational doctrine of God. We have already seen that the electing God in process theology is not aloof from the types of relations that characterize human experience, but instead is the perfect exemplification of those relations. What Williamson's argument does not cover, and which I would like to add to his observation, is that process theology also best articulates the vector of relationship that runs from the creature to God.

Relationship is not a state that must be chosen by both parties. If one party pursues a relationship and the other turns away, the two are still related by conflict and antagonism. Similarly, when God initiates a relationship and the creature rejects God's vision of what the relationship will become, there is still a relationship—a tragic relationship of rebellion to be sure, but nonetheless, God and the creature are related to each other, and nothing the creature can do will break the relationship. Process theology explains this irrevocability of relationship with the concept of physical prehensions. The emerging occasion does not have a choice whether or not it will be related to the occasions in its past, just as it does not have complete power over what occasions will be related to it in the future. The occasions of the past are the facts that unavoidably condition the present, and the occasions of the future are mere potentials, which may or may not come to be. The choice of the emerging occasion comes not in its decision to be related or not to be related, but in choosing *how* to be related. Whitehead insists that the stamp of individuality and free decision is found in the concrescent occasion's subjective mode of feeling. Some kind of relationship is inevitable, but what kind of relationship it will be is up to the decision of the entity. This decision will be discussed in more detail in the section on freedom. My point here is that process theology does not restrict to the divine initiative the creation of relationship. The individuals elected retain their freedom to choose what type of relationship results from the election, while God's establishment of the election relationship remains effective, and before the choice of the individual is redeemed in the consequent nature. All creatures are related to God by election, but every creature's response conditions that election relationship in a unique way. Because process theology describes how the particular creature expresses its particularity within the relationship, it is best equipped to express the free response of creatures to the electing act of God.

The Gift of Vocation

The initial aim that the emerging occasion receives from God is a proposed life-direction, a vocation the creature may accept or reject. Regardless of its decision, the vocation offered to the creature provides a context for the creature's life; it becomes the opportunity for the creature to define itself in reaction to or in acceptance of God's will. If God's aim for the creature is accepted, then the accomplishment of the creature in fulfillment of its given vocation finds an immediate place in the complex forward motion of the divine drive toward value. Its achievement can be built upon by its close-following successors, whose own initial aims will be tailored by God to take advantage of the progress in the last generation. If, on the other hand, the creature rejects God's optimum aim for its life in favor of a lesser good, or even for outright rebellion, then it may be many generations before God's inexorable persuasive power can turn that actuality into a positive contribution to the world process.[60] In the first case, the context given to the creature's act by the initial aim becomes, with relative simplicity, the context of the completed actuality in God's consequent nature. In the second case, what originally was a negative response to the initial aim can become, through the ordering of actuality in the consequent nature toward God's ultimate aim for God's self and the world, a positive contribution. The creature's response is recontextualized through God's redemptive inclusion of its act in God's self.

Does this mean that the original act of election, the gift of vocation in the initial aim, is irrelevant? Not at all. The initial aim functions in three ways when considered in abstraction from election's fulfillment in the consequent nature. First, it provides definiteness or concreteness to the emerging creature by placing it in a specific time and place with respect to its past and future. The ordered schemata given in the initial aim allow the physical data and the realm of viable possibilities to be aligned, so that a specific character for this creature can emerge. That this order is not imposed by God but chosen by the creature from possibilities provided by God does not lessen the necessity to have a specific order, provided by a specific agency, in order to create actualities. Second, the initial aim gives notice to the creature that it does not exist only for itself. It serves as a promise and a warning that what the creature does has meaning for other creatures and for God. In short, the initial aim reveals the inevitability of judgment, along with the standards by which that judgment will be conducted. Finally, God's initial gift of vocation provides direction both for the individual creature and for the world process as a whole. In it the potential good of the individual and the goodness of God, both immanent and economic, are reconciled *prior* to the individual's free response of actualization.

"Vocation" is an apt term for the invitation extended in election because it connotes a life direction that may be unknown to the individual until she "discovers" it. The image produced by the word is that of a hidden but always present aptitude, a calling that comes to conscious light only gradually, but that even as an unconscious predilection shapes the course of our lives. When a creature receives a purpose from God, and modifies it to suit the creature's own wishes, there need be no conscious awareness of the reception or the modification. I do not make this observation simply to allow the process doctrine of election to be extended to creatures that lack self-consciousness. Our experience as human agents informs us that many creatures with the capacity for self-consciousness never consciously formulate or embrace a specific purpose for their lives. At best, human beings often entertain only partial, half-formed, temporary, and contradictory notions of purpose in their conscious minds and wills. Nevertheless, they live toward certain unspoken, assumed goals that guide their subsequent decisions and actions. Purpose is a universal feature of existence, process thought holds; the conscious understanding and pursuit of a goal is the most concentrated experience of purpose, but not the sole experience. However, as human beings, we have the capacity to hold our goals in our conscious minds and wills, and this allows a higher degree of enjoyment in the pursuit of that goal. If we do not exploit our ability to hold conscious purposes, then we are falling short of true humanity and failing in our quest to create aesthetic value through our private experiences.

Similarly, the contact with God that produces the creature's response to the divine gift of vocation need not be recognized as such, yet it remains nonetheless an authentic relationship with divinity. Norman Pittenger writes:

> If people *say* that they have no rationally experienced sense of God's presence or activity, then it is thought that God cannot be at work in their life. But surely response to the divine initiative is possible at most diverse levels and through most various dimensions of existence. It is not necessary that we be vividly *aware* of what is going on.[61]

It is necessary for any doctrine of God's providence that God be able to be at work in those who do not recognize the work as God's work. It is necessary for any doctrine of election that is serious about God's freedom to choose based on God's self-determination, that God be able to choose those who do not know they have been chosen—even those who do not wish to be chosen. Where Calvin sees God's electing freedom in God's ability to choose those who do not believe and reject those who do believe, ensuring that God remains unconditioned by any creaturely reality, the process doctrine of election sees God's electing freedom in God's ability to use ignorance and rebellion as well as open acceptance and obedience in the construction of God's kingdom. The difference is subtle, but it turns on the concept of vocation and purpose. Calvin sees election as a *state:* one is either elect or reprobate, and this ontological status is unchanging since it has its basis in God's eternal will. Process theology sees election as a *call to service:* the call goes out and is received, but the response of the elected creature to serve or not to serve alters the election relationship.

In other words, the vocational aspect of the process doctrine of election tends to slant the explication of election forward—toward the future, and what the creature's accomplishment and God's persuasive power might bring about there. In Calvin's doctrine of election, the emphasis is on a pretemporal decision of God that determines each human being's fate. The future aspect of election is otherworldly blessedness or eternal punishment, toward which ends we are all destined because of God's primordial decision. All of the "action," so to speak, however, takes place in God's eternal and unknowable counsels, outside the scope of history. The process doctrine of election shifts this focus so that the action takes place in the present and becomes evident and meaningful in its impact on the future. Each divine act of election toward an individual looks forward to an anticipated state of affairs in the future, should that individual fulfill the vocation that election gives to him.[62] The electing act also has a "backward" reference, of course, toward God's primordial act of self-determination in which God constituted God's self to be *pro nobis,* and on which each divine act of individual election is predicated. But the emphasis on the historical future of the world, which, through its inclusion in the consequent nature, is the ongoing concrescence of God, is a salient characteristic of the process doctrine of election. Through the concept of vocation, it becomes clear that God directs history because the outcome of history matters to God, not as something predetermined and merely played out on a stage, but as the only—and therefore the crucial—theater in which God's own aims can be fulfilled.

Through the gift of vocation to each individual, the individual creature becomes related to God and at the same time becomes caught up in purposes greater than the creature's finite horizons admit on their own. Each recipient of the divine vocational call is thereby connected to the rest of history, in which the creature's own purpose is enmeshed as a vital cog in gigantic machinery. The unity of that history is found in God's universal purpose, given to each participant through the initial aim, and reinforced in the inclusion of each participant in the consequent nature. Without this one referent for history's purpose—the divine aim embodied in the primordial nature that orders the world's actualities—there can be no rationale for speaking of historical progress, or of a unified history at all for that matter. Some actual entity must be responsible for that unity, according to process thought, and that actual entity is God. Through God's coordination of creaturely vocations with the divine aim, there is a unity of purpose in the world, which allows creatures to extend themselves beyond narrow self-interest. We are not alone in our election; the vocational call experienced by a single individual is included in the call to societies, communities, and lineages. Pannenberg explains that election for service unifies the history of the world in terms of the history of a chosen people:

> The most fundamental category, however, in a theological description of history within the context of the Jewish-Christian tradition is the category of *election* as referring to the definitive intention in the corporate experience of the vocation of a people. The singularity of the elective act implied in that definitive intention precedes and underlies all the subsequent history of God's grace turned upon the people he chose once for himself. Thus the act of election constitutes the unity of that history since it provides a continuous direction to the course of events. All the particular promises or admonitions arising subsequently from particular situations have their place within that history which was constituted by the act of election.[63]

The service we are elected to perform is service to the past, because we are called to build upon the accomplishments of those who have gone before us, to whom we have a responsibility, and with whom we are called to keep faith. It is service to the present, which means service to ourselves, because our decision to constitute ourselves according to God's will defines the present moment as an occasion in and for God, and because as God's creatures coming to be through divine grace, we are called to enjoy our own experiences to the fullest. Most important, however, the service we are elected to perform is service to the future.[64] We are called to leave a legacy that will steer others toward productive lives in response to God's election. This service to the future is the most remarkable aspect of election because it steers our interests to those we will never know, those who can give nothing back to us. Here election calls us to disinterested love as an ideal not incompatible with our own interests, and enables us to continue serving God and the ongoing world process long after our momentary subjective experience has ceased to be.

Transformation of Initial Aim into Subjective Aim

Thus far I have described some theological ramifications of the process doctrine of election in terms of the creature's initial receipt of the divine call. With the consideration in this section of the creature's transformation of that call into its own subjective aim, the description of the creature's response per se—its free act—begins in earnest. Free will is a topic that has often been paired with predestination and election as their opposite, or at best as a concept that on its face is opposed to these doctrines of God's will and action and that must be reconciled to them. Process theology begins with the assumption that God and creatures are alike in their freedom of decision, which is the intrinsic ability shared by all actual entities to determine themselves in the privacy of their own concrescence. The exercise of free will admits of a range, with God having infinite latitude for decision among all possibilities but creatures having finite boundaries placed on their decision by conditions, which restrict what possibilities may be actualized to a greater or lesser degree depending on the type of occasion in question.

Does the process concept of God as principle of concretion and giver of the initial aim conflict with the process doctrine that every actual occasion has the freedom to determine itself? Robert C. Neville, in his criticism of process thought, believes that the two notions are contradictory:

> First, Whitehead and [Lewis] Ford must acknowledge God to be an external limit on human freedom in the same sense that other external things limit freedom. All objective things limit freedom in that they are given as initial data required to be harmonized in the prehending occasion's concrescence. God's datum is so important as to determine the initial state of the subjective aim. Whereas finite occasions determine themselves, God is rather like a smother-mother, structuring all possibilities and continually insisting on values of her own arbitrary choice. Considering creatures' immortality in God's life, in the long run there is a metaphysical guarantee that people cannot damn themselves, and the possibility of self-damnation seems to me a touchstone of freedom.[65]

This argument accuses process theology of perpetuating the traditional structure of predestination overriding a creature's free will, an ironic criticism considering that one of the reasons for the construction of the process system of metaphysics is to eliminate this conflict by metaphysically limiting God's power and guaranteeing creaturely freedom.[66] I will answer what I understand to be Neville's main contention. First, he is correct in saying that God is a conditioning factor on the exercise of an occasion's freedom in the same way as any actual occasions in the past prehended by the emerging occasion condition and limit the possibilities for its self-determination. He is also correct in stating that the prehension of God is a crucial factor in the concrescence since it determines the initial state of the creature's aim. However, this does not make God a "smother-mother" who leaves little or nothing up to the creature's own decision. The value system communicated in the initial aim is not imposed upon the creature; it is simply a fact of the universe that God has a definite value system of God's (gracious rather than arbitrary) choice, which creatures may or may not share. The initial aim that God provides contains graded alternatives awaiting the creature's decision. The freedom of the creature consists in its intrinsic, inalienable ability and right to choose an alternative based on its agreement or disagreement with God over what counts as its own good. In its self-determination, the creature is free to substitute a different value for the one that God endorses for its life, and to pursue that value in its own self-constitution. Does such rebellion amount to self-damnation? I have repeatedly described God's redemption of creaturely choices through the inclusion of all actualities in the divine consequent nature, and it is this to which Neville refers in the final sentence of the passage quoted. No, we are not free to damn ourselves past the extent of our own lives, because God's freedom to include us transcends and outlives our freedom in our own subjectivity. But is the possibility for (eternal) self-damnation truly a sine qua non for freedom? How can the authenticity of our freedom be measured by what occurs after we can no longer exercise it? If a creature is able to damn itself not eternally but temporally, not in the ultimate ordering of things in God's consequent nature but in the private ordering of things in the creature's own concrescence, then surely the ability to rebel against God has been demonstrated and with it, true freedom: doing what one wishes with the real possibility of doing otherwise. This exercise of freedom is what is judged against the absolute standard of God in Christ, and this exercise of freedom is what is redeemed in God's patient, persuasive work in the world of actuality.[67]

The process doctrine of election, so far as high-grade occasions are concerned, holds to a strong definition of freedom when elucidating the creature's response; that is to say, the creature's response as an act of will cannot be called "free" unless the creature has real alternatives to consider. Neville charges that God's primordial decision with regard to the value of possibilities, made effective in the world through the gift of the initial aim, eliminates real alternatives for the emerging occasion by pointing it toward a preselected range of possibilities for its concrescence. But Whitehead makes it clear that God gives us an opportunity to choose at the same time as God informs us of God's perfect will.[68] The limitations placed upon our choices by the past and by God as an element in the past do not smother our freedom of choice, but are the arena in which freedom is exercised.

> Accordingly, any given instance of experience is only possible so far as the antecedent facts permit. For they are required in order to constitute it. . . . The limitations are the opportunities. The essence of depth of actuality—that is of vivid experience—is definiteness. Now to be definite always means that all the elements of a complex whole contribute to some *one* effect, to the exclusion of others. The creative process is a process of exclusion to the same

extent as it is a process of inclusion. In this connection "to exclude" means
to relegate to irrelevance in the aesthetic unity, and "to include" means to
elicit relevance to that unity. (RM 112–13)

The grading of relevance in each concrescence is based on the valuation of
eternal objects in God's primordial nature, which is presented to us as an
ideal, but it is not constrained by the occasion's prehension of God into predetermined lines. Each occasion modifies the received aim, the received
gradation, to achieve a unique gradation, which is its own subjective aim.
The activity of God in providing the initial aim is essential for the exercise
of freedom, that is, for the determination of relevant identity and contrast
with the past that makes a creature what it is. Without order, there is no
freedom, because there is no actuality:[69]

> The order of the world is no accident. There is nothing actual which could
> be actual without some measure of order. The religious insight is the grasp
> of this truth: That the order of the world, the depth of reality of the world,
> the value of the world in its whole and in its parts, the beauty of the world,
> the zest of life, the peace of life, and the mastery of evil, are all bound
> together—not accidentally, but by reason of this truth: that the universe
> exhibits a creativity with infinite freedom, and a realm of forms with infi-
> nite possibilities; but that this creativity and these forms are together impo-
> tent to achieve actuality apart from the completed ideal harmony, which is
> God. (RM 119–20)

   In making the case that the process system preserves (and in fact enables)
real freedom for creatures and not just the illusion of it, one finds oneself
working to interpret Whitehead's writings in a direction opposite to the
author's original concern. The above passage from *Religion in the Making*
illustrates that Whitehead was less worried about preserving human freedom, which the liberal religion of his time seemed to be taking quite for
granted, than in showing how God's power to order the world was compatible with human self-determination. Neville's criticism shows that the
philosophical and theological tenor of our times is no longer inclined to
grant freedom as an assumption; hence, contemporary readers are liable to
be misled by Whitehead's extensive argument in favor of an active God into
thinking that Whitehead was willing to sacrifice creaturely freedom in
order to justify God's immanence in the world. To the contrary: The
process doctrine of election is built upon the fundamental tenet of process
thought that holds that each occasion is free in its own concrescence to
choose between real alternatives. Therefore, in its response to God's call,
the elected creature faces a true decision, and its action has consequences
for its own life and for the future.[70]

Consequences of Rejecting the Initial Aim

The result of my effort in the previous section to secure the doctrine of the creature's free will and freedom of decision against the threat of divine determinism is the appearance of the threat that God's will might be thwarted by the creature's action. What happens to the creature that rebels against the initial aim by choosing a subjective aim that is contrary to the vocation God gives in election? There are three categories of consequences: first, the effect upon the disobedient creature; second, the effect upon future creatures; and third, the effect upon God.

The creature is indeed free to choose for itself an aim that differs from God's perfect will for that particular occasion. However, as we have already seen, the creature is not absolutely free to actualize any possibility it wishes. The limits to action and decision that ensure order also prevent many instances in which a creature's will might turn toward wild destruction and reversal of God's plan:

> To worship God in dependence on his holiness does transform the self, far beyond its conscious intent and understanding. When we oppose God we discover the boundaries of our action, which are visited upon us whether we will or no. There are large coercive aspects in the divine governance of the world.[71]

So rebellion is not only prevented by God's persuasive action but also is limited by the inherent limitations to creaturely action that are built into the world process. One effect of the creature's rebellion, then, is humility: the discovery that the creature has overestimated its power to thwart God. In rebellion the creature may discover that although it has the power of self-determination, and although its conscious intellect and technology may give it power over other creatures, it is not a god that can set itself up against God. For God works the work of election in all creatures, and many small acts of obedience may fence in even the largest acts of disobedience.

The inevitable effect of a creature's rebellion on the creature itself is judgment. The creature is free to constitute itself in opposition to God's election, but the consequences of that free decision are clear to the creature in the process of its concrescence. The election of God is also the divine warning of judgment, because it provides to the creature the standard by which the creature's acts will be judged. In chapter 2, I discussed the judgment on the completed satisfaction of each creature by the consequent nature, and this topic will once again appear below. The judgment I am speaking of at this point is the judgment that the rebelling creature *anticipates* thanks to the gift of the initial aim. Even during the process of concrescence, the

disobedient creature's choice is made in the awareness (more or less conscious, depending on the grade of occasion involved) that the choice is
contrary to God's will and must result in judgment. The initial aim does
not disappear from the constitution of the occasion when it is modified
into the subjective aim. God's aim for the creature remains as a prehension
that must be ordered by the creature into its self-determination, whether it
is given a high or low value. It remains part of the creature's satisfaction,
judging the creature from within as it were, proving that the law is written
upon our hearts and that we are without excuse.[72] The standard of judgment given in election means that the creature in its rebellion judges itself,
for it includes within itself the aim that it has rejected.

The consequences of rebellion extend beyond the creature who rebels,
because the creature's action reverberates past its own cessation, continuing
to affect every creature who prehends it. The creature that responds negatively to God's election has the capability not only to bring judgment upon
itself but also to cripple the ability of future generations to serve God to
their utmost capacity. This effect manifests itself in two ways. First, the circumstances that limit and circumscribe the exercise of freedom of the
emerging creatures, in the world situation conditioned by an ancestor's
rebellion, are changed from what they would have been had the ancestor
fulfilled its vocation. No longer do the progeny have the option to build
upon their forebear's accomplishment, directly and unambiguously contributing to God's plan. Instead, their optimum vocations given in election
will be toward regaining the ground lost to the earlier generation. The
father has prevented his children from attaining the greater glory, and in
this sense, the sins of the father are indeed visited upon the children.[73] Second, the creatures that come to be after the rebellious creature prehend that
creature and its interpretation of the world in disobedience to God's aim.
The environment of purpose that informs the subsequent creatures thus
includes both God's perfect aims for them and the influential example of a
predecessor who rejected God's standard of value. Certainly it is easier for
a creature to slip into disobedience and sin if it is reared in an atmosphere
where one or more of its ancestors has left an example of defiance, its life
representing an alternate standard of value and a strictly personal goal,
which differs from those prehended from God. The choice of one occasion
to constitute itself contrary to God's will may be communicated through
many generations as subsequent occasions choose to follow that influence
and example rather than the example of the ideal forms, namely, the
example of Christ. Although the persuasive power of God to minimize the
consequences of error and disobedience is greater than the persuasive power

of any occasion to influence subsequent occasions, each creature is nonetheless free to choose the path of the demogogue, and experience shows that the rebellion of one well-placed person can lead thousands or millions into decisions that are rejections of God's election. The power of God to overcome this destructive pattern lies in God's personal and immediate relationship with every creature, a perfectly intimate, perfectly relevant relationship of particular election, which persists long after the influence of past creatures has become diffuse.[74]

Finally, the creature's choice of an aim in opposition to the initial aim offered by God in election affects God. The most obvious effect is that the consequent nature includes the satisfaction of every creature, including those that actualize a possibility for their lives against God's will. God's consequent nature is made up of the actualities of the world reordered toward God's purpose; when those actualities are formed by subjective purposes against the divine purpose, they form a challenge to divine power to include those actualities despite their subjective orientation. Once the subjectivity of the occasion has ended, God in the consequent nature is free and able to utilize that occasion toward God's own purpose, in a way that the occasion could not have anticipated. However, this divine reordering does not mean that the creature's choice is without effect. The free response of the creature means that God must *react* as well as act, that God's actions to bring about the kingdom change based on what possibilities creatures actualize.

Can God be surprised or caught off guard by the rebellion of a creature? No event is completely unexpected to God, since God knows all possibilities. God also has a complete knowledge of probabilities, since God gives the relevant eternal objects to each creature and knows fully the conditions that shape the creature's response. In the final analysis, the creature's free response is never a sure thing precisely because it is a free response between equally viable possibilities. The emotions of surprise or dismay no doubt manifest themselves differently in finite creatures, which are incapable of grasping possibilities fully and are likely to overlook some probable outcome. However, I think it is consistent with the Christian message and with process thought's emphasis on God's aesthetic experience that God is subject to some degree of surprise and dismay, just as God feels delight at obedience and sadness at disobedience. These emotions, however we choose to characterize them to differentiate our finite experience from God's infinite experience, are part of the harmony and intensity that God is able to derive from the world of actual occasions. So it is not beyond the scope of this discussion to suggest that the response of the

206 THE DIVINE DECISION

creature affects God emotionally—that God experiences joy or sorrow in reaction to the choice of the creature with regard to election.

Consequences of Accepting the Initial Aim

Having just discussed the effects of creaturely rebellion on the creature itself, the future world, and God, I turn now to the corresponding effects of the creature's positive response. What is the result in each of these three spheres—self, the community, and God—when the creature accepts the vocation given in election and fulfills God's perfect will for that moment? First, a caveat: the scriptural and creedal insistence that no one is without sin except the incarnate Son must be kept in mind when I speak of a positive response. The fulfillment of election is, in the end, left up to God in the redemption of creaturely choices. Practically speaking, human beings are unable to perfectly meet God's expectations. With the process understanding that free decision is a capability of all occasions from the lowest to the highest grade, it becomes clear that the higher the grade of the occasion, and consequently the more capability for choice among a wider range of alternatives, the less likely it becomes that the occasion will make a perfect choice. Hence, while a molecule of granite might be imagined to perfectly fulfill God's purpose for it by simply repeating itself generation after generation, this response to election is possible, even probable, primarily because the molecule has few options. The human response to election is much more complex, involving many responses over time. Human beings are not marked by consistency in their choices, and an honest assessment of human capabilities would lead to the conclusion that it is impossible to answer God's call in perfect obedience throughout a human life. The miracle of the incarnation is that Christ reveals the possibility hidden inside the practical difficulties that seem to human beings insurmountable. To summarize my warning, when I speak of a positive, faithful, obedient response to God's election by creatures, I am talking in relative terms. None but Christ responds perfectly; the rest of us strive toward obedience.

What constitutes a positive response to God's act of election? Even before the actualization of the vocational possibility God offers to the creature, the response comes in the subjective mode of feeling in which God's election is prehended. In other words, the first indication of the act by which a creature will respond is the way the creature experiences God's electing act. If election is perceived as an unmerited act of grace by which the creature is included in God's universal purpose, then election will be received with awe, wonder, and gratitude. The creature sees election as the miracle that even this one has been chosen, even I, that God has laid the future of the divine plan in my hands. The act of response to such a miracle is praise and worship:

> If it is necessary, then, to maintain the mystery of election—and it is absolutely necessary, for God's freedom is the sovereign liberty of the Creator, which our liberty may never dispute nor judge: "O Man, who art thou that repliest against God?" (Rom. 9:20)—it is only on the basis of knowing and preaching that this mystery is none other than the peace that passes understanding. It is unfathomable because the love of God is unfathomable. And the only act of adoration God expects of us is our wonder at a purpose that overwhelms us.[75]

In considering the response of the creature, what Barth calls the mystery of election appears. For it is as mystery that the primordial purpose of God to include us in the divine plan of creativity, and the consequent mercy of God in utilizing our finite efforts toward that purpose, comes to us. Any mystery of the Christian faith inevitably must be couched in the language of unfathomable grace, and election is no exception. The mystery of election, found in our experience of divine grace, is the mystery that God loves us. Process thought affirms and describes this gracious love because it is the final word on our experience as creatures—both the final word that God speaks to us, and the final word that we can speak in reflecting on our relationship to God. The mystery is not where and how God's love is applied, as in Calvin;[76] the mystery is that God's love is applied to us, to include us in the divine purpose:

> The logic of grace is a universalizing, inclusive logic. Being overwhelmed with the sense of being loved by God is only adequately articulated in the language of inclusion–I, too, am included, even me! Knowing oneself to be loved by God brings with it an amazement at being included.[77]

Actualization of the Subjective Aim

Once the creature has made its decision regarding the initial aim, the next phase of the concrescence is the creature's becoming actual and ending its self-creation. In process thought, the decision is equivalent to the action; it is what the occasion purposes to do that determines what that occasion is. This is the case because process thought speaks of the mental activity of the occasion in its ordering of the physical data as constitutive of the occasion itself. In complex, conscious creatures that carry out multifaceted purposes over time, it is conceivable that the creature will want to do something but will fail. This is not self-creation; this is not the subjective aim; this is not response to God's vocational call. The phenomenon of failure to achieve a complex aim comes from the fact that every occasion in a series of controlling occasions may not be able to hold the same aim, due to changing circumstances.[78] Our ability to respond to election is not limited by the physical conditions or the actions of others that constrain us. Election is for a service that we can perform, and further, that we alone can perform. The only reason for failure is a negative response; it cannot be blamed on any other circumstance.

The actualization of the creature's subjective aim has both intrinsic value and instrumental value. Its intrinsic value is the accomplishment of actuality for the occasion itself. Actuality is its own good, quite apart from what kind of actuality it is. But this intrinsic value is fixed and finite; it cannot bear more fruit over time. It depends only on the aesthetic intensity of the subjective experience of that creature. Once the creature's subjectivity ends, no more value can be added to its intrinsic worth. The creature's instrumental value, however, depends not only on its subjective decision (though that decision is a condition that cannot be escaped, since it determines what the creature is for all time). Instrumental value also depends on what is made of that creature in the ordered societies of which it is a part. Election gives every creature a role, and the creature can be defined and valued by how it functions in that role. The instrumental value of that creature can continue to multiply long after its subjectivity is gone, if its actuality provides the conditions for other creatures to create value. God can maximize the positive instrumental value of a creature by ordering its actuality in the consequent nature toward the divine purpose, and by providing subsequent creatures with aims that value the positive contribution of the creature highly, thereby encouraging others to carry on the work of the creature. The actualization of the subjective aim, then, is not the end of the story of the creature's contribution to the creation of value. Through God's redemptive grace, the creature can continue to give to the world and to God beyond its death.

Redemption: The Creature's Response Deified

"All we like sheep have gone astray; we have all turned to our own way" (Isa. 53:6). The doctrine of election recognizes that God does not do violence to human will and human decision in our process of self-creation; creatures are allowed to create themselves in whatever image they desire. This is the power God has graciously fostered in creatures. But God's power takes the creature's decision and purifies it in God's self, by including the actuality of the creature in the divine consequent nature. This is what Christian theology calls redemption: the transformation of the creature's response to election into the maximum possible contribution to God's plan. What we cannot make of ourselves as creators of value, God makes of us. Earlier I called this stage election's fulfillment, and by that I mean that God's choice to be God for us and for us to be for him is carried through into everlasting for each and every creature. God's election of the creature is reaffirmed in God's redemptive inclusion of the creature, not as a repetition or a mechanical following-through, but as a new creative act that responds to the creature's creative act in all its particularity.

Redemption is not only a divine event, however, but also an event for creatures. In the case of a social organism persisting over time, and especially in the case of a creature with self-consciousness such as a human being, the redemptive inclusion of each successive actuality that makes up that creature is experienced by the emerging actualities that follow it. Each occasion prehends the divine consequent nature and becomes aware that, just as the entities in its own past have been included and reordered toward God's purpose, the same will happen in the present case once its choice is made. In this way, redemption becomes a present experience for creatures, in recognition of the divine choice in favor of the creatures of the past and in anticipation that the choice extends to the present and the future.

Moreover, the redemption of a creature makes a difference for the creatures that follow it in the world process. Through God's inclusion of the creature in the consequent nature, its accomplishment is redeemed by being integrated into the flow of the divine plan. As part of that unity, the redeemed creature is rendered effective in the world as part of the consequent nature prehended by a new generation of emerging entities. God's initial aim for a concrescent occasion builds upon the foundation laid by the redeemed creature, which has already ended its subjectivity. So each divine act of election and each creature's response benefits from the service performed by previous creatures, as redeemed and included in God's self. Thanks to God's redemption of our finite inadequacies in service to the divine will, our judgment on what constitutes proper clay for God's use is not the same as God's judgment! Pannenberg writes:

> The intention of God's elective activity in human history is not limited to a particular community, nor to isolated individuals. The love of God is directed to mankind as symbolized in the life of individuals and to individual human beings embodying in their lives the destiny of all humanity. Therefore, individual men and women are chosen by God, but not as isolated atoms of salvation. They are chosen to exemplify the gracious intentions of God's love for

all human beings. Hence, there is no room for sectarian seclusion of the chosen. Such elitist exclusivism only renders the excluded ones the more suitable
examples of God's elective love.[79]

Our faith that election means our own inclusion should not lead us to
believe that others who may lack that faith, or who appear to be unable
to contribute, cannot be included in the same way. God turns all actuality
to the service of the divine aim, by turning each actuality into a part of a
whole oriented toward that service.[80]

The concept of redemption as outlined here raises the issue of the equality of creatures before God. As Schleiermacher notes, there is an apparent
conflict between the uniformity of creatures considered from the divine
point of view as objects of election, and the nonuniformity of creatures
considered from the human point of view as more or less sanctified.[81] In
process terms, this tension between uniformity and nonuniformity is also
present. God's subjective aim, which looks forward to his ultimate satisfaction, is what corresponds to Schleiermacher's "eternity," wherein all
creatures have an equal share in fellowship with God.[82] As with Schleiermacher, it is an eschatological notion. All life will contribute to God's satisfaction, since all experiences will be eternally included in God and
incorporated into the final harmony. Yet in the midst of process, in time
and history, the contributions of some entities are unfathomable, and the
contributions of others seem entirely negative, so that rather than steady
progress toward a universal goal, there seem to be countless setbacks. Not
all creatures make steps toward the goal. Indeed, from the point of view of
entities in time, there are setbacks and reversals. This inequality in the
response of creatures to God's call is evident and real.

What is less immediately evident—the eventual equality—is that the
contributions of every entity provide an equal chance for God to work in
history, for they all produce a set of new circumstances, or givens, which
God takes into account. To bring the tension to a more existential level,
process asserts that the environment, inheritance, and opportunities of
each entity are unique. It goes without saying, then, that these circumstances are unequal; it is simply observed fact that some creatures have a
richer legacy from their past and a more varied set of possibilities in their
future than others. Yet because God tailors the initial aim uniquely to each
entity, the goal given to every creature is equally attainable. Thus, our existential situation in time is equal, as are our contributions to God's eventual
satisfaction, which now appear in the form of points of data that God takes
into account at every moment in God's relationship with the world.

Sanctification: Growth in God-consciousness

Creation, redemption, and sanctification are traditionally seen as the three great acts of God toward creatures. I have explicated each of these acts as derived from and ultimately dependent upon the divine act of election—God's primordial act of self-election and the subsequent election of individual creatures. Sanctification, like creation and redemption, has both a temporal and an everlasting aspect. For a creature that endures over time, consistent positive responses to election lead to a temporal experience of redemption through dwelling in God's will. For creatures with self-consciousness, this experience extended over time becomes the experience of sanctification. The creature that knows its vocation and responds with obedience enjoys a relationship with God that grows closer and more intimate, thanks to the reciprocal openness of the parties to each other. As a result, the creature grows more in tune with God's purpose both for the creature itself and for the world. Not only does the creature increase in holiness in its own life, but it increases its ability to pass along holiness to its fellows. This twofold openness to God, both for the individual and communal vocations of the creature, is the effect of the creature's growth in God-consciousness through its life.

The everlasting aspect of sanctification once again refers to the purification of the creature's satisfaction in God's consequent nature. To the extent that the creature's positive response can be utilized by God to advance the world process, and to the extent that God orders the creature's actuality so as to give it a high value in the consequent nature, the process of sanctification of the creature can be said to continue everlastingly. Here sanctification is measured not by the creature's subjective experience, which ends with the creature's death, but by the objectification of the creature in God's experience and in the experience of other creatures. The creature's actuality can become more and more effective through time, rather than less effective, thanks to God's ordering of it in the consequent nature and presentation of aims based on that actuality to subsequent creatures.

To call sanctification an act of God toward the creature signifies that the growth in God-consciousness and increase in effectiveness of the creature's accomplishment is dependent upon the divine response to the creature's act. Norman Pittenger points out that the role of providence in the life of an enduring creature is the maintenance of that creature in God's will:

> Hence providence in its special sense is not some theoretical explanation of the odd coincidences with which life abounds, although it includes those coinci-

dences; essentially it is God's doing whatever is necessary to bring us to him as love and to keep us there once we have let him take possession of our lives.[83]

Certainly all sorts of results can be imagined, and are evident in experience, for the divine act of election in the life of a conscious, long-lived creature. The levels of response on a continuum shading from positive to negative are surely infinite, and given the specificity of the initial aim given to each creature, the progress or regress achieved by each creature can be thought of as unique to that instance. Sanctification refers to the success God achieves in luring us toward our optimum level of progress. Complex goals are not achieved by a single actual occasion in its momentary lifespan; they are appropriate to the kind of highly evolved organism that can maintain a direction toward a distant goal over an extended period of time, even an entire human lifetime. It is not the end of the story of election for such a creature to respond positively to God's call. God's persuasive action means that election for this creature is not a single event, but a progressive call to become holy, as God is holy.

The final question to be considered in the construction of the election doctrine arises from the topic of sanctification. Many theologians have argued that the process of becoming holy need not end with the creature's death. If a conscious, subjective life after death for the creature is postulated, then there seems to be no reason why sanctification should not continue everlastingly. There is a range of opinions among process theologians about life after death.[84] I have adhered to a conservative interpretation of Whitehead by refusing to speculate about any subjective immortality. Process metaphysics describes an objective immortality for every creature in God's consequent nature, but Whitehead seems to consider the subjective experience of the creature to have ended at its satisfaction. Perhaps he found the religious desire to overcome personal death to be a holdover from a more primitive past; he describes objective immortality in the divine consequent nature as "life" in the truest sense: "Each actuality in the temporal world has its reception into God's nature. The corresponding element in God's nature is not temporal actuality, but is the transmutation of that temporal actuality into a living, ever-present fact" (PR 350).

The model of immortality here is complete and perfect memory in complete and perfect immediacy, so that God's memory of the creature's actuality includes its subjective experience present forever in God's self. To redefine "living" to mean the everlasting existence of an unchanging fact in God's consequent nature is not to hedge process philosophy's commitment to becoming as the defining characteristic of process. Instead, here Whitehead uses "living" to denote the effectiveness of an agent. During its concrescence, the creature does not affect any other contemporary entity. It acts only upon the data from the occasions in its past—which, the satisfactions of those occasions having been reached, cannot be affected substantively by its actions. In exercising its agency upon these prehensions, the creature acts in the most proper sense only upon itself, since the emerging creature is constituted by the sum of the data it takes in and orders into a whole. It is only upon the completion of the creature's becoming that it becomes an actor on the world stage, able to "live" in an exterior rather than interior sense by affecting others. The inclusion of the fact of the creature's satisfaction in God's consequent nature means that its agency in the world need not dwindle and fade into insignificance after a generation or two. The creature in its immortality has been given a unique role in the actualization of the divine plan, and it will continue to enact that role everlastingly.

As important as the idea of everlastingly fresh, living agency for the individual creature is to the process notion of immortality, there is still a more crucial feature of Whitehead's insight. Process thought always seeks to articulate the eternal balance between the one and the many. The universal process does not begin with one and return at last to one, with the many scattered in between as a more or less inevitable middle step. This, to Whitehead, would mean a return to Neoplatonic monism. But neither does the universal process preserve the many only in their distinction from each other. Too strong an insistence on personal, subjective immortality may tend in the direction of absolutizing individuals, by suggesting that there can never be a decisive unification because the becoming of the potential components never ends.

It is crucial to both the freedom and creativity of creatures and the freedom and creativity of God that the many and the one remain in constant counterpoint to each other. The becoming of an individual occasion is the unification into an ordered whole of all its particular prehensions. So the creature's world is self-defined and included in the creature as a unity; "the many become one, and are increased by one," because that particular unity is a new individual. In God, the process is inverted. The unity of the individual creatures is defined by the primordial nature prior to their becoming. It belongs to God's unique creativity to mold the many into one world at every moment, according to the divine subjective aim. Without this ongoing unification, extending itself to encompass every creature as it reaches its satisfaction, the living agency of the individual creature in the consequent nature is impossible. Every ordering of the expanding consequent nature must be a definitive unity if God is to present the presently

emerging creature with its own vocation—if, that is, there is to be an
increase of the many by one so that a new One is made possible. And this
definitive unity of the consequent nature must be prehended by the creature if it is to unify its own experiences in terms of a definitively chosen
aim.

Whitehead attempted in his metaphysics to construct a system, provisional though it necessarily must be, to describe adequately the experience
both of freedom and aesthetic enjoyment—descriptions of which had traditionally been the domain of philosophy—and of the insights of empirical science. On the topic of immortality, the two realms Whitehead
sought to unify seem to be in conflict. Kant recognized that the idea of the
Self is infinite, in the sense that we do not conceptualize our own selves in
terms of the boundaries recognized in others (corporeality, death). Yet
biology describes the relentless death of individuals and species, and evolutionary theory posits the necessity of death to make room for others, if
life itself is not to stagnate and end altogether. The objective immortality
described in Whitehead's writing is a way of unifying these disparate
insights in such a way that the concept of everlasting life does not become
mere wish fulfillment and the truth of perpetual perishing does not spell
the end of hope. Process theology, in speaking of immortality, at the very
least must assert that the elected creature is resurrected by the power of
God's inclusive consequent nature, out of the death of the subject, into
the everlasting life of the effective fact. Whether there must also be an affirmation of the survival of personal subjectivity after death to describe accurately our experience and to secure religious adequacy for process theology
is a matter for further study.

Conclusion

The doctrine of election is the foundation for the doctrines of creation,
redemption, and sanctification, and as such it must receive careful attention from theologians working in any Christian system. Karl Barth also
recognized that rightly constructed, the doctrine of election is the foundation for the doctrines of humanity and God. In process theology—as
in other, more traditional theologies—the decision of God to be for creatures is the necessary condition for all the structures of relationships that
obtain between God and creatures. Furthermore, election leads to the self-
revelation of God, and hence to the self-understanding of conscious creatures. Without the context of the election relationship, anthropology as

well as the doctrine of God is severely truncated, even hypothetical. The creature with which theology must contend is a creature constituted by God's choice of it, and the God with which theology must contend is a God who chooses creatures. Process thought demonstrates its effectiveness as a framework for theological exploration by locating the establishment of this relationship at the center of its description of the world process.

Once the analysis of election in process terms is begun, it becomes clear that process thought will lead the construction of the doctrine in terms of the priority of God's act, the freedom of the creature's response, and the importance of vocation in a universe of purposes. Election remains first and foremost a free act of God: As Lord of possibilities, God is free to choose God's own subjective aim and, further, to choose God's own method for achieving that aim. The good news of Christianity is that God in fact chose and chooses to maximize value through the endeavors of creatures. The election of individuals is the divine gift to the creature of an aim that represents the highest possible value of its life and the best possible legacy it can leave for its descendants. The creature is likewise free in its response to the divine initiative, although this act remains a response and never a fully autonomous first step. The divine act must precede the creaturely act, because without the limits set and the purposes structured by the divine act, the creature cannot achieve in its own self-creation the order that actuality requires. The creature's freedom is to choose its own aim from the possibilities valued by God and presented to it by God—in other words, to accept the divine standard of value or to substitute its own theory of value. Because this creaturely decision is the creation of identity, the creature's choice to be itself defines that creature as a stubborn fact for all time. Its individual purpose becomes a communal matter of fact.

Election is completed, however, in the response of God to the creature's free act. The divine purpose has its absolute power in its ability to encompass and redeem all creaturely purposes. If the creature responds positively to the aim proffered by God and actualizes an aim close to the ideal, then God may order its satisfaction highly in the consequent nature in order that its accomplishment might bear the most fruit. The creature in its immortality, then, becomes ever more effective through God's ordering in the unified whole of the consequent nature toward the eternal divine subjective aim. If, however, the creature responds with rebellion to God's gift of vocation, then God's judgment upon its satisfaction is likewise negative. Judgment does not preclude everlasting inclusion, however; the rebellious creature is found in the consequent nature with its purposes, however objectively turned against God, turned through God's power toward the

divine aim. It may be that the event may only be transformed into triviality, so that the infection of its rebellion reaches only a few generations; this
is as close to destruction or reprobation as the process doctrine of election
comes. But as Lord of possibilities, God is able to use persuasive power to
produce progress in unexpected directions, out of the entire range of creaturely responses.

The adequacy of the process doctrine of election must be measured in
two ways. First, it is held up before the standard of Scripture, to discover
whether the direction in which process thought leads the doctrine of election is consistent with the Christian witness to God's self-revelation. I have
argued that the process concept of God and creature in the relationship of
election fits the biblical picture in both the Old and New Testaments. The
God who calls Abraham, Isaac, and Jacob, the God who covenants with
Israel, the God who calls the prophets to service is the God who has purposes for all creatures. The God who brings all humanity into the fellowship of the Trinity through Christ is the God who includes all creatures.
Process thought has resources to understand and recover parts of Scripture
that have coexisted uneasily at best with the classical concept of God.
Through the doctrine of election, it also restores the centrality of the
divine-creature interaction with which Scripture is so uniformly concerned, by ruling out talk of an abstract, unrelated, immutable, impassible
God. The revelation of God's relatedness in Scripture is not contrary to the
experience of creatures, but reveals the divine nature along with its continuity with human nature. The process doctrine of election endeavors to
take Scripture seriously as a record of divine and human experiences.

Second, the process doctrine of election is measured by the standard of
religious adequacy in our present experience. This is the standard of praxis,
and it cannot be denied that process theology has been little tested in this
realm. No established community of believers bases their doctrine explicitly on process thought, and therefore the religious adequacy of the doctrine constructed cannot be tested empirically at present. As the explication
of the doctrine has progressed in this chapter, I have attempted to indicate
the ways in which the process doctrine of election finds itself congruent
with established Christian concerns and traditions, and the ways in which
it can lead to new insights. For example, the process doctrine of the Trinity briefly sketched at the end of the second section of this chapter begins
from twin foundations: process metaphysics and the Christian dogma that
has been the basis of Christian worship since the early church. I indicated
that the process understanding of election can lead to a new appreciation
of Christ as judge, which conceivably might lead to an emphasis on moral

faithfulness and the seeking of God's will in Christian practice. The final evaluation of the religious adequacy of the process doctrine of election rests with the experience of individuals and Christian communities that adopt its concepts and discover its consequences. My hope is that the power of the process system of thought can be brought to bear upon the truth of the Christian witness in order to encourage human beings to respond positively to God's vocational call.

EPILOGUE

Process *thought* is a metaphysical system, a worldview whose categories aim toward the description of all experience. Even though Whitehead introduces the term *God* and utilizes some theological language, his system is basically designed to explain reality in secular terms. Religious experience and the particular problems and issues of the religious life are treated in process thought as special cases, but are not to be understood outside, or as exceptions to, the general categories that govern all descriptions. His opposition to dualistic descriptions leads to a system in which the secular is the primary term and the religious or theological is a subset of the secular rather than a separate type of reality:

> The secularization of the concept of God's functions in the world is at least as urgent a requisite of thought as is the secularization of other elements in experience. The concept of God is certainly one essential element in religious feeling. But the converse is not true; the concept of religious feeling is not an essential element in the concept of God's function in the universe. (PR 207)

Process *theology*, on the other hand, takes this subset of experience as its primary subject. This change of focus means that the encounter of revelation between God and creatures may be taken as normative event, informing all other aspects of reality and acting as the standard by which all descriptions and explanations are to be judged. A creature's experience of God is its prehension of the initial aim and the divine consequent nature, which, consciously or unconsciously, conditions the creature's becoming. A creature's experience of Christ is the recognition that this prehension constitutes divine revelation with its demand and promise. One aspect of the faith to which process theology testifies, however, is that there is continuity between the prehension of divine revelation and other prehensions. Since all existence is constituted through its relationship with God, there is only a difference in consciousness and degree between what we term religious experience and secular experience. God is involved in every occasion in the universe, but this involvement is not the result of God's reaching across an ontological divide that separates creatures from divinity. The affirmation of this confluence of divine and creaturely reality is a primary rationale for

219

basing a theology on process thought. Whitehead's contention is that ordinary experience is not intelligible without postulating the activity of a divine entity; this discovery of God "from below" informs us only of what God must do, not of who God is. For the latter inquiry, the Christian faith points to God's own revelation of who God is, in Christ and the Scriptures that witness to Christ.

The construction of a process doctrine of election, as in the present work, is by necessity also an argument for the theological use of process categories. The explanatory power of process thought—its adequacy as an inclusive metaphysics—faces a test in the construction of doctrinal systems in its terms. Can the categories of process thought, which purport to describe all experience but which are admittedly based on secular experience, be utilized to describe the encounter of revelation (viewed from the divine side) and the encounter of faith (viewed from the human side), both of which are aspects of the doctrine of election? Based upon the fact that process thought describes a universal experience of divinely given purpose, I have answered "yes" to this question, and have outlined the congruities between process theology's understanding of the initial aim and traditional theology's doctrine of election, especially as presented by Karl Barth. But process theology also involves an agenda of reinterpreting the doctrine of God and the ontological divide between divinity and creaturehood, which should not be played down for the sake of presenting a more harmonious convergence. It has been my contention in this work that process theology's revisions of classical concepts do not hinder the construction of a doctrine of election, and in some cases these revisions provide a more congenial and more fruitful framework for the doctrine than traditional theism.

As a postscript to the doctrine constructed in chapter 4, I present here some consideration of the specifically religious dimension of the election doctrine. The process doctrine of election is universal, in that it presumes that every creature is the object of God's election, and experiences purpose, subjectivity, self-creation, divine judgment, and objective immortality. But the Christian witness and the scriptural record speak of the election of some individuals and communities in a special way. To do justice to this message of election, it is necessary to speak of special cases within the scope of the universal, divinely initiated relationship between God and creatures that was the topic of the constructive effort in the previous chapter.

The first step in speaking of the religious dimensions of election within the parameters of process thought is to recognize that a religious relationship does not exist between every creature elected of God and the divine Elector. Religion, and therefore religious experience, is defined by a self-conscious, reflective, language-capable norm. That is to say, since human beings recognize only in themselves the ability to form religious concepts and organize religious communities, they define religiosity in human terms. It certainly cannot be ruled out that other types of creatures, especially those with highly evolved social structures and systems of communication, will be found to possess some analog to human religion. The ability to utilize symbolic language, for example, which has been demonstrated to occur in nonhuman animals, suggests that creatures other than human beings can recognize divine revelation in their prehensions of God and can conceive of the divine-creature relation in cognitive categories. Even at that, however, a narrowing-down of the field has taken place when we speak of a religious relationship between God and the creature. Not all creatures have the capacity for this type of relationship, and among these, not all choose to involve themselves in it. Among human beings, for example, we find a range of engagements in religious thought and action, from total immersion to total avoidance. The task of discovering the various alternatives along this continuum is best left to sociologists of religion and psychologists of religion. The point to be made here is that religious experience has certain preconditions that are not under the control of the creature (level of self-consciousness, social and cultural factors), and requires a certain amount of choice on the part of the creature to involve itself in religious reflection and activity. Only a tiny percentage of the world's entities fit these criteria and therefore experience an explicitly religious relationship to God.

Christians believe that the true nature of that religious relationship can be found in reflection on the life, death, and resurrection of Jesus Christ, the incarnate Son of God. Since process theologians are committed to a less anthropocentric view of the creatures who are the objects of election and God's saving grace, however, the idea that God incarnates God's self only as a human being raises some questions. How can the incarnation in a man, Jesus, bring divine revelation to all creatures? For example, Daniel Day Williams writes, "In Jesus Christ God has not only given us promises but has identified his life with us in love and thus created a new relationship which is the decisive content of hope and promise for all who respond to him in trust."[1] How does God identify with *all* creatures—since all creatures have the ability to respond in trust—through a human being? How do nonhuman creatures find God in solidarity with them? How are their unique sufferings and fallibilities redeemed?

Process theology, like all theologies, is an endeavor of human beings following the lead of God revealing God's self in human experience. The

Christian faith is the assurance that this revelation has taken place in the incarnation, and that all human beings can enter into fellowship with God through the incarnate Christ. It is not for human theologians to postulate that there might be other incarnations than the union with the human Jesus; since our prehensions of divine revelation put us in contact with Jesus Christ, God's incarnation as a human being, we can have no direct knowledge of other divine acts that bring the world into contact with divine revelation. But it is also not for human theologians to rule out the possibility that other creatures are brought into fellowship with God through the same Christ in another form. Not until human beings can enter into the concrescences of other creatures and meet God in the form of other creatures will we know whether something like this is God's plan of salvation for the world.[2] Certainly process theology renders the possibility easier to contemplate; its assertion that the gift of election and vocation comes to all creatures, not just human beings, forces us to consider the possibility that the universal Christ is not limited to the human Jesus Christ. The process doctrine of the Trinity that I outlined in chapter 4 also leaves the door open for the possibility. If the Son is understood as the eternal possibilities ordered and directed toward God's subjective aim by the Father, then one can imagine the highest possibility for every type of creature becoming actual at particular times. Whether this would be necessary for God's plan to be achieved depends on several factors; for example, is the content of the revelation essentially cognitive, making the incarnation useful primarily for creatures with reflective intelligence? Or is it experiential, so that all creatures could be brought into contact with the incarnate Christ through prehension of the consequent nature that it leads as its head? My purpose in raising the issue here is not to propose a solution, but to demonstrate that process theology raises specifically religious questions through its efforts to decentralize the image of the human being from the question of God-creature relations. It is debatable whether even a fully mature process theological system will be able to answer these questions more than provisionally.

Returning to the human experience of election, another religious consideration raised by the doctrine is the relationship of God's gift of vocation to the existential question arising out of human life.[3] Here I suggest that process theology is uniquely well equipped to provide a satisfying account of the convergence of meaning and meaninglessness in human existence. If the content of election is the connection of individual aims with the divine aim for the universe, then obedience to election's call places an individual within a structure of purpose and power infinitely larger than itself. As conscious beings, we may sense that depth of purpose and power in religious experience, cognitively assess its meaning, and feel humbled at the same time we know ourselves to be exalted. On the other hand, the reality and insidious intermingling of evil within our world confronts us with purposes at odds with the divine purpose, not only as experienced in election but as revealed in Jesus Christ. Process theology provides a framework for understanding evil that takes seriously the reality and consequence of creaturely agency, while insisting that this opposition to God still takes place within the election relationship initiated and fulfilled by God. The insights into the deepest nature of reality that Whitehead proposed as a basis for process philosophy, then, are confirmed and expanded through the religious quest of process theology, which takes an opposite tack in starting from the revealed nature of God and moving toward an answer to the questions of human experience.[4]

The final religious issue I would like to raise concerns what has been termed "special election." Scripture reports and Christian experience continues to acknowledge that within the general structure of God's decision to elect, which encompasses all individuals, there are instances of election that become especially crucial in world history. In fact, tracking these instances through the Bible means tracing salvation history itself, which is understood to unfold through God's choice of specific individuals and communities for special service. Certain persons, families, and nations are understood in Scripture as recipients of an unusually important call to service. The fulfillment of these vocations is considered crucial to the accomplishment of God's purpose for the world.

The paradigm of so-called special election in Scripture is the election of the nation of Israel. The children of Abraham, Isaac, and Jacob are the chosen people, chosen out of the community of nations to bring God's revelation into the world: "I will make of you a great nation, and I will bless you, and make your name great, so that you will be a blessing. I will bless those who bless you, and the one who curses you I will curse; and in you all the families of the earth shall be blessed" (Gen. 12:2–3). Already in this description of the nation of Israel we find ourselves acknowledging that this moment of election is not an isolated moment. With the litany "Abraham, Isaac, and Jacob" the Scriptures indicate that the election of the community of Israel depends on the election of its forefathers. And in the book of Genesis, Abraham is a figure who falls in an even more ancient line of those elected for special service—Noah, for example. The recitations of lineages in Genesis can be seen as histories of special election; it is through this particular line that God brought about the crucial occasions at which Abraham,

Isaac, and Jacob fulfilled their election, and the outstanding Israelites after
them. So as soon as we start to ask the question about special election, we
see that there is no clear line between these examples of vocation and "ordinary" election. Only by offering purpose to every occasion, and only by
ordering every instance of actuality into the divine plan, does God bring
about those pivotal moments through which the entire world is changed and
blessed. It is not a matter of a narrow corridor of election recorded in Scripture as opposed to a general landscape with which divine election is uncon-
cerned. Crucial events acquire their importance through two factors: first,
their appearance at a moment when critical service is required; and second,
the progress in the creation of value that takes place as a result of their
accomplishment. The first factor is prospective and divine, in that the
importance of the event is foreseen (by God) before its arrival, and is fostered (again by God) through the election of other entities to lead up to this
moment when critical service is to be required. The second factor is retrospective and creaturely, because the event is judged to be important (by creatures) by its results in the advancement of world history.[5]

   The prospective importance of Israel is demonstrated in Scripture by the
Genesis account of its origin, beginning with the Garden of Eden and continuing through the stories of Cain and Abel, the flood, and the lineage of
Abraham. Whatever the value of these events in themselves, there is no
doubt that Scripture presents them in a role beyond themselves, as forming the set of conditions necessary for the coming of Israel. But we should
not be blinded by Scripture's relative silence as to the divine activity of election beyond these events. Their importance is a reflection of the high value
placed upon them in the ordering of God's consequent nature, and their
resulting effectiveness in the unfolding of world history. This is a difference
of degree from other instances of election, not a difference of kind. The
process doctrine of election does not recognize, at least in its most general
categories, a "special election" of a different order from the election of other
creatures. It does speak of moments at which the service demanded of the
creature by God's electing act is particularly momentous, having decisive
ramifications for the entire universal process. It does acknowledge crucial
junctures in history toward which God has directed the world so that something of eternal significance can be achieved. It is unwavering in its insistence that these critical events represent the climactic revelations of God's
purposes to creatures, and that they acquire for us a cognitive and experiential significance even beyond their significance as historical turning
points. But the "specialness" of special election is a retrospective designa-
tion. Every divine act of election is unique in that it presents to a unique

entity the opportunity to become an occasion of unique service to God. There is no *metaphysical* rationale for singling out certain acts of election as "more unique" than others.

There is a compelling *theological* rationale for speaking of special election, however: the biblical witness. It was not human beings but God who told Israel that it had been chosen out of all the nations; it was not human beings but God who made Christ's election the basis for all other acts of election. The scriptural story of election is not the story of the many, but of the few. Again and again, one person is called out of a family, one tribe is called out of a nation, one prophet is sent to a city, one sacrifice is made for the world. Perhaps the "specialness" of special election is this singular quality, the sense that the service rendered has the potential to affect a far greater audience than the service asked of others. The term is still retrospective in our usage, in the sense that we apply it based on the vastness of the historical impact of the vocation fulfilled. The election described still is not divorced from the continuum of election; the elected one would not be able to fulfill her vocation were it not for the support of unnumbered others fulfilling roles that go unsung. But both from the divine point of view (high valuation in the consequent nature and expanded effect on the future) and the human point of view (as reflected in the selection of events recorded in Scripture), these instances of election have taken on an extra layer of meaning. They have been chosen to form the story of election, a story with characters, shape, movement, crises, and a satisfying conclusion. Their role in that story is special indeed, for in the story of election God reveals God's work toward creatures. A story is by nature limited to a narrow range of detail, even though it suggests the characters, actions, motivations, and consequences that extend out from it into its greater world. The election of these particular events to form the story of God's act toward the world can certainly be seen as an additional, special role given both prospectively and retrospectively—that is, it is always intended by God that these individuals and groups should fill these roles in the story, and human tellers of the story can appreciate their significance because of their fulfillment of these roles.

Israel, then, is elected by God to be the revelation of election in microcosm, the visible incarnation of the divine covenantal nature. Its history remains a history like that of any other nation. But when viewed in the light of Scripture, with Scripture's theocentrism, God's act is evident. Special election does not remove the elected one from the world with all its natural facets accessible to empirical study; it enables the elected one, in all its historical reality, to be understood in a new way, as a part of the divine story.[6] Through the existence of the specially elect in the world, we also come to understand that the acts of God in the world are indeed historical acts—part of the general stream of world history, and able to be apprehended as nondivine acts—as the objects of scientific study, for example. We incorporate a past event into our lives through the understanding of those who experienced the event directly, either accepting their interpretation of the event or reinterpreting it on our own terms. The testimony of Israel to God's election comes through the conviction of those who experienced chosenness, interpreted through our understanding of what kinds of acts are attributable to God. Not all events that claim inspiration by God are indeed experiences of God. Through the canonical story of election that is formed by the history of Israel and culminates in Christ, we say with the conviction of faith, yes, God made a great nation out of Abraham, but no, God did not inspire the burning of witches at Salem.

The gift of religious vocation is the instance of special election most often invoked today. In fact the term *vocation* can refer specifically to this experience of the divine call. The "specialness" of this election rests upon the idea that the call to a religious vocation is something given to only a few. Already we see that this type of special election is similar to the Israel paradigm, in that a few are called out of the many. It is similar in another respect, as well; just as there is a scriptural concept that the calling of Israel was to serve the world,[7] the calling to the religious life is to serve both God and the world. Israel is to mediate the blessings of God to the rest of the nations, and the clergy or priesthood is to mediate the blessings of God to their congregation, and through them to all people. Nothing less than a lifetime of service is the proper response to the miracle of being called out of the place one thought was one's limit, to be marked as God's possession in a special and unmistakable way. That service is not only to God, but to others; it is for this reason that one is marked at all, that one is separated physically or spiritually from the general mass of people, so that everyone can see the story of election written again in the life of the elected one.[8] In the divine call to religious vocation, we see a direct and conscious bond being forged through God's initiative with an individual for the purpose of service. Yet the individual who is called comes from a community with shared cultural and religious values, and enters, as a result of the call, a more selective community of those who also claim this special bond. The call is not an isolated encounter with God any more than "ordinary" election is unconditioned by the past, present, and future environment, nor does it contradict the tradition of the community to which the elected one seeks entrance. In fact, the call to religious vocation confirms that community by directing the elected one toward it, as the proper place to render his service.

Further work in the process doctrine of election might be fruitfully directed at this experience. Process thought contains resources for understanding communal transmission of value from the past, to analyze how history and shared experience form a living community. It could be utilized to describe how the divine call to service, ever renewed in the present generation, comes to individuals qua individuals and qua participants in a tradition. Wolfhart Pannenberg illustrates how this experience of election illuminates a tension and a communication between the individual and the group, between the past as fact and the future as anticipated communally, individually, and divinely:

> Again and again, individual Christians enter into the continuing history and mission of Christianity. They have to stand up to the heritage of Christian history, taking upon themselves the burden of the divisiveness and distortions that resulted from that history. At the same time, they must listen to the call that was received by past epochs and still points beyond their failures, thus illuminating the contours and responsibilities of the present situation.[9]

This postscript to the process doctrine of election has pointed out only a few of the religious consequences of adopting election, in the framework of process thought, as a central doctrine and a key to understanding God's way with creatures. The evidence adduced here in the form of reflection on Christian doctrine and practice also suggests that process thought is not a finished philosophical system that one either adopts or rejects as a framework for theology. Regardless of the attitude taken toward Whitehead's system, thinking along with process categories reveals new and potentially valuable emphases and insights into the relationship between God and the world. This meeting place between the divine and the creature, which I have described in terms of election, is the key to Christianity, for the Christian faith asserts that here is where God reveals God's self. Such a revelation is an infinite resource for new ways of thinking about ourselves and about the God who chooses us.

NOTES

Introduction

1. "There Is a Name I Love to Hear," words by Frederick Whitfield.
2. Donald G. Bloesch, "Process Theology and Reformed Theology," in *Major Themes in the Reformed Tradition,* ed. Donald K. McKim (Grand Rapids: Eerdmans, 1992), 386. Cf. the same author's "Process Theology in Reformed Perspective," *Reformed Journal* 29, no. 10 (October 1979): 19–24.
3. Michael Welker, "Barth's Theology and Process Theology," *Theology Today* 43, no. 3 (October 1986): 383–97.
4. RM 51.
5. Welker, "Barth's Theology," 393.
6. Ibid., 394.
7. Cf. Michael Welker, *Universalität Gottes un der Relavität der Welt: Theologische Cosmologie im Dialog mit dem amerikanischen Theologie,* vol. 1 (Neukirchen-Vluyn: Neukirchener Verlag, 1981).
8. Kenneth Surin, "Process Theology," in *The Modern Theologians: An Introduction to Christian Theology in the Twentieth Century,* ed. David F. Ford (New York: Basil Blackwell, 1989), 1:103–14.
9. Hans Küng, *Justification: The Doctrine of Karl Barth and a Catholic Reflection,* trans. Thomas Collins et al. (London: Burns & Oates, 1964), 16–24.
10. Hans Urs von Balthasar, *The Theology of Karl Barth,* trans. John Drury (New York: Holt, Rinehart & Winston, 1971), 155–64.
11. G. C. Berkouwer, *The Triumph of Grace in the Theology of Karl Barth* (Grand Rapids: Eerdmans, 1956).
12. Robert Jenson, *God after God: The God of the Past and the Future as Seen in the Work of Karl Barth* (Indianapolis: Bobbs-Merrill, 1969).
13. Bruce McCormack, Ph.D. diss., Princeton Theological Seminary, 1989.
14. See Part 2, pp. 595–625.
15. Bruce McCormack, *Karl Barth's Critically Realistic Dialectical Theology: Its Genesis and Development 1909–1936* (Oxford: Clarendon, 1995), see esp. 453–63.
16. George Hunsinger, *How to Read Karl Barth: The Shape of His Theology* (New York: Oxford University Press, 1991).
17. Anthony C. Yu, "Karl Barth's Doctrine of Election," *Foundations* 13, no. 3 (July–September 1970): 248–61.
18. Reformed thinkers are divided on whether Barth finally embraces universal salvation; see chapter 1 for a fairly detailed description of his position. My own interpretation is that Barth endorses (perhaps even demands) a Christian hope for universal salvation, on the grounds that human beings cannot put a limit on the grace of God. But it is unfair to reduce his position to simple universalism,

given his insistence on the reality of divine rejection and epic struggle with the implications of that doctrine. Perhaps "dialectic universalism" is the proper term to employ for such a doctrine, whose process of creation is as important as its propositional content.

19.   David Ray Griffin, "Barth: Much Ado about Nothingness" and "Calvin: Omnipotence without Obfuscation," in *God, Power, and Evil: A Process Theodicy* (Lanham, Md.: University Press of America, 1991), 150–73, 116–30. Cf. the same author's "Whitehead and Niebuhr on God, Man, and the World," *Journal of Religion* 53, no. 2 (April 1973): 149–75.

20.   Daniel Day Williams, "The Concept of Truth in Karl Barth's Theology," in *Essays in Process Theology,* ed. Perry LeFevre (Chicago: Exploration Press, 1985), 302–10. Cf. in the same collection, the same author's "Barth and Brunner on Philosophy" (199–212) and "Niebuhr and Liberalism" (213–32).

21.   John B. Cobb Jr., "Calvinism," in *Varieties of Protestantism* (Philadelphia: Westminster, 1960), 48–68.

22.   John B. Cobb Jr., *Living Options in Protestant Theology* (Philadelphia: Westminster, 1962), 197.

23.   John B. Cobb Jr., "Barth: An Appreciation from the Enemy Camp," *Christian Advocate,* March 20, 1969, 7–8.

24.   John B. Cobb Jr., "Barth and the Barthians: A Critical Appraisal," in *How Karl Barth Changed My Mind,* ed. Donald K. McKim (Grand Rapids: Eerdmans, 1986), 172–77.

25.   "On Barthian terms one must order one's life around a purported reality with which contemporary thought makes no contact, or else one must deny any transcendent God altogether. Barth's influence excluded for many any other course. Thomists, Tillichians, Niebuhrians, and we process theologians watched this reversal with keen interest, but few of us participated. We did not experience the alternatives in this way" (Ibid., 174).

26.   H. R. Plomp, "John Cobb und Karl Barth: Was macht die Prozess-theologie mit Karl Barths Theologie, besonders der Schopfungslehre?" *Zeitschrift Dialektische Theologie* 1, no. 3 (1987): 45–64.

27.   See, for example, Anna Case-Winters, *God's Power: Traditional Understandings and Contemporary Challenges* (Louisville, Ky.: Westminster/John Knox, 1990), which sets up a contrast between Calvin and Barth on the one hand, and feminist thought and Charles Hartshorne on the other; Colin E. Gunton, *Becoming and Being: The Doctrine of God in Charles Hartshorne and Karl Barth* (Oxford: Oxford University Press, 1978); John C. Robertson Jr., "The Concept of the Divine Person in the Thought of Charles Hartshorne and Karl Barth" (Ph.D. diss., Yale University, 1967); and Sheila G. Davaney, *Divine Power: A Study of Karl Barth and Charles Hartshorne* (Philadelphia: Fortress, 1986).

28.   Clark M. Williamson, "Reversing the Reversal: Covenant and Election in Jewish and Process Theology," in *Jewish Theology and Process Thought,* ed. Sandra B. Lubarsky and David Ray Griffin (Albany, N.Y.: State University of New York Press, 1996), 163–84.

29.   Daniel Day Williams, *The Spirit and the Forms of Love* (New York: Harper & Row, 1968), 35.

30.   Ibid., 160–65.

31.   Norman Pittenger, *God's Way with Men: A Study of the Relationship between God*

and Man in Providence, "Miracle," and Prayer (London: Catholic Book Club, 1970), see esp. 101–22.

32. D. W. D. Shaw, "Providence and Persuasion," *Duke Divinity School Review* 45 (1980): 11–22.

33. See, for example, Charles Hartshorne, *The Divine Relativity: A Social Conception of God* (New Haven, Conn.: Yale University Press, 1948).

34. John B. Cobb Jr., *A Christian Natural Theology: Based on the Thought of Alfred North Whitehead* (Philadelphia: Westminster, 1965), 176–92.

35. Peter Hamilton, *The Living God and the Modern World: Christian Theology Based on the Thought of A. N. Whitehead* (Philadelphia: United Church Press, 1967), see esp. 89–96.

36. Bernard Meland, *The Reality of Faith: The Revolution in Cultural Forms* (New York: Oxford University Press, 1962), 109–36.

37. Ibid., 222–30.

38. Ibid., 267–83.

39. Schubert Ogden, *The Reality of God and Other Essays* (London: SCM Press, 1967), 1–70.

40. Ibid., 164–87.

41. Ibid., 96.

1. Karl Barth's Doctrine of Election

1. This work appeared in its original German as *Kirchliche Dogmatik* (Zurich: Evangelischer Verlag Zöllikon, 1932–1970). All quotations attributed to Barth in this chapter, unless otherwise indicated, are from the translation by G. W. Bromiley and T. F. Torrance: *Church Dogmatics* (Edinburgh: T. & T. Clark, 1962). Volume, section, and page numbers are indicated in each note.

2. Karl Barth, "The Strange New World within the Bible," in *The Word of God and the Word of Man,* trans. Douglas Horton (Grand Rapids: Zondervan, 1935), 28–50.

3. *CD* II/2:3.

4. It occurs in the presentation of the doctrine of salvation, under the Trinitarian heading of the Holy Spirit, after the doctrines of God, creation, and Christ's work, and preceding only ecclesiology.

5. See *Institutes* 3.21.5: "We call predestination God's eternal decree, by which he compacted with himself what he willed to become of each man. For all are not created in equal condition; rather, eternal life is foreordained for some, eternal damnation for others. Therefore, as any man has been created to one or the other of these ends, we speak of him as predestined to life or to death" (926); and 3.21.7: "As Scripture, then, clearly shows, we say that God once established by his eternal and unchangeable plan those whom he long before determined once for all to receive into salvation, and those whom, on the other hand, he would devote to destruction" (931). All quotations from the *Institutes* are from the Library of Christian Classics edition, edited by John T. McNeill and translated by Ford Lewis Battles (Philadelphia: Westminster, 1960).

6. See *Institutes,* 3.21.6: "[F]or in the election of a whole nation God has already shown that in his mere generosity he has not been bound by any laws but is

free, so that equal apportionment of grace is not to be required of him. The very inequality of his grace proves that it is free" (929); and 3.21.7: "We assert that, with respect to the elect, this plan [to save some and destroy others] was founded on his freely given mercy, without regard to human worth; but by his just and irreprehensible but incomprehensible judgment he has barred the door of life to those whom he has given over to damnation" (931).

7.   *Institutes* 3.23.12, p. 960. Barth criticizes Calvin's doctrine of God's "absolute decree" in the following passage: "But there is a temptation here. . . . It is the temptation to think of God the Father, Son and Holy Spirit merely as a Subject which can and does elect, a Subject which is furnished, of course, with supereminent divine attributes, but which differs from other such subjects only by the fact that in its election it is absolutely free. . . . And it follows that its election is absolutely unconditioned, or is conditioned only by the Subject in and for itself and as such. And this means that the choice actually made must be regarded as a *decretum absolutum*" (*CD* II/2:100). Barth finds God's freedom in God's love rather than in an abstract notion of absoluteness.

8.   "[I]n Himself, in the primal and basic decision in which He wills to be and actually is God, in the mystery of what takes place from and to all eternity within Himself, within His triune being, God is none other than the One who in His Son or Word elects Himself, and in and with Himself elects His people. . . . Because this is the case, the doctrine of election occupies a place at the head of all other Christian dogmas. And it belongs to the doctrine of God Himself because God Himself does not will to be God, and is not God, except as the One who elects" (*CD* II/2:76–77).

9.   Election must precede and inform the doctrine of creation, for example, or there is a danger that the doctrine of reconciliation will appear as God's stop-gap remedy for sin: "On this view God Himself appears in a sense to be halted and baffled by sin, being pushed back into a kind of special 'world of God.' From this it might easily appear as if reconciliation is the corresponding escape from this dilemma, a mysterious wrestling with what is almost a rival God, a reaction against a different power, something not at all in keeping with the unity and omnipotence of God" (*CD* II/2:90).

10. This issue begins Schleiermacher's exposition of the doctrine, which is the first theorem in the doctrine of the church, and guides his inquiry throughout: "While we denote this ordinance by the phrase 'divine election,' because we hold firmly that its final ground lies in the divine good-pleasure, this does not hinder us from inquiring by what this divine good-pleasure is determined. Especially as we are not in a position to say that God makes no distinctions, but that some human wills place hindrances in the way . . . The demand for such an investigation has become still more pressing since whole peoples have accepted Christianity, of whom a considerable proportion at least attained regeneration, while on the other hand many a member of nations long Christian remained provisionally excluded from that inner circle" (Friedrich Schleiermacher, *The Christian Faith* [Philadelphia: Fortress, 1928], 538).

11. Barth finds that deterministic election is the result of mistakenly basing the doctrine on one's experience that there are those who have never heard the gospel, or, having heard it, reject or misuse it. Combined with a previously arrived at doctrine of efficacious grace, this leads some to conclude that God determines

the creature's response: "[T]he dubious basing of the doctrine on certain experiences has its root in the supposedly self-evident presupposition that the divine election is a direct determination of human existence as such. Once we are freed from this presupposition, there is no further point in attempting in some way or other to derive the divine election of grace from the existence of heathen and Christians, or of good Christians and bad" (CD II/2:44).

12. See CD II/2:257; the section title is "The Being of God as the One Who Loves in Freedom." This describes God's self-constitution, the divine being *in se:* "God is who He is in the act of His revelation. God seeks and creates fellowship between Himself and us, and therefore He loves us. But He is this loving God without us as Father, Son and Holy Spirit, in the freedom of the Lord, who has His life from Himself" (*Leitsatz,* 257). The *Leitsatz* of §32 (II/2:3), quoted above (see note 3), describes God as the One who loves in freedom not only in God's triune self, but also, graciously, for us.

13. Ephesians 1:3 gives Barth the scriptural imperative to find election "in Christ."

14. "If it is to be a question of the divine judgment, as it must be in dealing with the doctrine of election, then Scripture must not be brought in simply as an interpretation of the facts of the case as given by our own judgment. The very facts which we consider must not be sought in the realm of experience but in Scripture, or rather in the self-revelation of God attested in Scripture" (CD II/2:39). This is also Barth's criticism of Calvin—that the observation of election and rejection becomes an abstract principle that guides the doctrine in place of the story of Jesus Christ: "I could not say that [Calvin] made the experience in question the basis of his doctrine of predestination. But he did buttress his doctrine so emphatically by the appeal to it, that we can hardly fail to recognize that much of the pathos and emotional power with which he defended it, and to an even greater extent the form in which he did so, were determined by this experience, the effects of which were inevitably serious from the point of view of the purity of the doctrine" (CD II/2:39).

15. Hence, Barth also criticizes the Reformed dogmatic approach of treating election under the general tenet of the decrees of God: "We have already stated the reasons why we cannot adopt this approach. It takes God in His general relationship with the world as its first datum, and understands His electing as one function in this general relationship" (CD II/2:78).

16. CD II/2:45.

17. "That idea [of the *decretum absolutum*] does, of course, give us an answer to the question about the electing God. It speaks of a good-pleasure of God which in basis and direction is unknown to man and to all beings outside God Himself. This good-pleasure is omnipotent and incontrovertible in its decisions. If we are asked concerning its nature, then ultimately no more can be said than that it is divine, and therefore absolutely supreme and authoritative. But now in the place of this blank, this unknown quantity, we are to put the name of Jesus Christ. . . . How can the doctrine of predestination be anything but 'dark' and obscure if in its very first tenet, the tenet which determines all the rest, it can speak only of a *decretum absolutum?* In trying to understand Jesus Christ as the electing God we abandon this tradition, but we hold fast by Jn. 1:1-2" (CD II/2:103–4).

18. CD II/2:103.

19. *CD* II/2:3, italics mine.

20. Quoted in Ian Barbour, *Religion in an Age of Science: The Gifford Lectures, 1989–1991* (San Francisco: Harper & Row, 1990), 1:136.

21. For instance, God is love not only in relation to the creation, but also within God's self: "Even if there were no such relationship, even if there were no other outside of Him, He would still be love" (*CD* II/2:6).

22. Barth criticizes other theologians for succumbing to the temptation of asserting these extra-divine realities: "[T]here was a desire to be wise in respect of God before learning wisdom from God Himself. Thus there sprang up within the sphere of this doctrine all those attempts which resulted in violence being done to the freedom of God by the indication of certain external conditions of God's work in the light of which the validity and order of His election could again be measured by our conceptions of order, and thus acknowledged as righteous and worthy of God without that silence, without listening to God Himself" (*CD* II/2:22–23).

23. To anticipate for a moment the argument of the following chapters, it seems that a different but equally Christian notion of God's freedom could be achieved if different assumptions guide the discussion. If God and creatures occupy the same reality, which is constituted in its metaphysical orderliness by God's decision, then God's decisions might still be considered free although they "follow" regular laws and do not violate the categories that are applicable to all entities. To put it in the terms of Duns Scotus, *potentia ordinata* is the becoming concrete of *potentia absoluta*, not a limitation of it. If creatures have no particularity in advance of their own temporal becoming, then they cannot be foreknown as actualities and cannot exert any sort of influence on God except as potentialities. With these assumptions in place, God is free in God's own proper act of election while still with creatures in the same system of reality, and in election God freely opens God's self to the creative acts of creatures because foreknowledge and determinism are logically impossible. Cf. J. B. Korolec, "Free Will and Free Choice," in *The Cambridge History of Later Medieval Philosophy: From the Rediscovery of Aristotle to the Disintegration of Scholasticism, 1100–1600*, ed. Norman Kretzmann et al. (New York: Cambridge University Press, 1988), 639–40.

24. *CD* II/2:50. On the meaning of decision language in Barth, see my "Barth and Whitehead on Divine Self-Determination," *Encounter* 60, no. 4 (1999): 441–62.

25. The prevalence of freedom over power, of election over sovereignty in theology, is further guaranteed in Barth's theology by the doctrine of God's unity in act. That God elects, and does not both elect and reject as if there were two acts to be considered, follows from the fact that God elects God's self first and acts subsequently in harmony with that self-election. If there is also rejection to be found here (in Christ), then it is swallowed up by election as death is swallowed up in resurrection. If the act of God has two aspects, it is not a reflection of duality in God or in God's decision to elect, which is single and definitive. "It is certainly true that God's mercy and righteousness are both active in God's dealings with believers and unbelievers. But in view of the unity of the divine essence, we must at once ask whether it is possible to allocate the two attributes to different dealings of God, as though only His mercy

were at work in the one case and only His righteousness in the other" (*CD* II/2:16).

26. *CD* II/2:4.
27. *CD* II/2:22.
28. These errors may even be masked in the appearance of cleaving to revealed truth, according to Barth: "There must not be any systematization, no setting up of a principle. There must not be any delimitation by the assertion of the *benevolentia Dei universalis* as an assertion which binds God in advance and thus anticipates and secretly controls the reality" (*CD* II/2:73). Barth wants us to attend to the whole of revelation in describing God's ways and works rather than choosing one aspect of revelation (e.g., "God is love") and judging the rest by it.
29. *CD* II/1:7.
30. *CD* II/1:6.
31. *CD* III/1:340–44. I am indebted to George Hunsinger for bringing these pages to my attention.
32. *CD* III/1:340.
33. *CD* III/1:341.
34. *CD* III/1:341.
35. *CD* III/1:342.
36. *CD* III/1:340–41, italics mine.
37. *CD* III/1:341–42.
38. *CD* III/1:342.
39. *CD* III/1:342.
40. *CD* III/1:343.
41. Cf. Barth's assertion that God's freedom is found not in divine abstraction but in divine concretion—that is, in Jesus Christ: "God is free. Because this is the case, we must say expressly in conclusion that the freedom of God is the freedom which consists and fulfils itself in His Son Jesus Christ. In Him God has loved Himself from all eternity. In Him He has loved the world. He has done so in Him, in the freedom which renders His life divine, and therefore glorious, triumphant, and strong to save" (*CD* II/1:321).
42. "Now an eternal object, in itself, abstracts from all determinate actual entities, including even God. . . . Accordingly, the differentiated relevance of eternal objects to each instance of the creative process requires their conceptual realization in the primordial nature of God. He does not create eternal objects; for his nature requires them in the same degree that they require him" (PR 256–57).
43. Barth speaks of a "disproportion" between contrasting pairs such as good and evil, election and rejection: "And for this reason we do not find a proportion but a disproportion between the positive will of God which purposes the life and blessedness of man and the permissive will of God which ordains him to seduction by Satan and guilt before God. In this disproportion the first element is always predominate, the second subordinate" (*CD* II/2:172); "[D]ouble predestination can be understood only in this order, only in this disproportionate relation between the divine taking away and the divine giving, between the humiliation of God and the exaltation of man, between rejection and election" (174). In passages that are more troubling, Barth also sees and approves the

disproportion between Christians and Jews (II/2, §34) and between men and women (III/2, §45).

44. *CD* II/2:170.

45. This is George Hunsinger's interpretation, with which I agree; see his *How to Read Karl Barth: The Shape of His Theology* (New York: Oxford University Press, 1991), 185–88.

46. "The electing God creates for Himself as such man over against Himself. And this means that for his part man can and actually does elect God, thus attesting and activating himself as elected man" (*CD* II/2:177); "It is not that He [Jesus Christ] does not also elect as man, i.e., elect God in faith. But this election can only follow His own election" (103).

47. *CD* II/2:94.

48. *CD* II/2:94.

49. "In the beginning, before time and space as we know them, before creation, before there was any reality distinct from God which could be the object of the love of God or the setting for His acts of freedom, God anticipated and determined within Himself (in the power of His love and freedom, of His knowing and willing) that the goal and meaning of all His dealings with the as yet non-existent universe should be the fact that in His Son He would be gracious towards man, uniting Himself with him" (*CD* II/2:101).

50. Barth tends to use the term *immutable* not to denote a metaphysically necessary divine trait, but the biblical idea of divine faithfulness; for example: "With the traditional teaching of Scripture, we think of predestination as eternal, preceding time and all the contents of time. We also think of it as divine, a disposing of time and its contents which is based on the omnipotence of God and characterized by His constancy (or 'immutability')" (*CD* II/2:155). Here Barth redefines a nonbiblical term brought into theology from philosophy in order to rescue the older theology from itself, by recovering the meaning of God's revelation of God's own character in Scripture as opposed to the nonbiblical implication of the term (that God is inert and not living).

51. *CD* II/2:101–2.

52. Cf. Robert W. Jenson, "Eighth Locus: The Holy Spirit," in *Christian Dogmatics,* ed. Carl E. Braaten et al. (Philadelphia: Fortress, 1984), 2:125–42, on the necessity to go beyond Barth in affirming election by the Holy Spirit: "Barth unites God's rule in Christ and God's rule of all history by making the Christ-event itself to be the reality of eternity, and he does this by bringing the trinitarian dialectic to new life. These are indeed what must be done. But Barth unites the two wills of God by the relation of only the Father and the Son. Correspondingly, the eternity that Christ fills is defined as pretemporal, thus remaining within the traditional interpretation. . . . But the eternity of this moment must be established not by the prefix 'pre-' but by the prefix 'post-'; it is in that the man Christ *will* be the agent and center of the final community, that his will for us is the eternal determination of our lives. The trinitarian dialectic can be the appropriate conceptual scheme of predestination only if the whole scheme—of Father, Son, *and* Holy Spirit—is used and only if the Spirit's metaphysical priority ('God is Spirit') is affirmed. The speaking of the gospel is the event of predestination in that the gospel gives what it speaks about, but this eschatological efficacy of the

gospel is the Spirit. We must parody Barth: the Holy Spirit is the choosing God" (138).

53. Consider *CD* II/2:76–77: "[I]n the mystery of what takes place from and to all eternity within Himself, within His triune being, God is none other than the One who in His Son or Word elects Himself, and in and with Himself elects His people." With a mention of the Trinity coming just before a mention of the community, it would seem natural at this point to acknowledge the Holy Spirit as the one who draws the community together to form God's people.

54. See chapter 2 for a more detailed demonstration of this claim.

55. Eugene Rogers's article "Supplementing Barth on Jews and Gender: Identifying God by Anagogy and the Spirit," *Modern Theology* 14, no. 1 (January 1998): 43–81, argues that Barth's theology in the areas of interreligious dialogue and gender relations would be improved by a more Trinitarian structure. See especially pp. 66–67: "The eschatological community where Christians learn to see themselves as possessing no God of their *own*, but as brought by sheer grace into the worship of the God of the Jews, would lead to a doctrine of election of the community to which the Holy Spirit *calls* us. Unlike most Protestants, Barth has a rich doctrine of vocation, which Catholics might call glorification or Orthodox deification. He might have built his doctrine of election on that model."

56. *CD* II/2:10.

57. *CD* II/2:121.

58. *CD* II/2:5.

59. *CD* II/1:56.

60. Notice the repeated "in Jesus Christ" of the *Leitsatz* to §33.

61. *CD* II/2:147. The relative success or failure of prior theologians to see Jesus Christ as electing and elected is related in *CD* II/2:60–76.

62. *CD* II/2:110.

63. *CD* II/2:111. Barth begins §33, "The Election of Jesus Christ," with an exegesis of John 1 that identifies the Logos with election, both *ab intra* and *ad extra,* both as God's self-determination and as God's choice for creatures. This election was "in the beginning with God" (John 1:2) and governs the creation.

64. *CD* II/2:110.

65. *CD* II/2:100.

66. *CD* II/2:104.

67. "The eternal will of God which is the predestination of all things is God's life in the form of the history, encounter and decision between Himself and man, a history, encounter and decision which are already willed and known from all eternity, and to that extent, prior to all external events, are already actual before Him and for Him" (*CD* II/2:175).

68. *CD* II/2:17.

69. *CD* II/2:178.

70. *CD* II/2:107.

71. *CD* II/2:103.

72. "The Subject of this [election] is indeed God in Jesus Christ, and its particular object is indeed men. But it is not men as private persons in the singular or plural. It is these men as a fellowship elected by God in Jesus Christ and determined from all eternity for a particular service, to be made capable of this service and to discharge it" (*CD* II/2:196).

73. This attention to communal election provides a basis for process theology's attempt to explicate the election of "societies," composite individuals made up of specialized entities.

74. *CD* II/2:212.

75. "Who and what is Jesus Christ Himself in His relation to the community of God? . . . He is the promised son of Abraham and David, the Messiah of Israel. And He is simultaneously the Head and Lord of the Church, called and gathered from Jews and Gentiles" (*CD* II/2:197).

76. Katherine Sonderegger, *That Jesus Christ Was Born a Jew: Karl Barth's "Doctrine of Israel"* (University Park, Pa.: Pennsylvania State University Press, 1992), 170.

77. For an extended discussion of this issue, see Sonderegger, *That Jesus Christ Was Born,* especially chapters 2 and 3. Sonderegger aims to take full advantage of Barth's "discovery of Judaism for Christian theology," in the words of Friedrich Marquardt, while critically examining his supersessionism.

78. Michael Wyschogrod, a self-described "Jewish Barthian," makes this intriguing point at length in his book *The Body of Faith: God in the People Israel* (San Francisco: Harper & Row, 1983): "The election of the people of Israel as the people of God constitutes the sanctification of a natural family. God could have chosen a spiritual criterion: the election of all those who have faith or who obey God's commandments. . . . But God did not choose this path. He chose the seed of Abraham, Isaac and Jacob. There are, of course, religious and ethical demands made of the elect. When they do not live up to those demands, they are punished. But the essential belonging to the people of election is derived from descent from the patriarchs. The election of Israel is therefore a corporate election" (xv).

79. *CD* II/2:214.

80. *CD* II/2:212–13.

81. "[T]he Church lives by the existence of 'Christ according to the flesh.' It lives by Jesus Christ because and so far as He is, as man, the Son of Abraham and David, and is called Jesus of Nazareth; not in spite of this; not under the incidental assumption that He is this too and not only the eternal Son of God; but because and so far as He is an Israelite out of Israel" (*CD* II/2:204).

82. "But the miracle of the Church does not consist only in the fact that there were and are Jews who finally come to believe, i.e., to know the God of Israel who has taken away from it all its sins. Over and above this it consists also in the fact that Gentiles, many Gentiles, were and are called to the same faith in the God of Israel, an abundance of men from the nations beside and around Israel, from the nations who as such are not elected, who as such have no part in its promise, distinction and endowment, to whom its Messiah is a complete stranger. . . . Yet they had, as a rule, served only as the dark foil to Israel's history. Israel's sanctification was always its separation from them. Israel's grace was always its preservation from their might and hostility. Israel's distinction was always its discrimination from them. That God loved Israel always seemed to mean that He did not love the nations as such, but let them go their own ways, let them share in His work for the most part only as instruments of His wrath against Israel. . . . Is it not rather the case that God did not really concern Himself incidentally with Israel for the sake of the nations, but that He concerned Himself in such a special way with Israel for the sake of the nations?" (*CD* II/2:228–29).

83. *CD* II/2:229.
84. *CD* II/2:195.
85. *CD* II/2:288.
86. *CD* II/2:195.
87. *CD* II/2:198. Barth's struggle with the *Judenfrage,* the continued existence of Jews and Judaism in the era of the Christian gospel, threatens his scheme of "passing" and "coming" forms by allowing the symbolic Israel and church, the abstract communities, to replace their concrete actualities in his theology. A possible way out of this dilemma for Barth is indicated by the following passage, in which Barth depicts the church waiting for the conversion of the Jews not in time but at the end of time, as a resurrection: "From the very first 'life from the dead' has been the sign under which the history of Israel has stood. We think of Isaac's birth and sacrifice, of the deliverance of the Israelite first-born in Egypt, of the passage of the Red Sea, of the blooming and fruit-bearing rod of Aaron (Num.17:8f), of the experience of Jonah the unwilling prophet, of the well-known vision of the revivified bones in Ezek. 37. What is promised to it will in that day pass into fulfilment in the Church, indeed in the cosmos—in that day when all Israel believes in Jesus. But that will itself be in the divine miracle of a resurrection from the dead, the revelation of the end of all things in the beginning of a new world. It is quite impossible, therefore, that it should be made apprehensible as an expectation within history" (*CD* II/2:283). Perhaps Barth's doctrine of Israel might be made less abstract if the problem of applying its tenets to concrete, existing Jews were tempered by a more thorough recognition that both Israel *and* the church await the *eschaton* for their fulfillment. The church is, after all, the bride of Christ, charged as yet to wait and watch for the bridegroom; the wedding feast has not commenced.
88. *CD* II/2:199.
89. "[The Church] must call [the Synagogue] by joining with it as [God's] people, and therefore with Him. No particular function can be this call, but only the life of the community as a whole authentically lived before the Jews. It need hardly be said that the life of the community as a whole has not been nor is this call. . . . In this sense the Church as a whole has made no convincing impression on the Jew as a whole. It has debated with him, tolerated him, persecuted him, or abandoned him to persecution without protest. . . . But for the most part it has not done for the Jews the only real thing it can do, attesting the manifested King of Israel and Saviour of the world, the imminent kingdom, in the form of the convincing witness of its own existence. And thus it still owes everything to those to whom it is indebted for everything. . . . The recurrent Jewish question is the question of Christ and the Church which has not been and cannot be answered by any of its ministries" (*CD* IV/3:878).
90. *CD* II/2:200. Barth's christological methodology is utilized with great consistency in this section, but to the denigration of the Jewish faith in both its concrete and abstract forms. If "only in the knowledge of Jesus Christ and of His election, i.e., in the faith of the Church" can election per se be understood and actually experienced, then Jews outside the church are only ignorantly elect and can be accused of not grasping and fulfilling the promises of the Hebrew Scriptures. But Barth finds that the church is equally guilty of ignorance with regard

to its election insofar as it seeks to separate that election from Israel and separate Jesus Christ from his people. The difference in seriousness between the two accusations seems to be that the church is guilty of dismissing the truth of Jesus Christ that it pretends to acknowledge, while Israel is guilty of not recognizing the truth of Jesus Christ at all. Is the sin of unbelief greater in one case than in the other? See *CD* II/2:200–201.

91.   *CD* II/2:213–33 is largely concerned with this issue. In this passage, Barth explicates Romans 9 to discover what purpose is served by those who continue to resist their election: "God's purpose in the election of His community is executed through Pharaoh too, and not through Moses only. In the way marked by His deeds, which leads on to the day of His future, to the day of Jesus Christ, God finds and uses even him, and not Moses only. He stands fittingly beside Moses because he makes it clear that in respect of its fulfilment God's purpose in the election of His community is not bound up with (v. 16) the willing and running of any man (not even with that of Moses), that in one way or another it has to be carried out by the person concerned. He stands fittingly beside Moses because in his own very different way he bears witness to the righteousness of God and indeed to the righteousness of His mercy. In the same sense, too, Ishmael stands fittingly beside Isaac, Esau beside Jacob, and today the refractory Synagogue beside the Church" (220–21). God uses the synagogue, then, in the same sense as God used Pharaoh—hardening its heart for the greater divine glory. This is consistent with God's self-determined character to show mercy on whom God wills to show mercy (Rom. 9:16). Here Barth skirts dangerously close to finding concrete examples of rejected persons outside Jesus Christ, since the synagogue and its members are actual Jews who can be met—and, possibly, discriminated against and hated—by Christians who accept Barth's exegesis.

92.   *CD* II/2:313.

93.   *CD* II/2:314.

94.   *CD* II/2:314.

95.   *CD* II/2:234.

96.   *CD* II/2:238.

97.   *CD* II/2:238.

98.   *CD* II/2:6.

99.   *CD* II/2:25.

100.   *CD* II/2:246.

101.   *Institutes*, 1.1.1, p. 17.

102.   *CD* II/2:178.

103.   On human agency as miracle, see George Hunsinger, "Double Agency as a Test Case," in *How to Read Karl Barth*, 185–224. Hunsinger maintains that for Barth, God's working and the creature's working can never be described together under one conceptual scheme, but have a "difference in order" that remains in effect even when God condescends to enter creaturely reality: "That the divine otherness establishes a 'fellowship of intimacy' with the creature in which the integrity of each partner is maintained, that the divine omnipotence establishes a 'fellowship of freedom' with the creature in which the unconditional sovereignty of the divine partner is fully expressed without crushing and indeed by liberating the creature's full spontaneity—these assertions are

descriptions of the indescribable, conceptions of the inconceivable, and apprehensions of the inapprehensible" (199).

104. *CD* II/2:317.
105. *CD* II/2:118.
106. *CD* II/2:153.
107. *CD* II/2:179.
108. "The man Jesus is not a mere puppet moved this way and that by God. He is not a mere reed used by God as the instrument of His Word. . . . In His wholehearted obedience, in His electing of God alone, He is wholly free" (*CD* II/2:178–79).
109. *CD* II/2:179–80.
110. "While Christian sympathy is not disquieted by the earlier and later adoption of one and another individual into the fellowship of redemption, yet on the other hand there does remain an insoluble discord if, on the assumption of survival after death, we are to think of a part of the human race as entirely excluded from this fellowship" (Schleiermacher, *Christian Faith,* 539); "Only in this limited sense, therefore—that is, only at each point where we can make a comparison between those laid hold of by sanctification and those not yet laid hold of—ought we to say that God omits or passes over some, and that He rejects those He passes over, and hence that election always and only appears with reprobation as its foil" (548).
111. *CD* II/2:167.
112. *CD* II/2:327.
113. *CD* II/2:193.
114. *CD* II/2:194.
115. *CD* II/2:236.
116. *CD* II/2:208.
117. *CD* II/2:248.
118. *CD* II/2:208. Note that Barth's reference to the destruction of Jerusalem indirectly refers to a familiar Christian argument which holds that the Jewish faith is invalid because sacrifices can no longer be performed: "These traditional Christian critics point to verses in the Hebrew Bible that connect forgiveness of sin with the offering of sacrifices. With the destruction of the Temple, the bringing of sacrifices by Jews ended. The Christian argument then is that since forgiveness of sins requires sacrifices and since there are no sacrifices in Judaism, the guilt of the sinner cannot be alleviated by Judaism. While, in one sense, Christianity also lacks sacrifices, it insists that the death of Jesus was the ultimate sacrifice, which ended all further sacrifice" (Wyschogrod, *Body of Faith,* 245).
119. *CD* II/2:207.
120. *CD* II/2:241.
121. "We will proceed, then, on this presupposition. The elect individual in the Old Testament, so impressively and yet in so many different ways distinguished, set apart and differentiated in the Old Testament stories and pictures, is always a witness to Jesus Christ, and is indeed a type of Christ Himself" (*CD* II/2:364).
122. *CD* II/2:353.
123. *CD* II/2:371.
124. *CD* II/2:361.

125. *CD* II/2:390.
126. "The man who is isolated over against God is as such rejected by God. But to be this man can only be the godless man's own choice" (*CD* II/2:306).
127. *CD* II/2:317.
128. *CD* II/2:356.
129. *CD* II/2:391.
130. *CD* II/2:306.
131. *CD* II/2:181.
132. *CD* II/2:181.
133. *CD* II/2:183.
134. "In virtue of its character and content this decree can never be rigid and fixed. Because it is God's decree it must, of course, be constant, authoritative and powerful. But because it has pleased God to let it be a concrete decree, it never ceases to be event" (*CD* II/2:184).
135. "The historical multiformity of individual elect and non-elect, of those placed on the right and those on the left, cannot be ignored and no sound exegesis can afford to ignore it. . . . But this multiformity of historical appearances is best observed and maintained if here too the final word in exegesis is actually the name of Jesus Christ, if He is understood as the individual in whom we recover both the unity of that which they all commonly attest, and that which is the peculiar individuality of each" (*CD* II/2:366).
136. *CD* II/2:184.
137. Peter Barth, as quoted in *CD* II/2:188.
138. *CD* II/2:191.
139. *CD* II/2:315.
140. *CD* II/2:193. Notice in this passage and in the two previous long quotations that Barth evokes the language of the Spirit whenever he is discussing God's present activity in history to conform creation to the eternal divine will.
141. *CD* II/2:343.
142. *CD* IV/3:482.
143. *CD* IV/3:484.
144. *CD* IV/3:483–84.
145. *CD* IV/3:481.
146. "Hence the knowledge of God given to man through his illumination is no mere apprehension and understanding of God's being and action, nor as such a kind of intuitive contemplation. It is the claiming not only of his thinking but also of his willing and work, of the whole man, for God. It is his refashioning to be a theatre, witness and instrument of His acts. Its subject and content, which are also its origin, make it an active knowledge, in which there are affirmation and negation, volition and decision, action and inaction, and in which man leaves certain old courses and enters and pursues new ones" (*CD* IV/3:513).
147. "The essence of their vocation is that God makes them His witnesses. Only indirectly and by implication does this mean that He makes them only witnesses of the fact that He is, or of who and what He is in and for Himself in His hidden Godhead. He makes them witnesses of His being in His past, present and future action in the world and in history, of His being in His acts among and upon men" (*CD* IV/3:575).

148. *CD* IV/3:613.
149. *CD* IV/3:649.
150. *CD* IV/3:484.
151. *CD* IV/3:497.

2. Whitehead's Concept of the Initial Aim

1. As noted in chapter 1, Karl Barth does not consider it necessary to place the doctrine of election within a philosophical system or "worldview" to have it accurately reflect the divine-human relationship. However, all that is being asserted at this point is that process thought is in fact included in the range of viable approaches to describing this relationship. The range also encompasses descriptions within the bounds of revelation alone, such as Barth's. As noted by Robert W. Jenson, Barth constructs a "christological metaphysics," "an encompassing, flexible and drastically coherent interpretation of reality" by defying the inherited metaphysical rule "that the Ground [of Being] can be reached only by abstraction from time and its particularities" ("Karl Barth," in *The Modern Theologians: An Introduction to Christian Theology in the Twentieth Century*, ed. David F. Ford [New York: Basil Blackwell, 1989], 1:41). Process thought aims to construct a similar interpretation of reality by defining general categories that govern every event, including both divine and creaturely events; it also defies the inherited rule by stating that God is found in each event of creaturely history as an active partner and as final cause. Both Barth and process thought thus utilize a metaphysics, in Jenson's definition, to give election its proper terminology, structure, and place in theology. The claim that process thought possesses categories that render it uniquely suited to describe election is the substance of this volume.
2. See Emil Brunner, "Nature and Grace," and Karl Barth, "No! An Answer to Emil Brunner," in *Natural Theology*, ed. Peter Fraenkel (London: Centenary, 1946).
3. *CD* II/2:3.
4. "In the philosophy of organism, as here developed, God's existence is not generically different from that of other actual entities, except that he is 'primordial' in a sense to be gradually explained" (PR 75). This exception may indeed amount to a "species of the primordial" whose only member is God, but to take process thought in this direction is clearly against Whitehead's intention. God's primordiality has an analogue in the creature's mental pole, which guides its self-creation in terms of purpose; thus, the exception can be treated as a distinction without an absolute difference.
5. The need for contrast in aesthetic intensity does not mean that evil is necessary as a contrast to good. Process thought's commitment to the value of multiplicity means that many varied goods contrast with each other (as well as with the possibility of unrealized goods *and* evils); there is diversity in the good and the beautiful, unified in God's vision of order without being thereby collapsed into undifferentiation.
6. See John B. Cobb Jr. and David Ray Griffin, *Process Theology: An Introductory Exposition* (Philadelphia: Westminster, 1976), 61: "Likewise, the loss of a

notion of divine purpose that at its most general level is inflexible would lead to a complete relativism." To these authors, this "most general level" is the aesthetic goal.

7. "[T]he notion of 'power' is transformed into the principle that the reason for things are always to be found in the composite nature of definite actual entities—in the nature of God for reasons of the highest absoluteness, and in the nature of definite temporal actual entities for reasons which refer to a particular environment. The ontological principle can be summarized as: no actual entity, then no reason" (PR 19).

8. "That the potentiality for being an element in a real concrescence of many entities into one actuality is the one general metaphysical character attaching to all entities, actual or non-actual; and that every item in its universe is involved in each concrescence. In other words, it belongs to the nature of a 'being' that it is a potential for every 'becoming.' This is the 'principle of relativity'" (PR 22). Elsewhere Whitehead notes that this principle requires a single primordial entity with a nature not derived from any contingent particulars if *nonactual* entities, (i.e., possibilities) are to find their unity in a real concrescence: "So if there is a relevance of what in the temporal world is unrealized, the relevance must express a fact of togetherness in the formal constitution of a non-temporal actuality. But by the principle of relativity, there can only be one non-derivative actuality, unbounded by its prehensions of an actual world. Such a primordial superject of creativity achieves, in its unity of satisfaction, the complete conceptual valuation of all eternal objects" (PR 32).

9. "In each actuality there are two concrescent poles of realization—'enjoyment' and 'appetition,' that is, the 'physical' and the 'conceptual.' For God the conceptual is prior to the physical, for the World the physical poles are prior to the conceptual poles" (PR 348). "In the case of the primordial actual entity, which is God, there is no past. Thus the ideal realization of conceptual feeling takes the precedence" (PR 87).

10. George Allen, "The Aims of Societies and the Aims of God," in *Process Philosophy and Christian Thought,* ed. Delwin Brown et al. (Indianapolis: Bobbs-Merrill, 1971), 469–70.

11. "Here 'feeling' is the term used for the basic generic operation of passing from the objectivity of the data to the subjectivity of the actual entity in question" (PR 40). "Feelings are 'vectors'; for they feel what is *there* and transform it into what is *here*" (PR 87).

12. Cf. PR 7, 46. A God who could be past would undergo perishing from moment to moment; in effect, God would be a route of occasions rather than a single actual entity.

13. Cf., for example, PR 348, on the dipolar nature of both God and world: "In God's nature, permanence is primordial and flux is derivative from the World: in the World's nature, flux is primordial and permanence is derivative from God."

14. Cobb and Griffin, *Process Theology,* 105.

15. Cf. PR 57: "The creative action is the universe always becoming one in a particular unity of self-experience, and thereby adding to the multiplicity which is the universe as many. This insistent concrescence into unity is the outcome of the ultimate self-identity of each entity. No entity—be it 'universal' or 'partic-

ular'—can play disjointed rôles. Self-identity requires that every entity have one conjoined, self-consistent function, whatever be the complexity of that function." The actual occasion creates itself in the image of a role it has chosen for itself, but God is the first *and final* elector of the entity's role in the world process, free to transform and redeem the entity's choice into the ordered actuality of a place in the consequent nature.

16. On God as initiator of each occasion, Whitehead writes: "In this sense God is the principle of concretion; namely, he is that actual entity from which each temporal concrescence receives that initial aim from which its self-causation starts. That aim determines the initial gradations of relevance of eternal objects for conceptual feeling; and constitutes the autonomous subject in its primary phase of feelings with its initial conceptual valuations, and with its initial physical purposes" (PR 244).

17. Cf. PR 40: "By reason of the actuality of this primordial valuation of pure potentials, each eternal object has a definite relevance to each concrescent process."

18. "Abrupt" is a technical term in SMW for the imposition of finitude on infinity. In other words, the unlimited realm of eternal objects becomes the limited and delineated hierarchy of possibility prehended by the emerging occasion. Cf. SMW 171.

19. Cf. PR 31: "The primordial created fact is the unconditioned conceptual valuation of the entire multiplicity of eternal objects. This is the 'primordial nature' of God. By reason of this complete valuation, the objectification of God in each derivate actual entity results in a graduation of the relevance of eternal objects to the concrescent phases of that derivate occasion."

20. "The principle of the graduated 'intensive relevance' of eternal objects to the primary physical data of experience expresses a real fact as to the preferential adaptation of selected eternal objects to novel occasions originating from an assigned environment. This principle expresses the prehension by every creature of the graduated order of appetitions constituting the primordial nature of God" (PR 207).

21. "Thus the transition of the creativity from an actual world to the correlate novel concrescence is conditioned by the relevance of God's all-embracing conceptual valuations to the particular possibilities of transmission from the actual world, and by its relevance to the various possibilities of initial subjective form available for the initial feelings" (PR 244).

22. "An actual entity feels as it does feel in order to be the actual entity which it is. In this way an actual entity satisfies Spinoza's notion of substance: it is *causa sui*. The creativity is not an external agency with its own ulterior purposes. All actual entities share with God this characteristic of self-causation" (PR 222).

23. "But as soon as individual experience is not negligible, the autonomy of the subject in the modification of its initial subjective aim must be taken into account" (PR 245).

24. Cf. PR 254: "The low-grade organism is merely the summation of the forms of energy which flow in upon it in all their multiplicity of detail. It receives, and it transmits, but it fails to simplify into intelligible system. The physical theory of the structural flow of energy has to do with the transmission of simple physical feelings from individual actuality to actuality. Thus some sort of quantum

theory in physics, relevant to the existing type of cosmic order, is to be expected."

25. The division of the concrescence into phases does not indicate temporal succession, as indicated in PR 283: "This genetic passage from phase to phase is not in physical time: the exactly converse point of view expresses the relationship of concrescence to physical time. It can be put shortly by saying, that physical time expresses some features of the growth, but *not* the growth of the features." The phases do indicate growth in an ordered process which can be analyzed into component feelings, but the succession that obtains should not be understood as a temporal succession. For a more detailed treatment of the division of components in a concrescence, see Bowman C. Clarke, "God and Time in Whitehead," *Journal of the American Academy of Religion* 48, no. 4 (1980): 563–79.

26. The superjective nature of God as mentioned in PR 32 (see note 8) is the divine mediation of eternal objects through the primordial nature, making the unity of the divine subjective aim available to creatures along with the diversity of viable possibilities.

27. "According to this explanation, self-determination is always imaginative in its origin. The deterministic efficient causation is the inflow of the actual world in its own proper character of its own feelings, with their own intensive strength, felt and re-enacted by the novel concrescent subject. But this re-enaction has a mere character of conformation to pattern. The subjective valuation is the work of novel conceptual feeling; and in proportion to its importance, acquired in the complex processes of integration and reintegration, this autonomous conceptual element modifies the subjective forms throughout the whole range of feeling in that concrescence and thereby guides the integrations" (PR 245).

28. This term refers to the scientific notion of the space-time framework of the universe, but also to the network of relations that enables us to perceive that framework. "We must first consider the perceptive mode in which there is clear, distinct consciousness of the 'extensive' relations of the world. These relations include the 'extensiveness' of space and the 'extensiveness' of time. . . . In this 'mode' the contemporary world is consciously prehended as a continuum of extensive relations" (PR 61).

29. Whitehead uses this term to refer to the way each occasion forms its prehensions into a unified whole unique to itself: "The eternal objects are the same for all actual entities. The nexus of actual entities in the universe correlate to a concrescence is termed 'the actual world' correlate to that concrescence" (PR 23).

30. "The limitation whereby there is a perspective relegation of eternal objects to the background is the characteristic of decision. Transcendent decision includes God's decision. He is the actual entity in virtue of which the *entire* multiplicity of eternal objects obtains its graded relevance to each stage of concrescence. Apart from God, there could be no relevant novelty. Whatever arises in actual entities from God's decision, arises first conceptually, and is transmuted into the physical world" (PR 164).

31. Cf. David Griffin's clarification of the problems involved in describing God's dipolar nature in relation to the world in his *Reenchantment without Supernaturalism: A Process Philosophy of Religion* (Ithaca, N.Y.: Cornell University Press, 2001), 148–63.

32. Forest Wood Jr., *Whiteheadian Thought as a Basis for a Philosophy of Religion* (Lanham, Md.: University Press of America, 1986), 36.

33. Stephen C. Pepper, "Whitehead's 'Actual Occasion,'" in *Studies in Whitehead's Philosophy*, Tulane Studies in Philosophy 10 (New Orleans: Tulane University Press, 1961), 86. What is misleading about this quotation is that it presumes that the primordial nature of God (strictly speaking) knows actualities; the two natures are confused here. The proper formulation would treat God as a unitary whole in the divine knowledge of both possibilities and actualities.

34. On the immortality of the occasion in the world: "[A]ctual entities 'perpetually perish' subjectively, but are immortal objectively. Actuality in perishing acquires objectivity, while it loses subjective immediacy. It loses the final causation which is its internal principle of unrest, and it acquires efficient causation whereby it is the ground of obligation characterizing the creativity" (PR 29). On the immortality of the occasion in God's consequent nature, see PR 347, quoted below.

35. Heraclitus is the founder of a line of notable dissent from this quest, with his metaphysics of flux, and Whitehead acknowledges his debt to the early Greek thinker: "That 'all things flow' is the first vague generalization which the unsystematized, barely analyzed, intuition of men has produced. It is the theme of some of the best Hebrew poetry in the Psalms; it appears as one of the first generalizations of Greek philosophy in the form of the saying of Heraclitus. . . . Without doubt, if we are to go back to that ultimate, integral experience, unwarped by the sophistications of theory, that experience whose elucidation is the final aim of philosophy, the flux of things is one ultimate generalization around which we must weave our philosophical system" (PR 208).

36. "This double problem cannot be separated into two distinct problems. Either side can only be explained in terms of the other. The consequent nature of God is the fluent world become 'everlasting' by its objective immortality in God. Also the objective immortality of actual occasions requires the primordial permanence of God, whereby the creative advance ever re-establishes itself endowed with initial subjective aim derived from the relevance of God to the evolving world" (PR 347).

37. Cf. PR 345: "The completion of God's nature into a fulness of physical feeling is derived from the objectification of the world in God. He shares with every new creation its actual world; and the concrescent creature is objectified in God as a novel element in God's objectification of that actual world. This prehension into God of each creature is directed with the subjective aim, and clothed with the subjective form, wholly derivative from his all-inclusive primordial valuation. God's conceptual nature is unchanged, by reason of its final completeness. But his derivative nature is consequent on the creative advance of the world."

38. Compare Wood's summary of this process: "God in his consequent nature responds creatively to whatever actual occasions occur in the world. All occasions become a part of God's unified experience of the world. Since each actual occasion has some degree of self-determination, God does not determine what happens in the world. He does provide an initial aim that is the best for that situation. But the actual occasion modifies the aim in its actualization. God awaits the outcome—hence, his 'patience.' Whatever the response, God

creatively prehends it into a whole" (*Whiteheadian Thought as a Basis,* 53). Once again, care must be taken not to separate God's primordial and consequent natures to such an extent that it appears we are talking about two different entities. The consequent nature and the primordial nature respond together to the actualities of the world: As the consequent nature includes actual occasions, God orders them according to the subjective aim determined in God's primordial nature; the subsequent actual occasions, then, receive an initial aim derived from God's primordial valuation of possibilities but informed by the actual situations of the emerging occasions as God knows them in the consequent nature.

39. "[A]t present it is generally held that a purely spiritual being is necessarily immortal. The doctrine here developed gives no warrant for such a belief. It is entirely neutral on the question of immortality, or on the existence of purely spiritual beings other than God. There is no reason why such a question should not be decided on more special evidence, religious or otherwise, provided that it is trustworthy" (RM 110–11).

40. "There is then . . . a derived conceptual feeling which reproduces for the subject the data and valuation of God's conceptual feeling. This conceptual feeling is the initial conceptual aim referred to in the preceding statement. In this sense, God can be termed the creator of each temporal actual entity" (PR 225).

41. Cf. *CD* II/2:5–6: "To be truly Christian, the doctrine of God must carry forward and complete the definition and exposition of the Subject God. It must do this in such a way that quite apart from what must be said about the knowledge and reality of God as such, it makes the Subject known as One who by virtue of its innermost being, willing and nature does not stand outside all relationships, but stands in a definite relationship *ad extra* to another. . . . [P]ositively, in the free decision of His love, God is God in the very fact, and in such a way, that He does stand in this relation, in a definite relationship with the other."

42. Cf. passages on Judas in Barth, where the rejected appear as "place-holders" for the elect, having no actuality of their own by merely making room, while the elect are always the actual objects of God's free act: "In this situation the rejected cannot be awarded any other position than that of a *locum tenens* for the elect who is predetermined to disappear. But nothing else may be expected or conjectured of any rejected than that in his place, but God's wonderful reversal as it was accomplished in Jesus Christ, an elect will one day stand" (*CD* II/2:480); "[God] wills that the rejected should believe, and that as a believer should become a rejected man elected. The rejected as such has no independent existence in the presence of God. He is not determined by God merely to be rejected. He is determined to hear and say that he is a rejected man elected" (*CD* II/2:506).

43. Along these lines, it is interesting to note how Henry of Ghent and William of Ockham dealt with the question of God's knowledge of possibles (and impossibles) in their investigations of the distinction between essence and existence. The former argued that God's knowledge of possible essences gives them sufficient objectivity and consistency for them to be objects of knowledge as possibilities before becoming actualities. Ockham abandoned a theory that possibles and impossibles have a nonreal mode of existence that enables them to be

known, after he observed that since God has complete knowledge of actuals, possibles, and impossibles, any objective existence given to these would be independent of the divine will, making God's knowledge dependent and limiting God's power. Process thought does conceive of possibles as having an independent existence; this is the realm of eternal objects. But this existence is abstract and impotent without God's ordering in the primordial nature. See Marilyn McCord Adams, "Universals in the Early Fourteenth Century," 437; and John P. Wippel, "Essence and Existence," 403; both in *The Cambridge History of Later Medieval Philosophy: From the Rediscovery of Aristotle to the Disintegration of Scholasticism, 1100–1600,* ed. Norman Kretzmann et al. (New York: Cambridge University Press, 1988).

44. Another type of external relation occurs between an actual occasion and the future occasion that will prehend it. For the future occasion, the relation will be internal; for the completed and objective actual entity being prehended, it will be external. Cf. AI 191–200.

45. "It is evident that if the solidarity of the physical world is to be relevant to the description of its individual actualities, it can only be by reason of the fundamental internality of the relationships in question. On the other hand, if the individual discreteness of the actualities is to have its weight, there must be an aspect in these relationships from which they can be conceived as external, that is, as bonds between divided things" (PR 309).

46. "It is by reason of the body, with its miracle of order, that the treasures of the past environment are poured into the living occasion. The final percipient route of occasions is perhaps some thread of happenings wandering in 'empty' space amid the interstices of the brain. It toils not, neither does it spin. . . . In its turn, this culmination of bodily life transmits itself as an element of novelty throughout the avenues of the body. Its sole use to the body is its vivid originality; it is the organ of novelty" (PR 339).

47. On the difference between high-grade and low-grade occasions, Whitehead gives examples rather than strict definitions: "In our own relatively high grade of human existence, this doctrine of feelings and their subject is best illustrated by our notion of moral responsibility. The subject is responsible for being what it is in virtue of its feelings. It is also derivatively responsible for the consequences of its existence because they flow from its feelings" (PR 222); "The low-grade organism is merely the summation of the forms of energy which flow in upon it in all their multiplicity of detail. It receives, and it transmits; but it fails to simplify into intelligible system" (PR 254).

48. Cf. Heinrich Heppe, *Die Dogmatik der evangelisch-reformierten Kirche* (Berlin: Neukirchener Verlag, 1958), 201.

49. "A 'simple physical feeling' entertained in one subject is a feeling for which the initial datum is another single actual entity, and the objective datum is another feeling entertained by the latter actual entity. . . . A simple physical feeling is an act of causation. The actual entity which is the initial datum is the 'cause,' the simple physical feeling is the 'effect,' and the subject entertaining the simple physical feeling is the actual entity 'conditioned' by the effect" (PR 236).

50. "Adversion" is a Whiteheadian coinage for a positive valuation of data by a concrescing entity, and "aversion" is the corresponding term for a negative valuation: "The valuation values up, or down, so as to determine the intensive

importance accorded to the eternal object by the subjective form of the integral feeling" (PR 241). Cf. PR 253–54. The "Category of Transmutation" refers to "a transmutation of simple physical feelings of many actualities into one physical feeling of a nexus as one" (PR 251). Cf. PR 27.

51.   The more the organism is characterized by consciousness, the less important is the simple physical feeling and the more important is the order imposed on the raw data of the feelings by the dominant occasion of the organism: "But it is equally true to say that a simple physical feeling is the most primitive type of an act of perception, devoid of consciousness. . . . It seems as though in practice, for human beings at least, only transmuted feelings acquire consciousness, never simple physical feelings. Consciousness originates in the higher phases of integration and illuminates those phases with the greater clarity and distinctness" (PR 236).

52.   Cf. Thomas Aquinas: "Now it belongs to prudence, according to the Philosopher, to direct other things toward an end, whether in regard to oneself—as for instance, a man is said to be prudent, who orders well his acts toward the end of his life—or in regard to others subject to him, in a family, city, or kingdom. . . . In this way prudence or providence may suitably be attributed to God. For in God Himself there can be nothing ordered toward an end, since He is the last end. Wherefore Boethius says that *Providence is the divine type itself, seated in the Supreme Ruler, which disposeth all things*" (*Summa Theologica* Ia.22.1 [New York: Benzinger Brothers, 1947], 121).

53.   Cf. Thomas Aquinas: "Two things belong to Providence—namely, the type of the order of things foreordained towards an end; and the execution of this order, which is called government. . . . As to the second [of these], there are certain intermediaries of God's providence; for He governs things inferior by superior, not on account of any defect in His power, but by reason of the abundance of His goodness; so that the dignity of causality is imparted even to creatures" (*Summa Theologica* Ia.22.4, 124). Rather than God being the *sole* cause of events, as the Reformation tended to assert under the influence of Luther's repetition of the word *sola*, God is the *total* cause of events for Thomas, which does not preclude creatures from also being the total causes of events! "But since the very act of free will is traced to God as a cause, it necessarily follows that everything happening from the exercise of free will must be subject to divine providence. For human providence is included under the providence of God, as a particular under a universal cause" (*Summa Theologica* Ia.22.2, 123). For the contrast between the Reformation and Aquinas on this point, see Otto Hermann Pesch, "Alleinwirksamkeit" (368–77) and "Allwirksamkeit" (840–49) in *Die Theologie der Rechtfertigung bei Martin Luther und Thomas von Aquin* (Mainz: Matthias-Grünewald-Verlag, 1967).

54.   "Thus the transition of the creativity from an actual world to the correlate novel concrescence is conditioned by the relevance of God's all-embracing conceptual valuations to the particular possibilities of transmission from the actual world, and by its relevance to the various possibilities of initial subjective form available for the initial feelings" (PR 244).

55.   "'Order' in the actual world is differentiated from mere 'givenness' by introduction of adaptation for the attainment of an end. . . . 'Order' is a mere generic term: there can only be some definite specific 'order,' not merely 'order' in the

vague" (PR 83). "This is the conception of God, according to which he is considered as the outcome of creativity, as the foundation of order, and as the goad towards novelty. 'Order' and 'novelty' are but the instruments of his subjective aim which is the intensification of 'formal immediacy'" (PR 88).

56. "In the fourth phase, the creative action completes itself. For the perfected actuality passes back into the temporal world, and qualifies this world so that each temporal actuality includes it as an immediate fact of relevant experience. For the kingdom of heaven is with us today" (PR 351).

57. Cf. Heppe, *Dogmatik der evangelisch-reformierten Kirche,* 200.

58. While accepting the validity of this scheme, which balances the "push" (efficient causation) and "pull" (final causation or teleology) in reality, Whitehead also believes that it has been misused, in turn, by Christian theology and rational science: "This aspect [purpose] of the universe impressed itself on that great biologist and philosopher, Aristotle. His philosophy led to a wild overstressing of the notion of 'final causes' during the Christian middle ages; and thence, by a reaction, to the correlative overstressing of the notion of 'efficient causes' during the modern scientific period. One task of a sound metaphysics is to exhibit final and efficient causes in their proper relation to each other" (PR 84). Compare, however, Jonathan Lear's contention that Aristotle means by efficient and final causes not two different causes but two "fashions" in which the cause generally called "form," interior to the living thing, is cited: "The so-called formal, efficient and final causes are (at least in the wide variety of events that occur within the natural world) three different aspects of form itself. Aristotle says that these three causes 'often converge on one thing.' The one thing is form, and 'often' covers *all* cases of natural generation and creation of artefacts. So although Aristotle can talk about the three causes which coincide, he can also talk about the *primary* cause. He is not then picking out one of four causes for special honor; he is citing the one item, form, which can be considered either as the form it is or as the efficient cause or as the formal cause. The form really is the why of a thing" (*Aristotle: The Desire to Understand* [New York: Cambridge University Press, 1988], 27).

59. "It is to be noted that every actual entity, including God, is something individual for its own sake; and thereby transcends the rest of actuality. And also it is to be noted that every actual entity, including God, is a creature transcended by the creativity which it qualifies. . . . To be *causa sui* means that the process of concrescence is its own reason for the decision in respect to the qualitative clothing of feelings. It is finally responsible for the decision by which any lure for feeling is admitted to efficacy. The freedom inherent in the universe is constituted by this element of self-causation" (PR 88).

60. *CD* II/2:102. Cf. Barth's exegesis of John 1, pp. 95–106.

61. For a full description of this comparison, see my "Barth and Whitehead on Divine Self-Determination," *Encounter* 60, no. 4 (1999): 441–62.

62. "Evolution, on the materialistic theory, is reduced to the rôle of being another word for the description of the changes of the external relations between portions of matter. There is nothing to evolve, because one set of external relations is as good as any other set of external relations. There can merely be change, purposeless and unprogressive. But the whole point of the modern doctrine is the evolution of the complex organisms from antecedent states of less complex

organisms. . . . Thus in the process of analysing the character of nature in itself, we find that the emergence of organisms depends on a selective activity which is akin to purpose" (SMW 107).

63. An example of this phenomenon in the religious sphere: "Though religion can be a source of progress, it need not be so. . . . It is easy for a tribe to stabilize its ritual and its myths, and there need be no external spur to progress. In fact, this is the stage of religious evolution in which the masses of semi-civilized humanity have halted—the stage of satisfactory ritual and of satisfied belief without impulse toward higher things. Such religion satisfies the pragmatic test: It works, and thereby claims that it be awarded the prize for truth" (RM 28). Cf. RM 159–60, SMW 190–92.

64. The grace of God toward particular occasions must be contingent, since in the process system the existence of any particular occasion cannot be predicted before it arises: "The primordial appetitions which jointly constitute God's purpose are seeking intensity, and not preservation. Because they are primordial, there is nothing to preserve. He, in his primordial nature, is unmoved by love for this particular, or that particular; for in this foundational process of creativity, there are no preconstituted particulars. . . . His aim for [the occasion] is depth of satisfaction as an intermediate step towards the fulfilment of his own being. His tenderness is directed towards each actual occasion, as it arises" (PR 105).

3. Convergence and Divergence: What Process Theology Affirms and Denies

1. See especially the pairs of antitheses (PR 348).
2. For a "social trinity" that purports to be a process view, see Joseph A. Bracken, S.J., "Process Philosophy and Trinitarian Theology," *Process Studies* 8, no. 4 (1978): 217–30. For several analyses of what Trinity could mean in process thought, see Joseph A. Bracken and Marjorie Suchocki, eds., *Trinity in Process: A Relational Theology of God* (New York: Continuum, 1997). For my own proposal on Trinitarian doctrine (tailored to the needs of this constructive project and therefore quite speculative and preliminary), see the section "The Trinity in Election" in chapter 4.
3. It would seem to be prima facie possible to approach the Trinitarian solution to God's sociality by considering God in a Hartshornean sense, as a sequence of temporally ordered occasions. The consequent nature would then include the past occasions within God's self, which, being past, are fully actual. In this case, no world would be necessary as an object for God's contemplation, but God's nature as love would be severely curtailed if one had to maintain that God, existing alone, would only love God's past. A synthesis of the Bracken idea of a process Trinity, which opens the possibility that love exists within the three-member society of God, with the Hartshornean temporal sequence, might allow the construction of a process Trinity that could exist without a world. This approach would also, of course, entail taking on the problems associated with Hartshorne's and Bracken's views, problems that contradict Whitehead's view of God as the single nontemporal actual entity, and would require large sections of the system to be recast.

4. Daniel Day Williams, "Response to Wolfhart Pannenberg," in *Essays in Process Theology,* ed. Perry LeFevre (Chicago: Exploration Press, 1985), 315.

5. "In [election] God says Yes to the creature and not No. He says it of Himself. He says it without the creature having any right or claim to it. He says it, then, in freedom. But what He says, He says as the One who loves in freedom. . . . There is nothing inevitable against which the love of God must for its part be shattered. God elects, then, not the punishment but the undeserved rewarding of the creature, not its death but the life which it had forfeited, not its non-being but its impossible being. He elects. Neither to the creature nor to Himself is He under an obligation to elect in this way. But He does elect in this way" (*CD* II/2:28–29).

6. *Institutes* 3.23.8, 957.

7. Friedrich Schleiermacher, *The Christian Faith* (Philadelphia: Fortress, 1928), 547.

8. Ibid., 539.

9. *CD* II/2:453–54.

10. Cf. Donald G. Bloesch, "Process Theology and Reformed Theology," in *Major Themes in the Reformed Tradition,* ed. Donald K. McKim (Grand Rapids: Eerdmans, 1992), 386: "My reason for choosing to compare process thought and Reformed theology is that process thinkers generally see that particular strand of evangelical theology as their foremost adversary. It is the Augustinian and Calvinist doctrines of the sovereignty of God, the irresistibility of grace, revelation as divine intervention into history, and the shadow of a final irreversible divine judgement that seem to create special difficulties for process theologians. Just as Augustine and Calvin are considered the *bêtes noires* of the past, so Karl Barth is regarded as the main threat at present."

11. See Alan P. F. Sell, *The Great Debate: Calvinism, Arminianism, and Salvation* (Grand Rapids: Baker Book House, 1982), 14. The immediate emphasis of this point in the context of the Canons is not what human beings are able to do with their will *after* regeneration, but that human beings are culpable for what they do with their *enslaved* will.

12. Wolfhart Pannenberg, "Election and the People of God," in *Human Nature, Election, and History* (Philadelphia: Westminster, 1977), 51. Earlier in the essay, Pannenberg gives this definition: "Three elements characterized this classical doctrine of election: the timelessness of the divine decision in regard to its object, the restriction of its objects to individuals (in most cases to unrelated individuals), and finally the predominance of a transcendent salvation as constituting the purpose decided upon in the act of election" (46).

13. Ibid., 51–52.

14. Gen. 1:26–30; 2:7–8; Ps. 8:5–8.

15. Gen. 2:15–17.

16. Chapter 12 of SMW addresses the relationship between science and religion at length. Whitehead feels that science has exerted an ever widening influence in the modern age and that religion's influence has declined, in part because the former has accepted change as progressive while the latter sees change as destructive. He concludes at one point "that religion is the expression of one type of fundamental experience of mankind: that religious thought develops into an increasing accuracy of expression, disengaged from adventitious

imagery: that the interaction between religion and science is one great factor in promoting this development" (SMW 190).

17.   It would be remiss not to mention another prominent attempt to reconcile Christian theology with evolution: Karl Rahner's "evolutionary christology," which frames the doctrine of Christ in terms of an understanding of gradual material and spiritual improvement on the part of the human race. Rahner asserts that the incarnation must simultaneously represent the highest evolutionary stage for humankind *and* the necessary means by which this stage is to be reached by humanity as a whole: "The Incarnation would, of course, always appear as the highest stage in this world-reality because it is the hypostatic unity of God and a world-reality. But this does not yet make it intelligible as the goal and end, as the climax that can indeed be envisaged from below but always only as something unreachable. This seems possible only by presupposing that the Incarnation itself is to be made intelligible *in* its uniqueness and *in* the degree of reality given by it (in and not despite this uniqueness) as an intrinsic and necessary element in the process of God's giving himself in grace to the world as a whole and not only as an actually utilized means for this process" ("Christology within an Evolutionary View of the World," in *Theological Investigations* [Baltimore: Helicon Press, 1966], 5:180). Thus, Christ appears as the means by which "the cosmos evolves toward the spirit, transcendence and freedom" (185). Christ's grace enables the human being to balance individual and communal purposes, secure in the historically present existence of evolution's consummation but aware that the world is not yet perfected: "[H]e does not find the sole justification for his existence in using it up for the benefit of individuals of a future still to come, but also remains safe as an individual of eternal worth—safe in God and in his love; then is the community also justified and established with absolute validity in the face of this individual and his eternal dignity, for one cannot find the salvation of Christ unless one loves one's brothers and sisters—Christ's brothers and sisters; then is despair redeemed, for every fall into the abyss of the unspeakable and incomprehensible in spirit and life means falling into the hands of the one whom the Son addressed as his Father, when in death he commended his soul into his hands" (192).

     Thus far, Rahner's approach seems compatible with the process view that evolution is a divinely directed, gracious movement toward creaturely freedom, agency, and creativity. However, Rahner's matter-spirit dualism is not echoed in process thought. While Rahner finds "the final and absolute self-transcendence into God" only in "*spiritual* subjects" but in *all* of these (179)—restricting the spiritual stage, from which evolution can take its final leap, to human beings and angels—process thought would see purposeful activity, transcendence of its causes and therefore of itself as constituted by its world, and participation in God's consequent nature in *all creatures*, spirit not being something that appears in matter only for the purpose of freeing itself from it.

18.   Cf. MT lecture 7, "Nature Lifeless," and lecture 8, "Nature Alive."

19.   "Then the LORD opened the mouth of the donkey, and it said to Balaam, 'What have I done to you, that you have struck me these three times?' . . . The angel of the LORD said to him, 'Why have you struck your donkey these three times? I have come out as an adversary, because your way is perverse before me. The donkey saw me, and turned away from me these three times. If it had not turned

away from me, surely just now I would have killed you and let it live'" (Num. 22:28, 32–33).

20.   Frogs (Exod. 8:1–14), gnats and flies (8:16–32), cattle disease (presumably caused by microorganisms; 9:1–7).

21.   "He went up from there to Bethel; and while he was going up on the way, some small boys came out of the city and jeered at him, saying, 'Go away, baldhead! Go away, baldhead!' When he turned around and saw them, he cursed them in the name of the LORD. Then two she-bears came out of the woods and mauled forty-two of the boys" (2 Kgs. 2:23–24).

22.   Cf. Luke 19:39–40: "Some of the Pharisees in the crowd said to him, 'Teacher, order your disciples to stop.' He answered, 'I tell you, if these were silent, the stones would shout out.'"

23.   See also Psalms 104 and 148. For an interpretation of such passages that attempts to forge "a unifying view of worldly reality which brings God, the human, and the natural order together in an interconnected whole" (17), see Terence E. Fretheim, "Nature's Praise of God in the Psalms," *Ex Auditu* 3 (1987): 16–30.

24.   *CD* II/2:414.

25.   H. H. Rowley, *The Biblical Doctrine of Election* (London: Lutterworth, 1950), 31–32.

26.   Gen. 3:1–4:17.

27.   E.g., Exod. 3:11: "But Moses said to God, 'Who am I that I should go to Pharaoh, and bring the Israelites out of Egypt?'"; 4:10: "But Moses said to the LORD, 'O my Lord, I have never been eloquent, neither in the past nor even now that you have spoken to your servant; but I am slow of speech and slow of tongue'"; 4:13: "But he said, 'O my Lord, please send someone else.'"

28.   Num. 27:12–14; cf. Deut. 34:4–5.

29.   1 Sam. 9:15–17; 10:1–9.

30.   1 Sam. 16:1–13.

31.   2 Sam. 7:8–17; cf. 1 Kgs. 2:4.

32.   2 Sam. 12:13–14.

33.   2 Samuel 24. Interestingly, David was following God's command to number the people—this appears to be a case of entrapment.

34.   Hos. 3:1–3.

35.   Jonah 1:1–3:2.

36.   See, for example, 1 Kgs. 13:18–21, in which an old prophet prophesies falsely in order to bring the true man of God back to his house, but then prophesies truly that the man of God's disobedience will cause his death. The old prophet is truly called, but does not act in accordance with his call. Cf. Deut. 18:19–22 and 1 Kings 22 for the oft-encountered problem of distinguishing true prophet from false prophet.

37.   H. H. Rowley writes of the call to priesthood: "[W]hatever intrigues marked the course of the history of the priesthood, in the thought of the Old Testament writers the priests were chosen by God and were chosen for service; and the priestly office could be forfeited by the non-performance of that service" (102).

38.   Ibid., 108, italics mine.

39.   For the use in the Old Testament of *anointing* as an indication of election, see Lev. 4:3–16 and 2 Sam. 1:14–16. The use of the term in the Gospels is

pioneered in Matt. 1:16; cf. Matt. 26:63–64, 67; John 18:33; Mark 11:9–10; Luke 2:11; 9:20, 35.

40. "The apostolate consists of this sharing in Jesus' own mission. Those who possess it are to do what He Himself does: not because of their own will or choice, but because Jesus wills it and has chosen it for them; not in their own power, but in that might which is given them for the purpose by Jesus; not by their own decision, but both formally and in fact according to the strict instruction which they have received for the purpose from Jesus. Or conversely, His own action goes on in the world in the secondary form of the action to which the apostles are appointed, empowered and guided by Him. . . . They are themselves prophets, priests and kings (I Pet. 2:9) because He is this, and has made them His own" (*CD* II/2:432).

41. Matt. 4:18–22; Mark 1:16–20; Luke 5:1–11; John 1:35–49.

42. See, for example, Exod. 9:15–16.

43. See, for example, Isa. 8:7–8; 9:11; Jer. 5:15–17; and many other prophetic passages.

44. Rowley, *Biblical Doctrine of Election,* 130–31.

45. Pannenberg, "Election and the People of God," 49.

46. See, for example, PR 283: "The actual entity is the enjoyment of a certain quantum of physical time. . . . The quantum is that standpoint in the extensive continuum which is consonant with the subjective aim in its original derivation from God. Here 'God' is that actuality in the world, in virtue of which there is physical 'law.' "

47. Classical theologies with a strong sense of God's suffering, as in Barth and Hans Urs von Balthasar, also reject the docetism that results from allowing God to "hide out" in eternity, safe from temporal vicissitudes.

4. The Process Doctrine of Election: God's Call and the Creature's Response

1. As we have already seen, this assertion follows Karl Barth: "We mention of God that in Himself, in the primal and basic decision in which He wills to be and actually is God, in the mystery of what takes place from and to all eternity within Himself, within His triune being, God is none other than the One who in His Son or Word elects Himself, and in and with Himself elects His people" (*CD* II/2:76).

2. About this risk in the Reformed doctrine of election, Pierre Maury writes: "God's choice is none other than that in which the Lord chooses to give man life, whatever the cost to his own life, in which he chooses to be sacrificed for man, in which he takes man's part, in which he justifies him at his own expense. God is thus so seriously and completely in covenant with his creature that he can take upon himself the penalties of the covenant into which he has entered. He loves us enough, 'children of wrath' (Eph 2:3) as we are, to make of us, at the expense of his son, at his own expense, 'children of adoption,' of whom the prologue of St. John's Gospel says that the Word gives them 'power to become the sons of God' (1:12). Grace, free and sovereign, is there freely offered. There is no violation of justice. Love chooses, and pays the price. And we can praise 'the Father of lights, with whom is no variableness, neither shadow of turning,'

from whom all grace and every perfect gift comes down (James 1:17)" (*Predestination and Other Papers* [Richmond: John Knox, 1960], 54–55).

3. "The election of grace is the eternal beginning of all the ways and works of God in Jesus Christ. In Jesus Christ God in His free grace determines Himself for sinful man and sinful man for Himself. He therefore takes upon Himself the rejection of man with all its consequences, and elects man to participation in His own glory" (*CD* II/2:94).

4. "In the harmony of the triune God [Jesus Christ] is no less the original subject of this electing than He is its original object. And only in this harmony can He really be its object, i.e., completely fulfil not His own will but the will of the Father, and thus confirm and to some extent repeat as elected man the election of God. This all rests in the fact that from the very first He participates in the divine election; . . . that He too, with the Father and the Holy Spirit, is the electing God" (*CD* II/2:105).

5. Most traditional Christian theologies also reject divine coercion of creatures in practice, but prefer to reserve to God the theoretical power to coerce creatures as a feature of omnipotence while speaking of God's self-limitation in operating in creatures without violating their wills. Process thought differs by denying that God or any actual entity has the possibility of coercing the decision of any other actual entity.

6. Similarly, Barth's interpretation of "predestination" is God's reversal of the condemnation and rejection human beings have chosen for themselves. God destines the elect for the divine fellowship, even though their route may appear circuitous to the human observer.

7. Daniel Day Williams, "How Does God Act? An Essay in Whitehead's Metaphysics," in *Essays in Process Theology*, ed. Perry LeFevre (Chicago: Exploration Press, 1985), 107.

8. PR 345.

9. PR 73. The more general type of event is "a nexus of actual occasions, interrelated in some determinate fashion in one extensive quantum" (PR 73); this allows for a definition of change as "the differences between actual occasions in one event" (PR 80).

10. "Thus an actual entity never moves; it is where it is and what it is. In order to emphasize this characteristic by a phrase connecting the notion of 'actual entity' more closely with our ordinary habits of thought, I will also use the term 'actual occasion' in place of the term 'actual entity.' Thus the actual world is built up of actual occasions; and by the ontological principle whatever things there are in any sense of 'existence,' are derived by abstraction from actual occasions" (PR 73).

11. Cf. Kathryn Tanner, *God and Creation in Christian Theology* (New York: Basil Blackwell, 1988), 85: "If power and efficacy are perfections, the principle of direct proportions requires that creatures be said to gain these qualities, not in the degree God's agency is restricted, but in the degree God's creative agency is extended to them. Talk of the creature's power and efficacy is compatible with talk about God's universal and immediate agency if the theologian follows a rule according to which divinity is said to exercise its power in founding rather than suppressing created being, and created being is said to maintain and fulfil itself, not independently of such agency, but in essential dependence upon it."

12. John B. Cobb Jr. and David Ray Griffin, *Process Theology: An Introductory Expo-sition* (Philadelphia: Westminster, 1976), 119. This analysis is fully compatible with classical theology's view of divine and human freedom. In both systems, there is a possible relationship between God and creatures that is not compati-ble with the effective, creative agency of creatures, but that is not actualized. In classical theology, this hypothetical possibility is the creation of automatons; in process theology, it is the creation of low-level entities only. God's grace is demonstrated in process thought by the creation of *free* creatures, in the stronger sense involving real choice between significant viable alternatives. Classical theology does not necessarily require a strong sense of human freedom in order to affirm God's grace in creating free creatures.

13. "There is the becoming of the datum, which is to be found in the past of the world; and there is the becoming of the immediate self from the datum. This latter becoming is the immediate actual process. An actual entity is at once the product of the efficient past, and is also in Spinoza's phrase, *causa sui*" (PR 150).

14. "For the contemporary entities do not enter into the constitution of the per-cipient subject by objectification through any of their own feelings" (PR 318); "For the contemporary occasions in the presented duration are only efficacious through the feeling-tones of their sources, and not through their own immedi-ate feeling-tones" (PR 321); "[S]o far as physical relations are concerned, con-temporary events happen in *causal* independence of each other" (PR 61). This is not to say that contemporaries are not related—only that they are not *causally* related. See Bowman C. Clarke, "Process, Time, and God," in *Process Studies* 13, no. 4 (Winter 1983): 245–59.

15. Bowman Clarke's explanation of the future's relationship to past and future seem to me the most plausible description of Whitehead's own view: "White-head would reject this 'spatialization of time' [of McTaggert]. There are no 'fixed' future events, no fixed B series [sequential order of events] to move into the present. Earlier I suggested that it would be better to say that the 'is' of the relation: x is before y, which orders the B series, is 'tenseless' rather than 'fixed' or 'permanent.' To call it 'fixed' or 'permanent' is to spatialize it and suggest that it is settled and there in the future ready to become present. Whitehead would insist that there is, to use a term from Richard Cole, an asymmetry between the past and the future. The past, relative to a particular event, is fixed and settled; it is what has become actual. The present, relative to a particular event, is what is becoming actual. But future events must wait to see how the present becomes actual. There is freedom, to some degree, in the becoming of any actual entity, and consequently, in any event. Thus, the B series becomes fixed in its tenseless manner as events become. There is only 'a movement from earlier to later.' And this movement from earlier to later along the B series is the second type of process, the temporal process of transition." For further elaboration of Clarke's view, as well as an explanation of the A and B series to which the quoted pas-sage refers, see "God and Process in Whitehead," in *God and Temporality,* ed. Bowman C. Clarke and Eugene Long (New York: Paragon, 1984), 169–88. The quotation is from p. 177 of this essay.

16. "For although it is true that future occasions are potential and not yet real, their *anticipation* is real, and this anticipation is what gives rise to a final causality in the structure of the present occasion. This final causality, this fact of purpose or

aim in an actual entity, is the proof of a genuine immanence that the future exercises upon the present, even though the future is not yet actualized in individual actual occasions" (Robert B. Mellert, "The Relationship of God to Man and Nature in the Philosophy of Alfred North Whitehead" [Ph.D. diss., Fordham University, 1972], 38).

17. Williams, "How Does God Act?" 112–13.

18. Ibid., 111.

19. This is true even in God's self-election: God does not elect God's self as an already existing subject, but in a process of self-determination outside of which God does not exist.

20. Cobb and Griffin, *Process Theology,* 73.

21. Ibid., 125.

22. Williams, "How Does God Act?" 116.

23. "The view is then that God presents the individual occasions in the world with the possibility of participating in the society of being in certain definite ways, which involve elements of decision and novelty, but also strict conditions of novelty" (Williams, "How Does God Act?" 109).

24. Norman Pittenger, *The Holy Spirit* (Philadelphia: United Church Press, 1974), 107.

25. "We assert that, with respect to the elect, this plan was founded upon his freely given mercy, without regard to human worth; but by his just and irreprehensible but incomprehensible judgment he has barred the door of life to those whom he has given over to damnation" (*Institutes* 3.21.7, p. 931).

26. Karl Barth, *The Theology of Schleiermacher: Lectures at Göttingen, Winter Semester of 1923/24* (Grand Rapids: Eerdmans, 1982), 5.

27. See, for example, Matt. 25:31–46, in which Jesus links entrance into the kingdom with clothing the naked and visiting the sick and imprisoned, and Rev. 20:11–15: "And the dead were judged by what was written in the books, by what they had done" (v. 12b, RSV).

28. Wolfhart Pannenberg, "Election and History," in *Human Nature, Election, and History* (Philadelphia: Westminster, 1977), 97.

29. E.g., Ps. 59:16–17: "But I will sing of your might; I will sing aloud of your steadfast love in the morning. For you have been a fortress for me and a refuge in the day of my distress. O my strength, I will sing praises to you, for you, O God, are my fortress, the God who shows me steadfast love"; 46:1–3: "God is our refuge and strength, a very present help in trouble. Therefore we will not fear, though the earth should change, though the mountains shake in the heart of the sea; though its waters roar and foam, though the mountains tremble with its tumult"; 136:23–25: "It is he who remembered us in our low estate, for his steadfast love endures forever; and rescued us from our foes, for his steadfast love endures forever; who gives food to all flesh, for his steadfast love endures forever."

30. Tanner, *God and Creation,* 61.

31. Donald G. Bloesch, "Process Theology and Reformed Theology," in *Major Themes in the Reformed Tradition,* ed. Donald K. McKim (Grand Rapids: Eerdmans, 1992), 398.

32. Albert C. Outler, *John Wesley* (New York: Oxford University Press, 1964), 426.

33. In the story of the flood, for example: "The LORD saw that the wickedness of

humankind was great in the earth, and that every inclination of the thoughts of their hearts was only evil continually. And the LORD was sorry that he had made humankind on the earth, and it grieved him to his heart. So the LORD said, 'I will blot out from the earth the human beings I have created—people together with animals and creeping things and birds of the air, for I am sorry that I have made them'" (Gen. 6:5–7).

34.   "[W]hile perfection entails independence or absoluteness in some respects, it also entails dependence or relativity in other respects. . . . While there is a type of independence or absoluteness that is admirable, there is also a type of dependence or relativity that is admirable. And, if there is an example of absoluteness that is unqualifiedly admirable, this means that there is a divine absoluteness; and the same holds true of relativity. Process thought affirms that both of these are true. . . . God enjoys our enjoyments, and suffers with our sufferings. This is the kind of responsiveness which is truly divine and belongs to the very nature of perfection. Hence it belongs to the ideal for human existence" (Cobb and Griffin, *Process Theology,* 48–49).

35.   Clark M. Williamson, "Reversing the Reversal: Covenant and Election in Jewish and Process Theology," in *Jewish Thought and Process Thought,* ed. Sandra B. Lubarsky and David Ray Griffin (Albany, N.Y.: State University of New York Press, 1996), 179.

36.   Robert W. Jenson, "Second Locus: The Triune God," in *Christian Dogmatics,* ed. Carl E. Braaten et al. (Philadelphia: Fortress, 1984), 79–192. He adds that mutual emancipation and witness are intra-Trinitarian features as conditions for God's freeing of and witness to human beings: "The tradition could say how sending and obedience, giving and being given, are realities not merely between God and us, but in God—and so final goods. But it could not say how freeing and being freed, witnessing and being witnessed to, are equally realities in God. Thus the tradition could show that—to use Reformation language—God's *law* is his own true self-expression, but it could not show that the *gospel* is similarly anchored in his being" (157). "Using 'witnesses' for the Spirit and 'frees' for the Spirit with the Son, we may say the following. The Spirit's witness to the Son is equally God-constituting with the traditional relations. And so is the Son's and the Spirit's joint reality as the openness into which the Father is freed from mere persistence in his pretemporal transcendence" (156). Richard of St. Victor constructs a syllogism intended to prove that God's nature as love requires a Trinity, since creation is not sufficient as an object of supreme divine love: "Therefore see how easily reason clearly shows that in true Divinity plurality of persons cannot be lacking. Certainly God alone is supremely good. Therefore God alone ought to be loved supremely. A divine person could not show supreme love to a person who lacked divinity. However, fullness of Divinity could not exist without fullness of goodness. But fullness of goodness could not exist without fullness of charity, nor could fullness of charity exist without a plurality of divine persons" (*The Trinity* 3.2, in *Richard of St. Victor* [New York: Paulist Press, 1979], 375).

37.   David Day Williams, "Response to Wolfhart Pannenberg," in *Essays in Process Theology,* ed. Perry LeFevre (Chicago: Exploration Press, 1985), 315.

38.   It is possible, of course, that perfect and immutable divine foreknowledge is not inconsistent with free will—or at least with the contingency of creaturely

events. This has been a difficult case to make, however; both Augustine and Thomas Aquinas found solutions within their systems, but the problem endures. Most solutions have rested on a redefinition of freedom that runs counter to its prevalent Western usage. If real alternatives are not necessary for an act to be considered "free," then there is no problem. If that is not what we mean when we say "free," then something remains to be resolved. Thomas, for example, located contingency and freedom in the action of the agent as a secondary cause—real, but not primary. He thus avoids objections based on the need for alternatives. There is a long tradition of Christian thought, both Catholic and Protestant, that argues that the existence of alternatives is the smokescreen of a fallen world's definition of freedom—that, paradoxically but powerfully, true freedom consists of being a slave to Christ and eschewing "options" in favor of the divine will. While this formulation has many homiletic and theological advantages for anthropology, it does not touch the problem of the nature of God assayed here.

39. For a detailed description of the process notion of divine acts, see Williams, "How Does God Act?" This essay, which I have already quoted in previous sections, is perhaps too zealous in separating the acts of the primordial and consequent natures, without sufficiently emphasizing that neither nature acts on its own. For analysis, however, this separation is informative. Williams recognizes that as primordial, God acts by existing as an ordered, relevant resource for the emerging entity: "How does God in his primordial nature act? The most obvious answer is that he acts by presenting to the creatures the unity, the richness, and the limits of possibility as ordered by his vision. That is to say, God acts in his primordial gift of structures to the world by 'not acting.' He acts by being. He is the order upon which everything must draw if it is to be anything at all" (108). The omnipotence of this type of act is its comprehensiveness—an initial aim for every entity, drawn from a completely inclusive vision of possibilities. As consequent, then, God acts by knowing the world and ordering it toward the achievement of God's own aim. This knowledge unifies history and directs the provision of creaturely aims from the primordial nature.

40. Aristotle's Unmoved Mover does not conflict with this conception insofar as the Unmoved Mover is not an efficient cause, acting by "pushing," but a final cause, acting by attraction. Jonathan Lear interprets Aristotle's definition of the Unmoved Mover as "the object of desire" in the following passage: "God is the final cause: the order depends on him. The order of this well-ordered world must bear some relation to God if he is to be responsible for it. . . . Suppose that God is actively thinking the primary substances to be found in the world. Suppose, further, that his thinking forms a well-ordered whole. Then we can see the world as a whole as dependent on God: for the realization of form in the natural world depends upon the antecedent existence of form at its highest level of actuality. But form, or primary substance at its highest level of actuality simply is God. And the desire which God inspires is *none other than the desire of each organism to realize its form*" (*Aristotle: The Desire to Understand* [New York: Cambridge University Press, 1988], 295). That is to say, the organism's goal or purpose of self-determination and self-creation is in fact its movement toward God as its final cause.

41. "On the whole, the Gospel of love was turned into a Gospel of fear. . . . If the

modern world is to find God, it must find him through love and not through fear, with the help of John and not of Paul" (RM 74–76). Whitehead is certainly open to criticism here and elsewhere for a rather shallow understanding of the Bible and the finer points of the history of religious thought; he tends to overgeneralize about both. Fortunately, historical and biblical analysis is not the primary motivating factor behind his redefinitions of divine attributes. Rather, the necessities of his philosophical system find expression in his concept of God, with a reformation in religious thinking ensuing as a happy side effect.

42.	Whitehead himself usually uses "Unmoved Mover" as a term for a mistaken conception of God as "an aboriginal, eminently real, transcendent creator at whose fiat the world came into being, and whose will it obeys . . . the fallacy which has infused tragedy into the histories of Christianity and of Mahometanism" (PR 342). But he quotes Aristotle approvingly on God moving creatures by desire: "And since that which is moved and moves is intermediate, there is something which moves without being moved, being eternal, substance, and actuality. And the object of desire and the object of thought move in this way; they move without being moved. The primary objects of desire and of thought are the same. For the apparent good is the object of appetite, and the real good is the primary object of rational wish. But desire is consequent on opinion rather than opinion on desire; for the thinking is the starting-point. And thought is moved by the object of thought, and one of the two columns of opposites is in itself the object of thought" (quotation from *Metaphysics* 1072a. 23–32). Whitehead adds: "Aristotle had not made the distinction between conceptual feelings and the intellectual feelings which alone involve consciousness. But if 'conceptual feeling,' with its subjective form of valuation, be substituted for 'thought,' 'thinking,' and 'opinion,' in the above quotation, the agreement is exact" (PR 344).

43.	Daniel Day Williams, "Philosophy and Faith: A Study in Hegel and Whitehead," in *Our Common History as Christians: Essays in Honor of Albert C. Outler,* ed. John Deschner et al. (New York: Oxford University Press, 1975), 167.

44.	In this context, Gregory of Nyssa's thesis that "the word 'Godhead' does not refer to a nature, but to an *operation*," articulates God's unity as a single actual entity (therefore, a single cause or center of agency) in process thought, while demonstrating that this conception does not preclude Trinitarianism: "We do not learn that the Father does something on his own, in which the Son does not cooperate. Or again, that the Son acts on his own without the Spirit. Rather does every operation which extends from God to creation and is designated according to our differing conceptions of it have its origin in the Father, proceed through the Son, and reach its completion in the Holy Spirit. . . . For the action of each in any matter is not separate and individualized. But whatever becomes, whether in reference to God's providence for us or to the government and constitution of the universe, occurs through the three Persons, and is not three separate things" ("An Answer to Ablabius: That We Should Not Think of Saying There Are Three Gods," in *Christology of the Later Fathers,* ed. Edward R. Hardy [Philadelphia: Westminster, 1965], 261–62).

45.	If the term *aspects* were taken to mean "temporal manifestations," the process Trinity could not fail to be modalist: "Modalism is the teaching that God is above time and the distinctions of Father, Son, and Spirit, but appears successively in these roles to create, redeem, and sanctify" (Jenson, "Second Locus," 119). But the process Trinity being described presumes a continual role for Father, Son, and Spirit. The word *factors* might be substituted for *aspects* to express the doctrine's opposition to modalism.

46. This is the position of William L. Power, "The Doctrine of the Trinity and Whitehead's Metaphysics," *Encounter* 45, no. 4 (Autumn 1984): 287–302, which seems to me the most natural discovery of an immanent Trinity in Whitehead's doctrine of God.

47. Guilemus Bucanus is the source of the Latin motto that establishes the parameters of Trinitarian theology: "*Opera Trinitatis ad extra sunt indivisa*" (Heppe, p. 98, quoting Guilemus Bucanus).

48. For an overview of process Trinitarian concepts, see Joseph A. Bracken and Marjorie Suchocki, eds., *Trinity in Process: A Relational Theology of God* (New York: Continuum, 1997). For Whiteheadian Trinitarian theologies, see Lewis S. Ford, "Process Trinitarianism," *Journal of the American Academy of Religion* 43, no. 2 (June 1975): 199–213; Anthony J. Kelly, "Trinity and Process: Relevance of the Basic Christian Confession of God," *Theological Studies* 31 (1970): 393–414; and Power, "Doctrine of the Trinity." For a non-Whiteheadian view of the Trinity as a society of three actual entities, see Joseph A. Bracken, S.J., "Process Perspectives and Trinitarian Theology," in *Word and Spirit 8: Process Theology and the Christian Doctrine of God*, ed. Santiago Sia (Petersham, Mass.: St. Bede's Publications, 1986), 51–64; and "Process Philosophy and Trinitarian Theology—II," *Process Studies* 11, no. 2 (1981): 83–96.

49. Pittenger, *Holy Spirit*, 123.

50. Maury, *Predestination and Other Papers*, 35–36.

51. See David R. Griffin, *A Process Christology* (Philadelphia: Westminster, 1973); Lewis S. Ford, "The Possibilities for Process Christology," *Encounter* 35, no. 2 (Spring 1974): 281–94; Jerry R. Robbins, "A Reader's Guide to Process Christology," *Encounter* 53, no. 1 (Winter 1992): 78–92; and John B. Cobb Jr., *Christ in a Pluralistic Age* (Philadelphia: Westminster, 1975).

52. *Institutes* 3.22.1, p. 933.

53. Williamson, "Reversing the Reversal," 182.

54. Maury, *Predestination and Other Papers*, 23.

55. "For just as those engulf themselves in a deadly abyss who, to make their election more certain, investigate God's eternal plan apart from his Word, so those who rightly and duly examine it as it is contained in his Word reap the inestimate fruit of comfort" (*Institutes* 3.24.4, p. 969).

56. The consequent nature as described is the role of the Spirit in the economic Trinity—the relationship between God and the world as constituted by God's eternal self-determination and therefore enacted in fact and in history. The consequent nature consists of the world's actualities as received, ordered, and included in God. But if this relation does in fact hold, the immanent Trinity, in the process conception, must be constructed so as to provide the conditions in God's self-constitution for the possibility of God's reception of the world. These conditions are functions of the *primordial* nature, God in the abstract rather than in the concrete. The immanent Trinity in the primordial nature, as inferred from the concrete consequent nature, reveals God to be open to relation with another (represented by the Son) and to be open to freedom in the

other and increase by means of the other (represented by the Spirit). The economic Trinity, the subject of the current discussion, is nothing other than the abstract possibilities of the immanent Trinity enacted in an actual world.

57. Williamson, "Reversing the Reversal," 180.

58. Williams, "How Does God Act?" 114.

59. Williamson, "Reversing the Reversal," 179.

60. God's love for the world is revealed in God's steadfast pursuit of the good over many generations, while nonetheless the fruit of the evil that creatures actualize is passed from parents to children: "The LORD passed before him, and proclaimed, 'The LORD, the LORD, a God merciful and gracious, slow to anger, and abounding in steadfast love and faithfulness, keeping steadfast love for the thousandth generation, forgiving iniquity and transgression and sin, yet by no means clearing the guilty, but visiting the iniquity of the parents upon the children and the children's children, to the third and the fourth generation'" (Exod. 34:6–7); "Nothing is too hard for you. You show steadfast love to the thousandth generation, but repay the guilt of parents into the laps of their children after them" (Jer. 32:17b–18a); "For I knew that you are a gracious God and merciful, slow to anger, and abounding in steadfast love, and ready to relent from punishing" (Jonah 4:2b).

61. Pittenger, *Holy Spirit*, 20.

62. On this forward historical orientation of the process doctrine of providence, Norman Pittenger comments: "In the first place, it became clear to me that providence in its special sense is largely a *prospective* matter. It has to do with what I have styled, following Whitehead, the 'satisfaction of subjective aim.' Where am I going, in what direction am I moving, how am I becoming a fulfilled personality?—always remembering that to speak in this way entails also the community of men to which by virtue of my particular personalizing manhood I belong. Providence has to do with vocation in the proper sense, which is the call to every man to *become* a son of God 'in Christ'" (*God's Way with Men: A Study of the Relationship between God and Man in Providence, "Miracle," and Prayer* [London: Catholic Book Club, 1970], 117).

63. Pannenberg, "Election and History," 89.

64. Past, present, and especially future actualization of God's will can be equated to the scriptural concept of the kingdom of God. Pierre Maury writes, "Election is always the path by which God leads us towards his mysterious and freely given righteousness. It is thus also the path to righteousness of the Kingdom (Matt. 6:33) in seeking which we are seeking to be like Jesus Christ, which is our family-likeness, the path by which those who are justified by grace seek to be righteous toward their fellow-men in the way God is righteous—not, that is to say, in accordance with some law, but in charity. If, as we have indicated, election and vocation are for the Bible related and almost synonymous words, we shall not be surprised that election is invariably with a view to service" (*Predestination and Other Papers*, 67–68).

65. Robert C. Neville, *Creativity and God: A Challenge to Process Theology* (New York: Seabury, 1980), 9–10.

66. Process thought acknowledges the validity of a modern notion of freedom, wherein an individual is only free if she has equally viable options from which to choose; yet it also adheres to a certain evolutionary or hierarchical notion of

freedom, in agreement with Christian tradition, that true freedom is the ability to choose the good. In accordance with this latter concept, process thought holds that freedom cannot increase and be propagated among creatures in a progressively advancing world process unless creatures are given the opportunity to choose the good for themselves and others. A conditioned, ordered, and limited freedom is necessary in order that freedom may be enjoyed by ever increasing numbers and kinds of individuals, and may in turn be creative of value.

67. Compare this passage, by Daniel Day Williams, to Neville's argument: "For Whitehead there is an absolute importance for every individual occasion of experience, but this importance is not understood apart from the achievement and the failure of each act in experience to realize at least some of the possibility lying before it. 'Every act,' Whitehead says, 'leaves the world with a deeper or fainter impress of God.' (RM 152) If one takes this text as the real key to his view, then it is clear that there is loss and tragedy in all experience, but that God brings all such loss within the orbit of his understanding, his wisdom and his unflagging vision of the good" ("Philosophy and Faith," 170–71).

68. See, for instance, Whitehead's discussion of the gradations of relevance of eternal objects in the concrescence of an actual entity (PR 148–49), of the importance of negative prehensions as illustrations of "roads not taken" in conscious entities (PR 161–62), and of the Category of Conceptual Reversion: "In this second phase [of the mental pole] the proximate novelties are conceptually felt. This is the process by which the subsequent enrichment of subjective forms . . . is made possible by the positive conceptual prehension of relevant alternatives" (PR 249).

69. "What God does in freedom is in order," writes Barth. "And in that it is done in freedom, we can and must perceive and recognize that it is in order without first measuring it by our conception of order and only then recognizing it to be such" (CD II/2:22). Order is the result of God's infinite freedom being extended into the finite: "If we are to conceive of the true God, we shall do so only . . . as we conceive Him in the determination and limitation which are peculiar to Him, which He has not taken upon Himself as something additional, in His relationship with the world or as an accommodation to it, but which are the characteristics of His presence and activity in the world because they are the determination and limitation proper to His own eternal being, so assuredly has He decided for them by the decree of His eternal will" (CD II/2:50). That limitation and order is Jesus Christ, the concrete God.

70. Some confusion on the subject of God's influence over world events may be provoked by process thought's emphasis on purpose vectors proceeding from God to entities, to the exclusion of vectors from entities to God or arising from entities without divine interaction. While God does initiate each actual occasion into the realm of purposeful self-constitution by providing a model purpose, this vocation might be compared to God's pointing out a destination without "destining" that occasion. God provides a destination, but not a fate. David Ray Griffin writes: "[T]he specialness of an act of God also depends on the free response of the person in whom God is acting. Although the initiative is always with God, God's 'second move' depends on the person's response to the first. And this idea is only intelligible if the traditional views of God's

omnipotence and immutability are rejected. In fact, even Schleiermacher's views would be more intelligible within a modified doctrine of God's power, for his own doctrine of omnipotence makes unintelligible the variations in the degree to which the presence of God is an effective force in men. This variation would be understandable if man's free self-determination could limit God's effectiveness in him" (*Process Christology,* 144).

71. Williams, "How Does God Act?" 114.

72. Rom. 2:15; 2:1.

73. Exod. 20:5.

74. Norman Pittenger describes the effects of sin on the rebellious creature's future, along with the activity of God (here, of the Holy Spirit) to redeem that sin in history: "The decisions of people may be misguided leading to distortion or deviation in human affairs. When that is the case, correction is required. At such points, the Spirit who normally works only in gentleness, persuasion, and mercy, may work in judgment. He must bend people's evil wills to God's good will, not by breaking people but by showing them the error and absurdity of setting themselves at the center of things and proudly pretending that they are 'masters of all they survey.' He must lead people of the earth into obedience to God's will which is for their own best good, not by totally destroying them but by making plain to them the terrible results which follow upon selfish self-seeking, lust for power, attempts to dominate their fellowmen, and unjust treatment of helpless minorities. Such results will include the collapse of empires and nations, brought on themselves when they attempt to get along in supreme disregard of others or when they seek to control fellow human beings for their own ends. So it is that the Spirit speaks through the prophets, both ancient and modern; so it is that through him God raises up people who will put an end to oppression and wrong" (*Holy Spirit,* 70–71).

75. Maury, *Predestination and Other Papers,* 36.

76. "With Augustine I say: the Lord has created those whom he unquestionably foreknew would go to destruction. This has happened because he has so willed it. But why he so willed, it is not for our reason to inquire, for we cannot comprehend it. And it is not fitting that God's will should be dragged down into controversy among us, for whenever mention is made of it, under its name is designated the supreme rule of righteousness. Why raise any question of unrighteousness where righteousness clearly appears?" (*Institutes* 3.23.5, p. 952).

77. Williamson, "Reversing the Reversal," 172.

78. God's action over time toward the complex creature with a complex aim is to encourage the circumstances under which this aim can be entertained by every occasion in the dominant series, by encouraging the subordinate occasions to actualize aims consistent with the complex aim and by encouraging creatures outside the society in question to actualize aims that are consonant with the complex aim. This arrangement of aims and persuasion is what I called *gubernatio* in chapter 2, and what Pittenger means by "providential activity" in this passage: "What matters basically in God's providential activity is what happens to his children. In other words, God acts towards and in and for men to bring about that growing into personality of which we have spoken in our third chapter. If human life is a movement or a becoming, rather than a settled and finished product, then it is apparent that God's dealings with us will be toward

bringing about the fulfillment which is the initial aim that he has given us and which by our own decision we have made our subjective aim" (*God's Way with Men*, 113–14).

79. Wolfhart Pannenberg, "Postscript," in *Human Nature, Election, and History* (Philadelphia: Westminster, 1977), 108.

80. Bowman Clarke explains the relation of God to the actual occasions that constitute the consequent nature as follows: "[R]elative to God's subjective aim, each finite actual occasion has a certain incompleteness of form and aims at further integration with other occasions according to God's subjective aim, resulting in his consequent nature. . . . This is not to suggest that the temporal actual occasions are merely parts of God's satisfaction. They are that, but in concrescing into his satisfaction they concresce according to his subjective aim into his subjective form and become a part of his everlasting now. Such an interpretation would be true to Whitehead's technical vocabulary and, at the same time, do justice to his poetic language. He writes, for example, 'The world is the multiplicity of finites, actualities seeking a perfected unity' (PR 348). This perfect unity is found in their concrescence into God's everlasting satisfaction. God's consequent nature so interpreted, along with his primordial nature, appears also to do justice to Whitehead's statement, 'The theme of Cosmology, which is the basis of all religions, is the story of the dynamic effect of the World passing into everlasting unity, and of the static majesty of God's vision, accomplishing its purpose of completion by absorption of the World's multiplicity of effort' (PR 349)" ("Process, Time, and God," 258–59).

81. See Friedrich Schleiermacher, *The Christian Faith* (Philadelphia: Fortress, 1928), 536–45.

82. "The *second* consideration is an application of the truth that in regeneration each person becomes a new person. If that is so, sympathetic concern about a regeneration that occured too late is meaningless, for there is nothing originally present to think about; just as it would be a waste of pity, on the assumption of a creation of the world in time, to sigh that it was not created sooner. . . . And although such a regret may occasionally be felt on the grounds that the new life cannot now endure so long as if it had developed sooner, this too is a mere delusion, revealing a lack of acquaintance with the nature of the new life. For that life is in itself eternal, and gains no increment by the duration of time" (Schleiermacher, *Christian Faith*, 541).

83. Pittenger, *God's Way with Men*, 113–14.

84. See David Ray Griffin, "Life after Death in the Modern and Post-Modern Worlds," in *Religion and Parapsychology*, ed. Arthur S. Berger and Henry O. Thompson (Barrytown, N.Y.: Unification Theological Seminary, 1988), 39–60; John B. Cobb Jr., "The Resurrection of the Soul," *Harvard Theological Review* 80, no. 2 (1987): 213–27; and Marjorie Suchocki, *The End of Evil: Process Eschatology in a Historical Context* (Albany, N.Y.: State University of New York Press, 1988). Cobb and Griffin provide a summary of the options in *Process Theology:* "Some process theologians have believed that, though perpetual perishing is a more ultimate evil than death, personal death is also so fundamental that we must ask how God overcomes this evil as well. They have considered the possibility of renewed personal existence after death as contributing to the solution of the problem, and they have found that Whitehead's

conceptuality allows for such views even if he himself did not adopt them. He himself said that his philosophy is 'entirely neutral on the question of immortality' (RM 107). On the one hand, it gives no warrant for the belief that the human soul is necessarily immortal. . . . On the other hand, by its clear distinction of the soul from the body and its clarification of possible relations not mediated by bodies, it leaves open the possibility that the soul may live again after death: 'In some important sense the existence of the soul may be freed from its complete dependence upon the bodily organization' (AI 267). Whitehead writes that 'there is no reason why such a question should not be decided upon more special evidence' (RM 111). Some Christians believe that such evidence is provided in the resurrection of Jesus, and if so, process theology is open to affirming personal life after death" (123).

The Christian belief in bodily resurrection might be interpreted by process theology to refer to the continuation of a recognizably creaturely existence after death, as opposed to a metamorphosis into a new type of spiritual being and a severance of connections with the natural-historical past. Literal resuscitation of long-decomposed bodies seems to be ruled out by process thought because the movement of time requires physical entities to perish and contribute their physical resources to other entities. The recycling of matter into other forms precludes its definite assignment to any particular creature. And since complex individuals are conditioned by the specific single individuals that make up their bodies, the provision of a new body to house an immortal soul seems to pose a difficulty.

Epilogue

1. Daniel Day Williams, "Response to Wolfhart Pannenberg," in *Essays in Process Theology,* ed. Perry LeFevre (Chicago: Exploration Press, 1985), 315.
2. "Indeed, God did not send the Son into the world to condemn the world, but in order that the world might be saved through him" (John 3:17). Although the context of this verse is the belief of human beings, the larger context of Scripture supports the divine mission of Christ to nonhuman creatures (e.g., the new heaven and new earth of Rev. 12:1, and the peaceable kingdom of Isa. 65:25).
3. This issue is well framed by Langdon Gilkey in this passage: "The religious person, on the other hand, is primarily concerned with meaning rather than general structure. That is to say, he asks the question about a purpose in existence as a whole to which he can 'anchor' his own small purpose, and the question of a resource of power and love that can overcome the tragedy, the conflict, and the guilt that darken his personal and social existence" (*Maker of Heaven and Earth* [Garden City, N.Y.: Doubleday, 1959], 38).
4. Gilkey goes on to describe this reversal: "Religious thought thus tends to reverse the method of philosophical inquiry: instead of seeking to uncover the basic structure of reality by means of an empirical analysis of its general scope, it seeks to understand the ordinary levels of life in terms of an apprehension of its deepest meaning, discovered in some particular and irreplaceable experience. The method of religion is to see all things in the light of its special knowledge of

God; the method of philosophy is to see God in the light of what it knows generally of all things" (Ibid., 38–39).

5. A related view of the role of nations and other communities in the divine plan is articulated by George Allen in the following quotation; note that the scriptural assertion that God has a purpose for the nations can be taken in two senses, analogous to the prospective and retrospective senses I describe: "The conviction that God has a purpose for the nations is well grounded in biblical thought and accordingly reiterated in Christian theology, most notably by Augustine. The phrase 'God's purpose for the nations' is equivocal, however. It can be taken to mean that God *has a use* for nations, that they have a role to play in the divine economy. His purposes for institutions are in this sense akin to his purpose for other inanimate or nonhuman parts of his creation. They are necessary conditions for the fulfillment of human aims and of the divine aims for human beings. On the other hand, the phrase can be interpreted as asserting that God *provides a purpose* to the nations, that with respect to an institution, God entertains a goal-for-it just as he entertains a goal-for-me. He confronts the institution with that goal as a possibility for it to actualize" ("The Aims of Societies and the Aims of God," in *Process Philosophy and Christian Thought,* ed. Delwin Brown et al. [Indianapolis: Bobbs-Merrill, 1971], 471).

6. "[E]very 'act of God' is presented to us in, through and with the complex of nature and life in which we are. When we say God elected Israel, or that he sends down rain on the just and the unjust, we must not ignore the complex analysis of assignable causes and factors in Israel's history or in the cosmic record of rainfall. We have no way of extricating the acts of God from their involvement in the activities of the world" (Daniel Day Williams, "How Does God Act? An Essay in Whitehead's Metaphysics," in *Essays in Process Theology,* ed. LaFevre, 116–17).

7. See, for example, Gen. 12:3: "I will bless those who bless you, and the one who curses you I will curse; and in you all the families of the earth shall be blessed" (quoted by Peter in this form, in Acts 3:25–26); and Isa. 19:24: "On that day Israel will be the third with Egypt and Assyria, a blessing in the midst of the earth."

8. "We saw earlier that the presiding meaning of election in Exodus, underscored everywhere in Deuteronomy, was the paradox of God's sovereign choice of Israel as his 'own possession.' Surely, the inherent logic of the paradox calls for some breakthrough, some answer to the question, *For what?* And to this, weighty Old Testament scholarship answers, *election for service.* And what else is to square the astonishment, noted by the Deuteronomic author, of the unconditional grace of the Creator God allied with the destiny of a particular people?" (Robert E. Cushman, "Biblical Election as a Sacred History: A Study in the Ancient History of Ecumenism," in *Our Common History as Christians: Essays in Honor of Albert C. Outler,* ed. John Deschner et al. [New York: Oxford University Press, 1975], 195).

9. Wolfhart Pannenberg, "Postscript," in *Human Nature, Election, and History* (Philadelphia: Westminster, 1977), 108–9.

SOURCES CITED

Allen, George. "The Aims of Societies and the Aims of God." In *Process Philosophy and Christian Thought,* edited by Delwin Brown et al., 464–74. Indianapolis: Bobbs-Merrill, 1971.

Aquinas, Thomas. *Summa Theologica.* Vol. 1. Translated by the Fathers of the English Dominican Province. New York: Benzinger Brothers, 1947.

Balthasar, Hans Urs von. *The Theology of Karl Barth.* Translated by John Drury. New York: Holt, Rinehart & Winston, 1971.

Barbour, Ian. *Religion in an Age of Science: The Gifford Lectures, 1989–1991.* Vol. 1. San Francisco: Harper & Row, 1990.

Barth, Karl. *Church Dogmatics.* Translated by G. W. Bromiley and T. F. Torrance. 5 vols. in 13. Edinburgh: T. & T. Clark, 1962.

———. "The Strange New World within the Bible." In *The Word of God and the Word of Man,* 28–50. Translated by Douglas Horton. Grand Rapids: Zondervan, 1935.

———. *The Theology of Schleiermacher: Lectures at Göttingen, Winter Semester of 1923/24.* Translated by Geoffrey W. Bromiley. Grand Rapids: Eerdmans, 1982.

Berkouwer, G. C. *Studies in Dogmatics: Divine Election.* Grand Rapids: Eerdmans, 1960.

———. *The Triumph of Grace in the Theology of Karl Barth.* Grand Rapids: Eerdmans, 1956.

Bloesch, Donald G. "Process Theology and Reformed Theology." In *Major Themes in the Reformed Tradition,* edited by Donald K. McKim, 386–99. Grand Rapids: Eerdmans, 1992.

Bowman, Donna. "Barth and Whitehead on Divine Self-Determination." *Encounter* 60, no. 4 (1999): 441–62.

Bracken, Joseph A., S.J. "Process Perspectives and Trinitarian Theology." In *Word and Spirit 8: Process Theology and the Christian Doctrine of God,* edited by Santiago 51–64. Sia, Petersham, Mass.: St. Bede's Publications, 1986.

———. "Process Philosophy and Trinitarian Theology." *Process Studies* 8, no. 4 (1978): 217–30.

———. "Process Philosophy and Trinitarian Theology—II." *Process Studies* 11, no. 2 (1981): 83–96.

Bracken, Joseph A., and Marjorie Suchocki, eds. *Trinity in Process: A Relational Theology of God.* New York: Continuum, 1997.

Calvin, John. *Institutes of the Christian Religion.* Edited by John T. McNeill. Translated by Ford Lewis Battles. Philadelphia: Westminster, 1960.

Case-Winters, Anna. *God's Power: Traditional Understandings and Contemporary Challenges.* Louisville, Ky.: Westminster/John Knox, 1990.

Clarke, Bowman C. "God and Process in Whitehead." In *God and Temporality,* edited by Bowman C. Clarke and Eugene Long, 169–88. New York: Paragon, 1984.

———. "God and Time in Whitehead." *Journal of the American Academy of Religion* 48, no. 4 (1980): 563–79.

———. "Process, Time, and God." *Process Studies* 13, no. 4 (Winter 1983): 245–59.

Cobb, John B., Jr. "Barth: An Appreciation from the Enemy Camp." *Christian Advocate,* March 20, 1969, 7–8.

———. "Barth and the Barthians: A Critical Appraisal." In *How Karl Barth Changed My Mind,* edited by Donald K. McKim, 172–77. Grand Rapids: Eerdmans, 1986.

———. *A Christian Natural Theology: Based on the Thought of Alfred North Whitehead.* Philadelphia: Westminster, 1965.

———. *Christ in a Pluralistic Age.* Philadelphia: Westminster, 1975.

———. *Living Options in Protestant Theology.* Philadelphia: Westminster, 1962.

———. "The Resurrection of the Soul." *Harvard Theological Review* 80, no. 2 (1987): 213–27.

———. *Varieties of Protestantism.* Philadelphia: Westminster, 1960.

Cobb, John B., Jr., and David Ray Griffin. *Process Theology: An Introductory Exposition.* Philadelphia: Westminster, 1976.

Cushman, Robert E. "Biblical Election as a Sacred History: A Study in the Ancient History of Ecumenism." In *Our Common History as Christians: Essays in Honor of Albert C. Outler,* edited by John Deschner et al., 179–216. New York: Oxford University Press, 1975.

Davaney, Sheila G. *Divine Power: A Study of Karl Barth and Charles Hartshorne.* Philadelphia: Fortress, 1986.

Ford, Lewis S. "The Possibilities for Process Christology." *Encounter* 35, no. 2 (Spring 1974): 281–94.

———. "Process Trinitarianism." *Journal of the American Academy of Religion* 43, no. 2 (June 1975): 199–213.

Fraenkel, Peter, ed. *Natural Theology.* London: Centenary, 1946.

Fretheim, Terence E. "Nature's Praise of God in the Psalms." *Ex Auditu* 3 (1987): 16–30.

Gilkey, Langdon. *Maker of Heaven and Earth.* Garden City, N.Y.: Doubleday, 1959.

Gregory of Nyssa. "An Answer to Ablabius: That We Should Not Think of Saying There Are Three Gods." In *Christology of the Later Fathers,* edited by Edward R. Hardy, 256–67. Philadelphia: Westminster, 1965.

Griffin, David Ray. *God, Power, and Evil: A Process Theodicy.* Lanham, Md.: University Press of America, 1991.

———. "Life after Death in the Modern and Post-Modern Worlds." In *Religion and Parapsychology,* edited by Arthur S. Berger and Henry O. Thompson, 39–60. Barrytown, N.Y.: Unification Theological Seminary, 1988.

———. *A Process Christology.* Philadelphia: Westminster, 1973.

———. *Reenchantment without Supernaturalism: A Process Philosophy of Religion.* Ithaca, N.Y.: Cornell University Press, 2001.

———. "Whitehead and Niebuhr on God, Man, and the World." *Journal of Religion* 53, no. 2 (April 1973): 149–75.

Gunton, Colin E. *Becoming and Being: The Doctrine of God in Charles Hartshorne and Karl Barth.* Oxford: Oxford University Press, 1978.

Hamilton, Peter. *The Living God and the Modern World: Christian Theology Based on the Thought of A. N. Whitehead*. Philadelphia: United Church Press, 1967.

Hartshorne, Charles. *The Divine Relativity: A Social Conception of God*. New Haven, Conn.: Yale University Press, 1948.

Heppe, Heinrich. *Die Dogmatik der evangelisch-reformierten Kirche*. Berlin: Neukirchener Verlag, 1958.

Hunsinger, George. *How to Read Karl Barth: The Shape of His Theology*. New York: Oxford University Press, 1991.

Jenson, Robert W. "Eighth Locus: The Holy Spirit." In *Christian Dogmatics,* edited by Carl E. Braaten et al., 2:125–42. Philadelphia: Fortress, 1984.

———. *God after God: The God of the Past and the Future as Seen in the Work of Karl Barth*. Indianapolis: Bobbs-Merrill, 1969.

———. "Karl Barth." In *The Modern Theologians: An Introduction to Christian Theology in the Twentieth Century,* edited by David F. Ford, 1:23–49. New York: Basil Blackwell, 1989.

———. "Second Locus: The Triune God." In *Christian Dogmatics,* edited by Carl E. Braaten et al., 2:79–192. Philadelphia: Fortress, 1984.

Kelly, Anthony J. "Trinity and Process: Relevance of the Basic Christian Confession of God." *Theological Studies* 31 (1970): 393–414.

Kretzmann, Norman, et al., eds. *The Cambridge History of Later Medieval Philosophy: From the Rediscovery of Aristotle to the Disintegration of Scholasticism, 1100–1600*. New York: Cambridge University Press, 1988.

Küng, Hans. *Justification: The Doctrine of Karl Barth and a Catholic Reflection*. Translated by Thomas Collins et al. London: Burns & Oates, 1964.

Lear, Jonathan. *Aristotle: The Desire to Understand*. New York: Cambridge University Press, 1988.

Maury, Pierre. *Predestination and Other Papers*. Richmond: John Knox, 1960.

McCormack, Bruce. *Karl Barth's Critically Realistic Dialectical Theology: Its Genesis and Development 1909–1936*. Oxford: Clarendon, 1995.

———. "A Scholastic of a Higher Order: The Development of Karl Barth's Theology, 1921–1931." Ph.D. diss., Princeton Theological Seminary, 1989.

Meland, Bernard. *The Reality of Faith: The Revolution in Cultural Forms*. New York: Oxford University Press, 1962.

Mellert, Robert B. "The Relationship of God to Man and Nature in the Philosophy of Alfred North Whitehead." Ph.D. diss., Fordham University, 1972.

Neville, Robert C. *Creativity and God: A Challenge to Process Theology*. New York: Seabury, 1980.

Ogden, Schubert. *The Reality of God and Other Essays*. London: SCM Press, 1967.

Outler, Albert C. *John Wesley*. New York: Oxford University Press, 1964.

Pannenberg, Wolfhart. *Human Nature, Election, and History*. Philadelphia: Westminster, 1977.

Pepper, Stephen C. "Whitehead's 'Actual Occasion.'" In *Studies in Whitehead's Philosophy*. Tulane Studies in Philosophy 10, 71–88. New Orleans: Tulane University Press, 1961.

Pesch, Otto Hermann. *Die Theologie der Rechfertigung bei Martin Luther und Thomas von Aquin*. Mainz: Matthias-Grünewald-Verlag, 1967.

Pittenger, Norman. *God's Way with Men: A Study of the Relationship between God and Man in Providence, "Miracle," and Prayer*. London: Catholic Book Club, 1970.

————. *The Holy Spirit.* Philadelphia: United Church Press, 1974.

Plomp, H. R. "John Cobb und Karl Barth: Was macht die Prozess-theologie mit Karl Barths Theologie, besonders der Schopfungslehre?" *Zeitschrift Dialektische Theologie* 1, no. 3 (1987): 45–64.

Power, William L. "The Doctrine of the Trinity and Whitehead's Metaphysics." *Encounter* 45, no. 4 (Autumn 1984): 287–302.

Rahner, Karl. "Christology within an Evolutionary View of the World." In *Theological Investigations*, 5:157–92. Baltimore: Helicon, 1966.

Richard of St. Victor. *The Trinity.* Translated by Grover A. Zinn. New York: Paulist Press, 1979.

Robbins, Jerry R. "A Reader's Guide to Process Christology." *Encounter* 53, no. 1 (Winter 1992): 78–92.

Robertson, John C., Jr. "The Concept of the Divine Person in the Thought of Charles Hartshorne and Karl Barth." Ph.D. diss., Yale University, 1967.

Rogers, Eugene. "Supplementing Barth on Jews and Gender: Identifying God by Anagogy and the Spirit." *Modern Theology* 14, no. 1 (January 1998): 43–81.

Rowley, H. H. *The Biblical Doctrine of Election.* London: Lutterworth, 1950.

Schleiermacher, Friedrich. *The Christian Faith.* English translation of the second German edition. Edited by H. R. Mackintosh and J. S. Stewart. Philadelphia: Fortress, 1928.

Sell, Alan P. F. *The Great Debate: Calvinism, Arminianism, and Salvation.* Grand Rapids: Baker Book House, 1982.

Shaw, D. W. D. "Providence and Persuasion." *Duke Divinity School Review* 45 (1980): 11–22.

Sonderegger, Katherine. *That Jesus Christ Was Born a Jew: Karl Barth's "Doctrine of Israel."* University Park, Pa.: Pennsylvania State University Press, 1992.

Suchocki, Marjorie. *The End of Evil: Process Eschatology in a Historical Context.* Albany, N.Y.: State University of New York Press, 1988.

Surin, Kenneth. "Process Theology." In *The Modern Theologians: An Introduction to Christian Theology in the Twentieth Century,* edited by David F. Ford, 1:103–14. New York: Basil Blackwell, 1989.

Tanner, Kathryn. *God and Creation in Christian Theology.* New York: Basil Blackwell, 1988.

Welker, Michael. "Barth's Theology and Process Theology." *Theology Today* 43, no. 3 (October 1986): 383–97.

————. *Universalität Gottes und der Relativität der Welt: Theologische Cosmologie im Dialog mit dem amerikanischen Theologie.* Vol. 1. Neukirchen-Vluyn: Neukirchener Verlag, 1981.

Whitehead, Alfred North. *Adventures of Ideas.* New York: Macmillan, 1952.

————. *Modes of Thought.* New York: Free Press, 1968.

————. *Process and Reality: An Essay in Cosmology.* Corrected edition, edited by David Ray Griffin and Donald W. Sherburne. New York: Free Press, 1978.

————. *Religion in the Making.* New York: Fordham University Press, 1996.

————. *Science and the Modern World.* New York: Free Press, 1967.

Williams, Daniel Day. "Barth and Brunner on Philosophy." In *Essays in Process Theology,* edited by Perry LeFevre, 199–212. Chicago: Exploration Press, 1985.

————. "The Concept of Truth in Karl Barth's Theology." In *Essays in Process Theology,* edited by Perry LeFevre, 302–10. Chicago: Exploration Press, 1985.

————. "How Does God Act? An Essay in Whitehead's Metaphysics." In *Essays in Process Theology,* edited by Perry LeFevre, 98–117. Chicago: Exploration Press, 1985.

————. "Niebuhr and Liberalism." In *Essays in Process Theology,* edited by Perry LeFevre, 213–32. Chicago: Exploration Press, 1985.

————. "Philosophy and Faith: A Study in Hegel and Whitehead." In *Our Common History as Christians: Essays in Honor of Albert C. Outler,* edited by John Deschner et al., 157–75. New York: Oxford University Press, 1975.

————. "Response to Wolfhart Pannenberg." In *Essays in Process Theology,* edited by Perry LeFevre, 311–16. Chicago: Exploration Press, 1985.

————. *The Spirit and the Forms of Love.* New York: Harper & Row, 1968.

Williamson, Clark M. "Reversing the Reversal: Covenant and Election in Jewish and Process Theology." In *Jewish Thought and Process Thought,* edited by Sandra B. Lubarsky and David Ray Griffin, 163–84. Albany, N.Y.: State University of New York Press, 1996.

Wood, Forest, Jr. *Whiteheadian Thought as a Basis for a Philosophy of Religion.* Lanham, Md.: University Press of America, 1986.

Wyschogrod, Michael. *The Body of Faith: God in the People Israel.* San Francisco: Harper & Row, 1983.

Yu, Anthony C. "Karl Barth's Doctrine of Election." *Foundations* 13, no. 3 (July–September 1970): 248–61.

INDEX OF NAMES AND TOPICS

language, 169–70
law, 50, 60, 67, 164–66
Logos, 57, 184
Luther, Martin, 50, 164

materialism, 131
Maury, Pierre, 183–84, 187
McCormack, Bruce, 8
Meland, Bernard, 10
Messiah, 1, 40–41, 43, 45, 58–59, 138
    See also Jesus Christ
metaphysics, 3, 11, 13, 15, 21–25,
    27–31, 38, 52, 70, 75–79, 82–83,
    89, 91, 95, 99, 104, 106–7, 110,
    114–15, 117–18, 123–25, 128,
    135, 142, 144–45, 151–54, 158,
    166–70, 175, 177–80, 192–93,
    200, 212, 214, 216, 219–20, 224
miracles, 134
monism, 7, 30–31, 85, 108, 176, 213
Moses, 42, 137–38

natural theology, 8, 13, 16, 18–19, 77
nature, 10, 132–33, 135
neo-orthodoxy, 13
Neoplatonism, 136, 213
Neville, Robert C., 200–2
New Testament, 1, 9, 13, 73, 110, 133,
    139–40, 167, 192, 216
nexus, 120
Niebuhr, Reinhold, 11
Noah, 223
nonhuman, 130, 132–33
novelty, 79–80, 95–99, 101, 114, 119,
    122, 129, 161

obedience, 137, 187, 192, 197, 203,
    205–6, 211, 222
Ogden, Schubert, 10
Old Testament, 1, 13, 40–41, 51,
    62–63, 73, 133, 138–39, 164–68,
    192, 216
ontological principle, 81, 83, 85
order, 79, 97, 115, 117, 156, 196
ordination, 110
Outler, Albert C., 171–72

panentheism, 108

Pannenberg, Wolfhart, 125, 130, 140,
    166, 176, 209, 227
pantheism, 176
passion, 173
past, 10, 90, 195, 213
patripassionism, 173
Paul, 1, 59, 139, 181, 185
Pelagianism, 56, 110, 192
Pepper, Stephen C., 98
Perfect Being theology, 166–67, 179
persuasion, 113, 115, 117, 128, 150,
    154, 177–78, 184, 196, 198, 201,
    203–4, 212, 216
philosophy, 2–3, 5, 11, 13, 75, 81, 108,
    123, 131–32, 148–9, 153, 166,
    168, 170, 174, 214
    of organism, 4, 95, 132 (*see also*
    process philosophy)
    relationship to theology, 22–32, 71
Pittenger, Norman, 9, 163, 183, 197,
    211
Plato, 4, 48, 80, 96, 101, 106
Platonism, 136
Plomp, H. R., 9
pluralism, 85
prayer, 55
predestination, 2, 17, 36, 38, 54, 56, 61,
    64–67, 126–28, 199–200
    double, 30, 37, 151
prehension, 84, 148, 189, 204
    conceptual, 96, 108
    hybrid, 86, 96
    physical, 84, 94
process philosophy, 4–5, 11, 13, 73,
    118, 121, 124–26, 131, 144,
    147–48, 150, 154, 162, 167, 174,
    202, 207, 212–13, 215–16,
    219–20, 223, 226
process theology, 5, 7, 11, 16, 23,
    27–28, 31, 63, 71, 73, 77, 104–6,
    112, 115, 117–19, 123, 127, 130,
    134–35, 142–44, 150–1, 155, 160,
    164–66, 168–70, 172–75, 177,
    179, 184, 187–88, 191, 194–95,
    199, 214, 216, 221, 223
process thought. *See* process philosophy
progress, 99, 110, 112, 196, 198, 210,
    212

prophet, 138, 216
providence, 9, 93, 102, 104, 112,
   115–17, 163, 197, 211
Psalms, 135, 167

redemption, 2, 73, 105, 124, 148, 157,
   193, 196, 200, 206, 208–11, 214
Reformation, 1, 13, 28, 123, 136, 141,
   164
Reformed theology, 2, 4–6, 8–9, 11, 13,
   16, 50, 75–76, 78, 110, 123–24,
   126, 128–30, 136, 141, 144, 147,
   150, 164–65, 170–72, 188,
   191–92
rejection, 31, 43, 45, 50, 55, 63, 70,
   165–66, 188
relations
   external, 108, 132
   internal, 107–8
relativity, 130–31
religion, 28, 87, 111–12, 117, 131–32,
   148, 212, 214, 216–17, 219–21,
   225, 227
religious experience, 25, 27–28, 220
resurrection, 45, 59
revelation, 2–3, 5–6, 8, 13, 19, 23,
   26–27, 31, 46, 50, 53, 59–61, 73,
   77, 104, 117, 120–21, 168, 173,
   186, 216, 219–22, 225
Rowley, H. H., 137, 140

sacrifice, 99, 159, 164
salvation, 2, 6, 36, 59, 73, 110, 128,
   138, 141, 157, 162–64, 167,
   222–23
   universal, 163
Samuel, 61–62, 138
sanctification, 2, 70, 102, 105, 124,
   128, 148, 192–93, 211–12, 214
Satan, 35, 184
satisfaction, 82, 94, 96, 100–103, 108,
   114–15, 122, 155, 158, 161,
   163–64, 169, 175, 187, 190,
   204–5, 211–13, 215
   of God, 88, 210
Saul, 50–51, 61–64, 138
scapegoat, 62

Schleiermacher, Friedrich, 2, 15, 55,
   105, 123, 127–28, 164, 192,
   210
science, 3–4, 10, 92, 131, 214, 225
Scripture, 9, 13, 15, 17, 24, 37, 40, 47,
   50, 53, 55, 61, 64, 66, 73, 76, 110,
   130–31, 133–35, 137, 139, 145,
   147, 165–67, 169, 171, 173, 184,
   188, 192, 206, 216, 220, 223–25
   See also Hebrew Scripture; New Testament; Old Testament
Shaw, D. W. D., 9
sin, 18, 37, 52, 59, 62–64, 126, 138,
   162, 171
society, 72, 106, 120, 133, 143, 150,
   169–70, 176, 182, 199, 209
Son, 17–18, 33, 47, 52, 62–63, 68, 118,
   150, 168, 173, 175, 181–88, 191,
   206, 221–22
Sonderegger, 41
soteriology, 130, 161–62
soul, 133
subjective aim, 9–10, 107, 132, 154,
   199, 202, 207
   of creatures, 10, 85–86, 91–101, 122,
   163, 203–4, 208
   of God, 10, 78–84, 89, 101–2, 106,
   111–12, 116–17, 121, 124, 129,
   140, 142–43, 149, 151–52,
   157–60, 177, 189, 210, 213, 215,
   222
suffering, 173
superject, 80, 93–94, 100, 109, 111,
   121, 133, 137, 143, 158
supersessionism, 15, 41
Surin, Kenneth, 7
synagogue, 34, 45–46, 59

Tanner, Kathryn, 169
temple, 59
theism
   classical, 6
   neoclassical, 5, 10
theodicy. See evil: problem of
theology, 3, 51, 56, 61, 71, 75–76, 110,
   123, 128, 136, 141, 143, 154, 215,
   219–20